An advanced logic programming language

Vol 1 Prolog -2 User Guide

An Advanced Logic Programming Language

Volume 1
The Prolog-2 User Guide

Edited by

Tony Dodd

Expert Systems Ltd

intellect
Oxford, England

First published in Great Britain in 1990 by
Intellect Limited
Suite 2, 108/110 London Road, Oxford OX3 9AW

First published in the USA in 1990 by
Ablex Publishing Corporation
355 Chestnut Street
Norwood, New Jersey 07648

Copyright © 1990 Expert Systems Ltd

All rights reserved. No part of this publication may be reproduced, stored in a retrieval system, or transmitted, in any form or by any means, electronic, mechanical, photocopying, recording, or otherwise, without written permission.

Sole distributors outside North America
Blackwell Scientific Publications Ltd
Osney Mead, Oxford OX2 0EL, England

Consulting editor: Masoud Yazdani
Copy editor: Cate Foster
Cover design: Steven Fleming

British Library Cataloguing in Publication Data

An advanced logic programming language.
1. Computer systems. Programming languages: Prolog
I. Dodd, Tony, *1952–*
005.133

ISBN 1-871516-10-2 v.1
ISBN 1-871516-11-0 v.2

Library of Congress Cataloging-in-Publication Data available

Printed and bound in Great Britain by Billing & Sons Ltd, Worcester

Contents

PART ONE 1

1. Introduction 3
2. Prolog-2 as a logic programming language 9
3. The Syntax of Prolog-2 19

PART TWO 29

4. Lesson 1: Queries 31
5. Lesson 2: Variables 34
6. Lesson 3: The notepad 38
7. Lesson 4: A simple database 43
8. Lesson 5: Arithmetic, the Help System 47
9. Lesson 6: Built-in predicates 51
10. Lesson 7: Backtracking 57
11. Lesson 8: Repeating tasks 63
12. Lesson 9: Recursion 66

PART THREE 77

13. Compiling Prolog programs 79
14. Manipulating the clause store 88
15. Modules 98
16. How Prolog-2 uses memory 109
17. Arithmetic 115
18. Input/Output 128
19. High-level I/O 136
20. Error handling 155

The Prolog-2 User Guide

21. Debugging 160
22. Starting and stopping Prolog-2 169
23. External Code 174
24. Windowing facilities (P only) 245
25. The program development environment 274
26. Operating system interfaces 319
27. The LINT checker 375
Index 379

Preface

This is the first of two volumes describing Prolog-2, an advanced implementation of Prolog logic programming language. This volume is a topic-by-topic tour of Prolog-2 with examples and hints for use, plus a step by step tutorial. The second volume, the Prolog-2 Encyclopaedia, is an alphabetical reference of Prolog-2 facilities.

If you are not already a Prolog-2 user there is no cause for alarm. The first two thirds of the book cover facilities which exist in most implementations of the language. In addition, you'd find a voucher at the end of the book which entitles you to a free disk containing <u>Prolog-2 Tutorial</u>, sufficient for carrying out the exercises in Part Two of the book.

February 1990

PART ONE

THE PROLOG-2 LANGUAGE

1. Introduction

1.1 Some history

Prolog was first developed for large computers. The DEC-10 implementation at Edinburgh is the best known early implementation, but there were quite a few variants, as well, of course, as Pereira's portable C Prolog.

Expert Systems Ltd, later Expert Systems International Ltd, was founded in 1980 by Alex Goodall to promote expert systems technology. Though today that sounds a rather wide brief, the problem in 1980 was a shortage of things to promote, and Goodall advertised for suitable products that he could market. He was approached by Bill Clocksin and Chris Mellish, authors of the standard Prolog textbook, who had developed a Prolog system for the RT-11 operating system; and it was agreed that ESL would market this as Prolog-1. Later there was an RSX implementation, which was used to address the new but growing VAX market until Jocelyn Paine had completed a native code VAX Prolog-1. At the same time Charles Hardingham at ESL was worrying about porting to the Z80 processor; he solved the problem by translating the RSX version via an internal code of his own design, and the first or second microcomputer Prolog was born.

The first or second, not the first, because the claims of MicroProlog from LPA are at least as good: the two products appeared on the market at about the same time. Z80 Prolog-1 ran on a whole number of peculiar machines — making disks for customers was a nightmare, slightly alleviated by the use of a mysterious Cifer computer that could produce any format at all, given appropriate programming. Given sufficient ingenuity it was even possible to get the thing to run on an Apple, with a special processor board added. For this was before the days of the IBM PC.

When the 8088 and the IBM PC appeared it was decided that Prolog-1 should appear on the new platform. Again mechanical translation appeared to be the solution, and a Z80 to 8088 converter was written in Prolog. The bulk of the development was carried out on three LSI M4 microcomputers, which offered the advantage of Z80 and 8088 processors in the same box. Nobody can remember what the first benchmark was, but it was in three figures, which seemed pretty good in those days. Unfortunately the interpreter could only address 64K of data, but since the base configuration of the PC at the time offered 16K of memory that was not such a disadvantage as it seems in retrospect. Most of the demand was for CPM/86 systems, but a PC-DOS version was developed, and nervously put through its paces on a borrowed IBM PC. Daniel James was the main developer of this version.

Prolog-1 was a smallish system, but corresponded nicely with the subset of DEC-10 Prolog set out in Clocksin and Mellish, not surprisingly. Like DEC-10 Prolog it lacked real numbers, but there were other things missing too: there was no compiler, and the debugger was very primitive. Somebody had fiddled around to try and make it seem friendlier, introducing the **More (y/n)?** response after a goal solution instead of the standard ;. This and a few other foibles survived into Prolog-2. Prolog-1 had a surprisingly sophisticated garbage collector, atom garbage collection having been added to help minimise space usage. For the 8088 version, floating point support was added.

I[1] joined ESL late in 1983, just as the 8088 version was being completed; the floating point routines were driving a conscript to assembler-programming to distraction, and I was given the job of writing them myself, and promised that if they worked I would be kept on and allowed to write a compiler for calculating bus fares. I no longer remember why I agreed.

It quite soon became apparent that the 64K data restriction was a problem; on the other hand, it seemed unlikely that the program, now mechanically translated three times, would stand a full segmentation; though it was well commented — most of the comments seemed to escape the translation process unscathed — nobody really understood it well enough to introduce so fundamental a change. I experimented with some enhancements, such as tail recursion optimisation (important because LPA had it and we didn't) and some primitive windowing, and we produced what was to be the final release of Prolog-1, 2.20T, sold exclusively to a US software house for internal use.

At the same time I started work on a design for internal discussion that was to lead to a new interpreter that could address all the memory of the PC. By about March of 1984 this was ready, and debate raged as to whether we should choose the PC, the Mac or the QL as the target hardware. It was, as I recall, Alex Goodall's hard-nosed market assessment rather than any technical enthusiasm that led us to the PC; it was also his decision that the new system was to be a new product, Prolog-2.

There had long been a policy in ESL of developing a UNIX Prolog system. This was to be the target for the compiler, for everyone thought then that running a Prolog compiler on a micro was impossible. The UNIX development was the responsibility of Tim Irving. He and I would read through David Warren's papers on Prolog implementation and discuss technical details, without ever mentioning the conviction growing, I suspect, in both of us simultaneously that a PC compiler was perfectly feasible. For reasons best left undiscussed, and after a great deal of legal misery — I remember particularly standing in the car park in torrential rain with a gang of solicitors trying to set fire to some floppy disks — he took his design away and developed it into SD-Prolog while I quickly added the compiler to my Prolog-2 design. In retrospect I should have torn up my design, built a compiler and then added an interpreter, but at the time there were crucial projects dependent on the new system, and such a radical approach would have been unpopular.

Gary Noble, the first of many PIG (Prolog Implementation Group) programmers joined to help with the development of Prolog-2. For some reason we developed the system under CPM, fortunately with enough regard to DOS for a DOS version to follow easily. My recollection, perhaps exaggerated, is that we started coding on September 1st 1984 and had the first test release ready by Christmas. There was no windowing and no compiler, but the core of the system, with the PRM file mechanism, hashing and virtual memory, was present at that stage. Fortunately — though we did not think this at the

---

[1] I use the first person as editor of the volume and author of this chapter; later I shall try to apportion credit for the rest of the chapters.

The Prolog-2 User Guide

time — we had a paid army of critics trying to use the system. Don Smith, who looked after ESP Advisor, spent an age trying to get all the knowledge bases going in Prolog-2; every time one thing was mended something else broke. However, by the middle of 1985 the system was stable enough for me to add the compiler, with remarkable ease, thanks more to the clarity of Warren's papers than any skill of mine. In fact it wasn't what is now called a WAM (Warren Abstract Machine) system at all, and we hadn't heard of the WAM then. The abstract machine was my own development of the DEC-10 abstract machine, altered to use structure copying rather than sharing. The first benchmark on an old PC was 900 lips, but fortunately nobody was looking while I did it, and I was able to creep away and optimise the code templates in the small hours until I could announce that the official first benchmark was 1800 lips, about what we had predicted. The compiler itself was always mind-blowingly slow, 10 times slower then (on identical hardware) than now, though it is still slow. All in all, by late 1985 we were pretty pleased with our new system and thinking of new platforms for it.

The documentation for the first system, parts of which survive in what follows, were written by a technical author who preferred to remain anonymous. Given how little help we gave him, probably we were the ones who should have hidden away; I remember him having to picket my office for technical information, and of course, he had no system to try out because of the speed at which the thing was developed. We thought at first that we would sell Prolog-1 for beginners and Prolog-2 for experienced programmers, and so we designed the documentation to exclude any basic information about Prolog, a decision we rapidly regretted but which we had to live with. The first documentation was photocopied and bound in A4 binders.

The first obvious direction to go was to the 68000, and we reached an agreement with Sinclair which gave us a cheap QL and promised some money to develop a system. We also bought a Mac and a Lisa and recruited Dave Haines, who was to be the principal architect of the large machine Prolog-2 systems, but who made little headway on the QL because we never received any of the money from Sinclair; so he set out to overhaul the windowing system, producing in about a month the complete system as it stands today. To complicate his brief, we were not totally committed to the PC in those days: he had to address Apricot, Rainbow and other platforms too.

At the same time a team, usually of three programmers, started work on a C version of Prolog-2. The group leaders were, in succession, Gary Noble, Dave Haines and Bill Rivers; the VAX version was complete by the end of 1986, and SUN and Apollo versions followed. Dave Haines discovered the WAM and rebuilt the compiler around it, and also got compilation speeds down to a reasonable figure. Nick Wedd was briefly one of the implementers, and also got involved in an attempted port to the DEC PRO that foundered in the morass of DEC's corporate indecision. A fortunate side effect was that Nick was freed to rewrite the documentation, and the bulk of the core documentation, the early chapters of this volume and the more important BIP descriptions in the Prolog-2 Encyclopaedia, were his work.

Most of the interfaces were added then, largely in response to pressure from users. First Lattice and then MicroSoft C, 1-2-3, dBase and several others, some described in these volumes, some not. By then we had treated ourselves to a full time professional documenter, Martin Rush, and he would polish my garbled notes about new features

The Prolog-2 User Guide

and protect the users from my usual hasty scrawl. He touched every part of all of the product documentation in his time, and what is good and polished is usually a product of his professionalism and high standards. I take sole responsibility for the Prolog-2 tutorial.

Every silver lining has a cloud, and in retrospect it is clear that by the time all the Prolog-2 versions were released Expert Systems International was suffering from the general depression of the AI marketplace. Sustained longer than it would naturally have survived by some Alvey contracts, it nevertheless started to feel a very severe chill in 1987, and early in 1988 it was acquired by Chemical Design Ltd, a molecular modelling software company with money to invest, and conveniently situated at the end of the car park. In the course of 1988 the business was moved to a new office, the original directors left, and the chill turned into something more serious. It seems now extraordinary that so much technical work was done then; Prometheus, the AI toolkit was completed, the C Prolog version much enhanced (many of the extras that are not in the PC version were added then, largely by Bill Rivers, who also produced all the UNIX specific documentation, and the first coherent account of the tokeniser), and Sally Prime and I produced the 80386 version of Prolog-2, a complete rewrite of the 1984 assembler program that also gave us the chance to clean up a lot.

An impossibly bad trading outlook obliged the directors to appoint a receiver for ESI in January 1989. The products had been acquired separately by Chemical Design, so the demise of ESI did not mean the end of Prolog-2, and Bill Rivers and I joined the parent company to keep it going. Later Sally Prime replaced Bill and later still Dick Broughton replaced Sally; and after the shock of recent events passed we were able to return to development, with the Oracle interface and the Windows version produced in 1989.

Expert Systems Ltd acquired the rights to the products and started trading in January 1990.

1.2 The Prolog-2 family

The documentation covers Prolog-2 in general so far as is possible. In Prolog-2 we have always tried to reconcile maximum portability with maximum usage of each machine's particular facilities, and as a result there are quite a lot of machine specific parts in the system. Some of these are relegated to on-disk documentation, but to give a feeling for Prolog-2 it would be wrong to exclude all of them from this volume. There are, therefore, parts of the volume that do not apply to every system.

PC Prolog-2 is referred to as P. There are four versions:
    1   Personal
    2   Programmer
    3   Professional Plus
    4   80386

1 and 2 are stripped-down versions of 3 in which the capacity to build stand-alone systems is substantially reduced; 4 is a copy of 3 but can address the full memory of the 80386, despite running under DOS.

C Prolog-2 is available on VAX under VMS (V) and under UNIX on the following

The Prolog-2 User Guide

platforms:
- S   SUN-3 or 4
- A   Apollo (DN3000 or similar)
- H   HP 9000

These versions are very similar and are all referred to as U.

1.3 The Prolog-2 documentation set

This volume and its companion, the Prolog-2 Encyclopaedia, are intended as a complete account of the operation of a modern Prolog system. The reader may already have purchased the Prolog-2 program, or may intend to order Prolog-2. In that case the following information should be useful.

Prolog-2 documentation is supplied in two volumes:

The Prolog-2 User Guide describes the various features of Prolog-2 grouped according to the tasks they perform. For example, all the predicates for adding clauses to the database will be found together.

The Prolog-2 Encyclopaedia is an alphabetical catalogue of predicates, system states and many other things listed in its introduction.

Some aspects of Prolog-2 have been excluded from these volumes on the grounds that they would be unlikely to interest a general reader, or are liable to change often. Such documentation is supplied on disk.

In particular, each Prolog-2 disk or tape set will contain

- a READ.ME file, which should be read
- a CHANGES.DOC file, detailing any discrepancies between the software and the documentation
- a FILES.DOC file, explaining the purpose of each file in the distribution set.

Such details are not discussed in this volume.

The on-line help system gives short descriptions of Prolog-2's Built-In Predicates and other features.

The help system can be called during execution. It acts as a "quick reference" giving on-line help about various aspects of Prolog-2, and allowing you at every stage to ask for more help on related topics.

Full details of how to use the help system are given in the Program Development Environment (PDE) Manual contained in the accompanying Options Manuals volume; but you can find out how to use it just by typing **help**.

1.4 Further reading on Prolog

This is not a comprehensive booklist, but it contains the key texts on Prolog, including

The Prolog-2 User Guide

tutorial material.

For a simple account of Prolog:

Programming in Prolog

W F Clocksin & C S Mellish
Springer-Verlag
2nd edn, 1984

For a somewhat less elementary treatment:

The Art of Prolog

L Sterling and E Shapiro
MIT Press
1986

Prolog Programming for Artificial Intelligence

Ivan Bratko
Addison Wesley
1986

Prolog: a Logical Approach

Tony Dodd
Oxford University Press
1990

For a general introduction to logic programming, without particular reference to Prolog:

Introduction to Logic Programming

C J Hogger
Academic Press
1984

2. Prolog-2 as a logic programming language

2.1 A declarative language

The core of Prolog-2 is Prolog, the most commonly used logic programming language. Logic programming means, simply, using logic as a programming language. Habitually programmers have used languages that instruct the computer what actions it should take. Like parents of a growing child, they have foresaken the use of minutely detailed action by action instructions in favour of an approach that recognises that their charge has developed certain abilities of its own. They now feel confident in asking the value of a complicated arithmetic expression rather than giving a series of binary operations to be performed.

Many programming languages contain logical facilities. A logical expression is built up from propositions (which are either true or false) using connectives such as && (and) || (or) and ~ (not). Programming languages can evaluate such expressions, that is, given the value of the propositions they can tell whether the whole expression is true or false. However, before evaluating a logic expression the programmer must ensure that all the elements of the expression have their correct values, possibly be evaluating other expressions. Prolog differs in that it does not *evaluate* logical expressions: it *proves* them. If it does not recognise an expression element, it tries to prove that in its turn. There is no need to tell Prolog how to do this: it has its own mechanism.

A programming problem is a maze in which the inputs and outputs are defined but the space in between is blurred. In a procedural language, the programmer solves the problem by giving a path through the maze, a series of instructions 'turn left - turn left - turn right' and so on. In Prolog, the programmer produces a map of the maze and leaves the Prolog system to find a path through.

2.2 Relations

Prolog reduces a problem to a number of *relations*. A relation is a state of affairs that may or may not hold between a number of objects, the objects being called the *arguments* of the relation. Thus being married is a relation between two people; but not all relations have two arguments. Being happy is a property of a single object (Fred is happy, but Fred and Margaret are married), but we tend to speak of it as a relation with a single argument. We even allow the possibility of relations with no arguments, such as *It is sunny*, simply so as to have a uniform term. The number of arguments of a relation is fixed: although it is possible to say both *Fred is married* (one argument) and *Fred and Margaret are married* (two arguments) we would regard these as two different relations. Language misleads: *Fred and Margaret are happy* is not a two argument relation but two instances of a one argument relation (*Fred is happy and Margaret is happy*). Relations are classified by the number of their arguments, and because one argument relations are unary, two binary, three ternary and so forth it has become the practice to speak of an n-ary relation and, worse, to call n the arity of the relation.

The solution to a programming problem may be written as a relation. Thus, the problem of parsing a sentence into a tree of symbols may be solved by

The Prolog-2 User Guide

parse(String,Tree).

This is not helpful in itself; but Prolog allows us to define relations in terms of simpler relations, so that a problem may be broken down into its elements.

The simplest way of defining a relation is to write down an instance of the relation that is true. Thus

married(fred,margaret).

is a way of saying that Fred and Margaret are married. We probably do not want to solve the parsing problem by writing down all true instances of the relation **parse**, for there is an infinite set of such instances. Thus although we should like to be able to prove

parse([the,grey,cat,catches,the mouse],
       sentence(np(the,[grey],cat), vb(catch,pl), np(the,[],mouse))).

we do not want to have to enter it.

The simplest trick for avoiding multiple entries of data is the use of variables. A variable in Prolog is any sequence of letters, numbers and _ that begins with an upper case letter or _, but its significance is not a particluar object but every object. Thus

noun_phrase([the,Noun]).

says that any sequence beginning **the** is a noun phrase: the book, the ladder, the catches, the the ... This is a little broad, and we should prefer to restrict ourseleves to the cases where Noun is a noun. In this case we shall give a conditional rule, where the stated relation holds provided some other relation holds:

noun_phrase([the,Noun]) :- noun(Noun).

The term *clause* is used to describe the things that we have been writing; clauses that contain no :- are called *facts*, clauses with :- *rules*; the part of the clause to the left of the :- is called the *head*, to the right the *body* of the rule. The body of a rule may contain several different conditions, so

noun_phrase([the,Adj,Noun]) :- noun(Noun),adjective_list(Adj).

The comma in the body is read **and** (called *conjunction*).

It is possible to have several clauses for the same relation, so both the above clauses for **noun_phrase** could be used. For good measure we might add

noun_phrase([It]) :- pronoun(It).

as well. Then the pronoun relation could be defined as a collection of facts:

pronoun(it).
pronoun(he).
pronoun(she).

and so on.

The collection of clauses for a relation is called a *procedure*. The procedure is named by the name of the relation and the number of arguments, often written **Name/Arity**, as in **pronoun/1**; this latter name is called a *predicate*.

2.3 Goals

Prolog uses the clauses supplied as part of a program to solve queries. The usual mode of operation is that the prompt **?-** is displayed to solicit a query; to enter facts, the user may type **[user]**. causing the consult prompt **C:** to appear. The consult prompt indicates that clauses of the program should be entered.

Prolog-2 has a number of different ways of entering clauses, such as the editor for full-screen editing of clauses and the compiler for turning clauses into fast code. However, the effect of the program is not altered by the way in which it is entered, for it is a definition os a series of relations rather than a set of instructions.

When the user types a query, for example,

?- noun_phrase([the,[savage],lion]).

the Prolog systems looks to see whether it has a clause whose head is the same as the goal. In our program, of course, it hasn't. But it does have a clause whose head could be made into the clause given the right replacement of variables. The clause

noun_phrase([the,Adj,Noun]) :- noun(Noun),adjective_list(Adj).

represents every clause in which the variables are replaced by objects, in particular the clause

noun_phrase([the,[savage],lion]) :- noun(lion),adjective_list([savage]).

However, finding this clause is no guarantee of success; the two parts of the body (called *body goals*) must be checked.

Now as we said at the outset, Prolog does not merely evaluate a formula: it proves it. So there is no need for the programmer to arrange for the value of **noun(lion)** to have been established. Prolog will automatically go away and try to prove this in exactly the same way that it would had the user typed the query **noun(lion)** at the prompt. It keeps quiet about the result, though, noting the success of the query, and going on to the next query, **adjective_list([savage])**. Assuming that this can be proved too, the user will be told that the query has succeeded (the word **yes** will appear).

Had that clause failed, another matching clause would have been looked for. The process of going back and looking for another solution is called *backtracking*. Notice that the scope of a Prolog variable is the clause it occurs in: when another clause is tried variables with the same name will not receive the values of variables in the clause that failed.

In this case we saw how a variable rule could be used to solve a query with constant objects in it. The opposite situation may also arise. Suppose that we enter the query **pronoun(X)**; there is no clause with this as its head, nor any of which this is a special case; but there is a clause which is a special case of this one, **pronoun(it)**. So the query succeeds, and the resulting value of **X** is reported:

X=it.

Then the user may ask for another solution:

More (y/n)?

and type yes; this causes backtracking and the next solution

X=he

is offered.

In fact we may unify these two types of behaviour (fixed clause matches variable call, variable clause matches fixed call) under a more general notion. To see the need for this, suppose the clauses of the program were

a(3,X) :- divides(3,X).
a(7,X) :- divides(7,X).

and the query were a(N,9). Neither of the two patterns fits; yet clearly the solution N=3 should be returned. What Prolog actually does, given a goal and the head of the clause, is to try to find a *unifier* for them; that is, a term that is an instance of both of them. Thus a unifier of a(3,X) and a(N,9) is a(3,9). The terms are called *unifiable*. An extra subtlety is involved, though. Unifying a(3,X,Y) and a(N,9,YY) is easy; for example, a(3,9,55) is a unifier. The choice of 55 was arbitrary though. A better unifier would be a(3,9,Z), since

(i) this indeed unifies the two terms
(ii) anything that unifies the two terms is an instance of this.

Such a term is called a *most general unifier*, and it can be shown that whenever two terms can be unified, they have a most general unifier.

2.4 Lists

As an example, consider the way Prolog represents lists. A list is represented as a dotted pair, a term .(Head,Tail) whose first argument is the first element of the list and whose second is the list of all other members. This is a structure just like a(Head,Tail), it's just harder to write. In fact there is a preferred way of writing lists, [Head|Tail]. As an example consider the list whose only member is 19. Its first member is 19, but what is the list of other members? As there are no other members we use a special atom [], meaning the empty list. Thus the list is [19|[]]. The list whose two members are 19 and 20 is [19|[20|[]]]. However, we allow this to be abridged [19,20|[]]. Moreover, when the tail of a list is [] the part |[] may be omitted, so the list can be written [19,20].

A commonly used predicate that puts two lists together is **append/3**. This is defined as follows:

append([],A,A).
append([H|T],A,[H|TT]) :- append(T,A,TT).

It is worth examining what happens to the query **append([1,2],[3],L)** both to see unification in action and to see how Prolog answers a query.

Of the two clauses, the first does not unify with the query. To unify the second requires a bit of work. At first sight [H|T] and [1,2] look quite different (be very sure that you *never* match them by setting H to 1 and T to 2). However, remember that [1,2] is shorthand for [1|[2]] so the terms are indeed unifiable setting H to 1 and T to [2]. A clearly unifies with [3] and we are left with the task of unifying [1|TT] and L. This must work, as L can stand for anything. So we have:

H=1
T=[2]
A=[3]
L=[1|TT]

TT can be anything at all. However, this is not the end of the story, for this was a rule not a fact; we must prove the condition, which with substitutions made is

append([2],[3],TT).

When we look for a clause for this query we find that we must use the very clause we have just finished. Moreover, this has a variable called TT in the head, but the scope of a Prolog variable is restricted to its clause, so this will not be the same as the TT we already know about. To be safe we shall rename all the variables of the clause by adding 1 to their names. Thus the head of the clause is

append([H1|T1],A1,[H1|TT1])

and we must try to unify this with the query. Again, [2] and [H1|T1] don't look very unifiable, but the first is short for [2|[]], so they can be unified with H1 set to 2 and T1 to []. A1 will be [3] and TT [2|TT1] (so L is [1|[2|TT1]] or [1,2|TT1]).

Again, there is a further query: it is

append([],[3],TT1).

13

The Prolog-2 User Guide

This matches the first clause, however, setting TT1 to [3]; there are no further queries, as this was a fact. Thus L is [1,2|[3]], which is [1,2,3]; obviously this is the right answer.

Interestingly, the call **append(X,Y,[1,2,3])** can be used to find the different lists that may be added to give [1,2,3]; the relation once defined may be queried in many different ways.

2.5 Cut

The very simple system described is made more complicated by the addition of the cut operator, written !. The function of cut is to prevent backtracking. Suppose, for example, that we want to write a definition of the factorial of an integer (Prolog has built-in arithmetic that works in a reasonably intuitive way); this might be

factorial(0,1).
factorial(N,K) :- NN is N-1, factorial(NN,KK),K is N*KK.

Unfortunately this is wrong; the second clause should not apply in the case where N is 0. As it is, if I ask the query **factorial(0,33)** instead of answering **no** the system will go off and try to use the second clause, ending up in a bottomless pit. Of course, if we could say

factorial(N,K) :- not(N=0),NN is N-1, factorial(NN,KK),K is N*K.

then we should be safe, but trying to introduce **not** into Prolog is even more of a problem, as we'll see. The cut operator prevents any further clauses for this predicate from being tried (confusingly, it also prevents any goals to its left from being retried). Thus

factorial(0,K) :- !, K=1.
factorial(N,K) :- NN is N-1, factorial(NN,KK), K is N*KK.

is the correct solution. (Check that the first clause could not be **factorial(0,1) :- !**).

As an example of the extra cutting power of cut, consider the code

a :- b(X),!,c(X).

b(1).
b(2).
c(2).

Thanks to the cut this will fail, because the cut will prevent the second solution to b from being found. This is an irrational piece of code; and of you really do just want one solution from a multiple solution predicate, **once(Goal)** has the same effect.

Observe now that we are becoming dependent on the fact that Prolog evaluates goals

14

from left to right and clauses from first to last. Seen as pure logical definitions, the order of clauses and goals is irrelevant, but for cut to work the order is significant.

2.6 Built-in predicates

Prolog provides a number of built-in facilities, described at length in the remainder of this book. These are made to look like ordinary procedures, but they are not usually defined by Prolog clauses. As well as succeeding or failing as procedures do they may have side effects, effects that are not cancelled when the program backtracks. Thus if the code

```
a(X) :- X=1, fail.
a(X) :- X=2.
```

(**fail** always fails) is in he program and a(Y) is the query then at first Y will be set to 1, but then when **fail** causes the first clause to fail, X will be unset and then set to 2 just as though the first clause had not been there; but if the predicate is changed to

```
a(X) :- write(1),fail.
a(X) :- X=2.
```

then 1 will be displayed even though the first clause failed; output is a side effect.

In the first predicate the behaviour of the program was unaffected by swapping the two clauses, but in the second the order of clauses is critical. Once we write programs with side-effects, we come to rely heavily on Prolog's search strategy.

2.7 Terms

We have only spoken informally of the sort of objects manipulated by Prolog; a little more precision is now needed. Prolog-2 admits a number of (in effect) indivisible objects:

- atoms
- integers
- real numbers
- strings

Atoms are used as symbolic names for objects where the name is not significant. Integers and reals are used as numbers. Strings are used as a handy way to store text in a compact form. Not all Prolog systems have real numbers and strings.

As well as these atomic types, there are structures; a structure consists of a functor (syntactically just an atom) followed by a number of terms (called arguments) in parentheses. Of course, this is just what a Prolog goal is; goals are a special case of terms. Lists are special structures whose functor is .

There are a number of built-in predicates for term manipulation.

Firstly, for identifying the type of a term, the predicates **atom/1**, **integer/1**, **real/1**, and **string/1** identify the atomic types. **datatype(Object,Type)** binds **Type** to the appropriate type of **Object**. **numeric** succeeds of both integers and reals and **atomic** of any of the four atomic types.

What of the goal **integer(X)**? Since X can represent anything, it is hard to see whether the answer should be yes or no. Prolog answers no to such questions and treats unbound variables as a new type, supplying a predicate **var/1** to be true if its argument is a variable. Programs written using **var/1** may have very peculiar behaviour.

nonvar(X) is true if **var(X)** is false.

Secondly a number of conversions between different atomic types are supplied. The predicate **name(Atom,String)** is true if the string is the name of the atom, so **name(foo,"foo")** is true; either argument may be a variable but not both. **list(List,String)** is true if the list is a list of ASCII values and the string has the corresponding characters as its name. **number(No,String)** does for integers and reals what **name/2** does for atoms.

It should be noted that the behaviour of **name/2** in Prolog-2 is quite unlike the behaviour in other Prolog versions, where it converts between an atom and a list. In fact, the built-in predicate in Prolog-2 is called not **name** but **name1** and the definition

name(X,Y) :- name1(X,Y).

is supplied in the DEC10 library. The standard behaviour of **name/2** may be obtained by adding the clause

name(X,Y) :- name2(X,Y).

to the system before the DEC10 library is opened.

Finally there are predicates that manipulate structures. **functor(Term,F,N)** is true if **Term** has functor **F** and arity **N**; if **Term** is a variable then **F** must be an atom and **N** an integer; **F** will be set to a structure with the supplied functor and **N** variable arguments (a *most general instance* of F/N).

To extract or insert arguments use **arg/3**, **arg(N,Term,Arg)**, which is true if the Nth argument of **Term** is **Arg**; arguments are counted from 1. Although between then **functor/3** and **arg/3** supply all the functions one might need, there is an extra predicate **=.. /2** (pronounced *univ*) that combines the two:

Term =.. [F|L]

is true if **Term** is a term with functor F and arguments L. This is often useful, but if **functor** or **arg** will do, use them for preference; for example, don't write X=..[_|L],length(L,K) to extract the arity of X; use **functor(X,_,K)** instead.

2.8 Logical connectives

To conclude this brief tour of the core of Prolog we describe some extra logical connectives that are available.

A;B denotes **A** or **B**, the *disjunction* of **A** and **B**. The code

foo :- (a;b).

is equivalent to

foo :- a.
foo :- b.

but the latter is to be preferred.

(A -> B;C) is called *implication*. If **A** is true then **B** is evaluated; otherwise **C** is evaluated. For example, if the value **19** of **X** has to be corrected to **91**, but all other values are correct, the code

   (X = 19 -> XX = 91;XX=X)

will do the trick; unlike a disjunction, it does not create a choice point (subsequent failure will not set XX to 19). Experienced Prolog programmers use this a lot.

The construction **(A -> B)** is short for **(A -> B;true)**, which seems both logical and useful. Unfortunately some Prolog dialects treat it as **(A -> B;fail)**, so for portability the short form is better avoided.

not(X), the *negation* of **X**, could be defined

not(X) :- X,!,fail.
not(X).

The reader may check that if **X** can be proved then this will fail and otherwise it will succeed. This is peculiar if **X** contains a variable; **not(foo(X))** might be expected to set **X** to a value for which **foo(X)** was false, but in fact it fails if **foo(X)** is true for any value **X** at all.

true is always true, **fail** always false. **call(X)** is equivalent to **X**.

The predicate **bagof(X,Goal,S)** forms the set **S** of all **X** such **Goal** is true. Programmers should be aware that

• if **Goal** has variables that are not in **X** then they are not bagged but returned in successive calls. Thus in the code

a(1,1).
a(1,2).

17

The Prolog-2 User Guide

a(2,3).
a(2,4).

The call

bagof(X,a(_,X),S)

produces

X=1
S=[1,2]

and then

X=2
S=[3,4];

to just get the list [1,2,3,4] say

bagof(X,Y^a(Y,X),S)

(Y^ is called an existential quantifier.)

• if there are no solutions **bagof** fails; it never returns the empty list.

setof is like **bagof** but it sorts the answer in the canonical order and eliminates duplicates.

3. The Syntax of Prolog-2

3.1 Introduction

This chapter defines the syntax and semantics of compound Prolog terms. We first define the basic syntax of Prolog-2 for each of the primitive datatypes. We next consider structures, which are compound Prolog terms constructed from these simple terms. We then progress to the main elaborations on this basic syntax, lists, {} notation and operator declarations. We finish with a review of the principal components of Prolog programs and plus an outline of how Prolog-2 handles grammar rules.

3.2 Primitive data types

Primitive data types are data types which cannot be broken down into simpler types.

Prolog-2 programs are constructed from six such primitive datatypes:

(1) atoms
(2) integer numbers
(3) real numbers
(4) strings
(5) variables

Each type is discussed in turn below.

3.2.1 Atoms

An atom is a named symbolic entity. Any string of characters may be used to represent an atom by enclosing it in single quotes.

There are three special cases where an atom name need not be enclosed in single quotes:

(i)   Where the atom name is a sequence consisting only of letters, digits, and underscore characters, and starts with a lower case letter.

(ii)   Where the atom name consists only of the special symbol characters:

+ - * / \ ^ < > = ' ~ : . % ? @ # $ &

and is not a comment (see §3.2.6 below).

(iii)   Where the atom is one of these five special Prolog system atoms which do not follow the normal rules:
!
[]
{}
,
;

The Prolog-2 User Guide

The single quote character may be represented within an atom name in quotes by two adjacent single quote characters thus:

    'martin''s_atom'

3.2.2 Integer numbers

An integer is a whole number constant. An integer is represented by a sequence of digit characters; this may be preceded by a plus or minus sign. It must not contain a decimal point character, and must not be enclosed within quotes.

3.2.3 Real numbers

A real number is represented by a sequence of digits, possibly preceded by a sign character ("+" or "-"), and followed by a decimal part, or an exponent part, or a decimal part followed by an exponent part.

A decimal part consists of a decimal point character followed by at least one digit character. An exponent part consists of the exponent symbol E, possibly followed by a sign character, followed by a sequence of digit characters. (This is often called 'scientific notation' and is used to express very large or very small values concisely. A number containing E is read as: "multiply the number before the E by ten to the power of the number after the E".)

Examples of valid real numbers are:

    -2.3E4   10E-5   0.005E-56   2.9979E8   6.022E+27   0.0

3.2.4 Strings

A string is a sequence of ASCII characters; they are typically used for storing text. (This is more efficient than storing text as lists of characters.)

Syntactically a string is represented by zero or more characters enclosed in double quotes "". The body of a string (everything inside the quotes) may contain any ASCII character.

Within the body of a string, the following syntactic conventions apply:

(i) Any printable character (one with an ASCII code of 32 or above) except the backslash \ or double quotes " represents itself.

(ii) An unprintable character (one with an ASCII code below 32) may be represented by the backslash character \ followed by:

b	representing backspace
f	representing form-feed (newpage)
n	representing line feed
r	representing carriage return
t	representing horizontal tab
"	representing the double quote character
\	representing backslash itself

(iii) A backslash followed by an integer produces the character represented by that ASCII code number; the integer must be to base 10 with not more than three digits.

Examples of syntactically valid strings are :

"Ring the bell: \7 and newline\r\n"
"Not equal: =\008/"

3.2.5 Variables

Variable names may contain letters, numbers and underscore characters.

A variable name must start with an upper case letter or an underscore character. Thus:

    Var, Variable_name, _var, _22

are variables. As we shall explain in Chapter 5, the system is capable of storing the names of variables.

It is convenient to be able to represent a variable that does not share with any other variable. Such a variable is represented by a single underscore character _. This is known as the anonymous variable. If a term contains two variables represented like this, Prolog treats them as two different variables.

Named variables which occur only once in a clause are stored as if they were the anonymous variable.

3.2.6 Comments

Prolog-2, like most programming languages, allows you to document your code by including comments. A comment begins with /* and ends with */. Anything between these delimiters is ignored by the system. A comment may include any sequence of characters except */.

The Prolog-2 User Guide

Comments may appear anywhere in the program, provided individual tokens (atoms, numbers, strings, and variable names) are not broken up. They do not affect the program in any way. Comments may include any amount of text, and may occupy more than one line.

Comments cannot be nested. For example:

    /* some text including the /* sequence */

is treated as a complete comment.

3.3 Structures

A structure consists of a functor and a number of arguments. Here are three examples of structures:

    functor(argument)
    struct(99.9,_,"hello",sin(cos(2))).
    .(1,.(2,[])).

The functor is normally written as an atom; this is followed immediately by the brackets which contain the arguments of the structure.

An argument may be any Prolog term. Arguments in a structure are separated by commas. The number of arguments in a structure is called the arity of that structure; a structure may not have an arity of more than 255.

When you write a structure as a functor followed by brackets and a list of arguments, you must be careful not to leave a space between the functor and the opening bracket.

This, for example:

    append([a , b] , [c | D] , V)

is syntactically valid; but this:

    append ([a , b] , [c | D] , V)

is not, because of the space that separates the functor from its argument list.

A structure may also be written using an operator with one argument or two (see §3.6); an example is this elementary arithmetic structure:

    3 + 5

Two special ways of writing structures are to use list notation (see §3.4):

    [a,[b,c],d|e].

or grammar rule brackets (§3.5):

>   {term}.

If you want to use the atom , (comma) as an argument of a functor, or as an element in a list, you must enclose it in single quotes to prevent it from being treated as a separator:

>   assert(a:-b',',c').

3.4 Lists

A list is a structure with functor '.' and arity 2. The second argument is a list: either a list with members or the empty list.

The Prolog language provides a special notation for lists: this uses the symbols [,], and |.

This list notation is defined as follows:

(i)   [] denotes the empty list, a list with no members. The empty list is an atom.
(ii)   [A|B], where A and B are any terms, denotes .(A,B);
(iii)   [A1,A2|B] denotes .(A1,[A2|B]);
(iv) $[A_1,...A_n]$ denotes $[A_1,...A_n|[]]$;

Thus .(1,.(2,[])) may be written [1,2], and .(a,.(b,c)) may be written [a,b,c] or [a|[b,c]].

(Note that these terms are not necessarily lists; [a|b] is not a list for example. Note also that | is not an operator: it is a special character recognised by Prolog and used in the parsing of lists.)

The special symbol ,.. may be used instead of |, but will never appear on output.

3.5 {} notation

Curly brackets { and } play a special role in grammar rule notation (see §3.8); you can also use them for other purposes.

A term in curly brackets such as {Term} is read as a structure with principal functor {}, arity 1, and argument **Term**:

>   {}(Term).

A comma has no particular significance within curly brackets. It is just an operator, not an argument separator. So {T1,T2} would be parsed as {}(',',(T1,T2)). {} is an atom.

The Prolog-2 User Guide

3.6 Operators

The commonest extension to basic Prolog is operator syntax. The provision of operator syntax means that operator definitions can be made in Prolog. Operator definitions allow functors defined as operators to be used in a different way from normal functors. Consider the case of the ordinary '+' sign for addition. If we used unextended Prolog syntax '+' would have to be used as a functor to a structure, like this:

    +(2,2).

with the two numbers to be added supplied as arguments. This would be unfamiliar and annoying. Once '+' has been defined as an infix operator, however, it can be used in its conventional arithmetic form:

    2 + 2.

If + were not defined as an operator, Prolog would not understand this expression and would report it as a syntax error.

Prolog-2 provides a large number of standard predefined operators (sometimes called 'system operators'). Prolog-2 also allows you to define your own operators.

Any atom can be defined as an operator. You define an atom as an operator using the BIP **op/3**. The three arguments are the precedence number of the operator, the operator type, and the atom which you are defining as an operator. You must understand the notions of operator type and precedence before you can use **op/3**.

3.6.1 Operator type

The operator type declaration tells Prolog:

(i) whether the atom is infix, prefix or postfix;
(ii) what the "associativity" of the atom is — whether it evaluates right to left or left to right.

An infix operator must have two arguments, and lie between them; a prefix operator must have a single argument, which it must precede; and a postfix operator must have a single argument, which it must follow (postfix is the rarest of the three).

The associativity of operators is only relevant when parsing a structure which contains several operators and which can only be parsed unambiguously when the types (prefix, etc.,) and precedences of these operators are considered.

Your operator declaration must define an operator's type using one of the following atoms:

    fx, fy, xfx, xfy, yfx, xf, yf.

If the **f** of the type declaration comes at the start, the operator is prefix; if the **f** is in the centre it is infix; if the **f** is at the end it is postfix. The **xs** and **ys** represent the arguments. An **x** indicates that an argument in that position cannot be an unbracketed term in operator syntax with principal functor an operator of the same precedence; a **y** that such an argument is allowable.

This means that an operator of type **xfy** associates to the right, so that, for example: **a,b,c** is read as **a,(b,c)** and not as **(a,b),c**. Conversely **yfx** associates from the left, so that **a+b+c** is read as **(a+b)+c**. A type of **xfx** means that combinations such as **a=b=c** are illegal (because if there are two **xfx** operators with the same precedence the system does not know which of them as an argument of the other). But note that structures such as **a+b*c** and **a*b+c** are allowed, and are unambiguously parsed without reference to the types of the infix operators: their different precedences are sufficient to establish what is meant.

3.6.2 Operator precedences and precedence numbers

Operator precedences determine the order in which operations are carried out in an expression: one operator will always have precedence over another.

If + and * had the same precedence, an expression such as **a*b+c** might be ambiguous: it could be parsed as either *(a,+(b,c)) or +(*(a,b),c). In fact, * has a lower precedence than +, and therefore binds its arguments more tightly, so that the parser produces the latter interpretation.

The precedence number of an operator is an integer which determines how tightly it binds its arguments. The smaller the precedence number of an operator, the more tightly it binds its arguments.

Formally, an operator of a certain precedence cannot have an argument whose functor is an unbracketed operator of lower precedence. If you want to overrule the precedence of an operator, use brackets: **a*(b+c)** will be parsed as *(a,+(b,c)).

Prolog-2 operator precedence numbers range from 1 to 1200.

3.6.3 Using op/3 to define operators

The Prolog-2 BIP **op/3** defines an atom as an operator. The three arguments are the precedence number of the operator, the type of the operator, and the atom you are defining as an operator:

    op(450, xfy, atomname).

This defines the atom **atomname** as an infix operator with precedence number 450.

The last argument can also be a list of atoms; in this case the declaration is made for each member of the list in turn. For example:

    op(555, xf, [++,--]).

declares both ++ and -- as prefix operators with precedence number 555. It is possible to have up to three operator declarations for the same atom: one as a prefix operator, one as an infix operator, and one as a postfix operator.

You can also use **op/3** to clear an operator declaration and return an operator to ordinary atom status; you do this by making a new operator declaration for the atom, but using the atom **none** as second argument (operator type) to **op/3**:

> op(0, none, atomname).

This clears all operator declarations for the atom 'atomname'.

3.6.4 Retrieving information on operators

The Prolog-2 BIP **atomprops/3** will tell you the operator details of an atom. Like **op/3**, the first argument is the precedence number of the operator, the second its type, and the third the atom.

atomprops/3 is resatisfiable; if it is used with three variable arguments it will return all the atoms known to the system. Atoms which are not operators are returned with the first argument instantiated to 0 and the second argument instantiated to **none**.

If there are several declarations for an atom then **atomprops** will backtrack through the list and give you them all.

3.7 Syntax of programs

A Prolog-2 program is made up of "directives", which are called as soon as they are encountered, and "clauses" which are put in the database.

The main constituents of directives and clauses are "goals".

3.7.1 Directives

A directive is a command to the interpreter to prove/execute its constituent goals using data in the database. A directive consists of **?-** or **:-** followed by one or more goals separated by commas.

3.7.2 Clauses

A clause may consist of:

(i) A head only. This is known as a "fact".

> fact.
> is_a(bird,penguin).

(ii) A head followed by :-, followed by one or more goals separated by commas, called the "body". This is known as a "rule".

```
lays_eggs(X) :- is_a(bird,X), female(X).
```

A clause of type (ii) can be read as stating that its head is true provided that each of the goals in its body is true; in a program it provides a means of causing each of the tail goals to be executed by calling the head goal.

3.7.3 Goals

A goal is a term which forms part of a directive or clause. A goal can be thought of as being true or false, or as being proved or not proved, or as succeeding or failing when called.

An atom or a structure may occur as a goal, but a number or string may not.

A variable may be used as a goal, but only if it will have been instantiated when Prolog tries to prove it.

3.8 Grammar rules

Grammar rules are written to parse sentences of natural or artificial language, and use a special notation. They are useful because the Prolog code needed to parse natural language sentences is complex and difficult to read, while the grammar rule notation is clearer.

One of the Prolog-2 modules is a translator for grammar rules, **grules**. If this is open, and you include grammar rules in your program, they will be converted automatically into Prolog clauses.

When Prolog-2 encounters a structure with functor -->/2 during a consult, it assumes this is a grammar rule and turns it into a conventional Prolog clause. This is done by **expand_term/2**, which is exported by **grules**. The new Prolog clause is then asserted into the database in the usual way.

If you have a grammar rule with a tail goal written in Prolog instead of in grammar rule notation, you should enclose this tail goal in curly brackets { }. It will then be treated as a normal Prolog goal, and will not expanded by **expand_term/2**.

For example, if a consult session encounters two grammar rules as follows:

```
sentence(A,Z) --> subject(A,B), predicate(B,Z).
noun(plural,noun(RootN)) --> [N],
            {(name(N,Plname), append(Singname,"s",Plname),
             name(RootN,Singname), is_noun(RootN,singular))}.
```

then they are automatically translated into the following clauses, which are asserted into the database in the usual way.

```
sentence(A,Z,_194,_198) :-
     subject(A,B,_194,_222) ,
     predicate(B,Z,_222,_198) .

noun(plural,noun(RootN),_198,_202) :-
     'C'(N,_198,_202) ,
     name(N,Plname) ,
     append(Singname,"s",Plname) ,
     name(RootN,Singname) ,
     is_noun(RootN,singular) .
```

3.9 Compatibility notes

Most Prolog systems follow the Edinburgh syntax just described. Exceptions are older versions of MicroProlog from LPA, which use a LISP-like syntax, and Prolog systems descended from the Marseilles systems Prolog-II and Prolog-III, which again represent a clause as a list of goals, head followed by body.

Within the Edinburgh syntax there are some divergences, for example in the range of operator precedences allowed. Prolog-2 is non-standard in the following respects:

(i) It has real numbers (but most Prolog systems have added these)
(ii) It has strings (most Prolog systems read "abc" as the list [97,98,99])
(iii) It allows the declaration of operators of any precedence (to write portable code, avoid precedences above 1000)
(iv) It does not allow end of line comments of the form % comment
(v) It does not treat | outside a list as ;
(vi) It has no radix integers of the form 2'10101.

There is a token class **dec10** that can be switched on using the call

?- state(token_class,_,dec10).

that makes Prolog-2 compatible on (iv) to (vi).

The behaviour of **op** is reasonably standard, though the use of **none** to clear operator declarations is not. **atomprops** is more commonly called **current_op**, and this form is available in Prolog-2 and should be used for portable code.

PART TWO

THE PROLOG-2 TUTORIAL

The Prolog-2 User Guide

This tutorial is designed to be used with the special demonstration version of Prolog-2, but will work with any PC version of the system.

You will probably not want to do the whole tutorial in one session. To finish a Prolog session at the end of a lesson, when looking at the prompt, type

?- halt.

When you want to restart the tutorial, enter Prolog-2 as above but then as soon as the prompt appears type

?- lesson(N).

where N is the lesson you are starting with. The notepad will be set up as it should be for that lesson. This facility is only available in the demonstration version.

It is also possible to use the tutorial with a full version of Prolog-2, of course; with versions earlier than 2.15 you will notice minor differences in behaviour in the menu system and the debugger. You should note the following:

- make sure that there is no mouse installed. See the file CONFIG.PRO for details of how this can be done, or delete the mouse installation statement in the MNU file — the file READ.ME on diskette 1 tells you how to do this

- if you want to finish the tutorial at the end of a lesson, use the File save As facility of the notepad to save your work. When you start again, use the File Load option to retrieve the saved work.

The demonstration system will operate on an IBM-PC or close compatible running DOS 2.10 and above and having at least 512K of RAM.

4. Lesson 1: Queries

Prolog-2 is a programming system based on the theory of logic programming. That means that instead of supplying a program with instructions to be executed, you furnish Prolog-2 with a specification of the problem to be solved. In other words, instead of telling it what to do you ask it questions. You can do this in lots of different ways, but the simplest is just to type them in and read the answers.

When you start Prolog-2 the Program Development Environment (P.D.E.) is loaded. There are lots of facilities in the P.D.E. to help you develop Prolog applications; for the present we can safely ignore them. After the environment is loaded the characters

?-

are displayed on the screen and Prolog-2 sits and waits for you to do something. At the moment you are talking to the *top-level interpreter*, a simple Prolog-2 program that reads questions from the user and prints the answers.

The characters ?- are called the *prompt*. Whenever the prompt is displayed, Prolog-2 is waiting for you to type a *query*.

A query is just a question asked of the Prolog-2 system by the user. For example, try asking a question about arithmetic:

?- 5 > 2.

(Don't forget the full stop! Queries can run over many lines and Prolog-2 doesn't know that you've finished typing until it sees the full stop.)

Prolog-2 will reply

yes

meaning that the answer to your question was yes. The prompt is then displayed again and you can ask another question. If you type

?- 5 < 2.

then Prolog-2 will reply

no

as you would expect.

On the other hand if you throw caution to the winds and type something like

?- What are the thirty-nine steps.

then Prolog-2 will signal an error. It is as well to know from the start how to dispose

31

The Prolog-2 User Guide

simply and quickly of errors; read the error message and then press the <Enter> key. Take no notice of the little menu that appears in the top right corner for the time being; it offers a number of options we shall look at in a bit.

Once you have pressed <Enter> the message **Evaluation aborted** is displayed and then the prompt appears again.

Prolog-2 didn't like the question about the thirty-nine steps. In fact there are some quite strict rules about the queries that you can type in; they have to be in the correct syntax for Prolog-2. Prolog-2 reacts to a query in the wrong syntax rather as an English speaker would react to the question "Steps are the what thirty-nine?" — you can't say yes or no, because you don't know what it means, so you say "what?!?". An error message is Prolog-2's way of saying "what?!?".

You can find a full definition of Prolog-2 syntax in the reference manual. We'll only discuss the bits we need in these examples.

Let's look at another query: type

?- integer(44).

This is the way to ask Prolog-2 "Is 44 an integer?". Of course it is, so Prolog-2 will answer

yes.

The usual form of a Prolog-2 query is like this example: the query consists of the name of the property you are asking about (the *predicate*), an opening bracket, the thing that is to be tested for this property (the *argument*), a closing bracket and a full stop. In this case the property is being an integer, the object is 44.

There mustn't be a space between the predicate and the bracket! If you type

?- integer (44).

you'll get another syntax error.

Suppose, on the other hand, you get as far as the) and then you realise your mistake. Then you can go back and patch the input up. The arrow keys move you around just as you'd expect and the backspace and delete keys delete left of the cursor and at the cursor respectively. Be careful of the escape key — it clears all your input away, and you have to start all over again. Practice correcting the input in different ways.

Some questions concern more than one object. For example, the question which in English would be written "Does the cat sit on the mat?" asks whether the property sits_on applies to the objects cat and mat (sits_on is said to be a *relation* between cat and mat; you aren't allowed spaces in the middle of relation names, because they would be confusing for Prolog-2, so the convention is that if you want to join several words like this you use the underline character _). Prolog-2 also allows questions about relations; write first the relation, then the open bracket (no space in between, remember!), then all the arguments separated by commas, then the close bracket and a full stop.

?- sits_on(cat,mat).

Prolog-2 will answer

no.

If you think about it, this is rather a bold statement for Prolog-2 to make. You haven't specified which cat or which mat, and even if you had Prolog-2 had no way of knowing whether or not the cat was sitting on the mat.

Earlier we saw an English sentence that was nonsense, in that it was grammatically incorrect. On the other hand the question "Was the bandersnatch frumious?" is not grammatically unsound; you can't answer it because you don't know what the words mean, and are likely to reply "what?!?" just as to a grammatically incorrect sentence. But Prolog-2 isn't like that. If it doesn't know the answer, it says no. You must think that when Prolog-2 says yes it means "yes, I can see that that is true" and when it says no it means "no, I can't see that that is true, either because it isn't or because I haven't enough information".

As it stands at the moment Prolog-2 has some built-in information, so that it can answer questions about numbers; our first query

?- 5 > 2.

for example. The power of the system lies in the fact that as well as its built-in information it can be given extra information by the user and can then use that to answer queries. We shall see how to add information to the system in Lesson 3.

Summary

- We have seen how to enter simple queries

5. Lesson 2: Variables

In Lesson 1 we saw how to type in a query to Prolog-2. We saw a number of queries and learned that the usual form for a query is

predicate(argument_1,...,argument_n).

The number of arguments in a query is called its arity (this is because in logic one-argument structures are called unary, two-argument binary, three ternary. Someone had the idea of taking this ary suffix and making it into a noun, arity).

In the examples we saw the argument was in one case the number 44 and in the other the arguments were the words cat and mat. A word used as an argument in this sense is called an *atom*. To avoid confusion there are some restrictions on which collections of characters can be used as atoms, but you can be sure of the following:

(i) any collection of letters, digits and underline characters that begins with a lower case letter is an atom (the underline is there to make up for the lack of the space character)

(ii) most collections of symbols are atoms (+ * / =..)

(iii) anything at all enclosed in single quotes is an atom.

As well as atoms and integers Prolog-2 allows the use of real numbers, such as

1.2 0.001 44.4E10

and of strings, written in double quotes

"This is a string".

These are the four basic data types of Prolog-2.

As well as these simple types, there are also *structures* available in Prolog-2, and the most commonly used are lists. To write a list of objects just enclose them in square brackets and separate them with commas. For example, the list of numbers from 3 to 7 is

[3,4,5,6,7].

Prolog-2 knows a bit about lists without being told. For example, it can work out the length of a list. To ask whether the length of the above list is 5 type

?- length([3,4,5,6,7],5).

and the system will reply

yes.

Try it out with 6 instead to check that it isn't bluffing.

As a means of checking whether your assessment of the length of the list is correct, this is acceptable. As a means of determining the length of the list it is poor; you could try with each integer until it said yes, but that would be very tedious. In fact Prolog-2 can answer questions other than yes/no ones. A question like 'who is the Akond of Swat?' does not have a yes/no answer; it requires the name of an object instead. In Prolog-2 terms such a question is represented by a query containing a *variable*.

A variable is a sequence of characters consisting of letters, numbers and underlines (like an atom) but (unlike an atom) it must begin with an upper-case letter or an underline. So **X, Y, Foo, Akond_of_Swat** are variables and also **_448**. To make a query of a what question, use a variable in the place where you want the solution. So to find the length of the list [3,4,5,6,7] replace the guess, 5, with a variable (try to use meaningful names for variables)

?- length([3,4,5,6,7],Length).

and Prolog-2 says

Length = 5
More (y/n)?

Now Prolog-2 is asking you a question, and a pretty odd one too. Select n for the time being (you have to press <Enter> too).

Interestingly, you can make other questions out of the length query; for example "Which list has length 5?". This is an odd question to ask, but the rule is just the same: replace the argument you're interested in by a variable:

?- length(List,5).

Prolog-2 says

List = [_448,_452,_456,_460,_464]
More (y/n)?

(The numbers after the underlines may differ from these.)

Select n and <Enter>. Prolog-2 has returned a list with five variables as members. When Prolog-2 puts a variable in a solution it means "it doesn't matter what you put in that place", so it has found quite a neat way to tell you which list has five members. You have to excuse it for not using meaningful variable names; system generated variables always start with underline.

You are even allowed to have two variables in a query; consider the question "Which lists have which lengths?". Following the usual rule we replace each argument by a variable. Be careful, though! In any query two variables with the same name refer to

The Prolog-2 User Guide

the same thing, so we must use two different variable names.

?- length(List,Length).

gives the response

List = []
Length = 0
More (y/n)?

So the empty list has no members — true enough. This time select y then <Enter> and see what happens:

List = [_484]
Length = 1
More (y/n)?

We get another correct solution. The reason for the **More (y/n)** question is that some questions have lots of solutions; instead of printing them all, Prolog-2 offers them one at a time. Keep looking at the solutions to the last query until you get bored then select n <Enter>. It's a good thing that Prolog-2 only prints the solutions one at a time, because in this case there was an infinite number of them.

Consider next the question "Is the length of the list [3,4,5,6,7] greater than 3?". This poses a more complicated problem because we are looking for something that satisfies two conditions: it has to be the length of the list [3,4,5,6,7] AND it has to be greater than 3. To represent AND in a query use a comma;

?- length([3,4,5,6,7],Length),Length > 3.

Prolog-2 replies:

Length = 5
More (y/n)?

yes would have done as an answer, but Prolog-2 assumes that if there are variables you want to see their values. Incidentally, if you now select y and <Enter> the answer

no

will be printed; this does not mean that the original question was wrong, just that there are no more solutions.

(This can be confusing. If you answer 'no' to More (y/n)? Prolog-2 will reply yes; if you answer 'yes' it will often say no. You may get the idea that it enjoys disagreeing with you. The yes after your 'no' is unimportant; disregard it. The 'no' after your yes is significant: it means that there are no more solutions.)

In the above query it was important that we should use the same variable Length twice;

the fact that the name was the same meant that the same thing had to fit in each slot. Had we said something like

?- length([3,4,5,6,7],Length),Size > 3.

then Prolog-2 would have looked for one value for the length of the list and for another value, not necessarily the same, for the variable Size. This latter is beyond the built-in arithmetic knowledge of Prolog-2, and causes an error (again, just pressing <Enter> will clear it).

On the other hand, the significance of a variable name NEVER extends beyond the query it occurs in. If you type

?- length([3,4,5,6,7,8],Length).

then Length will be 6 — it's forgotten that it was 5 last time.

There is just one exception to this rule. A variable whose name consists just of the underline character is called an *anonymous variable*. Such a variable means something different every time it occurs; it's used as a don't care variable, when you want to know that something fills a slot but you don't care what. Type

?- length([3,4,5,6,7],_).

and Prolog-2 will just say

yes

"Something satisfies it; you said you didn't care what, so I'm not telling you."

Summary

- We have seen how to enter queries with variables

6. Lesson 3: The notepad

Now we have seen how to enter queries at the top-level interpreter prompt and exploit Prolog-2's inbuilt knowledge. Prolog-2's knowledge is a bit patchy, though. It knows lots about arithmetic and a bit about lists but nothing about cats and mats.

In this lesson we are going to start to teach Prolog-2 about cooking. The idea of the example — which we'll develop in later sections — is that in a recipe for, say, a sausage roll a number of things will be called for that are themselves the product of other cooking processes (making a sausage, making pastry ...). We have to tell Prolog-2 all the things it couldn't possible know, for example that pastry is made from flour, water and fat, and then at the end we hope to have a system that will give us full ingredients for making whatever we want to make.

First of all we have to find out about menus, but not in the usual cooking sense; we shall (unfortunately) not find sausage rolls on any of Prolog-2's menus. Instead we shall find things we can do with Prolog-2.

To enter some information, the simplest procedure is to enter the notepad. This can be speedily accomplished by pressing <F2> and then n. Try that now:

<F2>n

and the notepad appears on the right of the screen. Press

<Esc>

and it's gone!

Simple as that was, we shall sooner or later have to learn how to use the menus at normal speed; let's take it at walking pace this time.

As Prolog-2 explained when we started up, some of the keys have special significance. We have already used a good bit of the alphabetic keyboard, and in editing we have used the cursor keys. The function keys are used to give speedy access to the most important facilities of Prolog-2. We shall see most of them at work by the end of this tutorial. For the present, note the very useful <F6> key. Try it:

<F6>

and a table appears; this sums up what all the function keys do. Note that this table isn't always the same; some of the keys are sometimes disabled, and will then disappear from the table. So rule 1 when flummoxed is to press <F6> and see whether any of the resulting keys are helpful.

Now we are there, how are we to get rid of the box? The answer can be formulated as rule 2 when flummoxed; to get out of where you are press the escape key:

<Esc>

The box vanishes. If you are lost in Prolog-2 and would like to move back to safer ground, <Esc> is the key to help you.

(For completeness we also present rule 3 here. If there wasn't a function key, or the <F6> key had no effect, so that rule 1 failed you; and if <Esc> had no perceptible effect after a few tries then <Control-Break> will interrupt the existing program. If you then press <Enter> you should return to the top-level interpreter. This is a bit violent, and you have to start again from scratch afterwards. There are, as we shall see, other less violent things you can do after an interrupt.)

The function key we are after at the moment is <F2>. <F2> gives access to a menu system of Prolog-2 facilities. All Prolog-2 facilities can be accessed from the top-level interpreter too, but the menu system is sometimes faster and also useful if you forget what to type. Press the key then:

<F2>

and a menu appears. It looks like this:

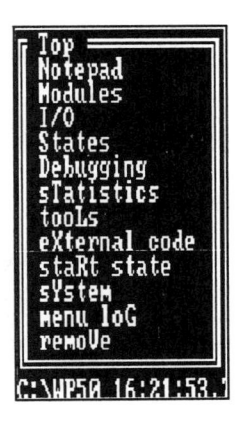

```
Top
Notepad
Modules
I/O
States
Debugging
sTatistics
tooLs
eXternal code
staRt state
sYstem
menu loG
remoVe
C:\WP50 16:21:53.
```

(In the demonstration version facilities on the menu that have been removed will appear in brackets.)

The bar is over the top option, Notepad. There are two ways to make a selection: you can move the bar to the item you want using the cursor up and cursor down key and then press <Enter> or you can press an alphabetic key. The rule is that one letter of an option can be used for fast selection of the item and that letter is the first upper-case letter in the option (to select system you key Y, for example). You can type the letter in upper or lower case. Move the bar around a bit for practice. Notice that the <Home> and <End> keys move straight to the top and straight to the bottom. Some menus are so long that they have to be scrolled up and down to see all the items; in

The Prolog-2 User Guide

this case the <PageUp> and <PageDown> keys are useful. You can abandon a menu without making a selection by keying <Esc>.

For now we want the notepad; later we'll explore the menu system a bit more. Either get the bar back to the top and select:

<Home><Enter>

or use the notepad selection key

N

and we are in the notepad again. (If you hunt around the menu system you'll find an option called Editor rather than Notepad. This is a more complex interface to the same editor, and allows you to edit several windows at the same time. Leave it alone until you feel happy with the notepad.)

Note: In subsequent menu selections, we shall just tell you which item to select and leave it to you whether to use the cursor keys or a letter. Thus

<F2> Notepad

means press <F2> and then either type N or move the bar to notepad and select by typing <Enter>.

The notepad behaves like most editors, that is, it sits and ignores you. There is no prompt and nothing happens when you press full stop. These are fairly superficial points. The important thing to remember is this:

- When you are typing at the ?- prompt in the top-level interpreter you are ASKING the system.

- When you are typing in the notepad you are TELLING the system.

It will remember what you tell it. At times it will demur; for example, if you tell it that 3<5, instead of saying yes, as the top-level interpreter does, it will reply, in effect "I'll be the judge of that"; you mustn't try to tell it about things that are built-in. At the moment, though, it appears totally inert and totally unconcerned about what you type in. Try typing in 'Mary had a little lamb' and editing it. For editing the following information is useful:

- All ASCII keys enter characters as expected; and in addition you can get control characters with <Control> and special characters with the <Alt> key just as when typing in DOS.

- The cursor keys can be used to move the cursor around as you would expect

- The <Delete> key deletes the character at the cursor, the <Backspace> key deletes the character left of the cursor.

The Prolog-2 User Guide

- You can see the word **Insert** in the top-right corner of the screen. That means that any characters you type will be inserted. By keying <Insert> you can toggle between Insert and Overwrite mode; in the latter characters entered delete existing characters.

All of these points are true when typing in the top-level interpreter and in the notepad.

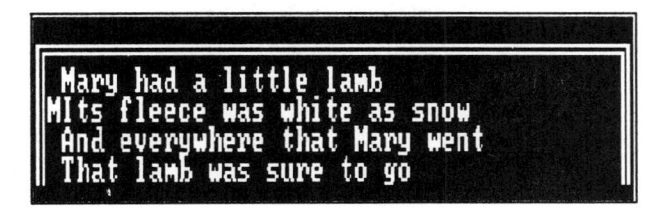

```
Mary had a little lamb
MIts fleece was white as snow
And everywhere that Mary went
That lamb was sure to go
```

We saw that the Top-level interpreter is quite choosy about syntax — the notepad appears not to care at all.

The key that unlocks the notepad is the <F2> function key. Just as in the top-level interpreter, this offers a menu of possibilities, but this time all the possibilities are related to the notepad. We'll see how a few of them work as we go along. Leaving 'Mary had a little lamb' in the window choose the item 'forM' and then 'Syntax':

<F2> **M S**

You will be told that the poem is not valid syntax.

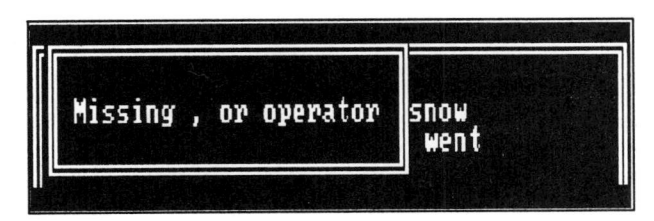

```
Missing , or operator   snow
                        went
```

Press <Esc> to clear the message. Press <F2> again to get the menu and this time select File and then New:

<F2> **F N**.

This clears the window. You will be warned that your work has not been saved; select OK and you are back to a clear screen.

The Prolog-2 User Guide

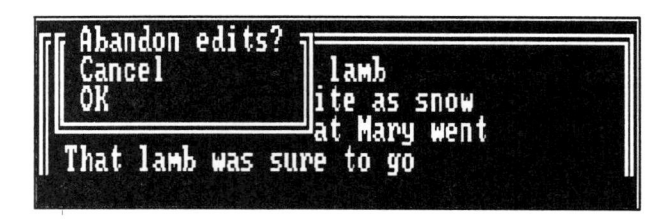

```
┌─Abandon edits?─┐─────────────
│ Cancel         │ lamb
│ OK             │ ite as snow
└────────────────┘ at Mary went
   That lamb was sure to go
```

In using the notepad what we shall do is:

- Type in the things we want to tell Prolog-2, using the notepad as an ordinary text editor.

- Tell Prolog-2 to learn all the things we've typed in.

Now leave the notepad and return to the prompt by typing <Esc>.

Summary

- We saw how to work menus
- We saw how to get to the notepad and use its menu

7. Lesson 4: A simple database

To tell Prolog-2 things, a syntax very similar to that of queries is used.

In effect, what you are saying is: "If I subsequently ask you this question, answer yes".

Let's try a very simple example. Use

<F2> N

to get to the notepad.

Type in the following:

contains(pastry,flour).
contains(pastry,water).
contains(pastry,butter).
contains(pastry,salt).
contains(sausage_roll,sausage).
contains(sausage_roll,pastry).

Now select the menu using <F2> and choose the options Predicate and then Consult. *Consult* is Prolog-2 terminology for learning some information from the user. Now we'd like to see whether this has indeed been learnt, so leave the notepad (typing <Esc>) and we are back at the top-level interpreter's prompt.

Type

?- contains(pastry,flour).

The system answers

yes.

Not only has Prolog-2 learnt to answer yes to these queries, but it can also use the information you gave to answer 'what' questions.

?- contains(pastry,Ingredient).

In other words, what does pastry contain? Back come the answers:

Ingredient = flour
More (y/n)?

and so on. Key y until it says no.

If you prefer to have all the answers at once you can use the setof construction:

The Prolog-2 User Guide

?- setof(Ingredient,contains(pastry,Ingredient),Set).

will return

Ingredient = _448
Set = [butter,flour,salt,water]

the list of solutions; it even sorted them alphabetically for us. There are no more solutions: after

More (y/n)?

type

N<Enter>

setof(X,Q,S) means: 'S is the set of X such that query Q is true'. It is useful if you need all the solutions to a query at once. For example, to find out how many ingredients pastry has:

?- setof(Ingredient,contains(pastry,Ingredient),Set),
   length(Set,Number).

Ingredient = _448
Set = [butter,flour,salt,water]
Number = 4

More (y/n)?

(We didn't want the set that time, but as we saw in Lesson 2, we get it anyway.)

There are no more solutions: type N<Enter>.

Now get back to the notepad, for we are going to add a very important extra piece of information:

<F2>N

Our previous information is still there.

To make a sausage roll you need a sausage and also you need all the things you need to make pastry. We now want to tell Prolog-2 this. More precisely we want a predicate that will be true if an ingredient is needed either directly or indirectly for a product.

One approach would be to type in all the things that were needed directly:

needed(sausage_roll,flour).

etc.

That would be tedious, though, and we should have to remember to change both predicates in the event that we updated the recipes in the system. Really what we want to tell Prolog is that

- sausages are needed for sausage rolls

- anything that is contained in pastry is needed for sausage rolls

The former is easy: get to the bottom of the contains predicate and add the line:

needed(sausage_roll,sausage).

The second thing that has to be added uses a new form, and one that is very important in Prolog-2. Up to now we have simply told Prolog-2 facts so that when we ask questions it will know they are true. In other words we have been using it as a simple database. Now we are going to tell it, not that something is true unconditionally, but that it is true conditionally on something else; X is needed for a sausage roll if it is contained in pastry. 'If' in Prolog-2 is represented by the symbol :-, that is, a colon followed by a minus sign.

Add the line

needed(sausage_roll,X) :- contains(pastry,X).

This is called a *rule*. Assertions to Prolog-2 with no :- are called *facts*. Rules and facts together are called *clauses*.

When Prolog-2 is asked a question and finds an appropriate rule it looks at the part after the :- (the *tail*), and treats that as a query to itself. In other words, it stops investigating the first question and asks itself the query in the tail. Unlike the transactions with the user, it keeps quiet about this internal questioning process, and does not print the answer to questions it asks itself. But if the answer is yes then Prolog-2 knows that the answer to the original question is also yes.

In the tail of a rule, as in a query, there may be several queries separated by commas; in this case it has to ask itself all the questions in the tail and only answer yes if the answer to each of them is yes. Queries in tails are usually referred to as *goals*.

Next we have to tell Prolog-2 to absorb this extra information. Use <F2> to get the menu and then select Predicate and Reconsult. (Reconsult is used when you have changed information; it means "alter the existing information", whereas consult means "here is some new information". If we had selected consult, we should have added all the clauses for contains again.) Then use <Esc> to leave the notepad.

From now on we often have to press <F2> Predicate Reconsult, so we'll shorten this and just say "commit the clauses".

Check that Prolog-2 knows now that water is needed for a sausage roll:

The Prolog-2 User Guide

?- needed(sausage_roll,water).

Get all the things needed for a sausage roll:

?- setof(Ingredient,needed(sausage_roll,Ingredient),Set).

It's just as though we had typed in all the ingredients separately; but much easier on the fingers!

Our next aim is to add some quantities to our data. We should like to know how much of each ingredient we need for some recipe. To decide this Prolog-2 has to be told how much of everything is contained in a given amount of the result. For example, half a pound of pastry contains four ounces of flour, four ounces of butter, four tablespoons of water and a pinch of salt. To avoid these quaint measures we shall simply use fractions; for each constituent, we shall record how much of the result by weight it makes up.

Return to the notepad and change the clauses for contains as follows:

contains(pastry,flour,0.4).
contains(pastry,water,0.19).
contains(pastry,butter,0.4).
contains(pastry,salt,0.01).
contains(sausage_roll,sausage,0.75).
contains(sausage_roll,pastry,0.25).

We want to ask Prolog-2 how much butter goes into a pound of sausage rolls. We'll see next how to do this.

Use <Esc> to leave the notepad.

Summary

- We saw what a rule looks like

8. Lesson 5: Arithmetic, the Help System

Use

<F2> N

to get to the notepad.

The rules for **needed** now need changing. Instead of just saying that we need butter for sausage rolls, we want to know how much.

The rule is simply enough stated: for 1 unit of sausage rolls we need 0.75 of sausage and quarter of each of the things required for one unit of pastry.

```
needed(sausage_roll,sausage,0.75).
needed(sausage_roll,Ingredient,Quantity_in_pastry*0.25) :-
     contains(pastry,Ingredient,Quantity_in_pastry).
```

Change the clauses to look like this, commit and leave the notepad. Try a couple of questions:

?- needed(sausage_roll,sausage,Amount).

The Amount is 0.75, as you would expect.

?- needed(sausage_roll,water,Amount).

Amount = 0.1900*0.2500

Surprise! Prolog-2 doesn't evaluate the result.

Prolog-2 can pass around as the value of variables not only the data types we saw in lesson 2, integer, real, atom and string, but also complex structures like 0.19*0.25. This is a source of great power and, in this case, minor annoyance because it has chosen this occasion to show off what it can keep in its variables and what we wanted was the answer. Back to the notepad.

Prolog-2 has built-in knowledge about arithmetic, and you can ask it to evaluate expressions for you. You do have to ask, though.

```
needed(sausage_roll,sausage,0.75).
needed(sausage_roll,Ingredient,Quantity) :-
    contains(pastry,Ingredient,Quantity_in_pastry),
    Quantity is Quantity_in_pastry*0.25.
```

Change the clauses to make them look like this. The second clause now requires Prolog-2 to ask itself two questions: one for which we supply the data and one we haven't heard of. Note the way the second clause is laid out; it makes things much easier to read if the tail goals each appear on a separate line.

The Prolog-2 User Guide

is is Prolog-2's arithmetic assignment statement. However, in line with thinking of Prolog-2 as a system to which you ask questions rather than to which you give instructions, you should think of is not as saying "evaluate the right hand side and assign the value to the variable on the left" (who said the thing on the left had to be a variable?) but as saying "Is the thing on the left equal to the value of expression on the right?". To get some practice, leave the notepad for a moment (<Esc>).

Try a few questions to the top-level interpreter.

?- 5 is 2+3.

Is 5 equal to 2 plus 3? Yes, of course.

?- 2+3 is 5.

No. The question was, is the left hand side equal to the value of the expression on the right, and the answer is no; the value of the expression on the right is 5 and the left hand side is 2+3, and these are different things in Prolog-2.

As usual you can insert variables and have Prolog-2 try to find values:

?- X is 2+3.

X = 5

So you can use is like an assignment statement in a conventional language. Try being a bit clever:

?- 5 is 2+X.

Unfortunately you have now hit one of the limitations of Prolog-2; though the question made perfectly good sense, the built-in arithmetic knowledge in Prolog-2 doesn't stretch that far.

Stop and look at the screen now. In addition to the usual display there are two extra windows: a menu in the top right and one at the bottom. The one at the bottom displays data about the error; there is a brief error message and also a record of the goal that caused the error (pretty obvious in this case, but not always).

```
Error no. 23
Unrecognised expression element
Error goal: 5 is 2+_102
```

Before clearing the error pause to look at the menu that appeared. You have several options: up to now we have aborted the operation. You can also ask Prolog-2 to treat the question as though the answer had been no and then carry on; this is useful if the

The Prolog-2 User Guide

question was one asked by Prolog-2 to itself because it can then go on and try and do something else without destroying all its work and returning to the prompt. You can exit Prolog-2, but that is too drastic a remedy for us at the moment. The option in brackets, correct, allows you to edit a term that contained a syntax error. This question was not syntactically wrong, it made perfectly good sense, indeed we know the answer; it just offended Prolog-2's way of doing things. So you can't edit the goal. This fact is shown by putting the option in brackets. You'll find that you can't get the bar onto it; it is disallowed for the present.

Select the Help option.

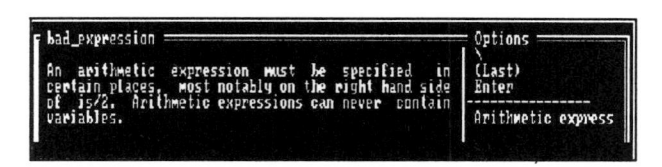

```
┌ bad_expression ═══════════════════════┬ Options ═══════
│ An arithmetic expression must be specified in │ (Last)
│ certain places, most notably on the right hand side │ Enter
│ of is/2. Arithmetic expressions can never contain │ ────────────
│ variables.                              │ Arithmetic express
```

This is our first encounter with the help system. The help system in Prolog-2 is very extensive and should be used whenever information is needed; there are lots of ways into it, and we shall see two of them in this lesson.

The left part is the help message. It reminds us that it was expecting a proper expression and that variables aren't allowed. The right hand part is a menu and gives access to other help screens. The first three options are always displayed: the top takes you to the root of the help system — we'll see this later — and the second to the previous screen displayed (there wasn't one so it's disallowed). The third allows you to type in a topic on which you want help, but that's for use as a last resort; the system is designed so that the items you are most likely to need are below the dotted line. In this case we might want to know more about valid expressions. Stop and browse around using the items below the line on the menu; you'll find out a lot about expressions. When you've finished, press <Esc>.

Notice the way help named the predicate causing trouble — is/2. This is the standard way to name a predicate in Prolog-2, separating the name and the arity with a /.

Now clear the error by typing A.

Before going back to the notepad we promised a second way into the help system. The expression information was useful, and it would be a shame if we had to make a mistake before we could see it. Prolog-2's help is context sensitive, and if it thinks you are trying to use one of its built-in facilities like is it will tell you about it. So imagine you type "X is" and then you think "what on earth comes next?". Try it now

?- X is

and now press the help key, <F1>. <F1> always offers you help of some kind, and at the moment it sees you hovering over is and offers you help on that; you can find your

49

The Prolog-2 User Guide

way easily to the arithmetic expression help from here.

Key <Esc> to leave help, <Esc> again to clear the partial term and then return to the notepad. This way into help is valid in the notepad too; steer the cursor to the right of the word is and press help and there you are again!

Leave help using <Esc>.

Now use <F2> and select Predicate and Reconsult to update Prolog-2's information about sausage rolls. <Esc> leaves the notepad and this time the query

?- needed(sausage_roll,water,Amount).

Amount = 0.0475

gives the expected answer.

Try out

?- setof(Ingredient-Amount,
    needed(sausage_roll,Ingredient,Amount),
    Set).

This gives a printout of the shopping list. Observe that the — did not mean subtract the **Amount** from the **Ingredient** because we didn't use **is/2**.

Summary

- We saw how to evaluate an arithmetic expression
- We learnt two ways to enter the help system

9. Lesson 6: Built-in predicates

We have seen some of the built-in facilities of Prolog-2 already; they are a sort of built-in database of information that it would be tedious for the programmer to have to enter explicitly. These predicates behave just like the ones we define ourselves; they can say yes, they can say no and they can give values to variables. We call predicates which are built-in to the Prolog-2 system, such as **is/2**, *built-in predicates*.

In fact up to now we have seen no possibility for getting Prolog-2 to do anything other than respond to questions in this way. However complex we make the question, Prolog-2 sits and thinks and then prints the answer. Writers of advanced applications may find this a bit restrictive (actually the notepad you are using is entirely written in Prolog-2, so there must be more facilities available).

Try typing

?- true.

Prolog-2 responds

yes

because true is built in and always succeeds. Now type

?- bell.

Prolog-2 responds

yes

because bell is built in and always succeeds.

There was a difference though; audible though not visible. As far as answering queries goes, bell is identical to true, but also it has what is called a *side-effect*; it sounds the computer's buzzer. Prolog-2 has many such built-in predicates; they have two functions, firstly to answer a question and secondly to do something. Often the first of these functions is quite trivial, as with bell; the only reason for including it in the language is to allow the side-effect.

It is impossible for the user to cause side-effects other than by writing predicates with tail goals that have side-effects; there are no other facilities (indeed, you have already seen pretty well all of the Prolog-2 language).

One of the most important side-effects is input/output. To illustrate this we shall amend our sausage roll system to print a shopping list. The idea is that the user enters

?- shop(sausage_roll).

The Prolog-2 User Guide

say, and the system will print out the shopping list for a unit of sausage rolls.

We shall use a built-in predicate, write, which outputs a term. It is always true, that is, there are no circumstances in which a question about this predicate will give the answer no; and therefore it is only interesting because it causes side-effects.

Of course, we always get output of variable values at the end of a query anyway, but now we want to take the output under our own control.

Back to the notepad then, and at the bottom we shall add our new predicate.

```
shop(Recipe) :-
    setof(Ingredient-Amount,
        needed(Recipe,Ingredient,Amount),S),
    write(S),
    nl.
```

This looks just like any other predicate except that two of the tail goals are only there for the side-effects. **write(S)** outputs the list S; **nl** starts a new line. Commit, leave the notepad and type the query:

?- shop(sausage_roll).

and you see the output

[butter-0.1000,flour-0.1000,salt-0.0025,
 sausage-0.7500,water-0.0475]

and then

yes

on the screen, meaning the answer to your question was yes. In this case you don't much care because you have your shopping list anyway. If you had typed

?- shop(duck_soup).

you would have been told no (it doesn't know anything about duck soup) and you'd have got no shopping list.

Now apart from looking unlike a conventional shopping list, this list of ours has another annoying property; it expects us to go out and buy some water. This is not really very helpful, because we only have to turn on the tap. In a bit we shall see how to leave out unwanted solutions.

If you have a printer attached you can redirect the shopping list to it by typing

?- tell(printer), shop(sausage_roll).

The Prolog-2 User Guide

tell/1 is Prolog-2's way of outputting to a device other than the screen. At the end of the output it is a good idea to close the stream to which the output has been sent; on some devices you won't see any output until this is done. So we need to close a stream.

Suppose we didn't know how to do that, and see how the help system guides us towards the solution. You can try to guess the required predicate name, type it and then press <F1> but that can be time-consuming. Here's a better way.

Press the <F1> key to enter help. Having no idea of the context Prolog-2 puts you at the top of the help system and you can read the root screen.

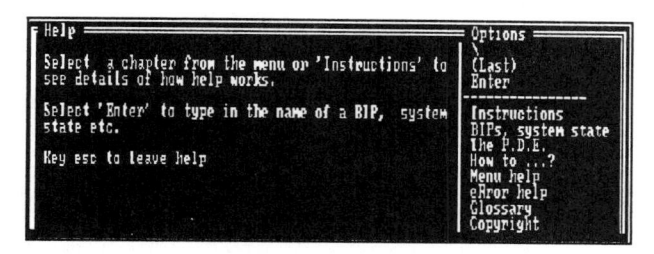

```
┌ Help ═══════════════════════════════ Options ═══════
│ Select a chapter from the menu or 'Instructions' to │ (Last)
│ see details of how help works.                      │ Enter
│                                                     │ ─────────
│ Select 'Enter' to type in the name of a BIP, system │ Instructions
│ state etc.                                          │ BIPs, system state
│                                                     │ The P.D.E.
│ Key esc to leave help                               │ How to ...?
│                                                     │ Menu help
│                                                     │ eRror help
│                                                     │ Glossary
│                                                     │ Copyright
```

A useful facility when you forget the name of a predicate is "How to?". Select it from the menu.

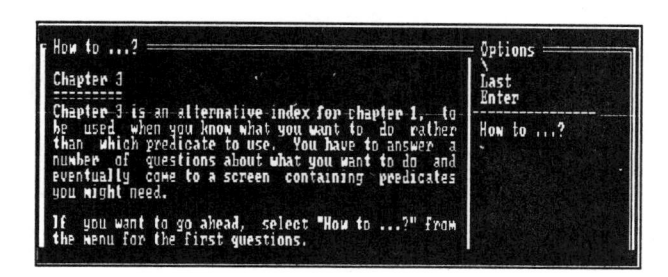

```
┌ How to ...? ════════════════════════ Options ═══════
│ Chapter 3                                           │ Last
│ ─────────                                           │ Enter
│ Chapter 3 is an alternative index for chapter 1, to │ ─────────
│ be used when you know what you want to do rather    │ How to ...?
│ than which predicate to use. You have to answer a   │
│ number of questions about what you want to do and   │
│ eventually come to a screen containing predicates   │
│ you might need.                                     │
│                                                     │
│ If you want to go ahead, select "How to ...?" from  │
│ the menu for the first questions.                   │
```

You feel brave: go ahead.

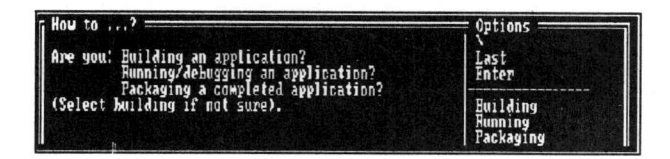

```
┌ How to ...? ════════════════════════ Options ═══════
│ Are you: Building an application?                   │ Last
│          Running/debugging an application?          │ Enter
│          Packaging a completed application?         │ ─────────
│ (Select Building if not sure).                      │ Building
│                                                     │ Running
│                                                     │ Packaging
```

Plainly we are building an application.

53

The Prolog-2 User Guide

```
┌ Building ═══════════════════════════════╤ Options ═══════
│ In an application you can write 'pure' code without │ Last
│ side effects, or you can write code with side-      │ Enter
│ effects. Side-effects affect the database and also  │────────────
│ are used to implement input-output.                 │ Free of side effec
│                                                     │ Database
│ Is the task you want to perform:                    │ Input/output
│       Free of side effects?                         │ Other
│       Related to the database?
│       Related to input/output?
│       Related to some other side-effect?
│
│ (If both database and I/O choose database).
```

No doubt about it!

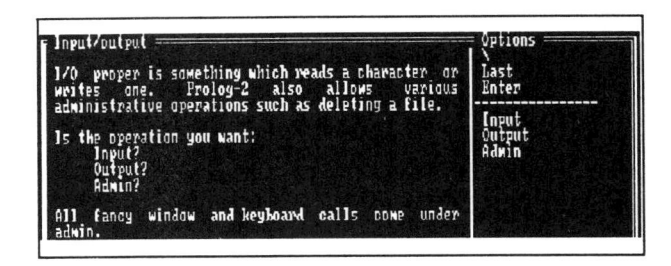

```
┌ Input/output ═══════════════════════════╤ Options ═══════
│ I/O proper is something which reads a character or  │ Last
│ writes one.  Prolog-2 also allows various           │ Enter
│ administrative operations such as deleting a file.  │────────────
│                                                     │ Input
│ Is the operation you want:                          │ Output
│       Input?                                        │ Admin
│       Output?
│       Admin?
│
│ All fancy window and keyboard calls come under
│ admin.
```

Closing a stream doesn't output any characters.

```
┌ Admin ══════════════════════════════════╤ Options ═══════
│ Is the operation concerned with token formatting?   │ Last
│                                                     │ Enter
│                                                     │────────────
│                                                     │ Yes
│                                                     │ No
```

That doesn't sound likely!

```
┌ No ═════════════════════════════════════╤ Options ═══════
│ Some operations, like opening and closing are       │ Last
│ relevant for all devices. Some, like scrolling, are │ Enter
│ specific to a device (window).                      │────────────
│                                                     │ General
│ Is the operation:                                   │ Disk
│       General?                                      │ Window
│       Disk related?
│       Window or keyboard related?
```

Closing is something you can do to any stream.

The Prolog-2 User Guide

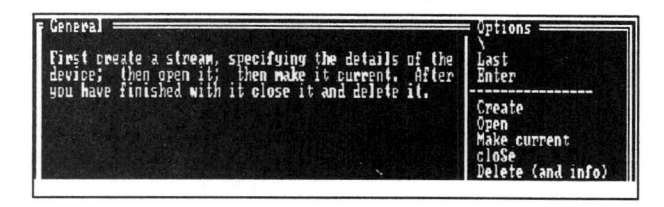

Now we appear to be almost there.

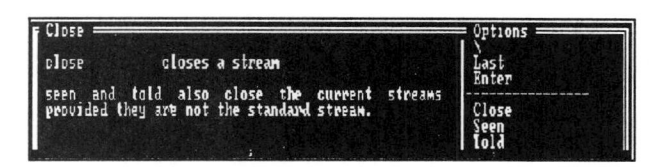

Close would do very well, but let's look at told.

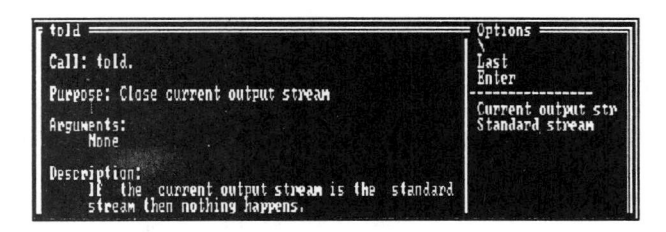

This is the screen we'd have got if we'd known the name told and just typed it and then <F1>. We'd probably have solved the problem in hand faster if we'd guessed **close** and typed <F1>, but the "How to" method is often useful.

Leave the help system with <Esc>.

So we can print the shopping list with

?- tell(printer),shop(sausage_roll),told.

Don't try this unless you have a printer!

Summary

• We saw what built-in predicates and side-effects are
• We discovered a method of getting help on a built-in predicate when we don't know its name

55

10. Lesson 7: Backtracking

Our next step is to stop sending people out to buy water. Of course we could just take the water out altogether, but then the proportions of the other ingredients wouldn't add up; and the database may be used for more than just shopping.

We can easily enough add some clauses saying which things are always in store (really we need to say how much of each, but we'll just list things that are either available on tap or are needed in such small quantities that we can assume they'll be around: water and salt).

Get to the notepad, and at the bottom add two facts:

in_store(water).
in_store(salt).

<F2> PR gets the information into Prolog-2 and <Esc> leaves the notepad. Try the query:

?- needed(sausage_roll,Ingredient,_),in_store(Ingredient).

The underline, remember, means we don't care about the amount.

The answers are water and salt, of course. But lets see what Prolog-2 does to get them.

You've asked the question "What is both needed for sausage rolls and in store?".

Prolog-2 first considers the first half of the query

needed(sausage_roll,Ingredient,_)

on its own. Had you just typed that in, the answer would have been that **Ingredient** was equal to sausage. So Prolog-2 assumes for the time being that **Ingredient** is equal to sausage and proceeds to the next query. This is now equivalent to:

in_store(sausage)

to which the answer would have been no. What Prolog-2 does now is to go back to the previous query, just as though it had asked you **More (y/n)?** and you had said y. It abandons the value of **Ingredient** it set just as it does when it goes back to look for another solution. This process is called *backtracking*. The next solution to needed sets **Ingredient** to flour; this suffers the same fate as **sausage**.

The next solution to **needed(Ingredient)** is water, **in_store(water)** is true so the solution

Ingredient = water

is printed. The test saves you from having to answer **More (y/n)?** questions in order to reject uninteresting answers; it filters the answers for you. Of course, there is no need to understand about backtracking to see that water and salt are the only solutions to the query; later, though, we shall find this approach very helpful.

For the time being we are actually interested in the things that aren't in store. Prolog-2 allows the word **not** to be placed before a query to reverse its meaning, so we want to replace the second goal in the last query with

not in_store(Ingredient)

Rather than type it in, press the <F3> key and you'll see the last term appear. It is easy to produce the desired term by editing this (play around a bit with <F3> and <F4> first; you can see the last ten terms you typed in, with <F3> giving older ones and <F4> newer).

Edit to

```
?- needed(sausage_roll,Ingredient,_),
   not in_store(Ingredient).
```

The answers now are as you would expect: sausage, flour and butter.

Get back to the notepad and add a new predicate at the bottom:

```
must_buy(Recipe,Ingredient,Amount) :-
    needed(Recipe,Ingredient,Amount),
    not in_store(Ingredient).
```

Then amend the shop predicate changing **needed** to **must_buy** and commit.

Printing the new list with

?- shop(sausage_roll).

you will find that water and salt have vanished.

A while back, we remarked that Prolog-2 conducts a sort of internal dialogue when it evaluates a predicate; for each goal in the tail it asks itself that as a query. We said that this dialogue produces no output. That is normally true, but Prolog-2 provides a tool to enable you to watch what's going on if you want to. This can be helpful when you are *debugging*, and the tool is called the debugger.

A special terminology is used when the debugger monitors a query.

- When Prolog-2 asks itself a question it is said to CALL the query.

The Prolog-2 User Guide

- When it gets the answer and asks **More (y/n)?** it is said to EXIT from the query. It then suspends that query and carries on with something else.

- If ever it backtracks and therefore has to look for more solutions as though it had answered Y to its own **More (y/n)?** question then it is said to REDO the query.

- When it looks for solutions but cannot find them (so that it answers no to its own query) it is said to FAIL the query.

Watch this at work in the shopping program. To do this type

?- trace.

A window appears in the middle of the screen. The reason the trace output is sent to a special window is to avoid disrupting the screen with trace output. Normally the window is there when you need it and not when you don't but you can make it disappear with <F8> and reappear with <F10>. This is particularly useful if you have to type behind the window.

Type

?- must_buy(sausage_roll,Ingredient,Amount).

The following line appears in the window:

(1) 0 CALL: must_buy(sausage_roll,_1968,_2002)?

The debugger has replaced your variable names with ones of its own. Repress your anger: it does this to avoid ambiguity (remember that two variables with the same name in different clauses are different variables).

(The numbers after the underlines are generated internally by Prolog-2 and will not necessarily be the same as those printed here.)

The question mark at the end indicates that you are required to type a key. Just typing <Enter> is the simplest thing to do.

Looking at must_buy we see that it is a rule and that first of all it requires Prolog-2 to ask the question

(2) 1 CALL: needed(sausage_roll,_1968,_2002)?

The answer to this is provided by a fact, so that immediately an answer appears:

(2) 1 EXIT: needed(sausage_roll,sausage,0.7500)

EXIT means the answer was yes (otherwise it would have said FAIL) and two variables have been given values. It is as though it had said

_1968 = sausage
_2002 = 0.7500

This time there was no ? and the thing continued at once. This behaviour is configurable.

The other thing to be worried about is whether sausages are available already.

   (3) 1 CALL: in_store(sausage)?
   (3) 1 FAIL: in_store(sausage)

No they aren't. That's what we wanted. So:

   (1) 0 EXIT: must_buy(sausage_roll,sausage,0.7500)

Ingredient = sausage
Amount = 0.7500
More (y/n)? y

This time it was you who told it to retry. It backtracks to must_buy, where there are more solutions:

   (1) 0 REDO: must_buy(sausage_roll,sausage,0.7500)?s

We know the answer will be flour this time. The s option tells Prolog-2 to revert to its usual uncommunicative behaviour on this query, that is, just solve it without nattering. This it does.

> (1) 0 EXIT: must_buy(sausage_roll,flour,0.1000)?

Note that after a skip the debugger pauses at the EXIT port.

So we have another solution:

Ingredient = flour
Amount = 0.1000
More (y/n)? y

Go back yet again.

   (1) 0 REDO: must_buy(sausage_roll,flour,0.1000)?
   (2) 1 REDO: needed(sausage_roll,flour,0.1000)?
   (4) 1 CALL: _262 is 0.1900*0.2500? [system]
   (4) 1 EXIT: 0.0475 is 0.1900*0.2500
   (2) 1 EXIT: needed(sausage_roll,water,0.0475)
   (5) 1 CALL: in_store(water)?
   (5) 1 EXIT: in_store(water)
   (6) 1 CALL: fail? [system]

The Prolog-2 User Guide

    (6) 1 FAIL: fail

(The fail predicate, which you didn't write in your program, is displayed to remind you that there was a not before in_store.)

So there won't be a solution from water.

    (2) 1 REDO: needed(sausage_roll,water,0.0475)?
    (4) 1 REDO: 0.0475 is 0.1900*0.2500?
    (4) 1 FAIL: _262 is 0.1900*0.2500
    (7) 1 CALL: _262 is 0.4000*0.2500? [system]
    (7) 1 EXIT: 0.1000 is 0.4000*0.2500
    (2) 1 EXIT: needed(sausage_roll,butter,0.1000)
    (8) 1 CALL: in_store(butter)?
    (8) 1 FAIL: in_store(butter)
    (1) 0 EXIT: must_buy(sausage_roll,butter,0.1000)

Ingredient = butter
Amount = 0.1000
More (y/n)? y

    (1) 0 REDO: must_buy(sausage_roll,butter,0.1000)?
    (2) 1 REDO: needed(sausage_roll,butter,0.1000)?
    (7) 1 REDO: 0.1000 is 0.4000*0.2500?
    (7) 1 FAIL: _262 is 0.4000*0.2500
    (9) 1 CALL: _262 is 0.0100*0.2500? [system]
    (9) 1 EXIT: 0.0025 is 0.0100*0.2500
    (2) 1 EXIT: needed(sausage_roll,salt,0.0025)
    (10) 1 CALL: in_store(salt)?f

At this point it strikes you that actually you've run out of salt. While debugging you can tell Prolog-2 not to solve a goal but instead to take the answer from you. In this case f overrides the fact that salt is in store as recorded in the database.

    (10) 1 FAIL: in_store(salt)
    (1) 0 EXIT: must_buy(sausage_roll,salt,0.0025)

Ingredient = salt
Amount = 0.0025
More (y/n)? y

So we actually used the debugger to change the behaviour of Prolog-2.

       (1) 0 REDO: must_buy(sausage_roll,salt,0.0025)?x
    => (2) 1 REDO: needed(sausage_roll,salt,0.0025)
    => (9) 1 REDO: 0.0025 is 0.0100*0.2500
    => (9) 1 FAIL: _262 is 0.0100*0.2500
    => (2) 1 FAIL: needed(sausage_roll,_228,_262)
    => (1) 0 FAIL: must_buy(sausage_roll,_228,_262)

x told Prolog-2 not to stop again unless it proved a new fact. As it didn't we got straight to the end.

In the full version you can get full help on the debugging options by typing h whenever you see the debugger's ? prompt.

Type

?- nodebug.

to stop debugging. As this is itself traced, you have to press <Enter> once more before the debugger will disappear.

Summary

- We learnt what backtracking is
- We saw how the debugger works

11. Lesson 8: Repeating tasks

The output from the shopping program is still not very pretty. A step in the right direction would be to place each item on a separate line.

Type the following:

?- must_buy(sausage_roll,Ingredient,Amount),
   write(Ingredient-Amount),
   nl.

Prolog-2 will display

sausage-0.7500

as expected and then the unwanted variable values and the More (y/n)? question. We have seen already that we can add a goal at the end to filter the solutions, and that the effect of that goal's failure is to backtrack into must_buy without the question, just as we want. We could add a completely implausible filter like

mostly_composed_of_yttrium(Ingredient)

which we assume we shall never want to add to the database for any ingredient; but Prolog-2 spares us the trouble by supplying the built-in fail which is guaranteed always to fail. Now change the last goal (use <F3>!) to

?- must_buy(sausage_roll,Ingredient,Amount),
   write(Ingredient-Amount),
   nl,
   fail.

and a nicer display will appear:

sausage-0.7500
flour-0.1000
butter-0.1000

Unfortunately it's not alphabetic any more.

Then, admittedly, it will say

no

but by now we have the list and don't care.

However, you should recognise that what we have written now differs a lot from the questions we asked in the early lessons. Not only does the goal have side-effects but the yes/no answer has no significance and, most importantly, we are relying on Prolog-2

The Prolog-2 User Guide

to behave in a certain way. Suppose a very clever Prolog-2 enhancement enabled it to tell straight away that the goal would fail and therefore that there was no need to work it out — we should not be grateful at all. On the contrary, we expect Prolog-2 to backtrack through the clauses in the order in which we entered them and we expect it to evaluate the tail goals from left to right. This is the price we pay for being able to control side-effects.

Let's amend the program in the notepad now. The shop program should be changed to read:

```
shop(Recipe) :-
    must_buy(Recipe,Ingredient,Amount),
    write(Ingredient-Amount),
    nl,
    fail.
```

It's ugly to have successful predicates failing, and also one day we may want to do something else afterwards; so to make the predicate succeed we add a second clause that will always be used after the failure of the first.

```
shop(_).
```

Using the _ is a conventional way to tell Prolog-2 that the argument isn't used in the second clause. Commit and leave the notepad.

To finish this lesson we are going to try to cut down on the number of figures in the decimal numbers being printed — our shoppers are getting depressed at having to weigh out such precise units. We'd really rather just have two decimal places.

Configuration parameters like the number of decimal places are usually to be found somewhere in the menu system and are collectively described as system states. Prolog-2 has a very large number of system states that allow the user to change the way it behaves — the simplest can be accessed from the state menu in the menu system. To get there type

<F2>

then select States. Another menu, with names of states appears, and one of them is called Decimals. Selecting it isn't likely to do any damage, but in case you're in any doubt move the bar to that entry and then press the help key, <F1> — you'll see a brief description in the help window of what the field is for. It looks right for us. Clear help with <Esc> and select the item; a box with a number appears. If you need instructions remember that <F1> will give them and that <F6> will tell you which keys may be used at the moment. However, in this case the operation is simple enough; use <Backspace> to remove the old entry, then just key 2 and then <Enter> then <Esc> to leave the menu system. Running

?- shop(sausage_roll).

The Prolog-2 User Guide

again will show that we succeeded in suppressing two of the decimal places.

There is still a problem, though: the information about this setting is not stored with our program. We need a way to set the number in the program.

There is a way and you could find it either by rummaging through the manual or by using the "How to" help system. For variety though note that if the menu system can do something then you can do it too. If you're feeling envious of the menu system, there is a way to find out how it gets its effects. It's a bit complicated, but it has other uses too, so we'll look at it here.

Select <F2> to get the menu. Select the menu loG item and another menu will appear. From this menu select log oN. The effect of this is that the commands issued by the menu system on your behalf will be logged in a window, so that you can use them in programs. Now go ahead and change the number of decimals to 2 as before and the term

state(decimals,_,2)

appears in the logging window. This is the answer to your problem, then. Of course you could just write it down on the back of an envelope and then type it in, but there's another way to move the term into your program: get back to the menu loG menu and then select copY log. This copies the most recently logged term to the clipboard (you can't normally see the clipboard, though there is an option on the Tools menu that displays it). Then switch off menu logging (just for tidiness) and return to the notepad. You want to insert the term on the clipboard into your program as a new first tail goal for the first clause of shop/1. Create a new line there and move the cursor to the start, then select the menu with <F2>, select Block and then Paste (you'll notice the copY option on the block menu; this puts a piece of text onto the clipboard). The line duly appears. You have to align it properly and add a comma at the end.

```
shop(Recipe) :-
    state(decimals,_,2),
    must_buy(Recipe,Ingredient,Amount),
    write(Ingredient-Amount),
    nl,
    fail.
```

Now the setting is saved for all future sessions. Commit and leave the notepad.

The clipboard was a slow way to transfer this term, but for very complex goals such as window definitions it can save a lot of time. Of course you can also use it within an edit just to move text around.

Summary

- We saw how backtracking could be used to repeatedly perform a task
- We discovered the menu log

12. Lesson 9: Recursion

Now we shall take an interest in sausage making.

To make a sausage you need sausage skin, pork and mixed spices. Skins and pork you get at the butcher, but mixed spices you make yourself depending on your fancy. You need a lot of pepper and probably a bit of cinnamon, some cloves, bayleaves and mace. These you grind up together and keep in a jar.

We can easily add all this to the contains predicate. Add the clauses after the other contains clauses, not at the end. This is good style and is compulsory if you want to compile the program.

Get to the notepad and add

```
contains(sausage,skin,0.01).
contains(sausage,pork,0.94).
contains(sausage,mixed_spice,0.05).
contains(mixed_spice,pepper,0.5).
contains(mixed_spice,cinnamon,0.1).
contains(mixed_spice,cloves,0.1).
contains(mixed_spice,bay,0.2).
contains(mixed_spice,mace,0.1).
```

I know that seems a lot of spice.

Unfortunately the needed program doesn't work any more because we didn't make it general enough. Remember it says

```
needed(sausage_roll,sausage,0.75).
needed(sausage_roll,Ingredient,Quantity) :-
    contains(pastry,Ingredient,Quantity_in_pastry),
    Quantity is Quantity_in_pastry*0.25.
```

Now we could generalise it a bit by changing the first clause to

```
needed(sausage_roll,sausage,Quantity) :-
    contains(sausage,Ingredient,Quantity_in_sausage),
    Quantity is Quantity_in_sausage*0.75.
```

Unfortunately that will not reduce the sausage roll to its 'shoppable' constituents, because it will give us a shopping list with mixed spice on, and we're supposed to make that.

Our problem is that we need to think more generally, so that our system can cope with any level of constituents. Roughly what we want to say is:

- to make something you need everything that it contains plus everything you need for something it contains.

The Prolog-2 User Guide

This sounds a bit circular! Let's try and reformulate a bit.

First of all, something is a basic ingredient if it doesn't contain anything.

Secondly, to make a basic ingredient you just need the same amount of that ingredient.

Thirdly, to make something that isn't a basic ingredient, and therefore has constituents, you need appropriate proportions of the things you need to make the constituents.

That isn't really circular, because knowledge of how to make a more complicated thing depends not on knowledge of how to make the same thing but only on knowledge of how to make simpler things.

Try that out in Prolog-2.

In the notepad delete the definition of needed (use the block facility for this: using the block menu, select a start and end surrounding the predicate. It will change colour. Now select cut from the same menu. The old version is still on the clipboard and will stay there until we do another cut or copy).

The new version is

```
needed(Recipe,Recipe,1) :- basic(Recipe).
needed(Recipe,Ingredient,Total) :-
    contains(Recipe,Something,Amount),
    needed(Something,Ingredient,Subamount),
    Total is Amount*Subamount.
```

To put this in words: first, to make something basic just take it. Secondly, if B is contained in C and A is needed for B then A is needed for C. For example sausage rolls contain sausages, so anything you need to make a sausage, you need to make a sausage roll.

Don't try it yet — we haven't defined basic.

In the case of the second clause Prolog-2 is trying to answer a question about whether something is needed and in doing that asks itself another question about what is needed — but the second question is about a different object, so it won't necessarily just loop round forever. In the end every question about things needed can be solved by a question about whether something is basic.

Our new definition is much nicer than the old — there's absolutely no knowledge of recipes coded in it.

We could add a lot of facts about which things are basic, but we don't need to, because we know that something is basic if there's nothing it contains. So we can write

basic(Recipe) :- not contains(Recipe,_,_).

66

The resulting program (as we must reluctantly call it — it really isn't a database any more) will cope with any level of nesting of constituents. Commit the new clauses and leave the notepad, then try it out:

?- shop(sausage_roll).

Unfortunately some of the quantities are too small and appear as zeros. Try setting the number of decimal places to 3. In the next lesson we'll see some much more powerful formatting ideas.

Let's make an erroneous version of this program and take it for a spin on the debugger. We'll keep the new version in the notepad and use a different editor window to store the old one. (We could keep it on the clipboard but that's risky — one little cut operation and it's lost.) The full editor is harder to use but very much more general.

Return to the notepad.

Mark the whole program as a block (it should all turn black) and copy it; all the operations you need are on the block menu.

Now leave the notepad, use <F2> to get the menu and select tooLs. There are several interesting things here. The compiler is used to speed programs up; the lint checker looks for errors. The clipboard contains all the stuff we've just clipped. Stop and admire the pocket calculator. Then select Editor.

All you get is another menu. This editor can have any number of windows that will fit in memory, but at the moment it has none at all. You can change the colour and position of the windows too, and this might be useful to help us distinguish between the versions. At the moment there are no windows at all, so all you can do is either create one or change the defaults for windows. We'll change the colour of the window to prevent its getting confused with the notepad.

Select deFaults from the menu. We're happy with the position and the size is OK; select Attribute and a little box appears:

```
┌─Attribute─┐
│»Foreground│
│ Background│
│   Bright  │
│  Flashing │
│     Go    │
└───────────┘
```

This allows you to select colours. We'll make the background red as a warning. Move the mark down to background with the cursor down key. Now the left and right keys will change the background while the bottom line shows the overall effect selected. Make the background red. Then move the mark to Go and hit <Enter>. We aren't changing

67

The Prolog-2 User Guide

any other defaults, so key <Esc>.

Now select New to create a window; it is indeed red! We've got the old program on the clipboard, so all we need to do now is select Edit and then use the block menu to paste the clipboard. The program reappears.

Leave the editor (3 escapes — extra escapes don't hurt, so the trick is just to keep pressing the key until you get back to the prompt) and get back to the notepad. Selecting End on the Block menu will clear the inverse video by setting the block empty.

We're going to try another version of needed.

You can see needed in the window, as it happens, but just to try out another feature select the Search menu. You can use this to search for text, but also it can recognise where in a window a predicate begins (even though the name is used elsewhere). Select Goto and you see a menu of predicates defined in the window. Select needed/3 (the /3 indicates that this is a predicate of arity 3).

The change we'll try is this: in our old definition, the second clause said: If A is contained in B and B is needed for C then A is needed for C. The following statement is also true: if A is needed for B and B is contained in C then A is needed for C. So edit the program to replace needed by contains and contains by needed in the tail of the second clause of needed/3. Now use <F2> Predicate Reconsult to commit the new version.

Let's see if it's any good.

?- must_buy(sausage_roll,Ing,Amt).

Nothing happens, a suspicious if not fatal sign. What you do on occasions like this is to interrupt the program by pressing <Control-Break>. You may spot that the letter I appears briefly in the top right hand corner of the screen. Prolog-2 cannot always deal with an interrupt at once, so it tells you that one is pending. This saves wear and tear on the control break keys.

(It may be that by the time you had read all this Prolog-2 had run out of space and given an error. In that case, clear the error and try again.)

Interrupting will never damage the execution of the program, though some of the options on the interrupt menu may. If you select Continue, the program will continue as though nothing had happened. A very convenient feature of interrupts is that you can invoke a new interpreter and ask it questions without disturbing your program. This is called breaking. Select Break from the menu.

The prompt has the number 1 against it to remind you that this is a break (if you broke again, so to speak, you would get the number 2). Although this is a completely new interpreter it can access the record of what the other one was doing. The predicate that does that is called backtrace.

The Prolog-2 User Guide

Note that the output you see may differ slightly from what follows depending on the precise moment when you pressed control break.

1?- backtrace.

You see the output

1. basic(sausage_roll)
2. needed(sausage_roll,sausage_roll,1)
3. needed(sausage_roll,_1350,_1354)
4. needed(sausage_roll,_1384,_1388)
5. needed(sausage_roll,_1418,_1422)
6. needed(sausage_roll,_1452,_1456)
7. needed(sausage_roll,_1486,_1490)
8. needed(sausage_roll,_1520,_1524)
9. needed(sausage_roll,_1554,_1558)

yes

The way to read this is as follows: the goal being tried when you interrupted was **basic(sausage_roll)**. That isn't the question you asked Prolog-2, so it must have asked itself. The next question listed is the one it was asking itself as a result of which it had to ask **basic(sausage_roll)**; in other words, this latter goal must be in the tail of some clause, and backtrace tells us that

needed(sausage_roll,sausage_roll,1)

was the head. Of course it had to be as that is the only place where basic is used, but in a more complicated example the information would be useful.

Incidentally goal 2 is called the *parent* of goal 1; and all the goals in the series are called *ancestors* of goal 1.

Next we do the same for goal number 2; this was asked because it appeared in the tail of goal number 3. Therefore Prolog-2 must have been trying the second clause of needed. Unfortunately it seems to be stuck in a loop doing this (the reason we only see 9 goals back is a limitation in backtrace — there are probably hundreds of them). Probably the best thing is to start again with trace on, but it may be worth tracing from where we are. To leave the break state type <Control-Z> and <Enter>.

1?- ^Z

and then select trace. Look at the output, pressing <Enter> every time a response is needed. You'll see something like

    (1) 0 CALL: fail? [system]
    (1) 0 FAIL: fail
    (2) 0 CALL: needed(sausage_roll,_372,_376)?
    (3) 1 CALL: basic(sausage_roll)?

69

The Prolog-2 User Guide

```
        (4) 2 CALL: contains(sausage_roll,_448,_452)?
        (4) 2 EXIT: contains(sausage_roll,sausage,0.7500)
        (5) 2 CALL: fail? [system]
        (5) 2 FAIL: fail
        (3) 1 FAIL: basic(sausage_roll)
        (6) 1 CALL: needed(sausage_roll,_416,_420)!?
        (7) 2 CALL: basic(sausage_roll)?s
      > (7) 2 FAIL: basic(sausage_roll)?
```

Not tremendously illuminating. The exclamation mark that appears after the goal for line (6) indicates that Prolog-2 thinks you are in a closed loop. It isn't always right about this, but if the ! appears, you should examine that possibility. You can look at the ancestors using the g10 option

```
        (8) 2 CALL: needed(sausage_roll,_460,_464)?g10
        (8) 2  needed(sausage_roll,_460,_464)
        (6) 1  needed(sausage_roll,_416,_420)
        (2) 0  needed(sausage_roll,_372,_376)
        (-)    needed(sausage_roll,_652,_656)
        (-)    needed(sausage_roll,_680,_684)
        (-)    needed(sausage_roll,_708,_712)
        (-)    needed(sausage_roll,_736,_740)
        (-)    needed(sausage_roll,_764,_768)
        (-)    needed(sausage_roll,_792,_796)
        (-)    needed(sausage_roll,_820,_824)
```

and they look much as before. The (-) indicates that this goal was tried before we switched trace on, so we can observe, ominously, that we have accumulated three more **needed** goals since we started tracing.

The **a** option aborts, that is, goes straight back to the prompt.

?a

Evaluation aborted

Try it tracing from the front. Abort turns off tracing, so we have to switch it on again.

?- trace.

yes

?- must_buy(sausage_roll,Ing,Amt).

```
        (1) 0 CALL: must_buy(sausage_roll,_802,_832)?
        (2) 1 CALL: needed(sausage_roll,_802,_832)?
        (3) 2 CALL: basic(sausage_roll)?s
```

70

We know sausage rolls aren't basic, and basic must be OK because we used it in the other version. Skip it then.

```
>  (3) 2 FAIL: basic(sausage_roll)?
   (4) 2 CALL: needed(sausage_roll,_1034,_1038)?
   (5) 3 CALL: basic(sausage_roll)?s
>  (5) 3 FAIL: basic(sausage_roll)?
   (6) 3 CALL: needed(sausage_roll,_1078,_1082)!?
```

That exclamation mark again!

Here we seem to have found the root of the problem. The other ingredients never get looked at at all; one **needed** question just tries basic and then falls into the same question about the same recipe with a different variable. Plainly this will never go anywhere. In this case recursion is indeed circular. The [option puts us straight into the notepad (the debugger options aren't always very intuitive. If you find them difficult typing ? gives you some menus of options). We can confirm that the second clause of needed is indeed circular.

needed(Recipe,Ingredient,Total) :-
    needed(Recipe,Something,Amount),
    contains(Something,Ingredient,Subamount),
    Total is Amount*Subamount.

Retrieve the correct version from the editor! (You should be able to do this by now. If you have difficulty the sequence is

<Esc>	out of notepad
a<Enter>	to abort the debugging session
<F2>LEE	to the red window
<F2>BS <F2> BC	to get the old version to the clipboard
<Esc>	out of the red window
D	to delete the red window — these windows use a lot of space
O	to agree to this
<Esc>	out of the editor
N	back to the notepad
<F2> FN	to clear the old version
O	to confirm this
<F2> BP	to copy the old version back.)

We could have left it in the editor and used that — all the notepad facilities are available — but as we've seen, it takes a few extra keystrokes to get into the editor. Now leave the notepad.

Summary

- We saw how recursion works
- We used the full editor

The Prolog-2 User Guide

Before we save the shop program we'd like to make its output more attractive. We've fiddled with the decimals system state to improve matters, but the output could still hardly be called beautiful.

Formatted output is controlled by using the predicate write/3. This differs from the usual write/1 that we have seen in accepting a format code to control output. The middle argument is of no use to us and we shall specify an _ every time we call the predicate.

Let's see yet another entry into help. This one is useful when we know what we want help about and don't want to fiddle about with menus. Type <F1> to enter help and then select Enter.

In the box that appears the name of a topic can be entered. This is not a good way to explore help — how are you to know the exact name of the topic? — but if you know the topic it gets there fast. In this case we want format, so type that in and press <Enter>.

By the way, in these one line edit windows you are often offered a default. If the first key you press is an edit key, you get to edit it. If you press another key it is cleared.

We definitely want output formats. The format system can be used to write full Prolog-2 terms (lists for example) but most control is achieved by specifying the type of the thing to be output (for example there is no point trying to output an atom in exponential format!). So select the tOkens item.

The two help screens give a complete table:

```
tokens
Formats designed to output one type are implemented
by token formats. The following are built-in:

a           atom
qa          quoted atom (if necessary)
s           string
qs          quoted string
r           real (fixed point)
i           integer
```

```
┌ More ... ═══════════════════════════════════════
│  m            money (using local format)
│  e            real (exponential)
│  v            variable, use name if supplied
│  v0           variable, underline form
│  b            blank
│  t            time
│  d            date
│
│  For time and date formats the first argument should
│  be  a  list  [Day,Month,Year]  for  date  and
│  [Hour,Minutes,Seconds] for time. If the argument is
│  a variable the current date or time is printed.
```

You can always supply an argument to the format to be used as field width, and with real number formats you can also specify the number of decimal places.

Leave help and try some examples.

?- write(33.3,_,r(10,1)).
    33.3

Numbers are right justified.

?- write(pastry,_,a(10)).
pastry

Atoms and strings are left justified. Money format differs from country to country.

?- write(33.3,_,m).
£33.30

in the U.K. You can amuse yourself by changing country and looking at local money format — country changes are done from the same menu as decimals. But remember that DOS will go on using the different country when you leave Prolog-2. (Country changes are not available under DOS 2).

Now let's tidy up the shopping; get to the notepad.

shop(Recipe) :-
    must_buy(Recipe,Ingredient,Amount),
    write(Ingredient,_,a(8)),
    write(Amount,_,r(6,3)),
    nl,
    fail.

shop(_).

To be really fancy we'll add the date automatically.

The Prolog-2 User Guide

```
shop(Recipe) :-
    write("Shopping list for "),
    write(Recipe),
    write(" on "),
    write(_,_,d),
    nl,nl,
    must_buy(Recipe,Ingredient,Amount),
    write(Ingredient,_,a(8)),
    write(Amount,_,r(6,3)),
    nl,
    fail.

shop(_).
```

As the help screen told you, **write(_,_,d)** adds today's date. This also uses local date format, so if you jetted off to some exotic place while playing with the money don't be surprised if the date looks odd.

Commit all this and try it out.

There are lots of features of Prolog-2 we haven't covered. Some you can read about in textbooks, some are specific to Prolog-2 and you'll find details in the rest of the book. Keep your finger over the <F1> key while you're learning. If you want to go on exploring now and feel happy with the material so far you should learn next about the following topics:

- Cut. The cut operation is vital for serious Prolog-2 programming.

- Structured data. We've only looked at lists, but in fact anything that's a goal can be used as a structure.

- Meta-programming. You don't always have to specify tail goals when you write the program — you can have Prolog-2 build them for you.

- Operators. Why could Prolog-2 understand 1 < 2 when our discussion suggested that <(1,2) was the right form?

- Grammar rules. There's a free parser in the Prolog-2 system.

- Changing the database as you go (assert and retract).

You'll also want to find out about:

- Modules — how to use them to structure a program, how to save a program in internal form for fast reloading, how to use virtual memory to gain access to up to 256 megabytes of database.

- External interfacing — to Lotus 1-2-3, assembler, Lattice C, MicroSoft C, Pascal and

FORTRAN, GEM graphics ...

- Creating your own windows.
- The tokeniser and formatted input.
- Packaging an application with your own error and interrupt handling.
- Compiling programs for greater speed; hashing predicates.

Summary

- We looked at output formats

PART THREE

THE PROLOG-2 GUIDE

13. Compiling Prolog programs

13.1 Introduction

The compiler transforms a Prolog-2 source file into a machine code module.

The advantage of compiling Prolog-2 is greater speed — compiled code is about 5 times as fast as interpreted code, rising to as much as 10 times in optimal circumstances

The disadvantages of compiling Prolog-2 are:

(1) compiled code is bulkier than interpreted code — though mode declarations (see §13.5.1 below) can reduce it.

(2) compiled code cannot be changed at runtime, nor can it be traced.

(3) the compiler program itself is slow.

Applications should therefore be developed using the interpreter and compiled only after debugging.

13.2 Format of compiler files

A compiler input file is an ordinary source file with a few restrictions. These are as follows:

(1) All the clauses for a predicate must be adjacent, and not separated by clauses for other predicates;

(2) Predicates not present in the module being compiled will be treated as undefined. If the predicate is a public predicate from another module (including the common module) then it must be declared external by a directive of the form:

?- external(Name/Arity).

(3) External declarations must be made before the first reference to the predicate involved. For preference put all directives at the start. Note that compiled code is not consulted into the database by the compiler; this means you cannot use predicates defined in the module in directives.

Note that any infringements of these conditions will be reported by the Lint checker (see §27.1). Because of the time the compiler takes to compile, it is worth running the Lint checker first: it is much faster than the compiler.

13.3 Running the compiler

13.3.1 Interactive mode

The Prolog-2 User Guide

To invoke the compiler you type

compile.

There is a pause while the compiler is loaded.

Eventually you will be prompted for a source file. This should be entered without its extension, which must be .PRO.

Next you will be offered the chance to specify an output file; if you simply press return your output file will take the same name as the compiler input file but extension .PRM.

Finally you are asked for a name for the module being compiled. Normally this is of no significance, but you should make it different from any other module name you are likely to use. If possible use the same name as the file.

Prolog-2 Compiler version X.Y0
Input file? slowprog
Output file? (<ENTER> for A:\SLOWPROG.PRM) quikprog
Module name? prog

The compiler now compiles the source file; this may take some time. As it proceeds the name of the predicate currently being compiled is displayed on the screen.

When the compiler has finished generating code it prints the message

END OF PASS ONE

There then follows a second pass (and, on some machines, a third) in which the symbol references are filled in. When this is done the compiler prints the message

END OF PASS TWO

and terminates.

13.3.2 Batch mode

Prolog-2 provides **compile/3** as an alternative to **compile/0**. The only difference is that **compile/0** provides prompts for file and module names; **compile/3** expects the programmer to supply these names as arguments:

compile("Inputfile","Outputfile",modulename).

The first argument to **compile/3** is the name of the compiler source file, written as a string: it should be entered without its extension, which must be .PRO.

The second argument is the name of the compiler object file, written as a string.

The third argument is the name of the module being compiled, which must be an atom.

13.4 Using compiled code

Compiled code can be used like other modules subject to certain restrictions. You have to open the module you created using the BIP **open_module/4**, with access **none** and mode **actual**. Once you have opened the module you can access any predicates you declared public in it just as though they were in an ordinary **none** access module.

The restrictions on compiled code modules are the following:

(1) access **none**, mode **actual**
(2) the module cannot be debugged
(3) the module cannot be modified or saved.

13.5 Writing code for compilation

You do not need this Section to run the compiler; however, it will help you write code that compiles into compact and efficient assembler.

13.5.1 Mode

You can cut down the size of compiled code by using mode declarations. This also gives a smallish increase in speed. Essentially, mode declarations enable the compiler to tell at compile time whether or not the input arguments of a predicate will be variables.

Precisely, an argument position where the input argument will contain no variables is called 'destructive' and one which will always be a variable is called 'constructive'.

For example, consider the predicate **append/3**:

append([],A,A).
append([H|T],A,[H|T1]) :- append(T,A,T1).

This can be used to append lists:

?- append([a,b,c],[d],X).

X = [a,b,c,d]

and to decompose lists:

?- append(X,Y,[a,b,c,d]).

X = []
Y = [a,b,c,d]

More? (y/n) y

The Prolog-2 User Guide

X = [a]
Y = [b,c,d]   etc.

In many applications only the former use is necessary; in that case we say that the first two arguments of **append**/3 are destructive and the third is constructive. You can tell the compiler this by placing a + or - mode directive in the file.

+ denotes destructive and - constructive occurrences, so you would write

?- **mode(append(+,+,-))**.

If you aren't sure about some of the positions you can use ? instead to indicate uncertainty.

Otherwise there are no special properties of compiled code. A few BIPs are compiled — **repeat**, **;**, **!**, **not**, **->**, **true**, **fail**, **once** for example — but generally BIPs are accessed as from the interpreter. You cannot, therefore, expect to compile a predicate like

a :- **write("Hello"),nl,put(7)**.

and have it run at five times the normal speed; the speedup will not be noticeable because of all the time spent in BIPs. If you are restricted for space reasons to compile only part of your source, you should compile a part where there is a high ratio of logic to side-effects.

13.5.2 Public

By default, predicates in compiled modules (unlike interpreted modules) will be private.

It is necessary to include a **public** directive for any predicate to be called from outside the compiled module. For example:

?- **public(append/3)**.

You can also make all the predicates in the module public by using **public**/0, just as you can in interpreted modules.

It is sometimes necessary to make public declarations in circumstances in which it looks as if the only uses of the predicate are internal to the module. Consider a module containing the following lines:

tom :-   t1, t2, etc.
dick :-   d1, run(tom), etc.

where the name **tom** does not occur anywhere else in the entire application. It might seem that as **tom**/0 is only mentioned within this module, there should be no need to declare it public. However, if the predicate **run**/1 is in another module, then **tom**/0 will have to be accessible from there — which it will not be if it has not been declared public.

Similarly, suppose your program contains this line:

tom(X):- t1, call(X), ... etc.

If X may be instantiated to a goal which matches a clause in the compiled program, then the predicate of which that clause is part must be declared public; otherwise the call will fail. This is an important difference between compiled and interpreted code.

13.5.3 Hashing directives

Code to be compiled may include hashing directives.

If you do not include a hashing directive for a predicate, the compiler will decide for itself whether to hash it. The compiler will aim for speed rather than for space optimisation. It hashes all predicates with more than four clauses and builds a hash table whose size is the smallest power of two greater than the number of clauses. This may give rise to two problems:

(1) the code generated can get quite big

(2) the compiler can run out of space trying to do the hash calculations.

For this reason it is possible to tell the compiler ') restrict the size of the hash table for a given predicate.

If you put a **hash/2** directive in the file the first argument must be a predicate rep and the second an integer. The hashing calculations for the predicate will then be based on this integer, not on the size of the predicate. Thus if you specify 10 you will get a 16-element hash table regardless of the number of clauses; if you specify 0 the predicate will not be hashed at all.

This is similar to the use of **hash/2** in interpreted code; but while the interpreter's default is not to hash, the compiler's default is to hash, so you will probably find yourself using this BIP for the opposite purpose.

13.5.4 State gc

One other directive which it can be sensible to include in a module that is to be compiled, is one to change the system state **gc**.

Such a directive will not be applied to the garbage-collection that happens within the compiler as it runs: it will be incorporated into the compiled code and obeyed when that is run. Thus you are able to specify the conditions under which garbage collection will take place when your compiled module is running.

The Prolog-2 User Guide

For example, your source to be compiled might include the directive

?- state(gc(cost),_,100).

which will cause your compiled code to continue running even if it has to spend all its time collecting garbage.

13.5.5 Symbol file

The directive

?- symbols.

causes the generation of a symbol file giving the offset in the compiled module of each clause. This is useful because errors in compiled code report the offset in the code rather than the goal that caused the error.

13.6 Compiler errors

Sometimes you will get a Prolog-2 error message while running the compiler.

Running out of memory

It is possible (especially with PCs) for the compiler to run out of memory while compiling. Should this happen to you the best course is to modify your program and then re-start the compilation.

What to do:

(1) **Out of workspace error** while compiling a predicate (Pass 1)

If you can increase the workspace, do so. This error is usually caused by either a clause with a very long tail, a predicate with a large number of clauses, or a combination of both.

If you cannot increase the workspace, chop up any long tails in the offending predicate into sub-predicates. If the predicate itself is large, break it down into a number of smaller predicates.

(2) **Out of heap space errors** (in Passes 1, 2 or 3)

This is usually caused by trying to compile large programs. If you cannot increase the size of the heap, chop the program up into two smaller modules.

Errors reported by the compiler itself

There are also a number of errors the compiler reports itself. These are as follows:

(1) A predicate was referenced but neither defined nor declared external. It will always fail. (PASS TWO)

(2) A public declaration for a predicate was encountered but the predicate was never defined. The predicate will not be exported by the compiled module. (PASS TWO)

(3) There were no public declarations. In this case the output is useless and will not be produced. (PASS TWO)

(4) Clauses for a system predicate were found. They have been ignored. (PASS ONE)

(5) A predicate with clauses split up by clauses for another predicate was found. The second block of clauses is ignored. (PASS ONE)

(6) An illegal mode declaration has been found. It has been ignored. (PASS ONE)

(7) An external declaration has been found for a predicate already known to be external. The second declaration is ignored. (PASS ONE)

(8) An external declaration has been found for a predicate already found in the module being compiled. The declaration is ignored. (PASS ONE)

There are also two errors specific to P.

(1) The support library, which is linked in at the start of pass 2, was not found in the appropriate directory (it should be in the Prolog directory). In this case the output was useless and has been deleted. (PASS TWO)

(2) In 123 only, the size of the compiled module would exceed 64K bytes. Compilation abandoned. (PASS ONE)

Compiler self-checking and internal error reports

The compiler checks a number of internal parameters while generating code. If these are incorrect it will generate an internal error, with a number greater than 100. This indicates an error in the compiler rather than your program. Please take a note of the exact message and contact your supplier.

13.7 Example

As an example, we take the following program, which generates prime numbers.

```
?- public(do/0).
?- mode(has_factor(+)).
?- external(is_prime/1).

do:-
```

```
            assert(seed(1)),
            repeat,
            retract(seed(X)),
            Y is X + 1,
            assert(seed(Y)),
            not has_factor(Y),
            assert(is_prime(Y)),
            write(Y),
            put(32),
            fail.

has_factor(N):-
            is_prime(P),
            0 is N mod P.
```

The following points about this program should be noted.

(1) It contains a **public** directive: this is to make one of its predicates accessible from other modules. If a module contains no public predicate, there is no way into it, and it is useless. Note that in compiled code the default is **private**.

(2) It contains a **mode** directive for has_factor/1. As this predicate is only ever called with its argument instantiated, this argument is destructive; and by informing the compiler of this, we can cause it to produce more compact compiled code.

(3) It contains an **external** directive for is_prime/1. This is because is_prime/1 is called from within the compiled code while it is not itself a clause of the compiled code. No **external** directive is necessary for seed/1, because although seed/1 is asserted and retracted by the compiled code, it is never called.

(4) If this program were to be interpreted, it would include one more predicate, the fact

seed(2).

This would work with interpreted code because the program would repeatedly retract and assert facts from and to the common module. But if we were to compile this version of the program, the fact would get compiled into the compiled module, where it would be impossible to retract it, or even to find it. It is therefore necessary to omit this fact from the source file, and to assert it (into the common module) at run time.

(5) It is a good idea to check a program with the lint checker before compiling it. If you test the above program with the lint checker, and you have typed it in correctly, you will get one lint error: "Repeat without subsequent cut" in do/0. Although this message sometimes indicates incorrect logic in a program, in this case it can be seen that the program is correct.

A sample session using the compiler

There follows a log showing how the above program, which was in the file PRIMES.PRO, was compiled, loaded, and run. The text produced by Prolog-2 is shown in bold type; the text entered by the user, in ordinary type.

?- compile.
Prolog-2 Compiler version X.Y0
Input file? primes
Code file? (<ENTER> for A:\PRIMES.PRM)
Module name? primes
do/0
has_factor/1
END OF PASS ONE
END OF PASS TWO
(END OF PASS THREE on certain machines)
Compilation complete

yes
?- open_module(M,"primes",none,actual).
M = primes
More (y/n)? n

yes
?- assert(seed(2)).

yes
?- do.
2 3 5 7 11 13 17 19 23 29 31 37 41 43 47 53 59 61 67 71

[etc.]

13.8 Compatibility notes

There is no general convention about exports and imports in Prolog; probably any different system will require changes to declarations. Some Prolog systems do not implement modes, though they probably simply ignore mode declarations rather than complaining.

Some Prolog systems will not accept expressions constructed at run-time in compiled code, so that X=1+2, Y is X will give an error. Prolog-2 can cope with these, but programs using them will give errors on other systems.

14. Manipulating the clause store

14.1 The Prolog-2 clause store: an overview

If a Prolog-2 program is compiled then the result is stored in a code module that is, in effect, locked. If the program is consulted then the clauses are stored in the clause store. Code in the clause store is called interpreted code.

This chapter explains how to add clauses to the clause store, how to examine clauses, and how to remove clauses from the clause store. The clause store is divided into modules, but discussion of these is deferred to the next Chapter.

The predicates in this chapter have a number of uses:

(i) to read a program into the clause store, **consult** is used. It is useful to develop a program in interpreted code, because facilities for editing and debugging the code are more extensive. Once the program is tested it may be compiled.

(ii) to record a piece of information. Ideally all information would be conveyed around in variables, but at times it becomes necessary to use a clause to record data; for example, the number of errors the user has made in a session could be recorded using a clause **no_errors** and when an error was detected:

once(retract(no_errors(N))), NN is N+1, assert(no_errors(N)).

(iii) to allow the program to modify itself on the fly. This is strongly discouraged.

Clauses can be added to ("asserted into") the clause store using the following Built-In Predicates (BIPs):

> **assert**
> **consult/1**
> **reconsult/1**

Whole files of clauses can be added to the database by typing a list of filenames at the ?- prompt, for example:

> [user].
> [file1,file2].

Clauses in a database can be examined using the following BIPs:

> **clause**
> **predicate**
> **listing**

Clauses can be removed ("retracted") from a database using the following BIPs:

> **retract**

retractall

In this Chapter we will frequently refer to variable-name structures: these are described in §14.5. Similarly, database references are treated in §14.7. §14.2, §14.3 and §14.4 summarise those Prolog-2 BIPs which manipulate clauses in the clause store.

14.2 Adding clauses to the database

All the BIPs described below add clauses to the Current Output Module.

The three arities of **assert** — **assert/1**, **assert/2** and **assert/3** — each inserts a single clause into the database. The first argument is always a clause to be asserted. **assert/1** simply asserts a Prolog clause into the database. **assert/2** exists in three forms: in the first form its second argument specifies the position the clause is to occupy within the list of clauses for that predicate; in the second form this argument is a variable-name structure; in the third form it is a database reference.

assert/3 has only one form: its second argument specifies the position the clause is to occupy within the predicate. The third argument is a variable-name structure. **asserta/1** adds a single clause to the database. The new clause is inserted in front of any other clauses for that predicate. **asserta/2** also adds a single clause to the database, again in front of any others for that predicate. In addition it returns a database reference for its second argument.

assertz/1 adds a single clause to the database, but places it after any other clauses for that predicate. **assertz/2** does the same, but returns a database reference for its second argument.

consult/1 reads a stream (which may be **user**) and copies the clauses it finds to the database. **reconsult/1** also reads a stream in the same way as **consult/1**. The difference is that when it first comes across a clause for a predicate, it retracts any clauses for that predicate already present in the database. **conlist/1** takes a list of streams as its argument: each stream is consulted unless it is preceded by - or $. Streams preceded by - or $ are reconsulted.

Generally it is best to build predicates by adding clauses on the end. There exists a mechanism for fast access to the final clause of a predicate, so that adding to the end is actually faster than adding at the start. The atom **max** must be supplied as argument position in versions of assert with clause number argument in order to take advantage of this fast access. The forms that implicitly use the last clause will use the fast form.

Therefore, try to avoid any use of **assert** other than **assert/1**.

In developing a program, you will normally reconsult the file after editing it so as to remove the old versions of changed predicates.

14.3 Examining the clauses in a database

All the predicates described below examine clauses in the Current Input Module.

The Prolog-2 User Guide

The three arities of **clause** — **clause/2**, **clause/3** and **clause/4** — all search the database for a single clause.

clause/2 exists in two forms. The first form takes a predicate-rep as its first argument and a clause for that predicate as its second; the second form takes the head of a clause as its first argument and the body of that clause as its second.

clause/3 also exists in two forms. The first is like the first form of **clause/2**; its additional third argument specifies the position of the clause within its predicate. The second form of **clause/3** is like the second form of **clause/2**; the third argument is a database reference.

clause/4 takes as arguments a predicate-rep (functor/arity), a clause for that predicate, an integer specifying the position of that clause within the predicate, and a variable-name structure.

Greatest portability is achieved by use of **clause/2** in its second form. Thus the clauses of **append/3** could be retrieved by the call clause(append(_,_,_),T). As the first clause is a fact, T will be returned as **true**. The other form of **clause/2** is more efficient but specific to Prolog-2. Variable name forms should be avoided; **listing** will automatically retrieve names, and if you do not intend to write the clause out you probably don't need the name. Use of clause numbers is sometimes inescapable.

It has three arities — **predicate/1, predicate/2, predicate/3** — all of which search the clause store for whole predicates.

predicate/?, whatever its arity, always takes a predicate-rep (functor/arity) for its first argument. The second argument, if present, is the scope (**public** or **private**) of the predicate; the third is the hashing status (**hashed, unhashed**) of the predicate.

listing has three arities, all of which produce a readable listing of one or more predicates in the database. **listing/0** lists the whole of the Current Input Module. **listing/1** lists the predicate specified by its argument, a predicate-rep. **listing/2** lists the predicate specified by its first argument to the stream specified by its second.

listing uses the pretty printer exported by **pretty**. If this module is closed, no clauses will be displayed.

predicate_size/2 takes a predicate-rep (functor/arity) for its first argument; it matches its second argument with the number of clauses for that predicate found.

14.4 Removing clauses from the database

All the predicates below retract clauses in the Current Output Module, which must also be the Current Input Module. It is an error to use any of these predicates while the Current Input Module and the Current Output Module are different.

The four arities of **retract** — **retract/1, retract/2, retract/3, retract/4** — each removes a single clause from the database. In each case the first argument specifies the clause to be removed.

Apart from **retract**/1, the versions of **retract** are all closely analogous to the corresponding versions of **clause**: they have the same arguments, and differ from **clause** only in that they have the side-effect of deleting the clause.

retract/1 simply retracts the clause specified. **retract**/2 takes a predicate-rep for its first argument and a clause for its second. **retract**/3 is like **retract**/2, but has a third argument specifying the position of the clause within the group for its predicate. **retract**/4 takes as arguments a predicate-rep, a clause for that predicate, an integer specifying the position of that clause within its predicate, and a variable-name structure.

deny/2 takes the head and the body of a clause as its two arguments.

retractall/1 retracts whole groups of clauses. It takes two forms: the first retracts all clauses for the predicate specified by its argument; the second retracts all clauses with the head specified by its argument.

Retracting clauses while running Prolog-2

It is safe to retract a clause while you can still backtrack through it. However this is not recommended, and can be confusing, especially if you assert a new clause to replace the one retracted.

The general rule is this: on backtracking into a predicate the interpreter will go to the next clause after the one it evaluated for that predicate last time. It will do this UNLESS the clause it was going to evaluate has been retracted: it that case, the interpreter moves on to the next clause after that, unless that one has been retracted, and so on.

The interpreter will fail to find a new clause asserted while it was busy evaluating the clause which had been, up to then, the final clause for the predicate. Look at this example:

```
?- assert(p(a)), p(X), write(X), assert(p(b)), fail.
a.
no
```

When the interpreter called the goal **p(X)** it noticed that there was no alternative clause for **p**/1; it therefore did not look for an alternative on backtracking. But

```
?- assert(q(a)),assert(q(b)),
   q(X),write(X),assert(q(c)),fail.
   abcccccccccccccccccccccccccccccccccccccccccccc [etc.]
```

This time, when the interpreter called the goal **q(X)** it noticed that there was an

The Prolog-2 User Guide

alternative. When it backtracked into it and found the second match **q(b)**, it noticed that there was still an alternative, as **q(c)** had by now been asserted once. And so on.

14.5 Saving variable names in the database

Prolog-2 allows you to store the names of a clause's variables in the database. This is not compulsory; in some programs the space the names would take up is not available.

There are two approaches to saving variable names: the 'automatic' and the 'bare hands'.

14.5.1 The automatic approach

Normally you do not need to worry about the format in which variable names are passed to and fro because the routines are packaged up in **consult**/1 and **listing**/1. If you consult a file then the names of variables are saved. If you list the database they are printed. If you want to stop this happening, you can use the system state **varnames** to switch off the saving of variable names in the Current Output Module:

>   ?- state(varnames,_,nosave).

listing/1 will then generate arbitrary names for variables.

Variables occurring only once in a clause are never stored and are always printed as an underline followed by a number, e.g. _. This is useful because it reminds you that such a variable does not share with any others; it may also help you detect misspelled variable names.

Variables in trace output are always printed in underline-number form. The use of variable names in trace output would conceal the fact that variables in different clauses were sharing.

14.5.2 The bare hands approach

If you must do it yourself, read on. There are four places where you need to know about variable-name structures:

>   (1) when you read a clause
>   (2) when you assert a clause
>   (3) when you retrieve a clause
>   (4) when you write a clause.

Therefore the predicates of the **read**, **assert**, **retract/clause** and **write** families all allow extra arguments for variable-name structures.

Variable-name structures: definition and use

A variable-name structure is either

(1) a term whose principal functor is . with three arguments: a variable, the name of the variable expressed as a string, and another variable name; or

(2) the empty list [].

This is an example of a variable-name structure:

.(FOOD,"FOOD",[]).

The principal functor is ., first argument the variable **food**, second argument the string **"FOOD"**, third argument the empty list [].

Even if you use the special forms of **read**, etc., you do not need to understand variable-name structures, because there is no need to handle them directly. A variable-name structure need only be decomposed if you intend to do something that involves looking at the names of variables. The lint checker program, for example, uses variable-name structures to look for single occurrences of variables with names other than _; the Top Level Interpreter uses them to print out the names of variables when replying to a query.

When you consult a file, **consult/1** automatically saves each clause into the database together with its variable-name structure. If you simply assert a clause with **assert/1** (or any other version of **assert** that does not take a variable-name structure for an argument), for example

assert((eats(bill,Food):-cheap(Food))).

it will be saved into the database without an associated variable-name structure; the spelling of the variable names will be lost, and will not be available on listing.

To save a variable-name structure into the database together with its clause you must use **assert/3**. This takes a variable-name structure as its third argument:

assert(eats(bill,FOOD):-cheap(FOOD),0,.(FOOD,"FOOD",[])).

You can also use variable-name structures to change the way the variable names in a clause are written. If you read in the term written as

term(Var1,Var1,Var2,Var2)

the variable-name structure will be

.(Var1,"Var1",.(Var2,"Var2",[])).

If you write it (using **write/2** or **write/3**) with variable-name structure

.(Var1,"Firstvar",.(Var2,"Secondvar",[]))

it will appear as

> term(Firstvar,Firstvar,Secondvar,Secondvar).

14.6 The hashing system

When the Prolog interpreter looks through the database for a clause it starts with the first clause for that predicate, tests whether it matches, goes on to the second clause, and so on. This can be unnecessarily slow with very long predicates. It is even slower if the predicate is stored in virtual memory and each clause has to be fetched from disk.

For example you might have a database of English words with their French translations, thus:

> e_to_f(pig,cochon).
> .
> .
> .
> e_to_f(wild,sauvage).

You can speed up the search process by having the interpreter generate a table of clauses which allows faster access. What then happens is that when a goal is tried — e_to_f(wild,X), for example — the interpreter looks up **wild** in an index and searches only for clauses with that as first argument. Thus it will not have to try all the clauses in between **pig** and **wild**.

The hashing procedure

This table-generating procedure is known as 'hashing' and is used in various areas of computing to compress extensive data structures into a more readily accessible form.

The hashing procedure works like this. The interpreter uses a hash function to generate a 'hash table' for the predicate. A hash function is a function that generates an integer called the hash value. The hash values generated by the hash function lie within a prescribed range, the hash range. For each hash value in this hash range the interpreter maintains a separate list of clauses whose first arguments have that hash value. Thus only the much shorter hash-value list has to be checked. Obviously, the larger the hash range, the quicker the search.

To be more precise, what the interpreter looks at is the principal functor of the first argument of the goal. Thus if the goal is

> try(a(b))

it is the **a** (and its arity) which determines the hash value. If the first argument is atomic then the hash value is calculated from it directly. This means that

> try(a(b),c).
> try(a(121),b(242)).

```
try(a(P),Q) :- P is Q*2.
```

will all hash identically, as the principal functor of the first argument of **try/2** is a/1 in each case.

Practical implications of hashing

Notice it is the first argument that is hashed. This has practical implications for the sequence of arguments in clauses: if the first argument is a variable then hashing is impossible and you force the interpreter to check every clause. Thus if you want to use your database to translate from French to English and you set this goal:

```
?- e_to_f(X,sauvage).
```

the interpreter will have to access the list the slow way. To avoid this you should arrange your arguments so that the first is usually instantiated: if you translate from French to English more often than the other way then swap the arguments over.

There are also practical implications for the sequence of clauses for a predicate. If you want to construct a hash table for the following predicate:

```
nickname(william,bill) :- !.
nickname(antony,tony) :- !.
nickname(andrew,ted) :- !.
nickname(X,X) :- director(X),!.
nickname(alexander,alex).
nickname(nicholas,nick).
nickname(peter,pete).
```

then you need to be aware that the hashing will only be effective as far as **andrew**; any first value must be checked with the fourth clause, so at this point the interpreter has to give up using its short chains [] and check all the clauses. You should therefore position any clause with a variable first argument as close to the end as you can.

BIPS available for hashing and unhashing predicates

You tell the system to hash a predicate by using one of the BIPS **hash/1**, **hash/2**, and **hash/3**. In all cases the first argument is the name of the predicate (functor/arity) whose clauses are to be hashed.

hash/1 is sufficient for most purposes, providing a hash table of initial size 8.

hash/2 allows you to specify the initial size of the hash table as second argument. We have already seen that the larger the hash size, the quicker the access; on the other hand a larger hash table takes up more space.

hash/3 provides a third argument allowing you to specify the desired ratio of number of clauses to hash size. The system will rehash the predicate from time to time to

The Prolog-2 User Guide

maintain this ratio. If you specify 0 for this rehash factor then automatic rehashing is disabled.

Default values for table size and rehash factor are 8 and 1.

There is little point in hashing a predicate with fewer than seven clauses; the improvement in access time is offset by the time lost computing the hash function. For predicates with seven or more clauses it is a question of trading gain in speed against loss of space. Remember that hashing is particularly useful with the slower access times of virtual memory.

unhash/1 unhashes the predicate-rep (functor/arity) specified in its argument. Space previously occupied by the hash table is reclaimed.

14.7 Database references

A database reference is a pointer to a clause in the clause store. Because clauses in the clause store move around, the reference is in fact to a location in a table. Database references are a fast way of remembering and recovering a piece of data from the clause store. In Prolog-2 the form of a database reference is '$db'(N), but the references should not be taken to pieces and should simply be used as handles to data obtainable by **assert** and redeemable using **clause**.

14.8 The recorded database

The recorded database is a fast internal store where data may be stored against a key. The predicate **record** is used to save the information. Instead of using a clause **no_errs** to record the number of errors in a session, the form **record(no_errs,N,Ref)** may be used; **Ref** is a database reference that can be used to retrieve the data faster, though until the database gets quite full searching under the key is efficient. **recorded** retrieves data by key and **instance** by reference; data may only be removed by quoting the reference, using **erase**.

14.9 Compatibility notes

These predicates are full of compatibility problems.

Among the assert tribe, only **assert/1** is at all standard. Some implementations suggest that the clause placing of **assert/1** is arbitrary, but they all place the clauses at the end. Consult and reconsult are both standard.

As already stated, **clause/2** in the form **clause(Head,Body)** is recommended for portability if not efficiency. **listing/1** is reasonably standard. **predicate/?** is unique to Prolog-2, but the limited form **current_predicate(Name,Functor)** is sufficient if you simply need names and arities; it returns a most general instance rather than a structure F/N.

The retract tribe are very complicated indeed. **retract/1** is the standard form, but the behaviour of a call like **retract(a(_) :- _)** varies: in Prolog-2 it retracts rules but not facts, in some systems it only retracts clauses whose body is **call(_)**, and in others, probably most sensibly, it retracts any clause at all.

The effect of retracting a clause and then backtracking into the predicate varies. Ideally a copy of the predicate would be made when it was first called, and this copy would remain unchanged by asserts and retracts and be used whenever that invocation of the predicate was resatisfied; however, this is difficult to implement. The best advice is to try to avoid using any variant of these devices.

retractall(Head) is sometimes called **retract_all(Head)**.

Hashing is unique to Prolog-2; in most systems the benefits are obtainable by either compiling the predicate or using the recorded database.

The recorded database is a more portable way of achieving fast data access without compilation, but unfortunately some implementations are rather half-hearted and unreliable during garbage collection. So for portability the only global data format (that is, data not undone on backtracking) is in a clause of a predicate.

15. Modules

15.1 Introduction to modules

Modules provide a way of dividing a large Prolog-2 program into discrete sections. This leads to greter power, speed, security and portability in programs. When you create a module you encapsulate a Prolog program, defining its features and how it can interact with the outside world. Large systems will typically be built up of many modules.

15.1.1 Creating a module

Suppose you have written a set of Prolog predicates to use as programming utilities. You decide you want to save these in a module. Your other programs will then be able to use these predicates without needing details of how they are implemented.

Some of the predicates defined in your file of utilities will probably be used only by their predicates within that file. These could be declared to be **private** so that their names could be re-used by other programs. You do this by typing **?- private:** in front of predicates you do not want 'exported' out of the module.

15.1.2 Constructing the module

You start by declaring that you want to create a module. You do this using **create_module(utility, actual)**. This creates a module called **utility** held in **actual** (rather than **virtual**) storage.

Next you need to re-direct output to your newly-created module: to do this you use the system state **state(output_module,_,utility)**. Now you can simply type **consult(myfile)** where **myfile** holds your utility predicates, written in Prolog-2. The effect of this is to read the contents of **myfile** into the module **utility**.

After writing your module you may save it. This is not essential: a module can be loaded from a text file with a module directive at the top. Nevertheless, having put the code into a module it is often advantageous to store the result in a form that can be accessed very quickly. You do this using **save(utility, "UTILITY", none, program, none)**. This saves your module called **utility** in a file called UTILITY.PRM. The module is saved without a start goal (a predicate that is run as soon as a module is opened). It is saved as a **program** module, and neither reading to it nor writing from it is permitted (the code can only be executed).

Your final step is to close the module: for this you use **close_module(utility)**.

15.1.3 Using the module

A Prolog-2 program can now call the utility encapsulated in the module. It first has to open the module, using the **open_module/4** predicate: in our case **open-module(utility, "UTILITY.PRM", none, actual)** opens any module called 'utility' held on a file called "UTILITY.PRM" with execute-only access and held in actual memory. The program would also have to close the utility after using it using

close_module(utility).

The nature of the programs you want to write will affect the way you use the module system. We have arranged this Chapter according to the functions needed to build and use modules. These include creating, opening, saving and closing modules. There is also a description of the public and private predicate system that is very important for the use of modules.

15.2 The attributes of a module

Modules have three definable attributes (qualities or properties, in other words):

(1) type
(2) language
(3) access.

15.2.1 Type

There are three types of module:

(1) data
(2) program
(3) library.

15.2.1.1 Data modules

A data module is loaded into the clause store as soon as it is opened.

15.2.1.2 Program modules

A program module is loaded into the clause store whenever one of its predicates is accessed. Typically this type will be used for a program that is invoked by a public, runs and then terminates, when the garbage collector will detect that it has finished and unload it. For example, the editor is a program module.

15.2.1.3 Library modules

The predicates in a library module are loaded one-by-one as they are needed — a program module is loaded all at once when any one of its predicates is needed. You can use library modules to hold collections of useful predicates that you will need frequently in your program but are too big to keep in RAM all the time. The sections of a library module not being used will be held on disk.

Once a predicate in a library module has been loaded, it remains in memory until removed by **trimlibs**. **trimlibs** removes all library predicates that are not directly or indirectly accessed by predicates in other modules.

15.2.2 Language

A Prolog-2 module can contain information in one of three forms:

    (1) Prolog clauses in Prolog-2 form
    (2) external code
    (3) compiled Prolog.

15.2.2.1 Prolog clauses in interpreted format

A file containing a module in interpreted format cannot be accessed by any other software than Prolog-2. Most modules in your program will probably be stored in this form. Heap format Prolog loads very quickly as it is already in the correct form for the theorem prover. This means that it does not need to be syntax-checked and tokenised. Information loaded from a source file using **consult**, or input directly by the user using **assert**, has to pass through the syntax-checker and the tokeniser before it reaches the theorem-prover. This makes it much slower than loading direct from a module.

15.2.2.2 External code

External code can be used to do things that either cannot be done at all in Prolog or are not very efficient in Prolog. Direct addressing of a port, for example, cannot be done in Prolog; number-crunching can be done but is slow. Both could be done using external code.

External code can take arguments from Prolog-2 and pass arguments back to it. For example, a program to carry out a chi-squared test on some statistics could accept the raw data (a sequence of numbers) fed to it from Prolog-2, carry out the calculations, and pass back the results of the test. These results would then be unified with a Prolog term and become available for use in the rest of the Prolog program.

External code modules are discussed in detail in Chapter 23.

15.2.2.3 Compiled Prolog

Compiled Prolog code is created from Prolog-2 using the Built-In Predicates **compile/1** or **compile/3** (see Chapter 13).

15.2.3 Access

There are four possible levels of access to modules:

    (1) readwrite
    (2) read
    (3) write
    (4) none

The first three levels are only available for data modules. The only level of access available for program modules and library modules is **none** (because these are execution-only modules).

15.2.3.1 readwrite

For data modules only, **readwrite** allows you full access to the module: you can add clauses, take them out, list them and execute them.

15.2.3.2 read

read allows you to inspect and execute clauses in the module; you cannot add or remove any.

15.2.3.3 write

write allows you to add clauses as well as execute them, but you cannot list clauses to see the contents of the module.

15.2.3.4 none

none only allows you to execute clauses. It gives data modules the same access properties as program and library modules.

15.3 Actual and virtual storage

In 123 the clause store may be extended by use of virtual memory. In all other versions the terms **actual** and **virtual** are synonymous.

In 123 data modules can be stored either in actual memory or virtual memory. Using virtual memory allows you to increase the size of a data module beyond the memory capacity of your computer. Only data modules can be stored in virtual memory: program and library modules must be stored in actual memory.

When you create a module it is automatically a data module and is open for **readwrite** access. The only thing you can specify about a module when you create it is the type of storage it is to occupy.

If the module is to occupy virtual memory it can be up to one megabyte in size. If you are only going to allow it to be stored in actual memory then it must be smaller: the size of your computer's memory less the space taken up by Prolog-2 and the operating system.

15.4 The current execution module

The Current Execution Module is the module to which the predicate being investigated (the goal which Prolog is currently trying to prove) belongs.

When you first start Prolog-2 the Current Execution Module is the common module. (You can never close the common module, even if you make another module the Current Execution Module.) To make a different module the Current Execution Module you call one of its public predicates. Prolog-2 will start to investigate this predicate, and the module to which it belongs will become the Current Execution Module. This is the only way of changing the Current Execution Module.

15.5 Public and private predicates in modules

There are two types of predicates in modules: public and private. The difference between the two is in whether they are accessible from other modules.

Public predicates are accessible from anywhere in an program: it does not matter whether the module is current or not. Private predicates are accessible only from within the module which contains them. This means you can have private predicates with the same name in different modules. Such predicates might or might not be identical. You cannot, however, use public predicates with the same name in different modules.

By default, Prolog-2 assumes that the predicates in a module are all public; but you can change this default.

15.5.1 Altering the scope of predicates

15.5.1.1 Making predicates private

Two BIPs make predicates in the current output module private:

    (1) **private/0**
    (2) **private/1.**

If you type **private** all the predicates subsequently created in the module, except those explicitly declared public, will be private.

If you type **private(predrep)** then only the clause explicitly identified by the argument **predrep**, which must be a predicate-rep, will be made private.

15.5.1.2 Making predicates public

Two more BIPs make predicates public:
    (1) **public/0**
    (2) **public/1.**

These are used in exactly the same way as **private/0** and **private/1**.

15.5.1.3 Changing the scope of a predicate

You can use **public/1** and **private/1** to alter the status of any predicate anywhere in the current output module: Prolog-2 will make the alteration when it obeys the directive.

public/0 and **private/0** have no effect on the status of predicates that already exist; they merely set the default status for predicates subsequently created without any specific status declaration.

An overall declaration made using **private/0** will be overruled by a subsequent call of **public/0**, and vice versa.

15.5.2 Public predicates in library modules

The public predicates of library modules are slightly different from the public predicates of other modules. It is useful to think of library module publics as 'soft' publics and program and data module publics as 'hard' publics.

There are two general rules:

(1) hard publics take precedence over soft publics
(2) new soft publics overwrite existing soft publics

Some of the implications of these rules are discussed below.

If you open a library module containing a public predicate (a soft predicate) with the same name as a public predicate already present in an opened program or data module (a hard predicate), then the soft library predicate will not load. No error message will be generated. (If you had tried to open two modules both containing a hard public with the same name then an error message would have been displayed.)

If you open a data or program module containing a hard public with the same name as a soft public in an open library module, then the hard public will replace the soft one. No error message will be generated.

Similarly, if you declare a new hard public with the same name as a soft public in an existing open library module, the new hard public will replace the soft one.

Finally, when you open a library module the publics it contains can have the same names as soft publics in another, already-open, library module. In this case the similar publics in the second library module opened will overwrite those in the first.

You can see an example of this if you create your own library containing public clauses with the same names as clauses in the **dec10** library module we supply. If **dec10** is open, any library of your own opened later may overwrite our own definitions and substitute yours.

For example, suppose you have open a library module containing a standard version of **append**. You then decide to open another library module holding your own version of append:

```
append([], X, X):- ! .
append([H|T], X, [H|Y]) :- append(T,X,Y).
```

When you next call append/3 you will find that your own version of the predicate has superseded the standard one. Note that your own version has had to include the first clause, even though this was the same in the version that already existed: a predicate

The Prolog-2 User Guide

cannot be split between modules, and if one of its clauses is in one particular module, then any clauses that it might once have had in another module no longer exist.

15.5.3 How modules use public and private predicates

Modules contain collections of public and private predicates. You cannot access any of these predicates unless the module is open.

When any predicate is called, Prolog-2 first looks for the predicate among the public and private predicates in the Current Execution Module. If it cannot find the predicate there, it goes on to search through the public predicates of all the other open modules. If Prolog-2 finds the predicate, it makes the module containing it the new Current Execution Module. The new Current Execution Module is then loaded into the computer's memory (if it is not already there).

When performing this search Prolog-2 must match both functor and arity to 'find' the predicate it is looking for. So if the call is to a predicate with two arguments with the functor 'arrange'

> arrange(Variable1,Variable2).

and Prolog-2 finds

> arrange(onlyarg).

in the Current Execution Module and

> arrange(firstarg,secondarg).

in another module it will switch to the other module. Although it has found a predicate with 'arrange' as a functor in the Current Execution Module, this version of 'arrange' only has an arity of one and so does not match the version the system is looking for. Prolog-2 therefore continues to look for a functor 'arrange' with an arity of two; if it finds one it executes it.

15.6 Creating a module

Before you can use a module you must first create it. This is done using the BIP **create_module/2**. You must specify the name of the module followed by the type of storage it is to occupy in memory:

> create_module(modulename,Storage)

The name of the module must be an atom.

Storage (actual or virtual memory) is specified using one of the atoms **actual** and **virtual**. (See Section §15.3 for more on module storage.)

When you first create a module, it will always be:

104

(1) **data** in type
(2) **readwrite** in access
(3) open for use

The new module is not made current for input, output, or execution (see §15.4 and §15.9). You may alter the type and access of the module later when you save it.

15.7 Saving a module

If you want to save the contents of a module you must save the module before you close it; if you close a module without saving it first its contents will be lost.

You save a module using the BIP **save/5**. This has five arguments:

save(modulename,"filename",predicate,data,readwrite).

The first argument is the name of the module: this is the name you gave the module when you created it.

The second argument is the name of the file you want to save the module to. If this is the same as the name of an existing file this file will be overwritten. If you do not specify an filename extension, Prolog-2 will add .PRM.

The third argument can be either the atom **none** or the name of a predicate (known as a start-goal). This predicate must not have any arguments. The next time the module is loaded it will immediately start to execute its start-goal. You can use this feature to set up modules which start to run as soon as one of their public predicates is called, or to carry out initialisations such as operator declarations.

The fourth argument is the type of the module: **data**, **program** or **library**. The only time you can change a module's type is when you are saving it. All modules are data modules when they are created. If you want a module to become a program or library module you must specify the new type when you save it.

You do not have complete freedom in selecting the type of the module at this stage. If your module is a data module, and you select data when you save it, you will still be able to change it to a program or a library module on some later save.

If you select program or library, you will never be able to alter the module's type or alter its contents. It is therefore advisable to save modules as data modules until you are sure that you have completed their development. The final save can then be to program or library modules as appropriate. You should also keep a backup copy saved as a data module.

The fifth argument sets the access permitted to the module. The possibilities are

readwrite, read, write or **none** (for a full explanation of these terms see §15.2.3). You cannot open a module with better access than you specified when you last saved it. Nor can you save a module with better access than you gave it when you opened it.

These two access limitations restrict the choices available to you when saving modules. If you save a module as anything other than **readwrite** you will not be able to use it as readwrite again. If, however, you save it as **readwrite** you can always restrict its access on later saves.

15.8 Opening modules

When you want to use a module, either one you have created and saved yourself or one you have obtained elsewhere, you first have to open it. Opening a module makes it available for use but does not automatically bring it into operation. A module will only start to operate if it has a start-goal, or if one of its public predicates is called as a goal.

To open a module you use the BIP **open_module/4**:

> open_module(computer,"module",readwrite,actual).

The first argument is the name of the module. Usually use a variable to select the name that the module was saved with, but if necessary use an atom to override that name.

The second argument is the name of the file in which the module is saved.

The third argument is the type of access required — **readwrite, read, write** or **none**. (If you defined the module as a program or library module when you saved it, the access level can only be **none**).

The fourth argument is the type of storage (see §15.3) the module is to occupy — **virtual** or **actual** for data modules, **actual** for program and library modules.

You cannot open a data module with better access than you gave it when you saved it. ('Better' here means 'more accessible' on the scale **none** to **readwrite**.) You can give a module worse access than you did when you saved it: you might want to do this, for example, to check that a module runs properly without risking changing it by accident.

15.9 Accessing modules

15.9.1 Current output module

You cannot put information into a module until you have made it the Current Output Module.

The system state **output_module** makes a module current for output.

state(output_module,Oldmodule,Newmodule).

The module you want to become the Current Output Module must already be:

(1) **data** in type
(2) **readwrite** in access
(3) open for use.

(A module you have just created will automatically be all three.)

15.9.2 Current input module

The Current Input Module passes clauses to the database editor and must also be specified. This is done using another system-state:

state(input_module,_,modulename).

which is used in exactly the same way as output_module.

15.9.3 Using the same module for input and output

The Current Output Module and the Current Input Module may be either the same module or different modules. When you are developing a program they should be the same module: you will have problems in developing programs if they are different. You will not be able to read the clauses you have asserted, and you will not be able to retract any clauses.

On startup, the 'common module' (the default module that opens automatically when you first start Prolog-2) is both the Current Output Module and the Current Input Module.

15.9.4 Adding and removing clauses

Once a module has been correctly set up as Current Output Module you can use the **assert** and **retract** BIP families to enter and delete clauses in it (see Chapter 14). The Current Input Module and Current Output Module must both be set to the same module for **retract**.

15.9.5 Inspecting clauses

The Current Input Module is used to read the database. You do this using the BIPs **listing** and **clause**.

listing/0 lists all the clauses in the current input module; **listing/1** takes a predicate name as its argument and lists all the clauses in the Current Input Module for that predicate.

The various versions of **clause** allow you to check on an individual clause; they all take

The Prolog-2 User Guide

a predicate-rep as first argument.

15.10 Closing a module

To close a module you use **close_module/1**

> close_module(modulename).

giving the name of the module to be closed as the argument.

15.11 Retrieving information on modules

module/6 tells you about modules which are open:

> module(Modname,File,Type,Access,Storage,Scope).

This matches its six arguments with: the name of a module; the name of the file in which it was found; its type (data, program, or library); its access (none, read, write, or readwrite); its storage (actual or virtual); and the default scope of its predicates (private or public). It is resatisfiable.

For example:

```
?- module(Modname,File,Type,Access,Storage,Scope).

Modname = common
File = none
Type = data
Access = readwrite
Storage = actual
Scope = public
More (y/n)? y

Modname = grules
File = "\GRULES.PRM"
Type = program
Access = none
Storage = actual
Scope = public
More (y/n)? n
```

15.12 Compatibility notes

The module system of Prolog-2 is unique; many other Prolog systems have module systems, no two are the same. However, programs from Prolog systems without modules, or that make no reference to modules, will work in Prolog-2 using the common module as input and output module.

16. How Prolog-2 uses memory

16.1 Prolog-2: program and modules

Prolog-2 consists of the Prolog-2 program and some modules. The modules supply extra facilities, which generally may be regarded as built in. Advanced users may alter the MNU file so that some modules are not opened: this will be discussed in Chapter 22.

The Prolog-2 program contains the Prolog interpreter, some support code for compiled modules, and code to implement some of the built-in predicates and system states. Some of this code is actually Prolog, but this is not apparent to the user.

Most of the modules are themselves written in Prolog-2.

16.2 The Prolog-2 program

16.2.1 The interpreter

The Prolog-2 core system contains the logical theorem prover which is the heart of interpreted Prolog. The theorem-prover is an interpreter that carries out all the logical operations needed to execute Prolog programs. The Prolog-2 interpreter is very efficient and ideally suited for development work.

The Prolog-2 program does not contain a user interface. The user can interact with the core interpreter via the Top-Level Interpreter or TLI, which is part of the program development environment (Chapter 25). The TLI is in the module **top**; like the rest of the development environment, it may be discarded in a packaged application.

16.2.2 Compiler support

Although much compiled code is in-line, more complicated code is kept in subroutines. Some of these are linked with the compiled code by the compiler, and others are resident in the Prolog-2 program.

16.2.3 Built-in predicates

Prolog-2 has a large number of "Built-In Predicates" or BIPs (catalogued alphabetically in the Prolog-2 Encyclopaedia). BIPs are names known to the Prolog system which cause it to perform various operations which would be difficult or impossible with user-written code. Examples include outputting a term or defining an operator.

DECsystem-10 Prolog has a standard set of BIPs, all of which are present in Prolog-2. But Prolog-2 also contains many new BIPs to give you access to numerous extra facilities. BIPs are part of the Prolog-2 program. They cannot be added to or altered by the user in any way. Trying to use a BIP name as an ordinary predicate — for example, by asserting one into the clause store — will generate an error.

If you want to define predicates which you will use regularly and which might take the place of some BIPs (although you must not give them the same name as any of the BIPs), you can create a library where you define these. This library will be a module, and you can arrange for it to be opened automatically whenever you start up the system.

One use of libraries is to avoid including in the Prolog-2 system bulky code that the user may not want. The **dec10** library contains the **setof** procedure and other bulky code; it also contains default code that the user may want to change: for example, the definition of **name/2** is stored in **dec10** so that the user can replace it by the standard **name/2** easily.

A source library of useful code is included in the Prolog-2 system; it is called **syslib**. The user may select useful routines from this, add personal favourites, and package this as a library module, to be opened at the start of each Prolog session.

16.2.4 System states

Prolog-2 has a number of system states. These are used to configure various aspects of the system, such as setting the input and output streams and specifying the time that may be spent on garbage collection.

A system state is a global variable that affects some aspect of the Prolog system. For example, the state **input** controls which stream input is taken from. System states are examined and altered using the predicate **state/3**; the first argument is the state name, the second the current value and the third the new value. To set input to a new stream **new** the form

state(input,_,new)

would be used, while to set the variable **Old** to the name of the input stream, the call

state(input,Old,Old)

is used. Systems states embody a principle adhered to throughout Prolog-2; anything that you can set you must be able to examine.

The system states are mentioned as appropriate in this volume and are catalogued in the Prolog-2 Encyclopaedia.

16.3 Fixed data

The Prolog-2 program uses a small fixed data area to store system tables, such as definitions of built-in streams, and other data. The user has no access to this area and its size is fixed.

16.4 Machine stack

Whereas most programming languages use the stack to store the record of procedure invocations, Prolog-2 uses a separate stack, the local stack, for this. The machine stack is used for subroutine calls within the Prolog program, and will therefore only grow noticeably in deep recursions. The creation of deep terms may eventually cause stack overflow, which will be detected in whatever way the machine architecture permits (e.g., on the 8086, not at all). A particular case to note is the unification of circular terms: although X=a(X) can be executed safely, the code

X=a(X),Y=a(Y),X=Y.

will overflow the stack.

16.5 The heap

The heap is used for data that will not be undone on backtracking; most notably, the clause store. Stream, window, module and tokenisation class definitions are also stored on the heap. The first part of the heap is built in to the Prolog system and contains definitions of built-in predicates in Prolog. The heap also contains the names of atoms. When items on the heap are not wanted they must be explicitly discarded; for example, a clause is discarded using **retract/1**. The space freed is not reclaimed until the user or the system decides to garbage collect using **trimcore**.

Exceptions to the explicit discard rule are **trimatoms** and **trimlibs** which detect unwanted atom names and library clauses respectively.

16.6 Virtual memory

8086 Prolog-2 (23) recognises two types of memory: actual and virtual. Actual memory holds information in the RAM itself. Virtual memory holds information on disk instead of in RAM, and swaps it in and out of RAM as needed.

Prolog-2 sees these two levels of memory as one and the same: it does not distinguish between the fast RAM portion and the somewhat slower disk storage.

A module stored in virtual memory is therefore not limited by the size of the computer's RAM. Actual memory modules are limited to the size of the RAM in your machine, less the space taken up by Prolog-2 itself and by the operating system.

If you are developing large programs, you can use the virtual memory facility to hold large Prolog databases.

16.7 Compiled code

Compiled code is loaded into the heap when opened and removed when closed; thus a number of compiled code modules can share memory; indeed, the memory can be used interchangeably for compiled code and anything else stored on the heap.

16.8 Global stack

The global stack contains copies of structures created at run time. For example, if the clause

The Prolog-2 User Guide

a(X) :- append([1,2,3],[4,5,6],X)

is in the clause store and a(X) is called then the structures [1,2,3] and [4,5,6] will be in the heap (perhaps in compiled form) but the structure [1,2,3,4,5,6] will be on the global stack.

The global stack is reset on failure but not when a goal succeeds. Thus garbage may collect on the global stack, and garbage collection can be used to clean this away.

16.9 Local stack

The local stack contains a frame for each goal call that is still active, that is to say, that is either in the course of proof or that may be backtracked into. It should be noted that the compiler is quite crafty in detecting that a predicate has no more solutions, but the interpreter always assumes that backtracking may occur if there is a clause that it has not tried, even if the head does not match. For this reason cut may be used in interpreted code to reduce the size of the local stack.

The local stack does not accumulate garbage. Firstly, it is reclaimed on failure and on deterministic success (true but no more solutions). Secondly it uses a mechanism called last call optimisation or tail recursion optimisation that allows early reclaim of entries for tail goals. The programmer needs to understand this to write efficient code.

If you write a predicate like the following:

a :- write("cabbage "),nl,a.

and then call it by typing

?- a.

then in some Prolog systems your cabbages will terminate after fairly short time. This is because each new Prolog goal takes up some extra space.

The evaluation of **a** is a loop, and the situation at the start of each evaluation of **a** is the same. Therefore the interpreter does not need to keep a stack of separate descriptions of the situation.

In general, when a tail goal reaches its last clause, and when there are no resatisfiable goals between it and its parent, and also the parent has no further clause, then the interpreter can throw away the information stored for the parent and replace it with the child. All these conditions are met trivially by **a**, but also can be met in the more general case where the tail goal is not an invocation of the same predicate as the parent invoked. This more general situation is not very aptly called 'tail recursion' in Prolog circles. A good account of this is given in C J Hogger "Introduction to Logic Programming" (Academic Press) 1984, pp. 208 - 212.

From the programmer's point of view the fact that Tail Recursion Optimisation is

112

implemented in Prolog-2 means that a few points should be remembered.

(1) Tail recursive code takes up less space. Therefore, other things being equal, you should put the recursive clause of a predicate last. For example

append([],T,T)
append([H|T],A,[H|T1]) :- append(T,A,T1)

and not the other way round.

(2) Tail recursion 'optimises' away some data you might have preferred to keep. This is especially annoying with the ancestor BIPs. If you write

a :- b.
b :- c.
c :- backtrace.

?- a.

you might hope to see the message

1. c
2. b
3. a

on the screen. In fact you will only get **a**; the others have been swallowed up by their children.

The moral of this story is to use the debugging system to debug programs. The debugging system churns out such a quantity of odd diagnostic information that it prevents Tail Recursion Optimisation from working at all. If you run the above program while debugging, or select the g option at the debug menu, then you will be able to ascertain that all ancestors are preserved.

Of course there will be times when you want to find out where you are after a mysterious error in a program you thought was working, and then you must rely on backtrace. But don't be surprised if you find that some of the ancestors are missing.

(3) You can switch Tail Recursion Optimisation off, using the system state **tro**. You should try to avoid this, because not only will your program take up more space in the stack of goal records (the local stack) as it runs, but also garbage collection of the global stack will be less efficient.

(4) In compiled code, Tail Recursion Optimisation is always used. Since the ancestor family does not work in compiled code anyway this will not matter.

16.10 Trail

The trail contains addresses to be set to undefined on backtracking. Generally it is very small.

16.11 Atom table

The atom table contains an entry for each atom. Internally atoms are stored as offsets in this table to save space; the table is only accessed when the atom name is needed, say by **write/1**, or when an interpreted predicate is sought. The atom table also contains information about the operator status of an atom.

16.12 Garbage collection

Prolog programs can use up a great deal of computer memory. Like other advanced implementations of Prolog, Prolog-2 has a memory management system that includes a "garbage collector" which periodically retrieves unwanted memory space.

It is normally automatic, but can be switched off if you want. This can increase the speed at which the system operates, but memory may fill up very quickly, depending on your program.

If automatic garbage collection is switched off, or if you want to force garbage collection at a particular time for some reason, there is a collection of Built-In Predicates that invoke it explicitly:

trimstacks/0
trimcore/0
trimlibs/0
trimatoms/0

It should rarely be necessary to switch off automatic garbage collection except in critical parts of a program.

16.13 Compatibility notes

Terminology varies. What we call the global stack is often called the heap, and the local stack is sometimes just called the stack. However, most Prolog systems have areas roughly corresponding to the ones described.

The garbage collector of Prolog-2 is modelled as closely as possible on that of DEC-10 Prolog, and the states **gcguide(_)** that limit garbage collection are taken from DEC-10. Generally the programmer should not rely on the configurability of garbage collection in Prolog systems. Quite a lot of Prolog systems do not garbage collect atom names, and this can pose problems.

17. Arithmetic

17.1 Introduction

Prolog-2 can evaluate two types of expression: arithmetic expressions and string expressions.

Arithmetic expressions are evaluated by **is/2** or a comparison operator; certain Built-In Predicates (BIPs) such as **tab/1** and **put/1** also evaluate their argument. String expressions are evaluated by **is_string/2**.

17.2 Arithmetic expressions in Prolog

An arithmetic expression is a structure which evaluates to a number. For example, the structure 5 + 3 * 2 evaluates to 11.

An arithmetic expression may be any of the following:

(1) a number;
(2) a non-null string;
(3) a non-empty list;
(4) an arithmetic functor: either a binary operator such as + with two arithmetic expressions as arguments; or a unary operator such as **truncate** with a single arithmetic expression as its argument;
(5) a transcendental function;
(6) one of the special structures **value/1**, **value/2**, **length/1**, **index/3**, or **?/2**.

17.2.1 Numbers

Numbers may be integers or reals. The integer and real ranges available are defined by the constants **max_real** and **max_integer**.

17.2.2 Strings

A single character Prolog-2 string is also a valid arithmetic expression. Its value is the ASCII value of its character. For example, the value of the string "b" is 98.

17.2.3 Non-empty lists

A list of integers or reals is a valid expression: its value is the value of its first element.

17.2.4 Arithmetic functors

Arithmetic functors cover the usual arithmetic operations such as addition and division. They are all listed below and described in detail in the Prolog-2 Encyclopaedia.

115

The Prolog-2 User Guide

Functor	Arity	Description
+	2	Addition
-	2	Subtraction
-	1	Negation
*	2	Multiplication
/	2	Division
//	2	Division of integers, with integer result
mod	2	Integer modulus
float	1	Converts integer to real number
fix	1	Converts real number to integer: rounds towards 0
truncate	1	Converts a real number to an integer: rounds towards zero, then back to a real number
real_round	1	As **truncate**, but rounds to the nearest whole real number instead of down

Prolog-2 also provides some operations that treat integers as bit patterns. The first six of these are recognised as operators.

/\	2	Bitwise and
\/	2	Bitwise or
\	1	Bitwise complement
<<	2	Bitwise left shift
>>	2	Bitwise right shift
$	1	see §17.2.7
!	1	see §17.2.7

17.2.5 Transcendental functions

17.2.5.1 Trigonometric functions: sin cos tan asin acos atan

These each take one argument, which must itself be an arithmetic expression. This argument is in radians.

17.2.5.2 Hyperbolic functions: sinh cosh tanh asinh acosh atanh

These each take one argument which must itself be an arithmetic expression.

17.2.5.3 log exp ^ sqrt

log evaluates to the natural logarithm of its argument; **exp** evaluates to the exponent of its argument; ^, which is an infix operator, evaluates to its left argument raised to the power of its right argument; and **sqrt** evaluates to the square root of its argument.

17.2.5.4 Arithmetic constants: pi and e

These are atoms and have no arguments.

17.2.6 Special Structures

Five types of special structure which can form arithmetic expressions:

Functor	Arity
value	1
value	2
length	1
index	3
?	2

17.2.6.1 value/1

value/1 takes a string as its argument. The contents of this string should parse to an arithmetic expression which is evaluated. For example

>   **value("12-33.")**

evaluates to -21. Note that the . within the string is necessary for the string to be a syntactically readable term.

value/1 may also be used in string expressions (see §17.4), provided the contents of the string parse as a string, list or atom.

17.2.6.2 value/2

value/2 is the same as **value/1** above, with the second argument being a format which is to be used to parse the contents of the string. For example

>   **X is value("23", ir).**
>
>   **X = 23**

value/2 may also be used in string expressions (see §17.4), provided the contents of the string parse as a string, list or atom.

17.2.6.3 length/1

length/1 takes a string expression (see §17.4 below) as its argument. It evaluates to the length of this string. For example,

>   **length("some string")**

evaluates to 11.

17.2.6.4 index/3

The **index**/3 structure locates the position of a substring within a string. The string is the first argument to **index**; the substring is the second argument. The third argument is an integer and specifies the character position in the main string where Prolog is to start looking for the substring. (The character positions start at 0.)

For example:

```
X is index("searching for a substring","for",0).
X = 10

X is index("searching for a substring","ing",10).
X = 22
```

If the substring cannot be found in the section of the string following the character position specified by the third argument, **index**/3 returns the length of the entire string instead.

```
X is index("searching for a substring","for",15).
X = 25

X is index("searching for a substring","not there",0).
X = 25
```

This form of arithmetic expression is useful when writing edit routines.

The first two arguments may be string expressions (see §17.4 below); the third may be an arithmetic expression. Note that the third argument must evaluate to an integer, not a real.

17.2.6.5 ?/2

When a term whose functor is ? with arity 2 is evaluated, its value is the value of its first argument when a match has been found for its second argument.

```
?- M is ?(X,wage(fred,X))/12.

M = 791.6667
X = 9500
```

Note that the variable X does not get instantiated by the call: it is placeholder, not a true variable.

17.2.7 $ and ! arithmetic functors

The effect of the $ and ! operators can only be understood relative to the internal representation of Prolog-2 integers on your particular machine.

During the evaluation of an expression, intermediate results may be generated: for instance, when evaluating the expression:

X is 2 + 3 * 5

the intermediate result 15 will be generated: 2 is added to this to produce the final result which will be matched with X. Intermediate results are held to the maximum integer precision of the machine you are running on (**max_internal_integer**). Prolog-2 integers, however, are held in a tagged data format. This means that the precision of a Prolog-2 integer is rather less than that of intermediate results. If the integer size for calculations is n bits, and the number of bits used for tag data is m, then the layout of intermediate integer results and Prolog-2 integers can be represented thus:

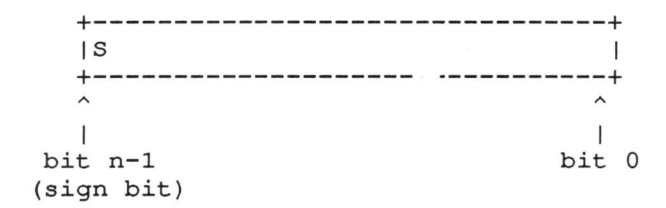

Intermediate result integer:

```
         +-------------------------------+
         |S                              |
         +---------------------   -------+
          ^                             ^
          |                             |
          |                             |
        bit n-1                       bit 0
       (sign bit)
```

Prolog-2 integer:

```
         +-------------------------------+
         |tttttS                         |
         +-------------------------------+
          ^^^^  ^                       ^
     tag bits   |                       |
           bit (n-m)-1                 bit 0
           (sign bit)
```

What the $ operator does

The effect of the $ operator is to sign-extend from bit (n-m)-1 of its argument into the area of the intermediate integer which would be occupied by the tag bits if the result were stored in a Prolog-2 integer.

The $ operator may turn a positive integer negative and vice versa: the point is that the

The Prolog-2 User Guide

result of the operation will squeeze into a Prolog-2 integer without generating an arithmetic overflow error.

What the ! functor does

The effect of the ! functor is similar, except that it zeroes bits (n-m) to n, thus always converting the argument to a positive integer.

Note that bit (n-m)-1 is left as is: this means that the result may still be out of Prolog-2 integer range, so

    X is ! <number>

may generate an arithmetic overflow at the point just prior to the match with X (at this point the result must be packed into a Prolog-2 integer format).

The two operators are provided largely for DECsystem-10 compatibility, but their exact result is perforce different on different machines.

Examples:

We will assume for the sake of argument that intermediate integer precision is 31 bits plus a sign bit, and that the Prolog-2 integer occupies 32 bits, the most significant five of which are tag bits: the sign of the Prolog-2 integer is therefore held in bit 26, giving an integer range of -2^{26} to $2^{26}-1$.

```
?- X is $ fix(2.0 ^ 26.0).
X = -67108864
```

This is because 2^{26} is an integer with bit 26 set, therefore the result after sign-extension will be negative.

```
?- X is $ fix(2.0 ^ 27.0).
X = 0
```

This is because 2^{27} is an integer where bit 26 is zero: therefore the result after sign extension will be positive. (It also happens in these two examples that all the bits to the right of bit 26 are zero also.)

```
?- X is !(fix(2.0 ^ 26.0)).
Error 29 : Arithmetic overflow
```

This is because 2^{26} has bit 26 set: when bits 27-31 are cleared, the result remains out of Prolog-2 integer range (because it is still 2^{26}). Compare and contrast with the effect of the $ operator.

Remember that these examples will behave quite differently on different machines.

17.3 Causing evaluation of arithmetic expressions

There are three situations where Prolog-2 will evaluate an arithmetic expression:

(1) with the infix operator **is/2**
(2) with arithmetic comparison BIPs
(3) with the BIPs **put/1**, **tab/1** or **skip/1**

is/2

The BIP **is/2** is an infix operator: it evaluates its right argument and matches the result with its left argument. If this left argument is a variable, it is instantiated to the result of the evaluation (provided this succeeds); if the left argument is a number, **is/2** will succeed or fail, depending on whether the evaluation matches the left argument or not.

For example:

    X is 2 + 2.

instantiates X to 4;

    12 is 2 * length("string").

succeeds; and

    10.0 is 1+2+3+4.

fails (because a real does not match an integer, even when they are equal).

Arithmetic comparison BIPs

The six arithmetic comparison BIPs are infix operators (with precedence 700): they work by evaluating both their arguments and comparing the results. They either succeed or fail depending on the result of this comparison. They cannot instantiate anything.

The arithmetic comparison BIPs are:

Operator	Description
<	Less than
>	Greater than
=<	Less than or equal to
>=	Greater than or equal to

121

The Prolog-2 User Guide

> =:=   Equal to
> =\=   Not equal to

For example

> length("string") < 5*5.

succeeds; but

> 1+9 =\= 2+8.

fails.

The comparison operators =:= and =\= may fail with real numbers because these are rounded up or down very slightly inside the machine.

put/1, tab/1, skip/1

Prolog-2 will also evaluate an arithmetic expression is when that expression occurs as an argument to **put/1**, **tab/1**, or **skip/1**. For example:

> put("K"+1).

will output a L, and

> X=5, tab(8*X).

will output 40 spaces. Note that the expression must evaluate to an integer.

17.4 String expressions

A string expression is a structure which, when evaluated by **is_string/2**, yields a string. A simple example is:

> ?- X is_string "Pro" & "log".
>
> X = "Prolog"

A string expression may be any of the following:

(1) a string;
(2) an atom;
(3) a list of ASCII values
(4) a structure with functor **string/2**, **?/2**, **&/2**, **substring/3**, **insert/3**, or **delete/3**.

17.4.1 Strings

The only way to evaluate a string expression in Prolog-2 is to use the BIP **is_string/2**. This is an infix operator (with precedence 700). It evaluates its right argument as a string and matches the result with its left argument. If the left argument is a variable, it will be instantiated to the result of the evaluation (provided this succeeds); if the left argument is a string, the call to **is_string/2** will either succeed or fail, depending on whether the result of the evaluation matches the left argument or not.

17.4.2 Atoms

When an atom is evaluated as a string, the result is the string which is the name of the atom. For example:

```
?- X is_string computer.
X = "computer"
```

17.4.3 Lists

A list of integers may also be evaluated as a string. They are regarded as ASCII values. For example:

```
?- X is_string [69,83,73].
X = "ESI"
```

17.4.4 Functors for string evaluation

Six functors assume special meanings when encountered in structures that are being evaluated as strings. These are:

Functor	Arity	Use
&	2	Concatenation
substring	3	Extracting a substring
insert	3	Inserting a string
delete	3	Deleting a substring
string	2	Writing a term
?	2	Obtaining information from the database

17.4.4.1 &/2

Joins two strings together. The strings are joined in the order they appear as arguments to &/2.

```
?- X is_string "computers " & "use " & "silicon".
X = "computers use silicon"
```

The arguments to &/2 can be any string expressions.

17.4.4.2 substring/3

123

The Prolog-2 User Guide

A substring can be extracted using the string operator **substring/3**:

```
?- X is_string substring("computers use silicon",10,3).
X = "use"
```

The first argument to **substring/3** is the string from which the substring is to be extracted. The second argument is the position at which extraction is to start (numbering from 0); the third argument is the number of characters to be extracted. All these arguments may be expressions.

17.4.4.3 insert/3

You can insert strings into other strings using the string operator **insert/3**.

```
?- X is_string insert("computers silicon","use ",10).
X = "computers use silicon"
```

The first argument to **insert/3** is the string which another string is going to be put into. The second argument is the string to be inserted and the third argument is the position in the first string where the insertion is to start (numbering from 0). All these arguments may be expressions.

17.4.4.4 delete/3

Substrings can be deleted using the operator **delete/3**.

```
?- X is_string delete("computers use use silicon",14,4).

X = "computers use silicon"
```

The first argument is the string from which the substring is to be deleted. The second argument is the start-position of the deletion (numbering from 0). The third argument is the number of characters to be deleted. All these arguments may be expressions.

17.4.4.5 string/2

The two arguments to **string/2** are a term and an output format (see Chapter 15 (Input/Output and Streams) for more information on formatted input and output). This evaluates to a string which contains the term expressed in the specified format.

For example:

```
?- X is_string string(a+b,display).

X = "+(a,b)"
```

17.4.4.6 ?/2

?/2 is used to implement functions which derive information from the database. For example, if the clause

> stored_in(sysmess,"SYSMESS").

is in the database, then

> ?- Y is_string "C:\\MYFILES\\" & ?(X,stored_in(sysmess,X)).

returns

> Y = "C:\\MYFILES\\SYSMESS"
> X = "SYSMESS"

Note the use here of pairs of backslashes within a string to produce single backslashes.

17.5 Term order: the canonical order of terms

As we have discussed the < predicate in this chapter, it is worth looking at the more general @< relation.

There is a canonical (i.e. arbitrary) ordering of all Prolog-2 terms defined by the system. This is also called the term order. The main reason for its presence is that **setof/3** needs an order to sort terms into. The order is similar to that in DECsystem-10 Prolog but more extended because of the extra data types in Prolog-2.

The canonical order is written @<. It is a total linear ordering of Prolog-2 terms. Objects of different types are ordered by their type only. For example, all integers are less than all atoms. Objects of the same type are ordered by a special rule for that type; this rule is specified below.

The ordering of types, from first to last, is as follows:

(1) variables
(2) integers
(3) reals
(4) strings
(5) atoms
(6) structures.

Within each type the ordering is as follows:

17.5.1 Variables

Variables are ordered in the sequence they were 'created'. Since you have no way of knowing this sequence you can regard the order as arbitrary. It is transitive, though, and consistent in that for given variables X and Y exactly one of the following holds.

> X == Y
> X @< Y

The Prolog-2 User Guide

        X @> Y

Note that if X or Y is subsequently matched with an "older" variable the order may change.

17.5.2 Integers

Integers are arranged in the conventional order.

17.5.3 Reals

Reals are arranged in the conventional order.

17.5.4 Strings

These are in dictionary order, assuming dictionaries use ASCII.

        "albatross" @< "ale"
        "ale" @< "alex".

This subset of the order is sometimes useful in its own right.

17.5.5 Atoms

These are ordered by their names as though they were strings (but be careful not to confuse the two)

        "zinc" @< aluminium

17.5.6 Structures

In ordering two structures, look first at the arities. If these differ the term with the lower arity is smaller.

If the two structures are of the same arity, look at the functors considered as atoms. If these differ then the smaller (as in (5)) gives the smaller structure.

Suppose the functor and arity are the same. If the structures are unequal, then some argument position contains different values for the different structures. Look at the leftmost position where this happens and apply the ordering already defined to that position. Whichever term has the smaller argument here is smaller. (The acute reader will have observed that this does not work with circular terms; but then, what does?)

Here is a list of terms in order:

[X, -9, 1, -7.2, 66E4, "Zeugma", "zebra", "zebras", fie, foe, fum, X=Y, fie(0,2), fie(1,1), foe(0,0), fie(3,3,3)].

17.6 Compatibility notes

Although DEC-10 Prolog had no real numbers, most Prolog systems now incorporate them. **is**/2 is the standard way to evaluate expressions, and the other operations that evaluate their arguments are also standard. Most arithmetic expression elements are found in most Prolog systems, but type conversion names vary and the hyperbolic functions are not to be relied upon.

The special expression elements in §17.2.6 are all unique to Prolog-2.

The bitwise operators are commonly found as described here. The description of $ and ! should make it clear that they are extremely machine specific.

String expressions are unique to Prolog-2.

18. Input/Output

18.1 Introduction to streams

All input and output (I/O) in Prolog-2 uses streams. Streams are pathways for data passing into and out of the system from input and output devices of various kinds. By looking at these data streams rather than at the devices themselves Prolog-2 avoids involving itself with the details of how they work; it leaves this to lower-level software.

Input streams carry information into the system, either from files or from other input devices such as a keyboard or serial port. Output streams carry information out of the system, again either to a file or to some output device such as the screen or printer.

The current input stream and current output stream

Although many different streams into and out of the system may exist, only two can be active at any one time: one for input and one for output. These are known as the current input stream and current output stream.

At startup the current input stream is set to run into the system from the keyboard and the current output stream to run out to the user screen. These streams are called **glass_tty**. However, a window-based front end will change these assignments at once.

Prolog-2 provides predicates which allow you to switch the current input and current output streams to any other streams available to you.

Streams: creating, opening, closing, deleting

You have to create and then open a stream before you can use it. When you no longer need a stream you can close it; if the stream will not be needed again in your program you can delete it.

You can create streams by using **create_stream/4**, described in §18.3. Some BIPs create streams automatically (see §18.6 for a list of these), and several streams are created by the PDE if loaded.

Certain special device streams are created automatically on startup but are not opened, such as **printer** and **glass_tty**. Each special device stream uses the special device of the same name.

There is no theoretical limit to the number of streams you can create in Prolog-2. But each stream takes up some memory; you may run out of space if you use too many.

18.2 Attributes of streams

All types of stream have the following four attributes:

(1) Name
(2) Access mode
(3) Data type
(4) Descriptor.

These four attributes are used with the various Prolog-2 stream-manipulation predicates described later in this chapter.

(1) Name

The name of a stream must be an atom. Two streams cannot have the same name.

(2) Access mode

A stream can be used for input, output or both. If it is to be used for input only, its access mode should be **read**; if for output only, **write**; and if for both, **readwrite**.

You set the access mode when you first create the stream (see §18.3 below). Once you have set a stream's access mode you cannot decide to make it less restricted; but you might choose to open the stream with a more restricted access m

(3) Data type

Streams can carry either 7-bit ASCII data or 8-bit binary data. You specify which you want, **ascii** or **byte**, when the stream is created (see §18.3 below). If you specify **ascii**, the seventh (high) bit of each character is set to zero as it is read in. Normally you will use **byte**.

(4) Descriptor

A descriptor differentiates the type of stream. The file descriptor is a structure **file/1** or **special/1**; its functor is the type of the stream and its arguments are its attributes.

18.3 Creating streams

Streams are created using the BIP **create_stream/4**. The four arguments to **create_stream/4** are the stream attributes described in §18.2 above:

> The name of the stream
> The access mode
> The data type
> A stream descriptor

Examples:

> create_stream(newstream,write,ascii,file("textfile")).
> create_stream(printout,write,ascii,special(printer)).

The Prolog-2 User Guide

The fourth argument is particularly important: it identifies the type of stream you are creating and its characteristics.

Types of stream: files

Files are mass storage devices recognised by the operating system, and can be either input or output devices. They can used sequentially or as random-access files.

The fourth argument to **create_stream**/4 for a file stream is:

>   **file(Filename)**

The filename must be a string, enclosed in double-quotes. If you do not specify a directory, the default directory will be assumed; if you do not specify a file extension, **.PRO** will be added.

Special devices

There are several special devices in Prolog-2. The only two available on all machines are:

>   **printer**
>   **glass_tty**

In §23.3 we shall see how the user may add special stream devices such as window handlers.

Creating special device streams

To associate a stream with a special device you also use the BIP **create_stream**/4.

The arguments are the four attributes of a stream described §18.2 above: the name of the stream, the access mode, the data type and the stream descriptor. For example:

>   **create_stream(punch,write,ascii,special(punch))**

The name of the stream can be any atom. Access and datatype are whatever is appropriate to the stream, and the stream descriptor is one of the structures **special(Device)** where support for **Device** is built-in or has been added by the programmer.

18.4 Manipulating streams

This Section discusses the following predicates:

>   **stream/5**
>   **open/2**
>   **close/1**
>   **delete_stream/1**

18.4.1 Getting information about streams: stream/5

stream/5 tells you what streams exist and what their attributes are.

The first argument is the name of a stream. Stream names must be atoms. If this argument is a variable it will be successively instantiated with the names of streams satisfying the other arguments of **stream/5**.

The second argument is the access mode set when the stream was created. If instantiated this must be one of the atoms **read**, **write** or **readwrite**. It can be a variable.

The third argument is the datatype of the stream, **ascii** or **byte**. You may use a variable here instead.

The fourth argument is the stream descriptor. This can be a variable or one of the structures used in the fourth argument to **create_stream/4**:

> **file(Name).**
> **special(Device).**

Such stream descriptor structures can be partly instantiated. Thus:

> **stream(A,B,C,special(D),E).**

finds information on all the special streams created.

The fifth argument to **stream/5** is the current open or closed status of the stream. Its possible values are **read**, **write**, **readwrite**, or **closed**. The argument may be one of these atoms or a variable.

If the stream is not closed, **stream/5** will indicate the access mode with which it was opened.

18.4.2 Opening streams: open/2

The BIPs **see/1**, **tell/1**, **consult/1** and **reconsult/1** open streams automatically: Section §18.6 below tells you about these.

In most cases you will need to arrange for any routines that use streams to open them when needed. **open/2** will open a stream for you: its two arguments are the name of the stream and the access required. The access argument must be one of the atoms **read**, **write** and **readwrite**.

Simply opening a stream does not make it the current stream. A stream must be made current before it can be used for input or output. Opening a file stream when the file does not exist will cause an error.

18.4.3 Closing streams: close/1

close/1 closes a stream. The single argument is the name of the stream. You cannot close the standard input-output stream (see §18.5 below).

Closing a stream when it is the Current Input or Current Output Stream will make the standard input-output stream current.

18.4.4 Deleting streams: delete_stream/1

You can delete streams to free memory space. **delete_stream**/1 takes the name of the stream to be deleted as its argument.

You cannot delete a stream until you have closed it.

18.5 The standard input-output stream

The standard input-output stream is the stream which automatically becomes the Current Input Stream if the existing Current Input Stream is closed; or automatically becomes the Current Output Stream if the existing Current Output Stream is closed.

The Top-Level Interpreter also causes the standard input-output stream to become current for both input and output every time its **?-** prompt appears.

The system state **stdio** specifies the standard input-output stream. The standard input-output stream is known to Prolog-2 as **user**. You switch Current Input or Current Output to the standard input-output stream by **see(user)** or **tell(user)**. The default value of the standard input-output stream is **glass_tty**.

18.6 Built-in predicates and streams

Prolog-2 provides a range of BIPs which:

(1) create streams
(2) provide information on streams
(3) close streams.

18.6.1 BIPs which create streams

The following BIPs may create or open streams:

    see/1
    tell/1
    consult/1
    reconsult/1

The single argument for all these predicates is the name of a stream. If this stream exists it is opened; if it does not exist it is created automatically.
If **see**/1, **tell**/1, **consult**/1, or **reconsult**/1 is used with an atom that is not recognised

as the name of a stream, a stream of that name is created: it is created as a file stream, and the atom used as the name of the file. If there is no extension, the default extension .PRO is assumed.

With **see**/1, **consult**/1, and **reconsult**/1, this will result in a "file not found" error if the file does not exist; with **tell**/1, a file of this name will be created.

Thus

> **consult(weather).**

will look for a file WEATHER.PRO on the logged-in drive, and consult it; and

> **tell(weather).**

will create a file WEATHER.PRO in the current directory (or truncate an existing file to 0 bytes) and put the Current Output into it.

The streams created by these BIPs are not deleted after they have been used. If you are short of space you may want to delete them yourself.

Creating the stream is not the primary purpose of any of these predicates. **see**/1 also makes its argument the Current Input Stream; **tell**/1 also makes its argument the Current Output Stream; **consult**/1 and **reconsult**/1 cause the stream to be read, and the clauses in it to be added to the database.

When a stream is created automatically, its data type is determined by the setting of the system state **file_type**.

tell should be used with caution: if the stream is open it is made current, but if you have inadvertently closed it, then the file will be deleted and a new one started. To open a file and append data at the end it is necessary to use **open** rather than **tell**.

18.6.2 BIPs which provide information about streams

seeing/1 matches its argument with the name of the Current Input Stream. **telling**/1 matches its argument with the name of the Current Output Stream.

18.6.3 BIPs which close streams

seen/0 closes the Current Input Stream. **told**/0 closes the Current Output Stream.

18.7 Switching streams

To make a stream the current input stream use the system state **input**; for output **output**. The general operation of the state mechanism was explained in Chapter 16.

The Prolog-2 User Guide

18.8 Performing I/O

Once the stream has been specified there are many predicates available for input and output. In this chapter we need discuss only the byte-by-byte predicates. For output the predicate **put**/1 is used. It evaluates its argument, so a single character string may be specified.

For input **get**/1 is used. Note that **get**(X) will never return a non-printing character; to get any character at all **get0**(X) should be used.

tab(N) emits N spaces. **skip**(N) gets characters until N is encountered.

18.9 Random-access streams

The use of streams as random access files requires a number of special operations.

For a random access file a pointer is maintained. This pointer determines where in the file the next input or output operation will take place.

There are two ways to specify a file position.

(1) the simplest method is to specify an offset in bytes from the start of the file

(2) the atom **end_of_file** may be used to specify the end of the file

The file pointer is automatically adjusted by read and write operations. It is also possible to adjust it using the BIP **seek**/2, which takes as arguments the stream and the desired position. It is permissible to position the pointer at or after the end of the file, but if you try to read from this area you will get first an end of file marker and then an end of file error, just as you would if you did sequential reads at the end of the file.

The current value of the file pointer can be accessed by the BIP **at**/2. This returns the pointer in the first form listed above. If you use one of the other forms in the hopes of testing whether the pointer is there you will be disappointed. For example:

    ?- at(file,end_of_file).

will fail even if file's pointer is at the end of the file; this is because the interpreter will match the integer position with the atom **end_of_file**.

18.10 Compatibility notes

Only the most primitive I/O operations may be regarded as standard. The stream system is unique to Prolog-2. In older Prolog systems, a stream name was assumed to be a file unless it was recognised as one of the special devices; there was no explicit creation of streams.

Thus, for complete portability, use **see, seeing** and **seen** to manipulate input streams and **tell, telling** and **told** for output streams. Avoid random access. **get0, get, put, skip** and **tab** may all be relied upon.

19. High-level I/O

This chapter describes the Prolog-2 facilities for reading and writing information in a formatted way. If you are not concerned to handle non-Prolog formats you should turn straight to §19.4.

These facilities are useful when you wish to read or write information in a format other than that of standard Prolog syntax. The token compiler, which is a utility for making formatted input easy, is also covered.

19.1 Overview

19.1.1 Input

Tokenisation is the process of dividing a stream of symbols into tokens. Tokens are primitive objects without structure and are in their turn parsed to form structures (i.e. Prolog terms).

The grammar of a token may usually be expressed by a right regular grammar; Prolog-2 provides a state table mechanism to deal with such tokens.

Simply speaking, with this grammar you can recognise whether a string of characters constitutes the token you are looking for by starting at the left-hand end and going forwards one character at a time. For more complicated tokenisation one can use combinations of state tables and even many-character look-ahead and context manipulation (§19.1.3).

Technical note: a right regular grammar is one in which the only non-terminal symbols on the right hand sides of the production rules occur in the rightmost place.

Formatted input can be done at one of two levels:

   (1) **term level**
   (2) **token level**

Term level input operates by means of a read term format in **read/3** and **decode/4**. These predicates use the token class and state table mechanisms to read in tokens and can build these tokens into complete prolog terms as well. Term level input is described in detail below in §19.1.2.

Sometimes term level input will not be adequate to your needs: you will want to write your own parser which takes tokens from the Prolog-2 tokeniser and combines these itself to form terms. This is **token level input**. Greater control and flexibility is provided at the token level, where you can work at the level of the state table mechanism.

Token level input is described in detail in §19.1.3.

19.1.2 Term level input

Term level input is input with a read term format.

Term level input reads tokens and parses them into complete Prolog terms. The tokens it can recognise are those defined in the state tables used by the system state token format. The input predicates **read** and **decode** take care of all housekeeping (such as maintaining the context buffer) and automatically return a variable name structure which records the names of the variables that were read in.

To change the existing term level input you supply a different token format and make this the default system state token format. This is useful when you wish to slightly modify the tokens that Prolog recognises whilst keeping Prolog's parsing method (i.e. its way of combining tokens into terms).

In the examples provided (§19.2) you will see how to change the term level input to read Advisor-2 syntax; you could also change the token class to use new state tables to recognise different tokens to the standard state tables.

Technical note: the term level parser only knows how to process certain types of tokens — to be precise, those tokens whose token identifiers (as specified in their state tables) are amongst those already used by the built-in state tables. The parser (being fixed) cannot cope with new types of token that you invent yourself — to do that you should write your own parser and work with token level input. As a consequence of this any new state tables that you use in the system state token format cannot return tokens of types other than those already built-in if they are to be used in term level input. The tokens returned should also match these token types (e.g. don't return token **foo** with token identifier i).

19.1.3 Token level input

Token level input is input with a token format or state table where tokens are read at this low level and interpreted by a user-written parser to form complete terms.

At the least ambitious level you may wish to read single tokens and use them as simple terms on their own. The simplest way to do this is by using **read** and **decode** which take care of all the housekeeping for you (see §19.1.2). As an example, consider **decode(" foo b",foo,[],prolog)**.

However not all tokens that you might want to read in can be sensibly read in this way because some tokens have particular significance to standard Prolog syntax and this may not be the tokenisation you had in mind. Consider **decode("[",none,[],prolog)**. You really need to use **get_token** in this case, as this returns the character class of the first character in the token and the token identifier in addition to the token itself. So we get **get_token([T,C,I],prolog)** with input "[" giving T = none C = 7 I = x.

Using the full information returned by **get_token** you should be able to write a parser which analyses this information to parse almost anything you have in mind. The state table mechanism will still be performing the basic tokenisation process for you but the flexibility afforded by creating your own character classes and state tables to use in this tokenisation is very great.

The main limit you are likely to come across is that this tokenisation operates by one-character look-ahead: this means, for instance, that a state table which looks a character of class 0, followed by one of class 1 and then of class 2 to succeed, will only succeed on the character of class 2 and will thus treat the class 1 character as part of the token. You are however allowed to manipulate the context buffer directly when using **get_token**, and so you could for instance rescue the character of class 1 from the context buffer so that this character will be the first looked at for the next token (use **restore_character/0**).

This leads us to the general point that when working at this lowest level of token input (using **get_token**) it is often useful to manipulate the context buffer in order to effect the standard housekeeping. The BIPs which do this are **get_character/1**, **restore_character/0** and **reset_context/0**. The contents of the context buffer can be examined and reset as a whole by **get_cbuff/4** and **set_cbuff/1**.

Technical note: Because **read** and **decode** perform their own housekeeping (as mentioned above) it is not permitted to perform predicates which themselves perform housekeeping from within **read** or **decode**, ie any token processor called by them cannot perform housekeeping functions itself (if it tries to then it will encounter the error "nested read").

Notice that **get_token** does not return a variable name structure, instead **process_variables/1** returns the variable name structure for all variables read using **get_token** calls since the last time the list of such variables was reset to []. This resetting is done when any of the following succeed: **decode**, **read**, **reset_context** and **process_variables**.

Technical note: Separate calls to **get_token** which return variables (via **token processor** variable) will return separate (ie non- sharing) variables even if the variables are the same. We do this because it is a feature of the semantics of Prolog but not necessarily of other syntax that variables with the same name are invocations of the same variable. If you wish to make these variables share then call **process_variables** to get the variable names and for all variables with identical names (except _ of course) call =/2.

19.1.4 Output

Prolog-2 also allows you to format output. This gives you the opportunity to present output to the user in forms that would not normally be recognised by Prolog: currency formats, for example.

To output in a certain format you must specify a **write format** in either **write/3**, **encode/4** or **term_length/4**. The examples we give (in §19.2) cover output of complete structured terms as well as of single tokens.

19.2 Examples of formatted i/o

All the examples in this chapter are given in consultable form, except for token compiler example (which is given in token compiler input file format).

Input

Example 1: reading Advisor-2 syntax
Example 2: parser for Reverse Polish Notation
Example 3: parsing sentences to tokens

Token compiler

Example 4: tokeniser for reading records from files

Output

Example 5: output negative integers enclosed in brackets
Example 6: using bracketed integers
Example 7: output in Reverse Polish Notation

19.2.1 Example 1: reading Advisor-2 syntax

Advisor-2 is a package for building expert systems. Advisor-2 uses a special syntax for representing the knowledge used by an expert system ('knowledge representation language').

To read Advisor-2 syntax we need to be able to treat } as an infix operator: this is so we can read { a } b as { (}(a,b)). The default Prolog-2 syntax doesn't allow this, since { a } is treated as a grammar rule and is read as {}(a).

To cope with this problem we need to modifiy the standard token class and character class of Prolog-2 to enable **read**/3 to handle the syntax change.

```
/* First create a character class that treats { and } as ordinary symbols */

?- create_character_class(advisor,
[26*13, 14, 6*13, 12, 5, 4*3, 6, 9, 10, 22, 17, 11, 17, 18, 21, 10*0, 3, 12,
5*3, 4*2, 19, 21*2, 7, 20, 8, 3, 4, 3, 26*1, 3, 15, 2*3, 13, 128*16]).

/* Now create a token class that is just like the built-in prolog one, except the character
class advisor just defined is used instead */

?- token_class(prolog,_,A,B),
        create_token_class(advisor,advisor,A,B).

/* Next make suitable operator declarations for { and } */
```

The Prolog-2 User Guide

```
?- op(1200,fx,'{'),
   op(1100,xfx,'}').
```

/* Finally set the token class used by the system to **advisor**; this will be used by default from here on */

?- state(token_class,_,advisor).

19.2.2 Example 2: parser for Reverse Polish Notation

We next present a parser which reads terms in Reverse Polish Notation.

This means that input such as:

    1 "bar" foo/1 hello fred/3

will be read as:

    fred(1,foo("bar"),hello)

To do this we replace **read/3** (which parses the tokens returned from **get_token/2**) with another parser **rpn_read/2** to handle the tokens returned from **get_token/2**.

```
rpn_read(Term,VNS) :-
        /* Find the term (we start with nothing read so far) */
        rpn_term([],Term),
        /* Get the variable name structure */
        process_variables(VNS).

?- private.

rpn_term(Sofar,Term) :-
        /* get next token and process this and remaining input */
        get_token([Token,_,Id],prolog),
        rpn_process_token(Id,Token,Sofar,Term).

rpn_process_token(end_of_file,_,_,_) :-
        !,
        rpn_error("End of input before term complete").

rpn_process_token(t,_,Sofar,Term) :-
        !,
        /* The term has terminated, so if there is just one term parsed so far
           then we can return this */
        (Sofar=[Term];
         rpn_error("Too many arguments for principal functor")).

rpn_process_token(a,Token,Sofar,Term) :-
```

140

```
        !,
        /* An atom was given, so look at next character to see if we have
        the atom/arity (i.e. a functor) case */
        get_character(Char),
        (Char==47,!,rpn_functor(Token,Sofar,Term);
        /* NOT the atom/arity case so restore character before continuing */
        restore_character,rpn_term([Token|Sofar],Term) ).

rpn_process_token(Id,Token,_,_) :-
        Token == none,
        !,
        /* No token (nb Id \== 'a' by previous clause) */
        rpn_error("Null token found").

rpn_process_token(_,Token,Sofar,Term) :-
        /* The general case where we add the read token to the list of parsed
        input and continue */
        rpn_term([Token|Sofar],Term).

rpn_functor(Functor,Sofar,Term) :-
        /* We have read Functor/ & now need to read the arity, note that this
        must follow immediately and can only be an integer so we use the
        built-n state table 'i'. */
        ( get_token([Arity,_,_],i) ;
          rpn_error("Missing arity")),
        !,
        ( Arity >=0 ;
          rpn_error("Arity negative")),
        !,
        /* Arity obtained, so get its arguments from the list of terms parsed
        so far in the input */
        rpn_move_args(Sofar,Arity,[],Arglist,Restsofar),
        !,
        Structure =.. [Functor|Arglist],
        /* Add the new compound term to the list of remaining terms input and
        continue */
        rpn_term([Structure|Restsofar],Term).

rpn_move_args(Sofar,0,Arglist,Arglist,Sofar).

rpn_move_args([Arg|Sofar],Arity,Arglist,Resultarglist,Restsofar) :-
        Newarity is Arity-1,
        rpn_move_args(Sofar,Newarity,[Arg|Arglist],
     Resultarglist,Restsofar).

rpn_move_args([],_,_,_,_) :-
        rpn_error("Not enough arguments for functor").

rpn_error(Message) :-
```

The Prolog-2 User Guide

```
            write("\nError in parsing input as rpn\nMessage : "),
            write(Message),
            write("\n\nContext : "),
            print_context,
            reset_context,
            !,
            fail.
```

?- public.

19.2.3 Example 3: parsing sentences to tokens

We next present a parser which reads sentences into a list of tokens.

This example follows the 'read_in' example in **Programming in Prolog** by Clocksin and Mellish (Chapter 5). Our version differs in that words are returned as string tokens (not atoms); this is more appropriate for a parser which is reading arbitrary text. (To return atoms instead insert a call to **name/2**.)

In implementation this example is very different from the book because we can use the character class and state table mechanism to do most of the work for us (and so avoid all the complications of reading ahead one character).

For simplicity we process words using the built-in processor **actual** and only perform the conversion to lower-case on the completed string token. As an alternative you could try creating a token processor for use with the **word_st** state table; this performs the same conversion as each character is passed to that state table.

```
/* Character class : read_in_cc
Class 0 = characters to be ignored (separators)
Class 1 = "," ";" ":" (i.e. a character that punctuates a sentence but doesn't end it)
Class 2 = Characters in a word (ie digits, letters and "'" "-" ).
Class 3 = "." "?" "!" (i.e. a character that ends a sentence) */

?- create_character_class(read_in_cc,
        [33*0,3,5*0,2,4*0,1,2,3,0,10*2,1,1,3*0,3,0,26*2,6*0,26*2,133*0]).

/* State table : end_sentence_st
        Recognises a character which ends a sentence */

?- create_state_table(end_sentence_st,read_in_cc,atom,
end_sentence,[[255,255,255,1],[2,2,2,2]]).

/* State table : special_st
        Recognises a punctuation character, which doesn't end the sentence */

?- create_state_table(special_st,read_in_cc,atom,special,
        [[255,1,255,255],[2,2,2,2]]).
```

```
/* State table : word_st
        Recognises a word (processing it as a string without case conversion at this
        point) */

?- create_state_table(word_st,read_in_cc,actual,word,[[1,1,0,1]]).

/* Token class : read_in_tc
        Declares the separator class and matches the state tables with the first
        character of the input */

?- create_token_class(read_in_tc,read_in_cc,[0],
[1-special_st,2-word_st,3-end_sentence_st]).

/* Read in a sentence */

read_in([Word|Otherwords]) :-
        get_token([Token,_,Id],read_in_tc),
        restsent(Id,Token,Word,Otherwords),
        !.

?- private.

/* Given the Token read and its identifier, read in the rest of the sentence */

restsent(end_sentence,Word,Word,[]). /* end sentence */

restsent(special,Word,Word,[NextWord|Otherwords]) :-
        /* punctuation character, NOT end of sentence */
        get_token([NextToken,_,Id],read_in_tc),
        restsent(Id,NextToken,NextWord,Otherwords).

restsent(word,Token,Word,[NextWord|Otherwords]) :-
        /* Obtain Word from Token */
        list(List,Token),
        convert_to_lower(List,LowerList),
        list(LowerList,Word),
        /* Get the next token and recurse */
        get_token([NextToken,_,Id],read_in_tc),
        restsent(Id,NextToken,NextWord,Otherwords).

/* Convert input list of ASCII values to all lower case list */
convert_to_lower([],[]).

convert_to_lower([A|Rest],[LowerA|LowerRest]) :-
        (A>64,A<91,LowerA is A+32;LowerA=A),
        convert_to_lower(Rest,LowerRest).

?- public.
```

The Prolog-2 User Guide

19.2.4 Example 4: a tokeniser for reading records from files

You are strongly recommended to read the file that the token compiler will generate for this input to make sure that you understand the workings of the tokeniser in detail.

/* Tokeniser for reading records from files */

record.

classes.

data --> 0...9;11...25;27...127. /* May be extended to 255 */
rterm --> 10. /* Record terminator */
fterm --> 26. /* End of file */

processors.

record_processor.

/* Note: It would be possible to use the built-in token processor **actual** but a user-defined token processor is given here as it is an informative example. */

record_proc_init :-
    /* Initialise at start of token */
    retractall(sofar/1),
    asserta(sofar("")).

record_proc_char(10) :-
    /* Strip record terminator */
    /* So that empty record = "" */
    !.

record_proc_char(C) :-
    /* Get string found so far */
    retract(sofar(STRING)),
    /* Add latest character to this */
    NSTRING is_string STRING & [C],
    asserta(sofar(NSTRING)),
    !.

record_proc_end(TOKEN) :-
    /* Return a complete token */
    retract(sofar(TOKEN)).

eof_processor.

eof_proc_init.   /* Stub */

eof_proc_char(_).   /* Stub */

eof_proc_end(end_of_file).

tokens.

record_st - record_processor - record_id.
eof_st   - eof_processor   - eof_id.

rules.

/* State table to recognise a record */
record_st --> rterm.

/* Records may be just LF */
record_st --> data,record_st.
/* or any number of 'data' chars */

/* State table to recognise end of file */
eof_st   --> fterm.

token_class.

record_tc - [].
/* No separator class as all characters are relevant */

19.2.5 Example 5: output negative integers enclosed in brackets

/* First create a token format which will hold the declaration of
this new format.

This format can be used as follows: write(-123,[],bi) */

?- create_token_format(bi, bracketed_integer).

/* Now define the predicate which will perform the output */

bracketed_integer(Integer_Token,_,_,_) :-
/* fail to output anything if not given an integer */
        not integer(Integer_Token),
        !,
        fail.

bracketed_integer(Integer_Token,Width,_,_) :-
/* if integer is not negative then write using standard i token format */

The Prolog-2 User Guide

```
                Integer_Token >= 0,
                !,
                write(Integer_Token,[],i(Width)).

bracketed_integer(Integer_Token,0,_,_) :-
/* (Integer_Token is negative) */
                !,
                Positive_Integer_Token is - Integer_Token,
                /* write the brackets and digits */
                write("(",[],s),
                write(Positive_Integer_Token,[],i),
                write(")",[],s).

bracketed_integer(Integer_Token,Width,_,_) :-
/* (Integer_Token is negative and Width is specified) */
/* set Inner_Width to be the width inside the brackets*/
                Inner_Width is Width - 2,
/* check that there is room for the digits to be written
inside the brackets, & put this output into a String */
                Inner_Width > 0,
                Positive_Integer_Token is - Integer_Token,
                encode(String,Positive_Integer_Token,[],i(Inner_Width)),
                !,
                String \== "",
/* write the brackets and digits */
                write("(",[],s),
                write(String,[],s),
                write(")",[],s).
```

19.2.6 Example 6: create a type-class which uses bracketed integers

To create a new type-class which is the same as the current system type-class except that it uses bracketed integers, and to make this the new system type-class.

/* First define the substitution of the first element of matching type by the given substitute. In none match then make no substitution */

```
substitute_new_token_format([Type - _|T],[Type - Token|T], Type - Token).
substitute_new_token_format([H|T],[H|New_T],Type - Token) :-
        substitute_new_token_format(T,New_T,Type - Token).

substitute_new_token_format([],[],_).
```

/* Now create the new type_class named 'bi_type_class' and make it the system type_class */

```
?- state(type_class,Old,Old),
        type_class(Old,List),
```

```
        substitute_new_token_format(List,New_List,integer - bi),
        create_type_class(bi_type_class,New_List),
        state(type_class,_,bi_type_class).
```

19.2.7 Example 7: output in Reverse Polish Notation

To create a new type-class which outputs terms in Reverse Polish Notation, quoting all atoms and strings if needed for readability and separating all tokens by a space (ie non-conditional spacing), with Width requirements ignored. (Thus foo(1,"bar") is output as 1 "bar" foo/2.)

(Note: this is a simple implementation which doesn't cope with recursive structure or use system state **write_depth**.)

```
/* First create a type class which quotes where needed (like prologq) and uses a new
token format (rpn_structure) to print out the structures. Also create this token format */

?- type_class(prologq,List),
        substitute_new_token_format(List,New_List,structure - rpn_structure),
        create_type_class(rpn,New_List),
        create_token_format( rpn_structure,reverse_polish_notation_structure).


/* Next define the predicate which will perform the RPN structure output */

reverse_polish_notation_structure(Structure_Token,_,Decimals,VNS):-
        Structure_Token =.. [Functor|Argument_List] ,
        rpn_arguments(Argument_List,Decimals,VNS,0,Number),
        write(Functor,VNS,qa),
        put("/"),
        write(Number,[],i).

rpn_arguments([Argument|More],Decimals,VNS,Start_Number,End_Number) :-
        write(Argument,VNS,rpn(0,Decimals)),
        put(" "),
        New_Start_Number is Start_Number + 1,
        rpn_arguments(More,Decimals,VNS,New_Start_Number,End_Number).

rpn_arguments([],_,_,Number,Number).
```

19.3 The token compiler

Character classes and state tables are complicated to create and tedious to type in; Prolog-2 therefore provides a special program, the **token compiler**, to build them for you. The **token compiler** also does some optimisation of the state tables.

The Prolog-2 User Guide

19.3.1 Invoking the token compiler

The token compiler is in the module 'tokens' contained in the file "TOKENS.PRM". You use the token compiler by means of the BIPS **compile_tokens**/0 and **compile_tokens**/2 which automatically load the 'tokens' for you (and close this module on completion).

19.3.2 What the token compiler does

The token compiler takes an input file which specifies the tokenising requirements (default extension .TKN) and produces an output file which contains the character class, state table (etc.) definitions in Prolog form (default extension .PRO).

The output file is in a form such that it can be consulted to create the lexical items you have defined. It is Prolog source; you can therefore edit it directly if you wish.

19.3.3 Format of the input file

The first (non-comment) line of the input file is the title of the file; the rest of the file is divided into sections headed by keywords.

These keywords may be:

   (1) **classes**
   (2) **processors**
   (3) **tokens**
   (4) **rules**
   (5) **token_class**

These sections may appear in any order, but each section may only occur once. Some sections can be omitted altogether.

19.3.4 Example input file

We first present an example of a file; then we will explain its various sections.

```
/* tokeniser for hex numbers */

hex.

classes.
digit    --> "0"..."9".
hexdigit --> digit;"A"..."F";"a"..."f".
white    --> 0...32.

processors.
hex_processor.
hex_start :-
        retractall(hexno/1),
        assert(hexno(0)).
```

```
hex_process(X) :-
        X =< "9",
        !,
        Y is X-"0",
        retract(hexno(H)),
        H1 is H*16+Y,
        asserta(hexno(H1)).
hex_process(X) :-
        X =< "F",
        !,
        Y is X-"A"+10,
        retract(hexno(H)),
        H1 is H*16+Y,
        asserta(hexno(H1)).
hex_process(X) :-
        Y is X-"a"+10,
        retract(hexno(H)),
        H1 is H*16+Y,
        asserta(hexno(H1)).

hex_end(X) :-
        retract(hexno(X)).

tokens.
hex_state_table - hex_processor - hex_identifier.

rules.
hex_state_table --> digit,hextail.
hextail         --> hexdigit,hextail.
hextail         --> nil.

token_class.
hex_token_class - [white].
```

(1) Classes

The **classes** are a convenience to enable you to abbreviate the later rules. They define sets of characters using a grammar-rule like notation.

To be precise, the left hand side is a class name and the right hand side is:

(1) a character, expressed as an ASCII value. This is evaluated, so you may use arithmetic expressions if you wish

(2) a range of characters, in the form A...B where A and B are as in (1)

(3) another character class that you have already defined

The Prolog-2 User Guide

(4) a disjunction of the above, indicating a union of the classes defined

In the above example:

classes.
digit   --> "0"..."9".
hexdigit --> digit;"A"..."F";"a"..."f".
white   --> 0...32.

digit is defined to be anything from 0 to 9; a **hexdigit** is a **digit** or else one of the letters A...F (upper or lower case); a **white** space is anything less than or equal to 32 (ASCII blank).

Note that these definitions are only for your convenience and do not correspond to the classes that the token compiler will generate. In the example above 3 belongs to the character class **digit** and also to the character class **hexdigit**. In a character class table sent to **create_character_class**/2, each character belongs to exactly one character class, whereas in the above 3 belongs to two and G to none. The token compiler straightens all this out for you. (The name of the character class created is taken from the title in the input file.)

(2) Processors

The **processors** are token processors.

The compiler creates a token processor with the first term read as the name and the next three predicates as the three processing routines. The predicate definitions themselves are simply copied into the output file.

(3) Tokens

Under the heading **tokens** you must list all the state tables you want generated. The tables are listed as triples connected by the - operator.

The first term is the name of the state table. This is the name you will use if you want to use the table as third argument to read.

The second argument is the name of the token processor to be associated with the state table; the third is the token identifier to be passed to the Prolog read routine when this token is recognised. Unless you are redefining the syntax of Prolog you need not worry about the last.

(4) Rules

The bulk of information is provided by the **rules**.

The rules are production rules for tokens; there may be several rules for the same token.

A rule is made up of a head which is an atom, the operator --> and a body defining that token. The body must be made up of terminals (which means things that would be valid right-hand sides for class definitions) and non-terminals (atom names defined elsewhere by rules), separated by commas.

Intuitively the rule

    hextail --> hexdigit,hextail.

means that a hextail is a hexdigit followed by a hextail. The following restrictions apply:

(1) A non-terminal may appear in the body only as its last element

(2) If two clauses have the same head, then the first item of their bodies must be disjoint non-terminals (so that the next character read will tell the tokeniser which clause to use)

(3) There must be at least one terminal in each body.

The only exception to the above is that a rule whose body is simply the atom **nil** is allowed and indicates that the empty string belongs to the category in question. Strictly speaking this introduces an ambiguity, which is resolved by the convention that a nil rule is never used while another one will do.

(5) Token_class

The (optional) **token_class** entry tells the system to generate a token class for all the state tables in the file.

The **token_class** entry is followed by a structure of the form Name-Sep: Name is the name of the token class and Sep is a list (possibly empty) of separator character classes.

19.3.5 Compiling the example file

As an example of the use of the token compiler, there follows a log of the compilation of the example file above, which compiles hex tokens. The output from the token compiler is shown in **bold** type, and the user's responses in normal type.

?- compile_tokens.

Prolog-2 Token Compiler version X.Y0

Token file (Default extension tkn) hex
Output file (<ENTER> for HEX.PRO) hex

The Prolog-2 User Guide

Read Input - Complete
Compile Token Processors - Complete
Analyse Character Classes - Complete
Analyse State Tables - Complete
Optimisation - Complete
Compile Character Classes - Complete
Compile State Tables - Complete
Compile Token Class - All Compilation Complete

yes

The token compiler has produced the following file (hex.pro):

```
?- create_token_processor(hex_processor,hex_start,hex_process,hex_end).

hex_start :-
        retractall(hexno/1),
        asserta(hexno(0)).

hex_process(X) :-
        X =< "9",
        !,
        Y is X-"0",
        retract(hexno(H)),
        H1 is H*16+Y,
        asserta(hexno(H1)).
hex_process(X) :-
        X =< "F",
        !,
        Y is X-"A"+10,
        retract(hexno(H)),
        H1 is H*16+Y,
        asserta(hexno(H1)).
hex_process(X) :-
        Y is X-"a"+10,
        retract(hexno(H)),
        H1 is H*16+Y,
        asserta(hexno(H1)).

hex_end(X) :-
        retract(hexno(X)).

?- create_character_class(hex,[33*0,15*1,10*2,7*1,6*3,26*1,6*3,153*1]).

?- create_state_table(hex_state_table,hex,hex_processor,
        hex_identifier,[[255,255,1,255],[2,2,1,1]]).

?- create_token_class(hex_token_class,hex,[0],[ 2 - hex_state_table ]).
```

The following log demonstrates the use of this file:

?- [hex].
hex consulted
?- repeat, read(N,_,hex), write(N), nl, fail.
22
34
1ce
462
0f00d
61453

19.4 Prolog read and write

Prolog, unlike most other programming languages, is equipped with predicates that can read and write terms in the same syntax as is used for programs. Naturally these are useful for writing programs that read Prolog clauses, but they are of limited use for other purposes. The Prolog programmer is confronted with the choice of character level I/O and term I/O in a format designed for writing programs rather than communicating with a user. The use of operators makes for some flexibility. However, the tokenisation system described earlier is the most comprehensive system for customising I/O.

The predicate **read/1** reads a single Prolog term. Input is terminated by a full stop as usual. The predicate **read/2** sets the second argument of the call to a variable name structure for the term. There is also a three argument form, where the third argument is a read format. This is handy for reading a single token, such as an integer, and a width specifier may be supplied, so that **read(X,_,i(8))** reads eight characters and turns them into an integer. The third argument may be the token class **prolog**, in which case the next token of whatever kind will be read.

read/1 parses terms using Prolog syntax rules, but the tokenisation rules used by **read/1** are determined by the current token class. It is possible to enforce strict DEC-10 tokenisation by setting the system state **token_class** to **dec10**.

As well as **read/1**, there is a predicate **decode**, which takes its input from a string rather than a stream. The string is inserted as an extra first argument, so, for example, to read the string "a + b." the call **decode("a+b.",X)** would be made.

The usual output predicate is **write/1**. **write** tries to use operators and lists to make the output as similar to input format as possible. There are two useful variants: **display/1** does not use operator or list syntax, so the internal form of a term may be assessed; and **writeq** strictly ensures that output is syntactically correct, quoting atoms if necessary and strings all the time. So the effect of write('Hello there!') is Hello there!, but of writeq('Hello there!') is 'Hello there!'.

Again a second variable name argument and a third format argument are available. Output formats allow different floating point representations to be used; thus **write(X,_,e(10))** writes X in scientific format in a field of width 10.

encode is the opposite of **decode**; it turns a term into a string. The various formats are formed from **write/?** by adding the string (probably a variable) as a new first argument. Thus **encode(X,a+b)** writes the term **a+b** as a string.

Finally we should mention **print/1**. **print/1** is just like **write/1** except that it first calls the goal **portray(Term)**. **portray/1** is not built-in (though there is a stub version in **dec10**), so the user may write a portray call to do whatever is wanted with the call. If the call to portray fails then the term is written. **print/1** is used by default by the debugger to display goals.

19.5 Compatibility notes

None of the features of §§19.1-3 will be found in other Prolog systems. **read/1** and **write/1** are almost universal, as is **writeq/1**; **display/1** is generally found but sometimes sneaks in a stream switch to standard output. **print/1** in Prolog-2 differs from many implementations is that the call to **portray** is only made of the whole argument and not of arguments of the argument. This substantially reduces its usefulness.

Token level I/O is available in many systems but with no standardisation. The programmer concerned with portability will do well to write a little library of calls needed and resign herself to rewriting this when the software is ported.

20. Error handling

20.1 Introduction

Prolog-2 has facilities for detecting errors in code. It also has facilities for handling the errors it detects.

The errors discussed in this chapter are Prolog errors: if you want to set up additional types of error (for example, selecting an invalid option on a menu) you must arrange for these to be dealt with separately. Prolog-2 does have facilities for handling this type of error; these are described in §20.4.

Prolog errors occur when a Built-In Predicate (BIP) encounters a situation in which it cannot continue processing. This causes a 'break' in execution. Execution itself is not disrupted unless a real disaster occurs. Often the user will be able to correct the error and return to the program being executed.

The error system has four components:

(1) The error-detecting mechanism in the interpreter;
(2) The error-handling routine in the interpreter;
(3) The error-handler, which determines what happens after the error has occurred;
(4) A file of error-messages.

Components (1) and (2) are part of the Prolog-2 program and cannot be altered; (3) and (4) are modules you can alter or replace. You can also define new errors of your own to add to the list the interpreter recognises. Section §20.4 tells you how to do this.

Thus there are Prolog errors and errors you can define yourself: in either case you can specify how they are to be handled.

20.2 Types of error

There are four types of error in Prolog-2: the difference between them is how serious they are. The error-types are numbered from 0 to 3; no other numbering is permitted.

> 0: syntax error
> 1: normal error
> 2: serious error
> 3: fatal error

You must continue to use this 0 - 3 scheme even if you write your own error-handler.

Syntax errors

A syntax error (0) is a mistake in the form of a term: typical examples are omitting the full-stop at the end of a clause or forgetting to close a bracket.

Normal errors

A normal error (1) occurs in response to various common blunders — getting BIP arguments wrong, for example, or attempting to open a non-existent file.

Serious errors

A serious error (2) occurs when the record of the current evaluation has been corrupted. After a serious error has been detected the only actions the interpreter's error-handler will permit on return from the external error-handler are

        abort

or

        exit from Prolog

Anything done before the error occurred is lost. The contents of the database will be unaffected and another goal can be tried.

Serious errors usually occur when Prolog has run out of space in the section of memory being used for execution: this can happen with deep recursion, for example.

Fatal errors

A fatal error (3) occurs then the interpreter cannot continue at all. Fatal errors normally result in a return to the operating system; everything done since starting is lost. This includes everything in the database.

Fatal errors are relatively rare: one cause is running out of space in the memory area Prolog uses to keep track of the atoms in use.

20.3 Detecting errors

The interpreter does three things when it detects an error:

(1)   It works out the type of error (0 - 3)
(2)   It finds the appropriate error-number
(3)   It invokes the error-handler and passes this information on to it, together with the goal that caused the error.

The error handler supplied as part of the PDE (see Chapter 25) is suitable for program development, because it gives maximum information about the cause of the error. In delivering a packaged application you will probably want to avoid Prolog errors by adding your own checking; if a Prolog error occurs this will be through a fault in your logic. In this case the user will probably be baffled by a Prolog-2 error message and goal, and you should write an error handler that simply prints an apology.

You will find that the interpreter sometimes reports an error in a BIP which has not been called directly. This is because many Prolog-2 BIPs are implemented in terms of calls to other BIPs. For example, if you call the goal

?- retract(666).

you should expect to be told this is an error because a number cannot be a clause; but what Prolog-2 actually tells you is this:

> Error no. 14
> Bad first argument to functor
> Error goal: functor(666,_102,_106)

What happens is that **retract/1** causes a call to **functor/3** and passes 666 along to it as an argument. **functor/3** finds an argument it does not like, and reports a normal error.

20.4 Defining new errors

You can add to the fixed set of error conditions recognised by the Prolog-2 interpreter by defining further errors of your own; you do this by calling the BIP **force_error/3** from clauses you write.

Calling **force_error/3** has the same effect as the occurrence of a recognised error. The error-type and number are arguments and so under programmer control.

The arguments to **force_error/3** are:

(1)   The type of the error (0, 1, 2, or 3: see §20.2)
(2)   The error-number
(3)   A structure which the error-handler will assume is the goal which caused the error.

You should only force errors with numbers known to the error-handler: you can cater for extra errors by modifying the error message file.

You are limited in what you can do with the various types of error when you use **force_error/3**. If the error-code passed is type 2 or type 3 the user will not be able to restart the execution in progress; a type 2 error will abort the execution and return the user to the Top-Level Interpreter; a type 3 error will stop the execution and return the user to the operating system.

Alternatives to **force_error/3** are **force_error/4** and **force_error/1**.

force_error/4 takes the same three arguments as **force_error/3** buts adds a fourth which is passed directly directly to **error/4** (see §20.5).

force_error/1 takes only one argument, the error number. Prolog supplies the remaining arguments as for **error/4** by default (error type 1; goal which called the error **none**; empty list).

Notice that you cannot remove an error from the fixed set recognised by the interpreter.

The Prolog-2 User Guide

All you can do is trap it to prevent the error-handler coming into operation.

20.5 Building your own error-handler

This section covers only alternative ways of handling existing Prolog-2 errors. If you want to define new error conditions for your programs you should go back and read §20.4 above.

Building your own error-handler allows you to specify how the system is to react when it encounters an error. You might want to invoke the debugger automatically when an error is detected; you might want to make other changes to the error-handler to protect users who know little about Prolog from error-messages that they may not understand.

The error-handler supplied with Prolog-2 is a module called **error**. It is called by the public predicate **error/4**. **error/4** is called by the core interpreter every time it encounters an error. The interpreter instantiates the four arguments for **error/4**:

>   The type of error (0 to 3)
>   The number of the error
>   The goal which called the error
>   []

In compiled code the goal is replaced by the offset of the error in the compiled module; the offending goal must then be located using the symbol table.

The fourth argument to **error/4** will normally be the empty list []; but it may, and in the case of error **system** usually is, used to pass a supplementary error-number or term to the external error-handler.

The default error-handler makes use of all these items of information. Your own error-handler need not do so, but it will still have to take the information from the interpreter. The error-handler you build must be made up of clauses for **error/4**. These define how the error-handler will behave. If you really must keep several error handlers in one prgram, it is possible to change the name of the goal called when an error occurs by setting the system state **error_goal**.

You may also wish to display the context of the error — the clause containing the error and an indication of where the error occurs. Prolog-2 has **print_context/0** for this. If you incorporate **print_context/0** into your error-handling routines you can make rejected clauses appear for re-editing and re-input.

20.6 Switching off the error-handler

You can switch off all error-handling by using the system-state **error_break**:

>   ?- state(error_break,_,off).

This means that **error/4** is not called: what happens instead when an error occurs depends upon the severity of the error:

```
Syntax error   (error type 0):   fail
Normal error   (error type 1):   fail
Serious error  (error type 2):   abort
Fatal error    (error type 3):   exit
```

To switch the error-handler on again use:

?- state(error_break,_,on).

Error handling should only be switched off locally while a task is accomplished (for example, to cause **read** simply to fail if the user types an incorrect term); it must be switched back on immediately. Programs that switch off errors globally are almost impossible to debug.

Having switched off errors it is possible to use the system state **error_number** to find out whether an error occurred and if so which one.

20.7 Error messages and symbolic names

The module **efile** exports a predicate **error_file/3** that supplies, for a given error number (first argument) an error message (second argument) and a string with the symbolic name of the error (third argument). Symbolic names ensure portability of error handling code between versions of Prolog-2 (though in practice the numbers are portable too) and are used to document errors in the Prolog-2 Encyclopaedia.

20.8 Compatibility notes

All of the facilities described are unique to Prolog-2, though they often exist under different names in other systems.

21. Debugging

21.1 Introduction

The purpose of the Prolog-2 debugging system is to help you find mistakes in the logic of your programs. Simple errors such as incorrect syntax or calling a Built-In Predicate (BIP) with inappropriate arguments are detected and reported by the Prolog-2 error handler (described in Chapter 20). Mistakes in the intrinsic logic of your program can be more difficult to detect; this is where an effective debugging system can help enormously.

The debugger lets you watch what is going on in a program while it is actually running. It can be set up either to report when it encounters a particular goal or aspect of the control of the goal, or to stop and allow changes to be made to the program using the Prolog Editor.

The debugging system supplied with Prolog-2 provides all the features of the DECsystem-10 Prolog debugger plus a number features of its own. The main difference is that in some versions of Prolog-2 the debugger operates in a special debug window: this means that output from the program itself and output from the debugger are clearly separated on the display. The debug window can be switched on and off easily if you need to see the whole screen.

The Prolog interpreter does not operate in its normal mode when the debugger is switched on. It does not minimise storage by using tail recursion optimisation in the way it normally does; if it did it would lose information that might be needed for debugging. An effect of using the debugger is to slow down the operation of the system as a whole and to use a lot more memory. It is not advisable to run the system with the debugger on unless you think you may need it.

The debugger is a PDE module and you can replace it with a debugger of your own design. The Prolog-2 core system includes all the hooks you need to do this. It is really most unlikely that you will want to do this; the facility exists in practice to allow different debuggers to be supplied with Prolog-2. However, §21.5 below tells you how to build your own debugger.

21.2 The 'box model'

To take full advantage of the debugger you need to understand the 'box model' of a Prolog goal. This 'box model' is described in detail in Clocksin and Mellish's "Programming in Prolog". What we give here is a summary of the essential features of this box model.

The diagram shows the box itself and its four ports:

```
        CALL                                    EXIT
      ─────────> ┌─────────────────┐         ─────────>
                 │    ┌───────┐    │
                 │    │ tail  │    │
                 │    ├───────┤    │
                 │    │ goals │    │
                 │    └───────┘    │
        FAIL     │                 │          REDO
      <─────────  └─────────────────┘         <─────────
```

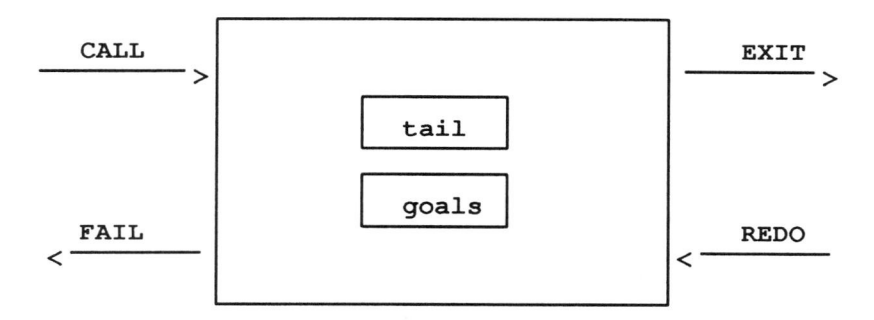

There are four ports labelled **call, exit, redo** and **fail**. The arrows show the direction of the system's control flow while trying to satisfy a goal (represented by the large box). Although Prolog is not a procedural language you can think of a goal as a procedure call. Control passes INTO the box through the **call** and **redo** ports, and OUT through the **exit** and **fail** ports.

When the system attempts to satisfy a subgoal as part of satisfying the main goal, control will pass through the relevant ports of the subgoal's box.

Call port: this is the first call to a goal. Control passes in through the **call** port with the aim of matching the head, and satisfying any subgoals.

Exit port: control passes out through the **exit** port when the goal has been satisfied. This will happen when the initial goal is matched and any subgoals proved.

Redo port: control passes into the box through the **redo** port when the system is backtracking from a subsequent goal (which has failed and therefore started the backtracking). The system will try to resatisfy the goal.

Fail port: control passes out of the box through the **fail** port if the goal fails. This will happen if the goal is not matched or the subgoals are not satisfiable (or resatisfiable). Once control has passed out of the **fail** port the system will backtrack into another goal.

The box is associated with an invocation number rather than a predicate. This is because each predicate may be called many times. It will have one box for each time it is called.

21.3 The Prolog-2 debugger

The debugger provides information about what is happening during the execution of Prolog clauses; it also allows you to select specific parts of an program to watch operating and will give you the chance to alter what is going on.

There are two ways of controlling the action of the debugger:

Trace or **spy**: you can choose to observe every predicate in the module (tracing) or just

The Prolog-2 User Guide

some predicates (spying).

Leashing: this selects the port or ports (call, exit, redo, fail) where the debugger comes into action.

21.3.1 Tracing and spying

The BIP **trace/0** switches on the debugger and reports on all the predicates in the Current Debug Module as they are executed. A separate report is displayed for each port every time a predicate is invoked.

The BIP **spy/1** allows you to check on specified predicates each time they are invoked. You can check on just one predicate or on a number of them.

21.3.2 Leashing

Using either **trace/0** or **spy/1** gives you the opportunity to do more than just watch messages go past. With both predicates you can select options (using the BIP **leash/1**) which cause the system to pause at one or more leashed ports. When it does you can use the facilities of the debugger to inspect more closely what is going on in your program and even to modify it if you wish.

You are still given a message when an unleashed port is passed, but the system will not pause to let you take further action.

There is a default leashing state for **spy/1** and **trace/0**. The default is **call** and **redo**. This means that when the debugger is reporting on a goal, either because tracing is on or because the goal is for a predicate with a spy point on it, it will just display a message and continue execution as it passes through the exit and fail ports; but it will display a message and wait for a response from the user (who can use any of the debugging options described below) as it passes through the call and redo ports.

You can change the leashing state so that the subset of ports at which you will be allowed to interact is different. **leash/1** will do this (see §21.4.1).

An example of leashed output, using the following database:

```
mortal(X) :- person(X).
person(X) :- athenian(X).
person(X) :- macedonian(X).
athenian(plato).
macedonian(alexander).
```

In this example, tracing has been switched on using **trace/0**. The **redo** and **exit** ports have been leashed: the system has been asked to provide more solutions to the directive **mortal(X)** on a small database:

X = plato
More (y/n)? y

```
(1) 0 REDO: mortal(plato)?              (stops and waits)
(2) 1 REDO: person(plato)?              (stops and waits)
(3) 1 REDO: athenian(plato)?            (stops and waits)
(3) 1 FAIL: athenian(_20)               (message only: no pause)
(4) 1 CALL: macedonian(_20)             (message only: no pause)
(4) 1 EXIT: macedonian(alexander)?      (stops and waits)
(2) 1 EXIT: person(alexander)?          (stops and waits)
(1) 0 EXIT: mortal(alexander)?          (stops and waits)
```

X = alexander
More (y/n)?

Debug in moderation

The Prolog-2 debugger can give you a great deal of information: sometimes too much to be useful. Setting spy-points carefully can help considerably by cutting out information on predicates you believe are operating correctly.

The other useful tool is the debug option **skip** (see §21.4.2). This allows you to pass over long sequences of uninteresting evaluations and move quickly from goal to goal.

21.3.3 Debug messages

The debugger ouputs messages at each port it passes. These are displayed unless the debug output is suppressed using one of the options on the debug menu (see §21.4.2).

The first two spaces are either blank or contain flag characters. If they are blank (as in the example) the message is a straight trace message. The flags relate to the debug options you get when you reach a leash-point. These options are described in §21.4.2 below.

The possible flags and their meanings are:

>   This is not a spy-point; the last time you were at this leash-point you skipped or quasi-skipped (see §21.4.2);
**   This is a spy-point
*>   This is a spy-point; the last time you were here you skipped or quasi-skipped
=>   You selected the x debug option (see §21.4.2); the system is taking you back to a call or exit port. You cannot halt at a leash-point flagged =>

The number in brackets is the unique number assigned to each box: the 'invocation number'.

The next number, not in brackets, is the number of ancestors this particular goal has: the 'invocation depth'.

The item after that is the name of the port the execution has reached.

The final item is the goal itself. This is printed with the variables as numbered variables, as you need to see what variables are sharing at this point.

A question-mark will be printed after the goal if the system pauses to allow you to interact.

21.3.4 Selecting the module to be debugged

The debugger can only operate with one module at a time. We recommend that you develop part of your program, debug it and then package it as a module.

Calling **trace/0** or **spy/1** will automatically switch on the debugger and make the common module the debugging module.

If you want to debug a different module, use the BIP **debug/1**. The single argument is the name of the module to be debugged. There is also a version of debug, **debug/0**, that has no arguments and makes the common module the debug module.

21.3.5 Switching the debugger off

Both spying and tracing can be switched off. However, although no debug output will appear from the point where they are switched off, the debugger itself is still on. This means that execution will still be slower than normal and will take up more memory than normal.

To ensure that debugging is completely switched off, use the BIP **nodebug/0**. This will automatically switch off tracing and remove any spypoints set. It is particularly important to use this if you already have tracing off and no spy points set: otherwise you might continue to run in debug mode without realising it, wasting time and memory.

Tracing itself is switched off using **notrace/0**. Spying is removed from named predicates using **nospy/1**, whose argument, like that of **spy/1**, can be a predicate-rep, the name of a predicate, or a list of predicates.

21.3.6 Information on debugging

The BIP **debugging/0** will display the following information:

> The module being debugged
> Whether tracing is on or off
> The leash mode
> A list of predicates with spypoints on them.

21.4 The Prolog-2 debugger in action

21.4.1 Tracing

Tracing is switched on using **trace/0**. All predicates invoked in the debug module will be reported.

To take action at particular ports, define the ports you need using **leash/1**.

The single argument for **leash/1** takes two forms:

The first is a list, enclosed in square brackets. Its members can be any or all of:

> call
> redo
> exit
> fail

If you just want reports and do not need a pause in execution, you can use the empty list [].

Examples:

> **leash([call]).**
> **leash([call,exit,fail]).**
> **leash([]).**

The second form of the argument to **leash/1** is one of the atoms **off, loose, half, tight,** or **full**. These are equivalent to combinations of the ports specifiers listed in the first form of the argument:

> off: []
> loose: [call]
> half: [call,redo]
> tight: [call,redo,fail]
> full: [call,exit,redo,fail]

Example:

> **leash(half).**

means exactly the same as

> **leash([call,redo]).**

This is the default.

21.4.2 Options at leash points

There are a range of possible options that you can choose among when the debugger encounters a leash-point. All are selected using a single letter or symbol: in three cases you can also add an integer to indicate what you want in more detail.

You can use the line edit keys to edit options in the same way as elsewhere: for example, if you mean to type **s3** but you accidentally hit **sw**, you can use the delete

The Prolog-2 User Guide

key to move back and delete the w.

The options may be presented to you in a menu. If so, you are given a simple prompt at the end of the line of debug output (?) and you enter the appropriate letter for the option you want. Type a carriage-return after the option you choose.

If the character you type is not one of the recognised options the debug prompt ? will be reissued.

The most important option to remember is **h**. This is the 'Help' option and will give you a list of the possible options.

The options are listed in the entry **debug_menu** in the Prolog-2 Encyclopaedia and described in separate entries.

21.5 Building your own debugger

21.5.1 Introduction

The DECsystem-10 style debugger supplied with Prolog-2 is a module, and can be replaced by a debugger of your own design.

You cannot write an entire debugger of your own. The switch to debug mode from conventional execution mode is a function of the core system. The basic tracing, spying and leashing mechanisms are also part of the core system. These cannot be modified.

The part of the debugger that you can rewrite yourself is the interactive control section, which provides the options listed in §21.4.2 above. This allows you to write a debugger that offers courses of action which are different from those of the DECsystem-10 debugger, or to present the DECsystem-10 options in a different way: through a displayed menu, for example, rather than through the command-prompt system that the DECsystem-10 version uses. You might also want to write a simplified debugger that allowed fewer courses of action than the debugger supplied.

21.5.2 Calling the debugger

The debugger comes into action when the goal **debug_goal** is called. This is not a Built-In Predicate, but a public predicate in the module **debug**. It is called whenever the debugging system traverses a leashed port.

To write your own debugger you will need to create new clauses for **debug_goal**. These will then be called whenever the system encounters a leashed predicate. **debug_goal** must be defined as a public predicate in your debugger module.

You will still turn debugging on using the BIPs **trace**/0 and **spy**/1. The module to be debugged is specified by **debug**/1 if you want to debug anything other than the common module. The equivalent **notrace**/0, **nospy**/1 and **nodebug**/0 will also be unaffected by your new debugger. **leash**/1 will continue to define the ports to be leashed.

21.5.3 Built-in predicates for debugging

The BIPs used for interactive debugging correspond to the options on the DECsystem-10 debugging menu listed in §21.4.2 above. These are the predicates that you will use to build routines for debug_goal.

The predicates corresponding to the options are:

>   **creep/0:**   c
>   **fail_out/0:**   f
>   **fail_out/1:**   fN
>   **leap/0:**   l
>   **retry/0:**   r
>   **retry/1:**   rN
>   **skip/0:**   s
>   **skip_out/1:**   sN
>   **xout/0:**   x
>   **goal_out/1:**   d, p, w
>   **or/0:**   ;

The arguments to **fail_out/1** and **retry/1** are integers and the predicates are equivalent to the debug options that require an integer.

The argument to **goal_out/1** can be any of the atoms **display, print, write,** or **writeq**. The break-goal will be displayed, printed or written complete with the standard debug message.

21.5.4 Ancestors

If you are writing your own debugger you will need access to the ancestors of a goal to implement the g and gN options on the debug menu. **print_ancestor/1** is used to find and display the ancestors of a goal.

The ancestors of a goal are the goals which led to it being called. The descendant goal is helping to satisfy the ancestor goals. **print_ancestor/1** will only work for ancestors in the same module as the descendant goal. It will not work for Built-In Predicates.

The single argument for **print_ancestor/1** is the number of generations back you want to go. It prints the ancestor(s) of the goal which called debug_goal on the Current Output Stream in standard debug format.

The other BIPs for retrieving ancestors, **ancestor/2** and **ancestors/1**, should not be used in a debugger as they cannot find goals at a different break level and they do not return the information needed for the debug messages.

21.6 Compatibility note

There is more compatibility here than you might expect, though this is little help to the

The Prolog-2 User Guide

programmer trying to develop portable code. On the other hand, once you have learned to debug Prolog programs on one system you will find using another one similar.

The whole debugging mechanism as described here, with all the options, leashing details and the like, was developed by Lawrence Byrd for DEC-10 Prolog. In Prolog-2 it has been reproduced as accurately as possible.

The BIP **ancestors**/1 is widespread as well.

22. Starting and stopping Prolog-2

22.1 Overview

When you load Prolog-2 from the operating system you first see the Prolog-2 banner and version number; then a series of announcements as each Prolog-2 module loads; and finally the Top Level Interpreter prompt ?-.

Various levels of configurability are available under the different versions of Prolog-2. The steps Prolog-2 goes through before producing this prompt can be configured by the user. The version supplied starts the program development environment.

The Prolog-2 startup routine is specified in a file called PROLOG2.INI, and in the 'menu file'.

PROLOG2.INI is an initialisation file whose contents are described in §22.2 below. The menu file is a Prolog source file which is consulted as soon as the .INI file has been read. It may contain clauses and will contain one or more directives, to open modules. Some of these modules may in turn have start goals, and so will start running immediately they are opened.

The menu file supplied with Prolog-2 is called PROLOG2.MNU. It opens several modules, including the Debugger and the Top-Level Interpreter.

22.2 Starting Prolog-2

The default startup procedure

Prolog-2 searches automatically for PROLOG2.INI when it is loaded: it will look first in the current default directory and then in the same directory in which it found the Prolog-2 program. Any new initialisation file should therefore be called PROLOG2.INI. The only alternative is to specify the name of an initialisation file on the operating system's command line at the same time as you load Prolog-2. For example, you might type:

> **PROLOG2 MYPROLOG**

where you want to use an initialisation file with a different name, or

> **PROLOG2 /MYDIR/MYPROLOG2**

where you want to use one that is not on the current directory.

If you do not specify an initialisation file when you load Prolog, then the default initialisation file PROLOG2.INI will be used. If the file specified does not exist, then it is assumed that there is no initialisation file. In this case some appropriate defaults are used and the name specified for the INI file is taken as the name of the MNU file.

Prolog-2 continues to remember the directory in which it found its initialisation file: it is

The Prolog-2 User Guide

known as the "system directory", as opposed to the directory where it found the Prolog-2 program, which is called the Prolog-2 directory.

Initialisation file contents

The minimum an initialisation file contains is the values of the configuration parameters, which will vary from system to system, and the name of the MNU file.

An initialisation file is not necessarily an ASCII file, and you may not be able to alter it directly by using an editor. If you want to create a new initialisation file, read Section §22.3 below.

The system directory

To simplify the process of running Prolog-2 from different directories there is a system directory that is remembered by Prolog-2.

The system directory is the directory in which PROLOG2.INI (or other initialisation file) was found on startup. All the special files used by the Prolog-2 system, such as EFILE.PRM, are looked for in the Prolog-2 directory. If you examine PROLOG2.MNU you will see how this is done. It is assumed that the user will set up files roughly as follows:

Prolog-2 directory	Prolog-2 system
System directory	MNU and PRM files for application
Default directory	Data for application

Thus the user of an application FOO may type **prolog2 /foo/foo** from any directory and be sure of getting the program from the Prolog-2 directory and the application from its directory.

The BIP **default_name_sys/3** is like **default_name/3**, but if no drive and/or \ (backslash character) precedes the file, the path leading to the system directory is supplied (instead of just using the current directory).

22.3 Altering the startup procedure

There are two ways to alter the startup procedure:

(1) modifying or replacing the initialisation file
(2) modifying or replacing the menu file

22.3.1 Altering the initialisation file

The initialisation file can be changed in either of two respects.

You can alter the sizes allocated to the various stacks and tables used by Prolog-2 by means of the system state **init_alloc**, and save the altered states in an initialisation file by using the BIP **save_state**(Filename).

You can also use the system state **setup_file** to alter the names in the menu file used by Prolog, and save the new names in an initialisation file, also by using **save_state**(Filename).

In UV the INI file is a text file and may be edited without the use of special predicates.

22.3.2 Altering the menu file

The menu file is consulted by Prolog-2 on startup.

The menu file is a simple text file: it can be modified to alter the startup procedure using an ordinary text editor.

You can alter the menu file by including other directives or by removing some of those already specified. For example, if you have developed an application which uses your own interface and not the Prolog-2 Top-Level Interpreter, you will want to remove from the menu file the directive that opens **top**, and replace it with a directive to open a module containing your own program.

The menu file should consist of a list of clauses which you want added to the database, and directives which you want obeyed. These directives may be to open modules.

Any module with a start goal will start to execute as soon as it is opened. If there is more than one module with a start goal, they will execute in the order they are opened by the menu file.

Generally you should use **default_name_sys** to parse modules of your application that are to be opened; this enables a user of your application to start it from a different directory.

The remainder of the command line (after the MNU or INI file has been removed) is available through the BIP **command_line**/1. This can be useful: for example, the following MNU file uses it.

```
go :-
       command_line(L),
       decode(L,Command),
       (Command -> true;true),
       halt.
```

?- go.

This file, conventionally called **do.mnu**, allows the command

PROLOG2 DO consult(prog),prog.

to be inserted in a batch file.

22.4 Aborting and restarting

You can restart Prolog-2 from within an execution. There are two Built-In Predicates that allow you to do this:

>   abort/0.
>   restart/0.

Both predicates stop the current execution and call the current **abort_goal**. The PDE sets up an abort goal that restarts the PDE. The only difference between the two predicates is that **abort/0** prints the message "Evaluation aborted" on standard output and **restart/0** does not.

Execution can also be aborted by selecting the **a** (for abort) option from a menu such as the error-menu.

Aborting or restarting execution does not affect the contents of the heap, so any clauses in the clause store at the time of the abort will be unaffected. The input and output streams are reset to the standard I/O stream (see §18.5).

If you are not using the Top-Level Interpreter supplied with Prolog-2 you must alter the system-state **abort_goal** to the name of the goal called after a call of **abort/0** or **restart/0**. Until you select an abort goal, any error that occurs will be treated as fatal, and pressing the break key will terminate Prolog at once.

22.5 Stopping Prolog-2

What happens when you leave Prolog-2

If you leave Prolog-2 by using **halt/0** or one of the other ways of leaving Prolog-2 (see below), the system will go through a closedown procedure before returning you to the operating system. The initial part of the halt procedure is specified by the system state **halt_goal**, and may be altered; for example, the editor uses this to ensure that the user has the chance to save work in the editor.

Closedown procedure

(1) any statistics being monitored are printed by the module **sysmess** on the standard stream. If you do not want these statistics reported, you can modify the menu file so that **sysmess** is not opened on startup
(2) all scratch files are closed and deleted
(3) all other files are closed
(4) the screen may be reset,to ensure the cursor is visible
(5) control is passed back to the operating system

The built-in predicate halt/0

A Prolog-2 program can be stopped by executing **halt/0**; this also causes Prolog itself to stop as described above. **halt/1** allows a status code to be passed back; this is useful in batch files.

Other ways of stopping Prolog

Other actions will also cause Prolog to halt. Those described below are:

    (1) **optional_halt**.
    (2) halt options in menus
    (3) control keys
    (4) fatal errors

22.5.1 optional_halt/0

The most significant from the system builder's point of view is the BIP **optional_halt/0**. This can be used to offer the user halt facilities on your own menus, and will print the message

    Leave Prolog (y/n)?

If the user answers **y** the system will halt just as if 'halt' had been typed. If the user answers **no** the goal will fail.

22.5.2 Exit options in menus

Some menus offer a halt option.

The halt option is always **e** for exit. You will be asked to confirm that you wish to leave Prolog.

22.5.3 Control keys

Typing control-C or control-break (in circumstances where it will be detected by the operating system) will interrupt the program and put up the interrupt menu; this includes the option **e** to exit from Prolog.

Typing control-Z when not in a break state will halt Prolog after a confirmation request. (Typing control-Z in a break state goes down one break-level.)

22.5.4 Fatal errors

A fatal error (see §20.2) will force you out of Prolog and into the operating system. The closedown procedure will not operate and virtual memory files will not be tidied up.

22.6 Compatibility notes

halt/0, abort/0 and restart/0 are all that can be relied upon in this chapter.

23. External Code

The external code facilities in P and in UV differ radically, and it is not possible to present a unified account. In this chapter §23.1 describes external code in P, §23.2 external code in UV, and §23.3 and 4 special streams and the system call compiler, two facilities only available in UV.

23.1 External code in P

There are two forms of external code in P; COM files may be packaged as Prolog modules and loaded onto the heap, where they share memory with other Prolog objects. This is very efficient, but of course depends on the code being relocatable, which often code generated by a high level language is not. We call this the assembler interface, since that is how you will probably use it. It is used internally for compiled modules. The interface is present in 4 but can be used only by those with access to an appropriate development system for 80386 protected mode code.

23.1.1 Assembler interface

23.1.1.1 Overview

External code can be used to do things that either cannot be done at all in Prolog or are not very efficient in Prolog. Direct addressing of a port, for example, cannot be done in Prolog. Number-crunching can be done in Prolog but is slow. Both these could be done using external code facilities.

External code facilities can also be used the other way around: Prolog-2 can be called from a non-Prolog program.

External code is stored in a data module with no access; to the user it looks like any other Prolog no access data module. The code may be accessed because the module must export at least one predicate.

When you call a predicate that is a public predicate exported by an external code module, control passes into that module. The external code program runs and may eventually pass control back to Prolog with a 'far return' statement.

External code modules can take arguments from Prolog-2 and pass arguments back to it. For example, a program to carry out a chi-squared test on some statistics could accept the raw data (a sequence of numbers) fed to it from Prolog-2, carry out the calculations, and pass back the results of the test. These results will then be unified with a Prolog term, becoming available for use in the rest of the Prolog programme.

Once a module has been built up in machine code (either by hand or using a high-level language compiler) it has to be 'packaged' by Prolog-2 itself before it can be used. First it must be turned into a COM file using EXE2BIN.

COM files can be packaged as modules using the BIP **pack_code**/4 to add a standard header. COM files are opened as ordinary modules and read onto the heap, where they can be moved around and where the occupied space can be reclaimed after they are closed. This interface is used chiefly for compiled modules, but can be used by the programmer as well. Its disadvantage is that the file to be packaged has to be a COM file and so is restricted to 64K in size and in addition cannot contain segment fixups. Compilers for high-level languages usually produce code that cannot be turned into a COM file.

COM files are compact, require no external free memory, and relatively simple to use if you are familiar with assembler programming; they are best suited to small tasks that cannot be done in Prolog, such as DOS and ROM BIOS calls.

23.1.1.2 The attributes of external code modules

Module type

External code COM format modules can be data, program or library.

Access

The only type of access possible for an external code module is **none**. This is because if the module is not in Prolog it makes no sense to try to see the contents of its clauses, nor to try to add new clauses to it.

Filenames

Packaged COM files are given extension PRM by default.

23.1.1.3 Packing COM files

The first stage in creating an external code module is to generate the program in machine code — by using either an assembler or a compiler. Once this has been linked it can be packaged by Prolog-2 into a Prolog-2 module.

It is packaged using **pack_code/4**, whose four arguments are:

The name of the module you want to create
The name of the assembly-code file
The start-goal, if any
The module type

The module name (first argument) can be any atom (just like any other Prolog-2 module).

The name of the file (second argument) can be any valid Prolog-2 filename, but it must have the extension .COM. Do not specify the extension or the . preceding it.

The third argument, the start goal, must be **none**.

The module type (fourth argument) can be data, program or library.

23.1.1.4 The information in the assembler code

In the following paragraphs we give an example of a COM format assembler module — there are no arguments and no calls to Prolog. The module will define a single predicate print_hello/0, which prints the message 'Hello!' on the screen. The first step is to use a text editor to produce source for the assembler. In this example we are using "asm" and "link" under MS-DOS.

The code is:

```
c_print_string      equ         9
msdos               equ         21h
string              equ         5
code                segment
prst                proc        far
                    assume      CS:code,DS:code

; Prolog header block

prolog_call         dw          0,0
scratch_arg         dw          0,0
no_predicates       dw          1

; Header for print_hello/0

                    db          string
                    dw          11           ; numberof bytes
                    db          'print_hello' ; name
                    dw          0            ; arity
                    dw          print_hello
hello_message       db          'Hello!$'
print_hello:        mov         AH,c_print_string
                    mov         DX,OFFSET hello_message
                    int         msdos
                    mov         AL,0
                    ret
prst                endp
code                ends
                    end
```

Note the use of a FAR PROC to get a far return; this is necessary.

Note also that when the assembler predicate receives control, registers CS and DS point to its start, so the assume statements in the code are safe. The ES register points to the PSP of the Prolog-2 interpreter; this can be used, for example, to obtain data from the environment. SS:SP points to the Prolog-2 machine stack, the size of which was determined from the .INI file. This will normally be sufficient, but if you do decide to move SS:SP you must restore them on return to Prolog.

The code in the example above simply calls DOS to print the string 'Hello!'. It then loads AL with 0 and returns. On return AL is interpreted as a status code. If it contains 0 then the call succeeded; if it contains 0FF hex then it failed; and if it contains any other value this is taken to be an error number, and that error is signalled. The start of the data segment contains information needed by Prolog to decide which predicates the routine exports, and where in the module these are.

The first three words of the data segment can be ignored for the time being. The next word is the number of predicate entries that follow.

The structure of each predicate entry is:

(1) the name of the predicate in Prolog string format;
(2) the arity of the predicate;
(3) the address of the code for the predicate in the code segment;
(4) argument information.

Prolog string format is described in §23.1.15; note that Prolog 0-terminated string format is *not* to be used.

In the example above there is no argument information, because there are no arguments.

To package the ASM file as a prolog module three steps are necessary:

Create the file HELLO.ASM, as above; a file BLD.PRO which consists of the following line:

```
get_string("file",X),name(N,X),pack_code(N,X,none,data),halt.
```

and a file BLD.BAT as follows:

```
masm %1
link %1
exe2bin %1
ren %1.bin %1.com
set file=%1
prolog2 <bld.pro
set file =
```

and type BLD.

The module is now usable. Open it:

```
?- open_module(_,hello,none,actual).
```

and then the goal

The Prolog-2 User Guide

        ?- print_hello.

causes the message

    Hello!
    yes

to appear on the screen.

23.1.1.5 Passing arguments between Prolog and external code modules

Prolog-2 allows you to pass arguments between Prolog modules and non-Prolog modules. The arguments can be passed in either direction.

An assembler predicate whose arity is not 0 will receive the arguments used in invoking it, and may pass out arguments to be matched with those arguments. The assembler routine does not need to do the matching itself; it is done automatically on return to Prolog.

The method of argument passing into an assembler routine is: in the header at the start of the data segment the third word is the offset of a scratch area in which Prolog may write input arguments. The fourth word is the size of this area. If the area is exhausted an error is signalled. The passing routine checks that the area does not overrun the data segment of the routine, but cannot check that it does not run into areas your machine-code may have reserved for other data.

Each predicate entry must contain, at the end, the 'argument vector'. This consists of one word for each argument. When the routine is invoked Prolog writes the arguments in the scratch area. The start of the Nth argument can be found in the Nth slot of the vector.

Before returning, the called routine must set up a similar arrangement to pass arguments back. These arguments are matched with the input arguments. If they fail to match then even if the success indicator is set (AL contains 0) the external predicate fails.

If the routine failed or gave an error no attempt is made to match arguments. The output arguments must match the input arguments to avoid failure. If, for example, you want to write an assembler routine to multiply a number by 2 you must give it two arguments, one for the input and one for the output. If you simply double the input and return it in the same slot the routine will fail.

The internal form of Prolog-2 terms

A few changes are made to remove space optimisations when the term is passed to an external-code routine, so do not be surprised if **core** statements suggest that internal terms are shorter than you would expect from what follows.

The Prolog-2 User Guide

A Prolog term consists of a byte which indicates the type of the object followed by the value of the object. There are seven possible types:

```
0    undefined
1    atom
2    pointer
3    functor
4    integer
5    string
6    real
```

Undefined

An undefined variable, represented in Prolog programmes as _, is passed to the machine-code interface as four zero bytes:

Byte 1:   The undefined tag, 0
Byte 2:   0
Byte 3:   0
Byte 4:   0

Atom

An atom is a special case of a functor, having arity 0, and therefore consists of:

Byte 1:   The atom tag, 1
Byte 2:   0
Bytes 3-n: The atom name as a 0-terminated string starting with the string tag 5 in byte 3

Pointer

The structure of a pointer is as follows:

Byte 1:   The pointer tag, 2
Byte 2:   0
Byte 3:   The low byte of the pointer
Byte 4:   The high byte of the pointer

The last two bytes constitute a pointer into the data segment of the called code.

Functor

The structure of a functor is as follows:

Byte 1: The functor tag, 3.
Byte 2: The arity.
Bytes 3-n: The functor name as a 0-terminated string starting with the string tag 5 in byte 3.

The arity is always greater than 0, because if it were 0 it would be an atom.

Integer

The structure of an integer is as follows:

Byte 1: The integer tag, 4
Byte 2: The low byte of the integer
Byte 3: The middle byte of the integer
Byte 4: The high byte of the integer

The integer is stored in standard Intel format, i.e. 2s complement with the sign in the most significant bit.

string

The structure of a 0-terminated string is as follows:

Byte 1: The string tag, 5
Bytes 2 & 3: The string length (less significant byte first)
Bytes 4 — n: The string itself, first character first
Byte n+1: This must be 0
Byte n+2: If n is even this must be 0, otherwise it is not needed

String format (only used in the predicate header) is similar but omits the final 0; again the total size must be even.

real

The structure of a real is as follows:

Byte 1: The real tag, 6
Byte 2: 0
Bytes 3-10: The real in IEEE long real format

Thus the atom **duck** would be represented as the following sequence of bytes (here represented in hex):

1	01	Atom tag
2	00	Arity
3	05	String tag
4	04	String length, less significant digit
5	05	String length, more significant digit.
6	64	d
7	75	u
8	63	c
9	6B	k
A	00	0

Example

Here is an example of an assembler predicate with two arguments. It takes the integer which is passed in to it as its first argument, doubles it, and passes it out as its second argument (Prolog will then try to match what the assembler predicate passes out with the second argument that was passed in).

Thus
    times_2(7, X)
will instantiate X to 14,
    times_2(7, 11)
will fail, and
    times_2(7, 14)
will succeed.

```
integer            equ            4
string             equ            5
scratch_size       equ            128
times_2_err        equ            133
tm2                segment
times2             proc           far
assume             CS:tm2,DS:tm2
prolog_call        dw             0,0
scratch_arg        dw             scratch,scratch_size
no_predicates      dw             1
; entry for times_2/2
                   db             string
                   dw             7
                   db             'times_2'
                   dw             2
                   dw             times_2
arg1               dw             0
arg2               dw             0
scratch            db             scratch_size DUP (0)
```

```
buffer          db      0,0,0,0
times_2:        mov     BX,arg1
                cmp     BYTE PTR [BX],integer
                jne     error
                mov     buffer,integer
                mov     AX,1[BX]
                add     AX,AX       ; double first two bytes
                mov     WORD PTR buffer+1,AX
                mov     AL,3[BX]
                adc     AL,AL       ; double third byte
                jo      error       ; error if too big
                mov     buffer+3,AL
                mov     arg2,OFFSET buffer
                mov     AL,0 ; succeed
                ret
error:          mov     AL,times_2_err
                ret
times2          endp
tm2             ends
                end
```

23.1.1.6 Calling Prolog-2 from external code

The external code interface in Prolog-2 works both ways. As well as calling non-Prolog code from Prolog-2, it can be used to call Prolog-2 from a non-Prolog program.

Calls to Prolog-2 have to be made from an external code module accessed from Prolog by the external code interface. When the system opens such a module it writes in the first double word address the address of a far location in the Prolog-2 system that may be used for calling Prolog goals. This is the address that we have called **prolog_call** in the examples above.

To make the call you have to tell Prolog-2 what goal you want evaluated. A goal is a Prolog structure just like any other, and what you have to do is to build the goal as though you were going to return it as the value of an argument. Load the SI register with the address of this goal and make a far call to the address provided. If you have altered the stack segment register SS, remember to change it back before calling Prolog-2; Prolog-2 uses it for all sorts of addressing and it must be right.

Control will be returned after the goal is evaluated regardless of whether it succeeds or fails. If it succeeds then AL is set to 0, and the goal is copied back to the address specified by the DI register. The reason for doing this is to allow you to recover the value of any variable that has been instantiated by the successful call. However, if you do not want to know the result you may set DI to 0, and nothing will be copied.

The following example shows a rather trivial routine to get a character from the current input stream. This makes it possible for an external code application to use the Prolog-2 windowing system.

```
ip                  segment
scratch_size        equ         128
integer             equ         4
                    assume      CS:ip,DS:ip
main                proc        far
prolog_call         dw          0,0
scratch_arg         dw          OFFSET scratch,scratch_size
no_predicates       dw          1
                    db          5,2,0,'ip',0
                    dw          1
                    dw          OFFSET ipt
arg1                dw          0
scratch             db          scratch_size DUP(0)
ipt:                call        input
                    mov         BX,arg1
                    mov         BYTE PTR [BX],integer
                    mov         1[BX],AL
                    mov         WORD PTR 2[BX],0
                    mov         AL,0
                    ret
main                endp
input               proc
                    mov         SI,OFFSET icall
                    mov         DI,OFFSET rewrite
                    xor         BX,BX
                    call        DWORD PTR [BX]
                    mov         AL,11[DI]
                    ret
icall               db          3,1,5,3,0,'get',0,0     ; functor get/1
                    db          0,0,0,0                 ; variable
rewrite             db          12 DUP (0)
input               endp
ip                  ends
                    end
```

23.1.2 MicroSoft languages interface

23.1.2.1 Overview

The Microsoft languages interface in Prolog-2 allows the user to write external functions in Microsoft C , Fortran or Pascal. These functions are linked together with the interface modules supplied to create an external code module. This module is loaded into memory space left free by the Prolog initialisation using the BIP **open_external/3** , and the functions are called as predicates from the Prolog code. It is also possible through the interface to call Prolog goals from the external code.

The Prolog-2 User Guide

A full set of commented example programs is provided. See §23.1.2.11 for a file summary.

23.1.2.2 Using external code

External code modules are opened by the BIP **open_external/3**:

> **open_external(Modname,File,Memory)**

Modname is a variable or an atom. If it is a variable it is matched with the module name given in the predicate table. If it is an atom, the module will be given that name.

File is a string. It is the file name of the external module. The default extension is .EXE.

Memory is an integer equal to the amount of memory (in bytes) that will be allocated to the module. The atom **max** means allocate all spare memory.

Note that **open_external/3** requires you to have left enough free memory when Prolog-2 started; see Chapter 22 to see how to do this. The file 64K.INI on the distribution diskette leaves 64K free which is enough to run the demonstration programs provided.

External modules are closed by the BIP **close_module/1**:

> **close_module(Modname)**

where **Modname** is the same module name as above. When the module is closed the memory allocated will be freed.

Once an external module containing suitable predicate declarations has been opened, the functions therein are accessed as Prolog goals in the normal way. Arguments may be read in and variables instantiated by the external code using the interface functions detailed in the remainder of this chapter.

23.1.2.3 Writing external functions

The programmer is required to write an external function of return type **char** for each external predicate declared. The single argument to this function is an array of 16 bit pointers to the arguments passed out by Prolog. The number of elements in this array is equal to the arity of the predicate. Using the interface functions provided, the user has access to the actual values of the Prolog arguments in a form suitable for the language being used, and may also set variable arguments to new values.

All these arguments are written to a special scratch area external to Prolog so the programmer does not have direct access to the internal data structures of the interpreter. The size of this area may be changed as needed (if for example, a scratch overflow error is encountered).

The BIP **open_external/3** calls the standard Microsoft start-up and there are no

The Prolog-2 User Guide

restrictions on the code that can be used. However, a few points need to be born in mind:

(1) The startup code returns all the memory it doesn't need to the operating system after it has been initialised. If you then do something to cause Prolog-2 to allocate more memory (another call to **open_external/2** is the obvious one) then the external module will not be able to expand and will therefore not allocate any more memory.

(2) Standard I/O may be used, but is not compatible with the Prolog windowing environment. Hence screen output may appear in unexpected places and vanish equally unexpectedly. The best way to get round this problem is to use calls to the Prolog routines for screen output. The demonstration programs show how to do this.

(3) You can return a value to Prolog-2 by using return(Value), and you should do this; normally you will say return(0) (it isn't safe just to say return). The value 0 causes the called goal to succeed and -1 to fail; any other value is treated as an error subcode for the multiplexed external code error **external_code**. Note that subcode 1 is reserved for buffer area overflow and 2 for a programming error.(A consistency check is done on the external predicate table whenever an external function is called, and the error 2 indicates a corruption of the table.)

(4) exit should not be used as this causes a direct return to the operating system.

23.1.2.4 Argument passing

The arguments passed to external code are actually near pointers to Prolog terms written in a scratch area of memory shared between the Prolog interpreter and the external code module. The size of this area may be controlled by the user. If you are familiar with the assembler interface, you will find what follows a little easier to understand.

The various input processing routines can decode arguments while protecting the user from the need to know the exact format of Prolog-2 terms.

A general description of interface functions is given here. Details particular to the language being used should also be read carefully before attempting to use any of these functions. The illustrations here are given in C, but the same principles apply to all the languages. The argument type PVAR is a generalised type defined for Prolog variables. Arguments to interfaces are pointers to Prolog variables, hence PVAR*.

Input functions

The input functions are as follows (note that all interface functions begin **pc_**).

pc_tag(p)

This extracts a tag saying what kind of Prolog-2 object is passed. Typically this tag will be passed to a case statement and the relevant value routine will be called. There are

The Prolog-2 User Guide

different value routines for each type of argument, and it is the programmer's responsibility to ensure that the right one gets called (calling the wrong one returns rubbish). On the other hand, if you are in control at the Prolog end, you may decide to omit type checking for the sake of speed.

The possible tag values are:

0 UNDEF
1 ATOM
2 POINTER
3 FUNCTOR
4 INTEGER
5 STRING
6 REAL

(literals for these tag values are defined for C and Pascal in the appropriate header files)

UNDEF means a variable. There is no value routine because variables don't have values.

ATOM means an atom. The value routine is **pc_a()** and returns the atom name as a string (**char *pc_a()**). For example

Prolog: foo(bar)

C: foo(PVAR* p[1])
{
    char *c;
    c = pc_a(p[0]);

assigns the string "bar" to c.

POINTER will not often occur; it is used when two uninstantiated variables are sharing. One of them (the leftmost in the call) will be UNDEF and the others will be pointers. The value function **pc_v()** returns the handle of the argument with which the pointer variable shares.

FUNCTOR means a Prolog-2 structure. Passing of non-circular structures is fully supported though it is not always very efficient. The value function **pc_f()** returns that functor name as a string. Another function **pc_arity** returns the arity and a third function **pc_arg** returns pointer to a desired argument; **pc_arg(p,i)** is a pointer to the ith argument. This can be accessed in the same way as function arguments.

INTEGER means a Prolog-2 integer. This is a long integer in C, and the header file contains the necessary declaration for the value function **pc_i()** that returns the long integer.

STRING means a Prolog-2 string. The value function is **pc_s()** and returns the string.

REAL means a Prolog-2 real. This is a double precision real(8 bytes). The value function is **pc_r()**.

Values are returned to Prolog-2 by passing the argument pointer and the desired value to a routine that has the same name as the input routine but with the characters _s appended. For example, the following routine calculates the sine of its first argument and returns the value as its second.

```
sine(PVAR* p[2])
{
    pc_r_s(p[1],sin(pc_r(p[0])));
    return(0);
}
```

(Note the lack of type checking!) This could be called from Prolog-2 by

?- sine(Argument,Value).

There is a subtlety that you can ignore unless you want to return structures to Prolog-2. You cannot directly reference arguments you have instantiated yourself; for example

```
pc_a_s(p2,"foo");
c = pc_a(p2);
```

will not necessarily assign the string "foo" to c. Usually you don't want to do this anyway, but in returning a functor you need to access it with pc_arg to get the argument positions before you instantiate them. The following (incorrect) code could be an attempt to return a(b) to Prolog-2:

```
getab(PVAR* p[1])   /* WRONG */
{
    PVAR* p1;
    pc_f_s(p[0],"a",1);  /* sets p to a(X) */
    p1 = pc_arg(p[0],1);      /* gets handle to X */
    pc_a_s(p1,"b");   /* sets X to b */
    return(0);
}
```

In fact any argument you have tampered with must be processed by a function **pc_deref()** before being accessed. Thus the 5th line of the above should read

```
        p1 = pc_arg(pc_deref(p[0]),1);     /* gets handle to X */
```

(In fact it's always safe to use pc_deref, but the arguments are passed in an optimised form that doesn't require it.)

Arguments passed back are matched with the arguments of the predicate. Though there is nothing to stop you from assigning to something whose tag isn't UNDEF it is not

The Prolog-2 User Guide

likely to do anything other than fail on return to Prolog.

23.1.2.5 Calling Prolog-2 from external code

The idea here is to build a Prolog-2 term in the same format as if you were going to return it to Prolog-2 but then pass it to the routine **pc_prove**() for proof.

To achieve this you need to get a new handle not associated with an argument; you can do this using **pc_grab**(). Then instantiate it as usual. Its value is either 0 (to indicate failure) or a handle to the same goal as rewritten in the course of proof with variables instantiated; these can be extracted as for a new call. You cannot resatisfy such goals.

All this processing uses up the buffer area, and you will be relieved to hear that there is a (final) function **pc_free**() that takes a single handle as its argument and returns all handles grabbed since that one (inclusive) to the pool. You can't do this if you have assigned an atom, functor or string to a variable since the handle was allocated unless you are willing to lose that too. In the following example it is used safely.

The example is a trivial string printing routine oc that outputs a string to the current Prolog output stream; for this it uses a call to the interpreter to 'prove' put.

```
#include "chead.inc"
hello(PVAR* pv[1])
{
    char *p;
    p=pc_s(pv[0]);
    while (*p)
        outchar(*p++);
    return(0);
}
outchar(ch)
char ch;
{
    register PVAR* p;
    pc_f_s((p=pc_grab()),"put",1);
    pc_i_s(pc_arg(pc_deref(p),1),(long) ch);
    pc_prove(p);
    pc_free(p);
    return;
}
```

23.1.2.6 Microsoft C interface

C language definitions

The following definitions are contained in the file CHEAD.INC which should be included in source files that do argument processing.

Prolog argument type

Actual Prolog arguments are stored in a special format that is not directly accessible to the external code programmer. They are accessed only by the routines below and a special type must always be used (by reference) for Prolog variables, defined as follows:

>   typedef char near PVAR;

Prolog type tag values

Prolog arguments may have any type. The individual types are recognised by their tag values, defined as follows:

>   #define P_UNDEF   0
>   #define P_ATOM   1
>   #define P_POINTER 2
>   #define P_FUNCTOR 3
>   #define P_INTEGER 4
>   #define P_STRING 5
>   #define P_REAL   6

Input functions

These functions take a pointer to a Prolog variable as argument and return the value of the variable in C format.

```
int     pc_tag(PVAR *); /* get type tag of variable */
char*   pc_a(PVAR *); /* get atom (string) */
char*   pc_f(PVAR *); /* get functor (string) */
int     pc_arity(PVAR *); /* get arity of functor */
long    pc_i(PVAR *); /* get integer (long integer) */
double  pc_r(PVAR *); /* get real (double) */
char*   pc_s(PVAR *); /* get string */
PVAR*   pc_v(PVAR *); /* get pointer to shared variable */
PVAR*   pc_arg(PVAR*,unsigned arg); /* get pointer to numbered arg of functor
                                       (numbering starts at 0) */
```

Output functions

Values may be assigned to Prolog variables with the routines below. In each case, the first argument is the pointer to the variable being instantiated and the second argument is the value it is being assigned with. Assigning values to arguments that are not of type P_UNDEF is illegal, and will at best cause the matcher to fail on return to Prolog, and may cause other undesirable effects!

```
void pc_v_s(PVAR *,PVAR*);   /* set a pointer */
void pc_s_s(PVAR *,char *);  /* set a string */
```

The Prolog-2 User Guide

```
void pc_a_s(PVAR *,char *);    /* set an atom */
void pc_f_s(PVAR *,char *,unsigned arity);
                               /* set a functor with given arity */
void pc_i_s(PVAR *,long);      /* set an integer (long) */
void pc_r_s(PVAR *,double);    /* set a real (double) */
```

Variable management

New variables may be allocated and freed in the scratch area with the following two functions. When pc_free() is called, all variables allocated since, and including the given variable will be freed.

```
PVAR*  pc_grab(void);         /* allocate an undefined variable */
void   pc_free(PVAR *);       /* release space in scratch area */
PVAR*  pc_deref(PVAR *)       /* de-reference a pointer */
```

Calling a Prolog goal

The argument to pc_prove() is a pointer to a Prolog-2 term built up by the programmer. It returns a pointer to the structure with any variable instantiations included.

```
PVAR* pc_prove(PVAR *);       /* Prove a Prolog goal */
```

23.1.2.7 Microsoft Pascal interface

Pascal language definitions

The following definitions are contained in the file PHEAD.INC which should be included in source files that do argument processing.

Prolog argument type

Actual Prolog arguments are stored in a special format that is not directly accessible to the external code programmer. They are accessed only by the routines below and a special type must always be used for Prolog variables, defined as follows:

```
type PVAR = ADR OF CHAR;
```

Passing strings to Prolog

The interface routines accept and return argument values in standard Pascal formats. The only type which has special problems is the string, because Pascal strings start with a length byte, whereas the interface strings have no length byte and are terminated by a null byte. Thus when setting Prolog strings from Pascal, the user must explicitly terminate the string with a null byte. This is done using the Pascal concatenation operator (see your compiler guide). The string is then passed by far reference to an interface function using the Pascal ADS (segmented address) operator. For example,

```
pc_s_s ( p1 , ads 'Pascal_to_Prolog' * chr(0) );
```

sets the variable pointed by p1 to the string 'Pascal_to_Prolog'.

The following type definitions are used in the interface functions:

```
type
    STR40      = string(40);
    ADS_STRING = ADS OF STR40;
```

Values of strings are obtained by dereferencing an ADS_STRING type into a STR40 type variable. e.g.

```
var
    Pascal_atom : STR40;

Pascal_atom := pc_a (p1)^ ;
```

Strings in the external code interface are limited to 39 characters plus one null byte.

Prolog type tag values

Prolog arguments may have any type. The individual types are recognised by their tag values, defined as follows:

```
const
    P_UNDEF   =   0;
    P_ATOM    =   1;
    P_POINTER =   2;
    P_FUNCTOR =   3;
    P_INTEGER =   4;
    P_STRING  =   5;
    P_REAL    =   6;
```

One of these values will be returned by the pc_tag function.

Input functions

Input functions return the actual value of the Prolog variable given as argument. Type tags are not checked. It is the responsibility of the programmer to ensure the correct function is called. The pc_tag function returns the type of the actual argument.

```
function pc_tag(i:PVAR):integer;      { get type tag of variable }
function pc_a(i:PVAR):ADS_STRING;     { get atom as string }
function pc_f(i:PVAR):ADS_STRING;     { get functor as string }
function pc_arity(i:PVAR):integer;    { get arity of functor }
function pc_i(i:PVAR):integer4;       { get integer (long) }
function pc_r(i:PVAR):real8;          { get real (double) }
function pc_s(i:PVAR):ADS_STRING;     { get string }
function pc_v(i:PVAR):PVAR;           { get pointer to shared variable}
function pc_arg(i:PVAR;j:integer):PVAR;
```

{ get pointer to jth arg in functor (starting at 0) }

Output functions

Values may be assigned to Prolog variables with the routines below. In each case, the first argument is the pointer to the variable being instantiated and the second argument is the value it is being assigned with. Assigning values to arguments that are not of type P_UNDEF is illegal, and will at best cause the matcher to fail on return to Prolog, and may cause other undesirable effects!

String arguments must be passed by far reference and terminated with a null byte.

```
procedure pc_v_s(i,j:PVAR);                     { set a pointer }
procedure pc_s_s(i:PVAR;s:adsmem);              { set a string }
procedure pc_a_s(i:PVAR;s:adsmem);              { set an atom }
procedure pc_f_s(i:PVAR;s:adsmem;j:integer);    { set functor,arity j}
procedure pc_i_s(i:PVAR;j:integer4);            { set an integer }
procedure pc_r_s(i:PVAR;a:real8);               { set a real }
```

Variable management

New variable pointers may be allocated and freed in the scratch area (default data segment) with the next two functions.

```
function  pc_grab:PVAR;            { allocate an undefined variable }
procedure pc_free(i:PVAR);         { release space in scratch area }
function  pc_deref(i:PVAR):PVAR;   { de-reference a pointer }
```

Calling a Prolog goal

The argument to pc_prove is a pointer to a Prolog-2 term built up by the user. The return value is a pointer to the same structure with any variable instantiations included.

```
function pc_prove(i:PVAR):PVAR;{ Prove a Prolog goal }
```

23.1.2.8 Microsoft FORTRAN interface

Fortran interface definitions

The following definitions are contained in the file FHEAD.INC which should be included in source files that do argument passing.

Prolog argument type

Arguments to Prolog variables are written to a shared memory area called the scratch block. All the interface functions use near pointers to the variables to reference them. In Fortran, near pointers should be typed integer*2.

Passing strings to Prolog

The normal Fortran string type is incompatible with Prolog, because Fortran strings are simple character arrays with a size attribute whereas the Prolog interface expects strings to be terminated by a null byte. Thus when setting Prolog strings from Fortran, the special C-compatible Fortran string format must be used. This is done by placing the character c after the string itself. For example

    call pc_s_s (p1 , 'Fortran_to_Prolog' c)

sets the Prolog variable pointed to by p1 to the string 'Fortran_to Prolog'.

Interfaces to input functions

Input functions return the value of the Prolog variable given as argument to the function. Select the type of input function you need by testing the tag value first, which returns the type code. Type tags are not checked by the input functions. Requesting an argument using the wrong input function will give garbage.

```
CPC_TAG returns type tag of variable
        interface to integer*2 function pc_tag (i)
        integer*2 i [value]
        end

CPC_A returns far pointer to atom as string
interface to integer*4 function PC_A (I)
integer*2 I [value]
end

CPC_F returns far pointer to functor as string
interface to integer*4 function PC_F (I)
integer*2 I [value]
end

CPC_ARITY returns arity of functor
          interface to integer*2 function PC_ARITY (i)
integer*2 I [value]
end

C  PC_I returns Prolog integer as long integer
         interface to integer*4 function PC_I (I)
integer*2 I [value]
end

C  PC_R returns Prolog real as double
interface to real*8 function PC_R (I)
integer*2 I [value]
end
```

The Prolog-2 User Guide

```
C  PC_S returns far pointer to Prolog string
interface to integer*4 function PC_S (I)
integer*2 I [value]
end

C  PC_V returns pointer to shared variable
interface to integer*2 function PC_V (I)
integer*2 I [value]
end

C  PC_ARG returns pointer to jth argument of functor (starts at 0)
interface to integer*2 function PC_ARG (I,J)
integer*2 i [value], j [value]
end
```

Output functions

Values may be assigned to Prolog variables with the routines below. In each case, the first argument is the pointer to the variable being instantiated and the second argument is the value it is being assigned with. Reassigning variables that have already been instantiated is illegal. String arguments must be terminated by a null byte (use the C string mechanism provided by Microsoft).

```
C  PC_V_S makes the variable referenced by I into a pointer to J
interface to subroutine PC_V_S (I,J)
integer*2 i [value], j [value]
end

C  PC_S_S sets a string
interface to subroutine PC_S_S (I,S)
integer*2 I [value]
integer*4 s [value]
end

C  PC_A_S sets an atom
interface to subroutine PC_A_S (I,S)
integer*2 I [value]
integer*4 s [value]
end

C  PC_F_S sets a functor
interface to subroutine PC_F_S (I,S,J)
integer*2 I [value]
integer*4 s [value]
integer*2 J [value]
end
```

```
C PC_I_S sets an integer
      interface to subroutine PC_I_S (I,I)
      integer*2 I [value]
      integer*4 I [value]
      end

C  PC_R_S sets a real
      interface to subroutine PC_R_S (i,r)
      integer*2 i [value]
      real*8 r [value]
      end
```

Variable management

New variables may be allocated and freed in the scratch area with the next two functions.

```
C  PC_GRAB returns a pointer to a new undefined Prolog variable
      interface to integer*2 function PC_GRAB
      end

C  PC_FREE releases all space allocated from I onwards in scratch area
      interface to subroutine PC_FREE (i)
      integer*2 i [value]
      end

C  PC_DEREF dereferences a pointer variable
      interface to integer*2 function pc_deref (i)
      integer*2 i [value]
      end
```

Calling a Prolog goal

The argument to pc_prove is a pointer to a Prolog-2 term built up by the user. The return value is a pointer to the same term with any variable instantiations made.

```
C  PC_PROVE calls a Prolog goal
      interface to integer*2 function PC_PROVE (i)
      integer*2 i [value]
      end
```

23.1.2.9 Declaring external predicates

The names, arities and function addresses of external predicates are communicated to Prolog by means of a special predicate table which is built when **open_external/3** is called. This information must be supplied to the interface by the user in a special module. Examples of this module are given in CPREDS.C, PPREDS.PAS and FPREDS.FOR for the three languages. These should be copied, modified and linked with the external functions and interface routines. The name of this module is not

The Prolog-2 User Guide

significant.

Four parts of this module are of significance to the user. (The rest should not be changed.)

1. There must be a list of external declarations of the external predicate handling functions. These are just external references to be picked up later by the linker so explicit function typing is not necessary. e.g.

    C: extern char far mypred();
    Pascal: procedure mypred; extern;
    Fortran: external mypred

2. Two manifest constants must be defined:

    (a) The number of predicates in the module, e.g.

    C: #define N_PREDICATES 1
    Pascal: const N_PREDICATES = 1;
    Fortran: parameter (N_PREDICATES = 1)

    (b) The size of the scratch block used to read and write arguments into, e.g.

    C: #define SCRATCH_SIZE 512
    Pascal: const SCRATCH_SIZE = 512;
    Fortran: parameter (SCRATCH_SIZE = 512)

3. The name of the module must be given (a valid Prolog atom). This is declared as a string. Note that in the case of Pascal all strings must be explicitly terminated with a null byte using the catenation operator (*), and a reference to the string passed to the interface using the special **ads** operator (see your Microsoft compiler guide). For Fortran the C-compatible string type should be used.

    C: #define MODNAME "mymod"
    Pascal: p_module(ads 'mymod'*chr(0),N_PREDICATES,SCRATCH_SIZE);
    Fortran   p_module('mymod' c , N_PREDICATES, SCRATCH_SIZE)

4. N_PREDICATES lines must be supplied to the function init_header() which is called when the module is opened, one line for each predicate. These lines are function calls of the form:

        predicate (name, arity, entry)

where,
    name = the name of the predicate as it appears to Prolog
    arity = arity of the predicate
    entry = pointer to your function for handling the predicate
    (as named in the extern declarations above)

e.g.
    C: predicate("cpred1", 2 , mypred);

```
Pascal:    predicate( ads 'ppred1'*chr(0) , 2 , ads mypred);
Fortran:   predicate('fpred1' c , 2 , locfar (mypred) )
```

The remaining lines in the file must not be changed.

23.1.2.10 Compiling and linking

Make files for the example programs are provided (?DEMO.MAK). Since Prolog has to call external functions by far reference, a large code model must be used for compiling and linking external code. The user is free to choose any floating point option as detailed in the appropriate compiler guide.

The Prolog interface routines are supplied as two object files; PROLMS1.OBJ and PROLMS2.OBJ. They contain an external reference to the Microsoft common start-up code (compatible across the three languages), and the main program is declared there.

Thus the programmer must write external code as far functions, produce a predicate declaration module, and compile each of these in the large code model to produce object (.OBJ) files.

The last step is to link these object files with the Prolog interface modules PROLMS1.OBJ and PROLMS2.OBJ using the large model language libraries, e.g.

link prolms1+prolms2+cpreds+cdemo,cdemo.exe /NOI /NOE;

The resulting .EXE file can now be loaded by Prolog as an external code module.

Note the link option /NOI (NOIGNORECASE) is needed for the C language which is case sensitive, but should not be used for Pascal and Fortran. /NOE prevents the linker from loading environment processing routines, which are unnecessary. Generally, the default library specifications are placed in the object files by the compiler, but in case of any difficulty, these can be overridden by explicitly named libraries, provided the linker option /NOD (NODEFAULTLIBRARY) is set.

23.1.2.11 File summary

64K.INI
    Prolog initialisation file leaves 64K bytes memory clear for external code.

PROLMS1.OBJ PROLMS2.OBJ
    Prolog interface module

CHEAD.INC FHEAD.INC PHEAD.INC
    Include files containing interface definitions for each language

CPREDS.C FPREDS.FOR PPREDS.PAS
    Predicate table declarations for the demo programs which should be customised to the user's application

The Prolog-2 User Guide

CDEMO.C FDEMO.FOR PDEMO.PAS
Demonstration programs illustrating the use of each interface function in each language

CDEMO.MAK FDEMO.MAK PDEMO.MAK
Make files for the Microsoft Make utility to build the demonstration programs

23.2 External code in UV

23.2.1 Introduction

Prolog-2's External Code facility enables you to write BIPs in C, Fortran, Pascal or other languages: such BIPs can then be called from Prolog in the same way as Prolog-2's own BIPs.

The External Code facility is particularly useful for functions which cannot be done very efficiently in Prolog-2 proper (e.g. number crunching) or are not available in a high-level language (e.g. specialised graphics). The user simply writes the desired function in an appropriate language and then links it with the existing Prolog-2 interpreter to produce an extended Prolog interpreter.

23.2.2 Using external code

External code BIPs are accessed by one BIP, **external_code/4**:

> **external_code(Op,Input,Output,[Return,Errcode1,Errcode2])**

Op is an integer: its value corresponds to the external code function to be performed

Input is a list of input values: note that these are read-only

Output is a list of values which are output by the external code function: this list is only matched if the external code function succeeds (e.g. **Return** is **none**). **Return** indicates if the external code function succeeded (**none**) or the type of error codes returned (e.g. **prolog, unix, vms** or **fortran**).

Errcode1 and **Errcode2** are integers which are only set when the external function has errored. Errcode values are set by the external code routine in conjunction with the **Return** value to indicate the reason for error. Two errcode integers are provided because some error codes use a full 32 bit integer whilst Prolog-2 integers are limited to 27 bits.

The values that can be passed into and out of external code functions are atoms, strings, integers, reals and anonymous variables (_).

Accessing external code functions via external_code/4

Individual external code functions are identified by unique **Op** values assigned by the

198

user. For instance

>   external_code(3,[],[],[Return,Errcode1,Errcode2]).

will cause external code function 3 to be executed.

A more user friendly interface can be provided by assigning individual functions to separate predicates. Thus external code function 16 can be used as predicate solve/3 as follows:

>   solve(In,Out1,Out2) :-
>   external_code(16,[In],[Out1,Out2],[none,_,_]).

External code calling sequence

When **external_code/4** is used the interpreter sets up the input arguments and **Op**, initialises the output arguments to be anonymous variables and then calls the external subroutine called externalcode(). Within externalcode() the particular function that corresponds to **Op** is performed, some data is set to show the result of the function and control is returned from externalcode() to the interpreter and the **external_code** goal finishes.

The input data is read and the output data written by means of some interface functions, control of the call itself (including reporting of success/failure/error) is done using variables shared with the interpreter. See §23.2.4.1 for details.

Success/failure/error of external_code/4

If externalcode() wishes to fail then it simply returns a fixed value (P2FAILRETURN) in one of the interface parameters (**ecreturn**) and the **external_code/4** will fail.

However if externalcode() wishes to signal an error then under Prolog semantics it must succeed in order to pass the error information out. We deal with this by having the **external_code/4** goal succeed if externalcode() signals success OR error, and we set the 4th argument of the goal to indicate which case applies. These cases are set out in detail below.

If externalcode() wishes to succeed then it returns a fixed value (P2OKAYRETURN) in an interface parameter (**ecreturn**) and when control returns to the interpreter then the output arguments set in externalcode() will be matched with the 3rd argument of the goal and [none,_,_] will be matched with its 4th argument when the goal succeeds.

If externalcode() wishes to signal an error then it returns a fixed value appropriate to the kind of error it is signalling in the interface parameter **ecreturn** and details of the error — as a full 32-bit integer — in parameter **ecstatus**. When control returns to the interpreter the 3rd goal argument will NOT be matched (ie no output data is passed out) but [Return,Errcode1,Errcode2] will be matched with its 4th argument, where **Return** and **Errcode** have values specifying the error, when the goal succeeds.

The Prolog-2 User Guide

Suppose, for example, you have written a Fortran external code function. You call it function 5. What function 5 does is compute the cube root of its input; if the answer is outside the required accuracy it sets **ecreturn** to P2FORTRANRETURN and **ecstatus** to 5. The interpreter will succeed the goal with **Return** set to 'fortran', **Errcode1** set to 0 and **Errcode2** set to 5.

You could call this function as follows:

```
cube_root(In,Out) :-
    external_code(5,[In],[Out],[Return,Errcode1,Errcode2]),
    ( Return == none
    /* success of external code function 5 */ ;
    handle_error(Return,Errcode1,Errcode2), fail ).

handle_error(fortran,_,5) :-
    write("cube_root too inaccurate"),nl.
handle_error(Return,Errcode1,Errcode2) :-
    write("Error type        : "),write(Return),nl,
    write("Error code (high) : "),write(Errcode1),nl,
    write("Error code (low)  : "),write(Errcode1),nl.
```

Passing structures and goals

You may have noticed that only atoms, strings, integers, reals and anonymous variables can be passed to and from the external code functions. However, with a little cleverness you can pass structures and even goals as well, by making Prolog do the work for you.

To pass a structure you simply use =.. to convert it to list format and pass such lists instead. For example, to pass the structure x("y",z) to external code function 6 (**esi_personnel**) you would write:

```
esi_personnel(Structure ) :-
    /* check that we were passed a structure of arity 2 */
    functor(Structure,_,2),
    Structure =.. Input,!,
    external_code(6,Input,_,[none,_,_]).
```

To pass a goal back to Prolog and have it executed you must write the goal to an atom and call this goal. For example, to pass the goal 'sales_staff' back to Prolog from external code function 7 (hire) you would write:

```
hire:-
    external_code(7,[],[Goal],[none,_,_]),!,
    call(Goal).
```

23.2.3 Creating external code functions

You create an external code function in two stages:

(1) **Write** functions in external language (eg C), producing source code.

(2) **Compile** external functions source code to produce object code and **link** external code object with Prolog-2 objects to produce a new executable extended Prolog interpreter.

The following sections describe these stages in full detail, with particular reference to C. §23.2.5.3 explains the differences for other languages.

(The example program "userc.c" contains illustrations of the use of all the features described below. The reader is strongly recommended to look at this program while studying these sections.)

23.2.4 Writing external code functions

To write external code functions you first need to understand the interface provided between external code and Prolog-2.

Data is passed between external code and Prolog via an area of shared memory; the external code accesses this data by means of the external code interface functions and some parameters.

23.2.4.1 External code parameters

The external code parameters are variables shared between Prolog and external code. Some are read-only (external code should only read these); others can be both written and read by external code.

The programmer should note that writing to read-only parameters will cause unpredictable and certainly undesirable results, and that meaningless results will be obtained by reading the writeable parameters before anything has been written to them.

The external code parameters are either 4-byte signed integers or the address of an array of signed 4-byte integers. See "cglobdat.h" for the formal declarations of these parameters. Which type is indicated by **integer** or **array** in the notes below.

ecop   (read only, int)

The value of **Op**

ecnmin   (read only, int)

The number of elements input (ie passed to the external code)

ecin   (read only, array)

The address of an array which holds the input elements. The external code need never examine this address, only pass it to the appropriate interface functions

ecnmout   (read/write, int)

The number of elements output (ie passed back to Prolog)

ecout   (read/write, array)

The address of an array, which holds the output elements. The external code need never examine this address, only pass it to the appropriate interface functions

ecreturn (read/write, integer)

The value indicates either the recognised **Return** values (eg **none, fortran, unix, prolog** etc) to be returned when the function succeeds, or the fail value to indicate failure. These **ecreturn** values are listed in the "cglobdef.h" include-file

ecstatus (read/write, integer)

The value is the full 32 bit error code value which is returned when the external code function returns error information. This error code is split into two 16-bit integer values, which are then assigned to **Errcode1** and **Errcode2**. **Errcode2** holds the low word (bits 0-15), **Errcode1** the high word (bits 16-31)

23.2.4.2 The external code interface functions

The external code interface functions allow the programmer to read the Input list elements and write (and read) the Output list elements.

When reading a data item you must first determine its type (integer, real, atom, string or anonymous variable); once this is done you can call the read function appropriate to the type to obtain the value of the item (note that there is no value to be obtained for an anonymous variable, its type tells you everything).

To write a data item you simply call the write function appropriate to the type being written, together with the value to be written. All output arguments are initially set to be anonymous variables when the external code is called, so to output an anonymous variable you simply leave the output argument unchanged.

Four sorts of arguments are passed to interface functions:

(1) **direction**: the address of an argument array, either **ecin** or **ecout** according to whether input or output arguments are being referenced. Input arguments should only be read, so the interface functions which set values (e.g. **ecpatom()**) should never be

used with **ecin**, only with **ecout**. Output arguments can be written (but only once) and read (many times) so **ecout** is always a valid **direction**,

(2) **index**: an integer indicating which of the arguments (for the given direction is to be accessed. 0 indicates the first argument. **ecnmin/ecnmout** indicate the number of arguments there are, so this number minus 1 is the highest index value allowed,

(3) **pointer**: address of the external code data item which holds or is to hold values passed to and from the interface. The data items are reals, strings, integers and atoms — see §3.3 for details,

(4) **value**: an integer holding either the value of the integer to be set (**ecpinteger()**) or the length of the atom/string to be set (**ecpatom()/ecpstring()**).

The address arguments (**direction** and **pointer**) are passed by passing the item they point to by reference. The integer arguments (**index** and **value**) are passed by value in Pascal and C, by reference in Fortran (i.e. the default passing mode appropriate to the external language is used). Some interface functions return an integer value, such functions are preceded by **integer** in the descriptions that follow.

integer ectype(direction,index)

Returns an integer which specifies the data type (atom, string, real, integer or anonymous variable) of the item indicated. These types are listed in the "cglobdef.h" include-file.

ecginteger(direction,index,pointer)

Used to transfer an integer value from the indicated interface data item into the location pointed to.

ecgreal(direction,index,pointer)

Used to transfer a real number value from the indicated interface data item into the location pointed to.

ecgatom(direction,index,pointer)

Used to transfer an atom from the indicated interface data item into the location pointed to.

ecgstring(direction,index,pointer)

Used to transfer a string from the indicated interface data item into the location pointed to.

integer ecatomlength(direction,index)

Returns an integer which specifies the length of the indicated interface data item (assumed to be an atom).

integer ecstringlength(direction,index)

Returns an integer which specifies the length of the indicated interface data item (assumed to be a string).

ecpinteger(direction,index,value)

Sets the indicated interface data item to the given signed integer value.

If the data item has already been set to something other than the anonymous variable then it is not reset.

integer ecpreal(direction,index,pointer)

Sets the indicated interface data item to the value of the real number pointed to.

If the data item cannot be set (because of insufficient workspace or because it has already been set to something other than the anonymous variable) then P2IFALSE is returned; otherwise P2ITRUE is returned (these constants are defined in the include-file "cglobdef.h")

integer ecpatom(direction,index,pointer,value)

Sets the indicated interface data item to the value of the atom pointed to, the number of characters in the atom being the **value** passed.

If the data item cannot be set (because of insufficient atom table space or because it has already been set to something other than the anonymous variable) then P2IFALSE is returned; otherwise P2ITRUE is returned (these constants are defined in the include-file "cglobdef.h").

integer ecpstring(direction,index,pointer,value)

Sets the indicated interface data item to the value of the string pointed to, the number of characters in the string being the **value** passed.

If the data item cannot be set (because of insufficient workspace or because it has already been set to something other than the anonymous variable) then P2IFALSE is returned; otherwise P2ITRUE is returned (these constants are defined in the include-file "cglobdef.h").

23.2.4.3 Data Representation within external code

The external code needs to be able to store four types of data passed to and from the interface — integers, reals, atoms and strings (remember that anonymous variables are also passed but these have no value, only a type). These four data types are as follows:

(1) integer: 4-byte signed integer,

(2) real: 8-byte IEEE double precision (11 bit exponent) real in U or D-floating point format in V,

(3) atom: stored as a contiguous character array, each character being a byte. Each array should have space for one extra byte at the end of the array — which is used by the interface routines to hold a terminating null byte. The length of the array (excluding the extra byte) is stored as a 4-byte signed integer,

(4) string: as for atoms above.

23.2.4.4 Validation and error checking

It is the programmer's responsibility to check that the right routines are called for each data type; this is why **ectype()** is supplied.

If your Prolog calls to external code functions can guarantee the data type of the items passed then you will not need to check their type: but be warned that calling the wrong routine will cause unpredictable and certainly undesirable results.

Strings and atoms can potentially be very long; their maximum lengths (excluding the extra byte mentioned above) are P2LNATM and P2LNSTR, as listed in the "cglobdef.h" include-file. When getting a string or atom from the interface it is of course important that there is enough space for them to be written to, otherwise corruption will occur. Because of this we have included functions to return the lengths of these items (**ecstringlength()** and **ecatomlength()**), so that the space allocation can be checked before potentially corrupting routines are called.

23.2.5 Version-specific notes

23.2.5.1 Calling conventions and external code restrictions

(1) On entry to EXTERNAL_CODE

In V EXTERNAL_CODE should be defined as a subroutine with no arguments (i.e. it need not save any registers via the entry mask).

In U externalcode() should be defined as a procedure with no arguments and no return

The Prolog-2 User Guide

value.

(2) Execution of the external code

In V the external code must obey the VAX calling conventions at all times. Within these conventions the external code can allocate its own virtual memory by suitable calls to VMS, but it should never access absolute addresses which lie outside such areas.

You must take care that any new global names defined in the external code are not also declared within the Prolog interpreter already. The easiest way around this is to prefix all new global names with "ec".

If your external code contains subprocesses then you should avoid using the global section name "ESI$GLOBAL_SECT" and Prolog's subprocess flags.

In U the external code can allocate its own virtual memory by suitable calls to UNIX library functions, but it should never access absolute addresses which lie outside such areas.

You must take care that any new variables or functions with global scope defined in the external code are not also declared within the Prolog interpreter already. The easiest way around this is to prefix all new global names with "ec".

(3) On return from EXTERNAL_CODE

In V, first set EC_RETURN to indicate failure, success or error. For the success case make sure that all output values are set and that EC_NMOUT records the number of these values. For the error case set EC_STATUS to record the error code itself.

Finally return to Prolog by using RETURN; do not use an EXIT statement.

In U, first set **ecreturn** to indicate failure, success or error. For the success case make sure that all output values are set and that **ecnmout** records the number of these values. For the error case set **ecstatus** to record the error code itself.

Finally return to Prolog by using a 'return' statement (NOT an 'exit').

23.2.5.2 Compiling / assembling external code

In V, external source code will normally include declarations of the interface functions provided by Prolog-2 (these can be found in the include-file "mglobfns.h01"). Declarations of the interface parameters and of the constants used to interface to Prolog would also need to be included in the source file (these can be found in the include-file "mglobdef.h01").

When complete the source should be compiled/assembled to produce an object file called EXTERNAL.OBJ. To link you must have available the VAXCTRL Object Library.

First of all the files to be linked together should be specified in an options file — the file "buserm.opt" does this for your object file EXTERNAL.OBJ . Then you should link the files to produce the executable image — the file "buserm.com" will link the files named in "buserm.opt" to produce an image called "userm.exe". To do this you must of course have all the object files named in the options file available for linking.

The executable file so produced should be run just like the Prolog interpreter "prolog2.exe".

In U, external source code will normally include declarations of the interface functions provided by Prolog-2 (these can be found in the include-file "pglobfns.h"). Declarations of the interface parameters and of the constants used to interface to Prolog would also need to be included in the source file (these can be found in the include-file "pglobdef.h") and declarations of the globals ("pglobdat.h").

When complete the source should be compiled to produce an object file and should be linked with the Prolog Interpreter and the interface functions appropriate to the external language you are using to produce the executable image. The executable file so produced should be run just like the Prolog interpreter ("prolog2.exe").

The supplied makefile ("makefile") will compile and link the supplied example files. Thus executing the UNIX command **make userp** will cause "userp.p" to be compiled and linked with the Prolog-2 interpreter ("prolog2.o"), Pascal interface routines ("pfns.o") and the Special Streams Pascal stub ("ss_stubp.o") to produce the executable ("userp.exe").

See §23.3 for details of the Special Streams facility. You can also build an executable file which includes the Special Stream example code as well as the External Code example by using the command **make userssp** — see "makefile" for details.

23.2.5.3 Language differences

'C' external code in V

To conform to normal 'C' standards, character strings (ie atoms or strings) passed to interface functions should terminate with a null ('\0'). Similarly, when they are set by these functions they will have a terminating null. Atom or string lengths should never include these terminal nulls.

Pascal external code in U

All character strings (i.e. Prolog atoms or strings) passed to and from interface functions should have space for one extra byte (which must be writeable) in the character array holding the string. These interface functions will put a null byte ('\0') into the array to signify the end of string (a C convention). Atom or string lengths should never include these terminal nulls.

This is illustrated in the following example, where the atom has 4 characters and therefore the array in which it is held must be at least 5 characters long;

```
atom : packed array [1..5] of char;
```

The Prolog-2 User Guide

```
atom := 'fred';
if ecpatom( ecout, 2, atom, 4) <> P2ITRUE then
    ...
```

The **index** and **value** parameters passed to interface functions (see §23.2.4.2) are passed by value not by reference. This is the default passing mechanism for Pascal and is illustrated in the previous example as the 2nd and 4th arguments to **ecpatom()** are **index** and **value** parameters, respectively.

Fortran external code in U

All character strings (i.e. Prolog atoms or strings) passed to and from interface functions should have space for one extra byte (which must be writeable) in the character array holding the string. These interface functions will put a null byte ('\0') into the array to signify the end of string (a C convention). Atom or string lengths should never include these terminal nulls.

This is illustrated in the following example, where the atom has 4 characters and therefore the array in which it is held must be at least 5 characters long;

```
character*5 atom
atom = 'fred'
if (ecpatom( ecout, 2, atom, 4) .ne. P2ITRUE) then
    ...
```

The **index** and **value** parameters passed to interface functions (see §23.2.4.2) are passed by reference not by value. This is the default passing mechanism for Fortran and is illustrated in the previous example as the 2nd and 4th arguments to **ecpatom()** are **index** and **value** parameters respectively.

C external code in U

To conform to normal C standards, character strings (ie atoms or strings) passed to interface functions should terminate with a null ('\0'). Similarly, when they are set by these functions they will have a terminating null. Atom or string lengths should never include these terminal nulls.

The **index** and **value** parameters passed to interface functions (see Section 3.2) are passed by value not by reference. For instance **ecpatom()** uses such parameters in the 2nd and 4th arguments (respectively) so we use it like

```
if ( ecpatom( ecout, 2, "fred", 4) != P2ITRUE )
    ...
```

instead of

```
int arg2 = 2;
int arg4 = 4;
```

```
        if ( ecpatom( ecout, &arg2, "fred", &arg4) != P2ITRUE )
            ...
```

23.2.5.4 Debugging

You can use the VMS debugger to debug an external code function by compiling/assembling your source with the /DEBUG qualifier and by altering the link command file to include the /DEBUG switch on linking.

To make the debugger pause when Prolog calls your function, give the debugger command:

    SET BREAK EXTERNAL_CODE

23.3 Accessing external code via special streams (UV only)

§23.3 describes the facilities that Prolog-2 provides for interfacing to devices other than files. Some devices are provided as standard (**glass_tty** and **printer**) and you can add your own to these.

You will recall that a single integrated method is used for all I/O in Prolog-2, the streams mechanism. A stream is either a file stream or (and these are the streams we are concerned with here) a **special** stream.

23.3.1 Overview

Prolog provides some types of special stream as standard (see the entry **special** in the Prolog-2 Encyclopaedia) and gives you the ability to add others yourself. The great advantage of using special streams is that their use is integrated with Prolog I/O; thus if **printer** is made the current output stream then all calls to **write** and **put** will output to the printer.

There are some I/O bips which only work with file streams (because they are not appropriate to an arbitrary device, eg **seek/2** and **at/2**), and these simply fail if used on special streams. However most I/O bips work with both special and file streams. We list the most important of these below, see §23.3.2 for an exhaustive list of the bips which work with both special and file streams:

create_stream/4	get/1	open/2	read/1/2/3
close/1	nl/0	put/1	write/1/2/3

With some types of special stream you are allowed to create multiple streams. Some special streams, such as **printer**, cannot usefully control several devices.

23.3.2 Bips which work with special and file streams

The following I/O bips work with both special and file streams:

    create_stream/4

The Prolog-2 User Guide

close/1
close_stream/1
delete_stream/1
display/1/2
get/1
get0/1
getbyte/1
listing/1
nl/0
open/2
print/1
put/1
putbyte/1
read/1/2/3
seeing/1
seen/0
skip/1
stream/5
tab/1
telling/1
told/0
ttyflush/0
ttyget/1
ttyget0/1
ttynl/0
ttyput/1
ttyskip/1
write/1/2/3
writeq/1/2

All the formatted i/o bips work with both types of stream, e.g.

get_cbuff/1/4
get_character/1
get_token/1/2
print_context/0

The following bips work with special streams so long as the stream name that they are passed names an existing special stream. (If it doesn't then they assume that the stream name corresponds to the name of a file and they attempt to use that file stream.)

consult/1
listing/2
reconsult/1
see/1
tell/1

23.3.3 Using your own special stream

23.3.3.1 General remarks

You can create your own types of special stream in addition to the standard types described in the preceding section. You might wish to do this to use for instance a graphics package or a foreign device driver. All you have to do is to provide a small number of routines through which Prolog can access your streams and then these streams will be available via the normal stream bips.

One of the examples in §23.3.7 describes the routines needed to interface to a SunView 'canvas' window. Once these routines have been linked into the Prolog-2 interpreter you could output to a window on the screen by doing the following:

```
?- create_stream(ex,write,byte,special(canvas,30,50)),
   open(ex,write),
   state(output,Old,ex),
   write("Hello"),           /* Write into the window */
   canvas_line(ex,5,17,45,17),       /* Draw line */
   state(output,_,Old).
```

Standard stream accessing predicates such as **create_stream/4**, **open/2** and **write/1** work with your own types of special stream. They do this by using a set of routines that you supply; one routine per action to be performed (eg routine **sscreate()** for **create_stream**/4), ten such routines in all. The routines can be written in any of the languages available via the external code interface. §23.3.4 explains how these routines relate to Prolog predicates.

It is quite likely that you will wish to perform some actions on a special stream that don't sensibly come within the scope of the standard i/o predicates. The above example has an instance of this in the instruction to draw a line (**canvas_line/5**). All this extra interfacing to your special streams is done via the bip **special_stream_control/3** which uses one further routine that you supply (**sscontrol()**). §23.3.5 explains this control interface in full.

23.3.3.2 Predicate / routine interface

When devices are used for I/O there is usually some general information to be kept about the device and a 'handle' associated with the device if it is open. For example, the SunView example in §23.3.7, a window driver, needs to keep general information about the window (current writing position) and the address of the 'pixwin' associated with the open window. (A pixwin is a construct used to draw or render images in SunView.)

The special stream interface deals with this by associating two signed integers with each special stream and passing these to each special stream routine. They are passed 'by reference' so that any routine can reset as well as access their value. The routines are then free to use these integers to keep the device information. In our example one integer is used to index the element (for that stream) in an array which holds the current writing position (along with other information) and the other integer holds the

The Prolog-2 User Guide

address of the pixwin. We call these two integers the 'handles' of the special stream.

There is no restriction on the uses that you make of these handles in a routine, the Prolog interpreter does not process the handles — it only passes the same integer pair for a given stream to each called routine. In the most general case you could use them as pointers to areas of memory maintained by your routines and hold the stream information in these areas. In addition to the handles, a routine may also have parameters particular to its function (thus **ssput()** is also passed the byte value to be output).

The return value of all routines is a pointer. If the routine succeeds this should be a null pointer but on error this should point to some error text terminated with a null character (i.e. ASCII 0). When a routine reports an error to Prolog, Prolog then calls the error handler for error 1022 which uses the user-defined predicate special_stream_error/1, passing the error text. If you haven't defined this predicate then the default error handler is used.

If you are using Pascal or Fortran then it is difficult to pass back a return value which is a text pointer and which may be the null pointer. Because of this we recommend that you define the return values as integer in these languages and use the specially supplied **ssretval()** to set the return value (this function takes some null terminated error text and returns its address).

We supply a function called as **ssunixtext(status)**, which will take a UNIX error **status** (integer) and return the address of the corresponding UNIX error text (null terminated). This address can then be passed back to Prolog as the return value of a special stream routine. This error text corresponds to that which would be obtained by the Prolog goal **sys_unix_error(STATUS,TEXT)**.

We also supply a function, **ssostext()**, which returns machine specific error text, corresponding to that returned by the BIP **sys_os_error/2**. VMS and AEGIS systems may be returned in this way.

The data type of a special stream (ie either **ascii** or **byte** as defined in **create_stream/4**) is used by the Prolog-2 interpreter to mask the data read from the special stream; this masking is not seen by the special stream routines, which operate as if all streams were byte streams.

23.3.3.3 Creating special stream routines

You create a set of special stream routines which will perform the special stream functions in two stages:

(1) **Write** routines in external language (eg Pascal), producing source code

(2) **Compile** the source code to produce object code and **link** this object with Prolog-2 objects to produce a new executable Prolog interpreter that can handle your special streams.

§23.3.4-6 explain the workings of the special stream routines and their relation to Prolog in full detail. §23.3.7 takes you through a number of complete examples for varying systems.

Various constant values alluded to in this manual (they appear in capitals and are prefixed by "SS") are defined for each external language in files supplied with Prolog-2.

23.3.4 Standard I/O via the special stream

This section describes how the standard stream accessing predicates relate to the special stream routines. This description is in functional terms, §23.3.6 contains a complete formal definition of these routines.

23.3.4.1 create_stream/4

To create a special stream you must specify the type of stream it is and then any other parameters associated with that stream. Thus

> create_stream(temp,read,ascii,special(monitor))

is a goal to create a stream — called **temp** — which is a **monitor** special stream, and (in an example of section §23.3.7)

> create_stream(example,write,byte,special(canvas,30,40))

is a goal to create a stream — called **example** — which is a **canvas** special stream with width 30 and height 40.

The routine called by these goals is **sscreate()**.

In addition to the handles passed to **sscreate()** there are four more parameters passed which are used to access the input arguments of functor **special** in the **create_stream** goal. This access is done using the external code access functions documented in §23.2.4.2.

For instance the goal

> create_stream(temp,read,ascii,special(monitor))

generates a call **sscreate(handle1,handle2,ssin,ssnmin,ssinl,ssinu)** where **ssnmin** is the extra parameter representing the number of arguments for **special** (in this case 1) and **ssin** is the extra parameter used to examine this input argument by means of the external code functions. So **ectype(ssin,0)** is **P2TATOM** (indicating that the first input argument is an atom), **ecatomlength(ssin,0)** is 7 (the length of **monitor**) and **ecgatom(ssin,0,buffer)** will place this atom name into **buffer**.

There are two forms of call to some of the routines. The first form passes an array as an argument and also the length of the array. Unfortunately this format is not suitable

The Prolog-2 User Guide

for use with versions of Pascal that implement the rules about conformant arrays strictly, and so a second form passes the array with its bounds. In the calls below both forms are given where they differ. Currently form 1 is used on V and A, form 2 on S. In form 2 the bounds of array **ssin** are given by the integers **ssinl** (lower bound) and **ssinu**. These are fixed bounds — only **ssnmin** indicates how many array elements were set for any particular call.

Passing further input arguments is often very useful (providing set-up data for the stream being created). The goal

    create_stream(example,write,byte,special(canvas,30,40))

generates a call **sscreate(handle1,handle2,ssin,ssnmin,ssinl,ssinu)** where **ssnmin** is 3 (indicating that there are three input arguments) and one can access the second argument as follows: **ectype(ssin,1)** is **P2TINTEGER** (indicating that the second input argument is an integer) and **ecginteger(ssin,0,pinteger)** will place the value 30 into the integer pointed at by **pinteger** (similar remarks apply for the third argument).

Note that **stream/5** only reports the type of special stream in its fourth argument, not the extra parameters that you supplied, thus:

    stream(example,write,byte,special(canvas),_)

23.3.4.2 open/2

To open a special stream you simply name the stream and the mode of access wanted (just like file streams). Thus

    open(example,write)

is a goal to open stream **example** for output.

The routine called by this goal is **ssopen()**.

In addition to the handles passed to **ssopen()** there is one more parameter passed which is a constant which indicates the access mode requested (SSWRITE in this case).

Prolog-2 will not call **ssopen()** for an access mode that is incompatible with the mode declared when the stream was created, nor will it call **ssopen()** if the stream is already open. Errors of this nature are trapped within the Prolog interpreter and handled by the default error handler just like non-special streams.

23.3.4.3 put/1

If the special stream is the current output stream then a goal like **put(100)** will generate a call to the routine **ssput()**.

In addition to the handles passed to **ssput()** there is one more parameter which is an integer holding the byte value to be output.

Prolog-2 implements nl/0 as **ssput()** of SSNL (representing 'new line'). Your stream may need to output this as carriage return plus line feed depending upon its characteristics.

23.3.4.4   write/1/2/3

If the special stream is the current output stream then a goal like **write(foo)** will cause a call to the routines **sswbuffer()** and/or **sswbyte()** followed by one call to **sswflush()**.

In addition to the handles passed to **sswbuffer()** there are extra parameters passed which specify a character array holding the data to be output. Similarily **sswbyte()** is passed two extra parameters; an integer holding the byte value to be output and an integer stipulating the number of times this is to be output.

When complicated output is to be written by the Prolog interpreter it does this by outputting the term piece by piece. Some of these pieces that consist of one repeated character may be output by calls to **sswbyte()**, all other output will use **sswbuffer()**.

The output of **write/1/2/3** can be buffered — by buffering the output of **sswbuffer()** and **sswbyte()** — for greater efficiency. To ensure that all output is sent by the end of **write** the Prolog Interpreter calls **sswflush()** (passing just the two handles) at the end of each **write**. If you are buffering the output of **write** then you should flush your output buffers in **sswflush()**.

When any error is detected by Prolog a call to **sswflush()** will be made to flush any pending output, but to avoid obscuring the original error condition, any error reported by such calls to **sswflush()** will be ignored. Note also that Prolog will always call **sswflush()** before any **ssput()/ssprompt()** call once **write** has commenced — because of this you need never bother to check that your output buffers are empty before performing the unbuffered **ssput()/ssprompt()**, the intervening call to **sswflush()** will guarantee that this is so. In some circumstances **sswflush()** may be called without a preceding **sswbuffer()** or **sswbyte()** call (for instance the goal **write("")**, or when an error occurs at the start of **write**).

Thus a goal like

   write(foo(23))

might use the call sequence

    sswbuffer(handle1,handle2,"foo",0,2)
    sswbyte(handle1,handle2,'(',1)
    sswbuffer(handle1,handle2,"23",0,1)
    sswbyte(handle1,handle2,')',1)
    sswflush(handle1,handle2)

The Prolog-2 User Guide

Whereas the goal

    write(1.26,[],r(5,1))

might use

    sswbyte(handle1,handle2,' ',2)
    sswbuffer(handle1,handle2,"1.3",0,2)
    sswflush(handle1,handle2)

Any control characters embedded in a term to be output (e.g. **write("foo\n")**) are just passed as they are to the routines (i.e. no interpretation is put upon them). So **"foo\n"** when output by your **sswbuffer()/sswbyte()** might for instance be "foo" and line feed only. If you wanted "foo" followed by carriage return line feed then you could change your Prolog code to be **write("foo\r\n")**, alternatively you can search any buffer given to **sswbuffer()/sswbyte()** for occurrences of '\n' and translate these to '\r\n'. As a general point, embedding control characters in strings is not recommended practice as it is rarely portable.

23.3.4.5 get/1 get0/1 getbyte/1 read/1/2/3

If the special stream is the current input stream then a goal like **get(X)** will cause a call to the routine **ssget()**.

The masking/selection of data that distinguishes the functionality of **get/1**, **get0/1** and **getbyte/1** are handled by the Prolog interpreter — all **ssget()** need do is to return the next byte read. The interpreter handles a **read/1/2/3** goal by making repeated calls to **ssget()** (note that **ssget()** is expected to perform any buffering that is needed for efficiency).

In addition to the handles passed to **ssget()** there is one more parameter passed which is the address of an integer which is to receive the input byte.

When reading from a special stream (via **read/1/2/3**) Prolog makes the special call **ssprompt()** whenever the read prompt should be output on that stream. This happens when Prolog has detected the end of a previous 'record' and so needs to prompt for a new 'record'. The **ssprompt** call is only made if the stream is the current output stream as well as being the current input stream and if the read prompt is not '$null'.

In addition to the handles passed to **ssprompt()** there are extra parameters passed which specify a character array holding the read prompt. This read prompt is defined by the system state **read_prompt**. Depending on the characteristics of your stream you may choose to output the prompt, to output another form of prompt or to output nothing at all.

The formatted input facility of Prolog-2 treats input as if it is composed of 'records'. This is significant in three places:

(1) A read prompt is output before a new record is read,

(2) In analysing a syntax error the context for that error is considered as extending up to the end of the last record read so far in parsing,

(3) Input is guzzled (i.e. thrown away) up to the end of the current record at various places in the Prolog-2 environment (e.g. when getting the response to the 'More (y/n)' prompt and when recovering from a syntax error).

So we recommend that **ssget()** should set the byte value to be SSRETURN when a record terminator is read (or when the RETURN key is read from the keyboard) and to be SSEOF when EOF is read.

23.3.4.6   close/1 close_stream/1

To close a special stream you simply name the stream and use **close/1** or **close_stream/1**, thus

    close(example)

is a goal to close stream **example**.

The routine called by this goal is **ssclose()**.

Prolog-2 will not call **ssclose()** unless the stream is already open.

23.3.4.7 delete_stream/1

To delete a special stream you simply name the stream and use **delete_stream/1**, e.g. **delete_stream(example)**.

The routine called by this goal is **ssdelete()**.

Prolog-2 will not call **ssdelete()** unless the stream exists (i.e. has been created with a **create_stream/4** goal) and is closed.

23.3.5 General access to special streams (special_stream_control/3)

The standard I/O predicates that affect special streams only cover the essential operations that you might wish to do with any type of stream (creating, opening, reading, writing, closing and deleting). You may well wish to perform other operations on your special streams, operations that don't fall with the standard i/o predicates. The bip **special_stream_control/3** is provided for this purpose; it gives a completely general interface to your special streams.

The Prolog-2 User Guide

The BIP **special_stream_control/3** calls routine **sscontrol()**, passing the stream handles and any input values and the routine can pass back output values on successful completion. The passing of all values is performed by means of the external code access functions. The full bip definition is:

    special_stream_control(Stream,Input,Output)

Stream is an atom naming the special stream to be accessed. The reserved name **none** should be given if no special stream in particular is intended (in which case the handles passed to **sscontrol()** will be **SSNULL**).

Input is a list of input values which are used in **sscontrol()** to determine the control action to be performed (note that these values are read only).

Output is a list of values which are output by **sscontrol()** (this list is only matched if **sscontrol()** succeeds). These values are used to return data obtained by the control action back to Prolog.

To use the first example in section 8, the goal

    special_stream_control(example,[3,10,20],[])

is a goal which sets the current writing position in the window associated with stream **example** to be at pixel (10,20) whilst

    special_stream_control(example,[2],[X,Y])

is a goal which instantiates X and Y to be the pixel coordinates of the current writing position of this window.

The first two parameters passed to **sscontrol()** are the handles and the remaining eight parameters are used to access the **Input** values and set the **Output** values (all of which is done by means of the external code access functions).
For instance the goal

    special_stream_control(example,[2],[X,Y])

calls **sscontrol(handle1, handle2, ssin, ssnmin, ssout, ssnmout)** (type 1) or **sscontrol(handle1, handle2, ssin, ssnmin, ssout, ssnmout, ssinl, ssinu, ssoutl, ssoutu)** (type 2) where **ssnmin** is 1 (indicating that there is one input argument) and **ssin** is the 'direction' parameter used to examine this input argument. So **ectype(ssin,0)** is P2TINTEGER (indicating that the first input argument is an integer) and **ecginteger(ssin,0,pinteger)** will place the value 3 into the integer pointed at by **pinteger**.

Calling **ecpinteger(ssout,0,17)** sets X (the first argument) to 17 and **ecpinteger(ssout,1,45)** sets Y to 45. Then just set the value of **ssnmout** to 2 to indicate that there are two output arguments (**ssnmout** is passed by reference so that

218

its value can be set inside **sscontrol()**).

ssnmout is set to 0 before **sscontrol()** is called, so if there are no output arguments then there is no need to set **ssnmout** to 0 to indicate this.

In type 2 calls the bounds of array **ssin/ssout** are given by the integers **ssinl/ssoutl** (lower bound) and **ssinu/ssoutu** respectively. These are fixed bounds — only **ssnmin** indicates how many array elements were set in **ssin** for any particular call and only **ssnmout** records how many were output.

The formal definition of **sscontrol()** is in the next section.

23.3.6 Calling definitions and building in special streams

This section contains the calling definitions (in alphabetical order) of the routines which perform special stream I/O, it does not describe the circumstances and purpose for which these routines are called — these are in §23.3.4-5.

All arguments are typed as signed 4-byte integers or as arrays.

Some integers must be passed by reference (i.e. the address of the integer is passed) so that you can change the value of the parameter from within the called routine; **variable-integers**. All other integers are passed as read-only values to the routine (i.e. the actual integer value is passed directly); **read-integers**.

Arrays are character arrays or integer arrays, they are always passed by reference (i.e. the address of the start of the array is passed) to conserve space and their lower and upper bounds are passed as **read-integers** (these are always inclusive bounds).

If you are using Fortran then as Fortran passes all arguments by reference we have to treat all **read-integers** as **variable-integers**.

All routines return a pointer, which should be SSNULL (i.e. the null pointer) to indicate success and otherwise should be the address of some error text terminated with a null character (i.e. ASCII 0).

If you are using Pascal or Fortran then you should define the return values to be integer and indicate success by setting this to SSNULL. Indicate an error by calling **ssretval()**, passing it the null terminated error text, and using its return value.

The first two parameters to all routines are the handles; see §23.3.3.2 for a description of these. They are **variable-integers** and are called **handle1** and **handle2** in the definitions that follow.

ssclose(handle1, handle2)

Has no parameters other than the handles.

The Prolog-2 User Guide

sscontrol(handle1, handle2, ssin, ssnmin, ssout, ssnmout) (type 1)
sscontrol(handle1, handle2, ssin, ssnmin, ssout, ssnmout, ssinl,ssinu, ssoutl, ssoutu) (type 2)

ssin — The 'direction' parameter which is used to access the **special_stream_control/3** input arguments by means of the standard external code access functions. Passed as an array of integers, with bounds **ssinl** and **ssinu**.

ssnmin — The number of input arguments used in this call (**read- integer**).

ssout — The 'direction' parameter which is used to set the **special_stream_control/3** output arguments by means of the standard external code access functions. Passed as an array of integers, with bounds **ssoutl** and **ssoutu**.

ssnmout — The number of output arguments, set by this routine (**variable-integer**).

sscreate(handle1, handle2, ssin, ssnmin) (type 1)
sscreate(handle1, handle2, ssin, ssnmin, ssinl, ssinu) (type 2)

ssin — The 'direction' parameter which used to access the **create_stream/4** input arguments by means of the standard external code access functions. Passed as an array of integers, with bounds **ssinl** and **ssinu**.

ssnmin — The number of input arguments used in this call (**read-integer**).

ssdelete(handle1, handle2)

Has no parameters other than the handles.

ssget(handle1, handle2, byte)

byte — The integer which is to be set by this routine to the value of the byte read from the stream (**variable-integer**).

ssopen(handle1, handle2, mode)

mode — Indicates to this routine the sort of access required to this stream; it is one of the constants SSREADWRITE, SSWRITE or SSREAD (**read-integer**).

ssprompt(handle1, handle2, string, length) (type 1)
ssprompt(handle1, handle2, string, stringl, stringu) (type 2)

string — The address of a character array which constitutes the prompt. Its length is **length**, or its bounds are **stringl** and **stringu**.

ssput(handle1, handle2, byte)

byte — The ASCII character code to be output (**read-integer**).

sswbuffer(handle1, handle2, string, length) (type 1)
sswbuffer(handle1, handle2, string, stringl, stringu) (type 2)

string — The address of a character array which constitutes the data to be output. Its length is **length**, or its bounds are **stringl** and **stringu**. The array is always at least one character long.

sswbyte(handle1, handle2, byte, number)

byte — The ASCII character code to be output (**read-integer**). The number of times this character should be output for this call of the routine is indicated by **number**.

number — The number of times that the **byte** character should be output (**read-integer**), which is always greater than zero.

sswflush(handle1, handle2)

Has no parameters other than the handles.

23.3.6.1 Utility functions

There are three utility functions available to the special stream routines defined above. They all return values which can be used as the return values of the special stream routines, indeed that is their purpose.

ssunixtext(errno)

Returns the address of the error text associated with the UNIX error number **errno** (**read-integer**). This text is identical with that returned by the Prolog BIP **sys_unix_error/2**.

ssostext(status)

Returns the address of the error text associated with the system error number **status** (**read-integer**). This text is identical with that returned by the Prolog BIP **sys_os_error/2**.

ssretval(text)

Returns the address of the passed error message passed in the character array **text**. This array should be passed by reference (i.e. by address of the start of the array) and must be null terminated. Constant strings (e.g. 'ab' in Pascal or Fortran and "ab" in C) are always in this form. This routine is not provided for the C interface because it is simplest to pass the **text** itself as the return value directly.

23.3.6.2 Building your special streams into Prolog-2

Special stream source code will normally include declarations of the special stream constants and utility functions provided by Prolog-2 (these can be found in the include-file "?ssdef.h"). Some declarations used in the external code interface will be needed as well (these are found in "?globdef.h" and "?globfns.h").

When complete the special stream source should be compiled to produce an object file. This object should be linked with the Prolog-2 Interpreter (object file "prolog.o"), any external code object and the supplied external code / utility functions ("?fns.o") to produce a new executable image. The executable file so produced should be run just like the Prolog-2 interpreter ("prolog2.exe").

In U the supplied makefile ("makefile") will compile and link the supplied example files. Thus executing the UNIX command **make ssexap** will cause the Pascal version of the SunCore example to be made (using source "ssexap.p", supplied files "pssdef.h" "pglobdef.h" "pglobfns.h", interpreter "prolog2.o", functions file "pfns.o" and external code stub "ec_stubp.o" to produce "ssexap.exe"). In V a linker options file is provided instead.

You can also build an executable file which includes the external code example code as well as a Special Stream example, for instance by using the command **make userssp** — see "makefile" for details. If you do use both Special Streams and External Code facilities then these must both be in the same external language.

If you examine the linker details provided you will see that when the example special streams are linked a file called EC_STUB is included; this resolves references that would normally be filled by user external code. Similarly, linking the external code example you will find a file SS_STUB provided to fill special stream stubs. If you are using both external code and special streams then you should omit both stubs.

23.3.7 Examples

23.3.7.1 Examples for S

This section takes you through two complete examples, the first uses a SunView 'canvas' window and the second uses SunCore graphics. Source files for these examples are supplied with Prolog-2. As Pascal and Fortran are not explicitly supported by SunView the first example is only given in C. The second example is given in all three languages.

Each example is written to be self-contained so you will find that there is some duplication of material between the two.

23.3.7.1.1 SunView canvas window example

This example gives simple 'canvas' window output using SunView functions. For details of these functions see the SunView Programmer's Guide. The first step is to create a source file which contains the special stream routines — the source file for this example is supplied with Prolog-2 and is called "ssexavc.c".

23.3.7.1.1.1 Remarks on the example source

We decided that to create a 'canvas' stream the user must use a structure of the form **special(canvas,WIDTH,HEIGHT)** as the fourth argument to **create_stream/4**, where **WIDTH** is the number of canvas window columns and **HEIGHT** is the number of columns.

We keep track of the 'current writing position', by which we mean the pixel position where the next piece of text (e.g. by **write(foo)**) will output. We buffer output internally and only output it when a **sswflush()** call is made. This buffering strategy is simplistic in its handling of overflow, reporting an error, but could easily be made more sophisticated. (For contrast the example in §23.3.7.1.2 uses unbuffered output.)

In our example we use the first special stream handle to hold the address of the Pixwin structure that is obtained whenever the special stream is opened (using the **canvas_pixwin()** function). We keep one static array with an element for each special stream that could be created, the second handle is used to index into this array.

A call to **sscreate()** will assign an unused array element to that new stream and the second handle will be set to indicate that array element at that point. (When **ssdelete()** is called that array element will be re-marked as unused).

Each array element is a structure with nine entries:

(1) a flag to say if the element is in use,

(2) the WIDTH of the canvas window as specified to **create_stream/4**,

(3) the HEIGHT of the canvas window as specified to **create_stream/4**,

(4) the X pixel co-ordinate of the current writing position,

(5) the Y pixel co-ordinate of the current writing position,

(6) the next free character in the internal output buffer,

(7) the internal buffer itself,

(8) the Canvas details returned by SunView function window_create() when the canvas window is created,

(9) the Frame details returned by SunView function window_create() when the frame which will hold the canvas window is created.

Having a static array hold stream details does limit the total number of special streams that can exist at any one time, but has the advantage that we don't have to allocate space each time **sscreate()** is called.

The **sswbuffer()** and **sswbyte()** routines simply insert characters into the stream's internal buffer, it is up to **sswflush()** to write these out (using SunView function pw_text()) and reset the buffer to empty.

ssput() first calls **sswflush()** to output anything in the internal buffer before proceeding to output its given character. It deals with SSNL by repositioning the current writing position, no character is output to do this.

There are four control operations in the example source, **sscontrol()** differentiates between them by examining the first input argument (which is an integer which we therefore expect to be in the range 0 to 3).

The initialisation operation is of particular note, this finds the size of the characters in the default font and stores these dimensions in a pair of static variables ready for subsequent calls to SunView functions. Because this is a general initialisation operation, independent of any particular special stream (indeed it should be called before any special stream is created at all) it is called from Prolog with the stream name **none** and no attempt is made to use the handles (which will be passed by null pointers anyway) for this particular control operation. We also take the opportunity here to initialise all elements of the stream array to 'unused'.

There are two different programming styles, known as 'mainline' and 'event-driven', see the SUN leaflet "The Hacker's Corner" (December 1987) for an explanation of the distinction. Prolog-2 is essentially 'mainline' in style, performing cpu intensive jobs (i.e. inferencing) with occasional recourse to asking the user for input! Because of this we perform implicit dispatching using the SunView functions notify_dispatch() and notify_do_dispatch() in **ssopen()**. See the SUN leaflet for a full explanation of this and the other options available.

23.3.7.1.1.2 Using the example

Having created the source file "ssexavc.c" we then compile it into the object file "ssexavc.o" and link it into a new Prolog-2 interpreter (called "ssexav.exe") by the UNIX command

    make ssexavc

which uses the supplied "makefile". This executable file should be run from within suntools (as it expects to find the suntools environment already loaded) just like the standard interpreter "prolog2.exe".

You will find it useful to define the separate control functions as separate predicates. In our example we add the following Prolog rules (from "ssexav.pro"):

```
canvas_initialisation :-
    special_stream_control(none,[0],[]).

canvas_line(Stream,X1,Y1,X2,Y2) :-
    special_stream_control(Stream,[1,X1,Y1,X2,Y2],[]).

canvas_at(Stream,X,Y) :-
    special_stream_control(Stream,[2],[X,Y]).

canvas_seek(Stream,X,Y) :-
    special_stream_control(Stream,[3,X,Y],[]).
```

Some higher level abstraction may be useful as well, for instance defining a predicate which writes a single pixel in terms of the line writing predicate.

```
canvas_point(Stream,X,Y) :-
    canvas_line(Stream,X,Y,X,Y).
```

We have put these rules and more besides in "ssexav.pro" so that with this file consulted into your adapted Prolog-2 interpreter ("ssexavc.exe") you can perform the following sequence of goals:

```
/* Initialise window driver */
?- canvas_initialisation.

/* Create an output window with 30 rows and 50 columns */
?- create_stream(example,write,byte,special(canvas,30,50)).

/* Open the window */
?- open(example,write).

/* Write a simple piece of text and underline it */
?- state(output,Old,example),
   write("Hello"),          /* Write into the window */
   canvas_line(example,5,17,45,17),   /* Draw line */
   state(output,_,Old).

/* Move the current position to pixel (200,200) */
?- canvas_seek(example,200,200).
```

The Prolog-2 User Guide

```
/* Draw cross and fill it with "Prolog-2" */
?- demo_cross(example,"Prolog-2").
```

23.3.7.1.2 SunCore graphics example

This example gives simple 2D gfxtool window output using SunCore functions. For details of these functions see the SunCore Reference Manual. This example is supplied in C, Fortran and Pascal source form; the next two subsections will explain the example with particular reference to C and §23.3.7.1.2.3 details the differences for Fortran and Pascal.

The first step is to create a source file which contains the special stream routines — the source file for this example is supplied with Prolog-2 and is called "ssexac.c".

23.3.7.1.2.1 Remarks on the example source

We decided that to create a 'core' stream the user must use a structure of the form **special(core,Xlower,Xupper,Ylower,Yupper)** as the fourth argument to **create_stream/4**, where **Xlower/Xupper** are the X co-ordinate bounds and **Ylower/Yupper** are the Y bounds of the graphics window in which the output will be displayed.

In our example we use the first special stream handle to hold the address of the view surface structure that is obtained whenever the special stream is opened (using the **get_view_surface()** function). We keep one static array with an element for each special stream that could be created, the second handle is used to index into this array.

A call to **sscreate()** will assign an unused array element to that new stream and the second handle will be set to indicate that array element at that point. (When **ssdelete()** is called that array element will be re-marked as unused).

Each array element is a structure with six entries :

(1) a flag to say if the element is in use,

(2) the **Xlower** bound of the graphics window as specified to **create_stream/4**,

(3) the **Xupper** bound of the graphics window as specified to **create_stream/4**,

(4) the **Ylower** bound of the graphics window as specified to **create_stream/4**,

(5) the **Yupper** bound of the graphics window as specified to **create_stream/4**,

(6) the view surface details returned by SunCore function get_view_surface() when the stream is opened.

Having a static array hold stream details does limit the total number of special streams that can exist at any one time, but has the advantage that we don't have to allocate space each time **sscreate**() is called. In this example the number of streams is limited anyway by the SunCore implementation and so we've used this limit (constant MAXVSURF) explicitly.

The **sswput**(), **sswbuffer**() and **sswbyte**() routines are implemented in terms of the SunCore function text(), but must also move the writing position on as they do so. Notice how **sswbyte**() iterates for the number of times the given character is to be output and how **ssput**() deals with SSNL simply by repositioning the writing position. All output is done directly so **sswflush**() has no use in this example. (For contrast the example in §23.3.7.1.1 buffers its output.)

Technical note: We use temporary segments for all our output, which means that the images we create cannot be translated or redisplayed in any way. Using retained segments would provide a more sophisticated stream facility.

There are seven control operations in the example source, **sscontrol**() differentiates between them by examining the first input argument (which is an integer which we therefore expect to be in the range 0 to 6).

The initialisation operation (operation 0) is of particular note, this performs some general SunCore initialisation and initialises all elements of the stream array to 'unused'. Because this is a general initialisation operation, independent of any particular special stream (indeed it should be called before any special stream is created at all) it is called from Prolog with the stream name **none** and no attempt is made to use the handles (which will be passed by null pointers anyway) for this particular control operation.

23.3.7.1.2.2 Using the example

Having created the source file "ssexac.c" we then compile it into the object file "ssexac.o" and link it into a new Prolog-2 interpreter (called "ssexa.exe") by the UNIX command

    make ssexac

which uses the supplied "makefile". This executable file should be run from within a gfxtool window from within suntools (as it expects to find the gfxtool environment already loaded) just like the standard interpreter "prolog2.exe".

You will find it useful to define the separate control functions as separate predicates. In our example we add the following Prolog rules (from "ssexa.pro"):

```
core_initialisation :-
    special_stream_control(none,[0],[]).

core_polyline(Stream,LIST) :-
    special_stream_control(Stream,[2 | LIST],[]).
```

227

The Prolog-2 User Guide

```
core_at(X,Y) :-
    special_stream_control(none,[3],[X,Y]).

core_seek(X,Y) :-
    special_stream_control(none,[4,X,Y],[]).
```

Some higher level abstraction may be useful as well, for instance defining a predicate which moves the write position relative to its current position (instead of the absolute move that core_seek/2 does).

```
core_move(X,Y) :-
    core_at(OldX,OldY),
    NewX is OldX + X,
    NewY is OldY + Y,
    core_seek(NewX,NewY).
```

We have put these rules and more besides in "ssexa.pro" so that with this file consulted into your adapted Prolog-2 interpreter ("ssexac.exe") you can perform the following sequence of goals:

```
/* Initialise window driver */
?- core_initialisation.

/* Create an output window with 100 by 100 co-ord range */
?- create_stream(example,write,byte,
    special(core, 0.0, 100.0, 0.0, 100.0)).

/* Open the window */
?- open(example,write).

/* Move the current position to (40,55) */
?- core_seek(40.0,55.0).

/* Draw "Prolog-2" in different sizes and directions */
?- demo_text(example).

/* Move current position up by 5 */
?- core_move(0.0,5.0).

/* Draw a martini glass */
?- demo_glass(example).
```

23.3.7.1.2.3 C, Pascal and Fortran example differences

The Fortran SunCore library expects 64 bit real numbers, so no conversion from the Prolog-2 real type is needed. The Pascal (and C) libraries expect 32-bit reals and so must perform conversion. The Fortran example also uses a second source file, "ssexaf.h", as this is the most convenient way of repeating definitions within a function subprogram ("ssexaf.f").

The Pascal SunCore library has a bug in inqcurrpos2(), so we use inqcurrpos3() instead, and variable '_argv' is unresolved, so we define this (and set it to zero) in "pfns.o". We also found it easiest to compare the atom value obtained in **sscreate**() (which is in C string form) with a Pascal constant string ('core') by using the C library function strncmp().

In the C version we used the first handle to point to the view surface structure, in the other versions we don't use the first handle at all but instead just access the structure as part of the stream array.

The Fortran and Pascal examples use **ssretval**() as explained in §23.3.6.1.

23.3.7.2 VMS Example

This section takes you through a complete example, in this case a simple window driver which uses Screen Management Guidelines (SMG) functions. For details of these functions see the VAX/VMS Run-time Library Manual (April 1986 version, Volume 8C, Part II, pages RTL-538 to RTL-759). The first step is to create a source file which contains the nine special stream routines — the source file for this example is supplied with Prolog-2 and is called "ssexac.c01".

23.3.7.2.1 Remarks on the example source

In our example we decided to use the first handle to hold the virtual display identifier that is obtained whenever the special stream is opened (using the **smg_create_virtual_display**() function). We keep one static array with an element for each special stream that could be created, each element is a structure with two entries — a flag to say if the element is in use and an integer to store the video attributes associated with that particular stream. The second handle is used to index into this array. A call to **ss_create**() will assign an unused array element to that new stream and the second handle will be set to indicate that array element at that point. (When **ss_delete**() is called that array element will be re-marked as unused.)

Having a static array hold stream details does limit the total number of special streams that can exist at any one time, but has the advantage that we don't have to allocate space each time **ss_create**() is called. It is quite likely that any useful window driver would keep more information other than just the video attributes in each array element, eg the position of the virtual display on the screen.

The **ss_put**(), **ss_wbuffer**() and **ss_wbyte**() routines are implemented in terms of smg$put_chars(); notice how **ss_wbyte**() iterates for the number of times the given character is to be output and how **ss_put**() translates SS_NL into carriage return plus line feed. All output is done directly so **ss_wflush**() has no use in this example.

There are four control operations in the example source, **ss_control**() differentiates between them by examining the first input argument (which is an integer in the range

The Prolog-2 User Guide

0 to 3).

The initialisation operation is of particular note, this creates a pasteboard for the subsequent calls to SMG functions (the identifier for this pasteboard is stored in **pbid**). Because this is a general initialisation operation, independent of any particular special stream (indeed it should be called before any special stream is created at all) it is called from Prolog with the stream name **none** and no attempt is made to use the handles (which will be SS_NULL anyway) for this particular control operation.

After every VMS function call we execute **ss_check(status)** where **status** is the return value of the function call. **ss_check** is defined by means of a macro and it checks to see if the success bit of this return value is set, and if it is not then it calls **ss_error_text()** to return the error text associated with this value and returns this as the special stream return value (ie reports an error with this as the text).

23.3.7.2.2 Compiling and linking the example

Having created the source file "ssexac.c01" we then compile it into the object file "ssexac.obj" by the DCL command:

    cc ssexac.c01 /nodebug

Then link this object with the other Prolog-2 objects to produce a new Prolog-2 interpreter which supports these special stream routines. To do this we use the supplied command file "ssexac.com" which references the options file "ssexac.opt", using the command:

    @ssexac

23.3.7.2.3 Using the example

The executable file ("ssexac.exe") produced by the previous subsection should be run just like the standard interpreter "prolog2.exe".

You will find it useful to define the separate control functions as separate predicates. In our example we add the following Prolog rules ("ssexa.p01"):

```
ssexa_initialisation :-
    special_stream_control(none,[0],[]).

ssexa_show_at_row(Stream,Row) :-
    special_stream_control(Stream,[1,Row],[]).

ssexa_hide(Stream) :-
    special_stream_control(Stream,[2],[]).

ssexa_read_from_display(Stream,Message) :-
    special_stream_control(Stream,[3],[Message]).
```

Some higher level abstraction may be useful as well, for instance defining a 'show' predicate which defaults to showing the window in the middle of the screen.

>   ssexa_show(Stream) :-
>   ssexa_show_at_row(Stream,12).

With the adapted Prolog interpreter ("ssexac.exe") and the preceding Prolog rules ("ssexa.p01") you can perform the following sequence of goals:

>   /* Initialise window driver */
>   ?- ssexa_initialise.
>
>   /* Create an output window with blink attribute (4) */
>   ?- create_stream(example,write,byte,special(ssexa,4)).
>
>   /* Open the window */
>   ?- open(example,write).
>
>   /* Write a message to it */
>   ?- state(output,Old,example),
>   write("Hello"),
>   state(output,_,Old).
>
>   /* Show the window, and hide it when the user hits any key */
>   ?- ssexa_show(example),
>   get0(_),
>   ssexa_hide(example).
>
>   /* Read what was in the window */
>   ?- ssexa_read_from_display(example,Message).

23.3.7.3 Example for A

This section takes you through a complete example based on the DOMAIN 2D GMR facilities, for details of these facilities see see the DOMAIN manuals "Programming With DOMAIN 2d Graphics Metafile Resource" and "DOMAIN 2D Graphics Metafile Resource Call Reference". This example is supplied in C, Fortran and Pascal source form; the next two subsections will explain the example with particular reference to C and §23.3.7.3.3 details the differences for Fortran and Pascal.

The first step is to create a source file which contains the special stream routines — the source file for this example is supplied with Prolog-2 and is called "ssexac.c".

23.3.7.3.1 Remarks on the example source

In this example each 'gmr' special stream corresponds to one viewport on a shared pad. The example only covers output, so we use a transcript pad and furthermore it only uses one GMR segment per viewport (instead of a hierarchy of segments).

The Prolog-2 User Guide

For simplicity we decided that each viewport would extend for the full width of the pad but would share the available height, so when creating the stream one only needs to specify **special(gmr)**. A more sophisticated example would allow you to specify the shape of the viewport in this pad at the time the stream is created, in which case the stream creation call would specify (as the fourth argument to **create_stream/4**) say, **special(gmr,Width,Height)**.

In our example we keep one static array with an element for each special stream that could be created, the second handle is used to index into this array. The first handle is unused.

A call to **sscreate()** will assign an unused array element to that new stream and the second handle will be set to indicate that array element at that point. (When **ssdelete()** is called that array element will be re-marked as unused).

Each array element is a structure with four entries :

(1) a flag to say if the element is in use,

(2) the viewport id of this stream,

(3) the segment associated with this viewport,

(4) the current output position within this segment.

Technical note: Having a static array hold stream details does limit the total number of special streams that can exist at any one time, but has the advantage that we don't have to allocate space each time **sscreate()** is called. In our example we limit the number of streams to NUMSTR.

We keep track of the 'current writing position' in the (single) segment associated with the stream's viewport. We buffer output internally and output it when a **sswflush()** call is made. As the GMR text output routine we use, GM_$TEXT_2D16(), is limited in the length of string that it will output we have limited our internal buffer to this size and have to output the buffer before a **sswflush()** call if it is about to overflow.

The **sswbuffer()** and **sswbyte()** routines copy the text into the internal buffer (with the overflow checking mentioned above). When they or **sswflush()** write out the buffer we also update the current writing position. Notice how **sswbyte()** iterates for the number of times the given character is to be output.

ssput() writes the character it is given directly and deals with SSNL simply by repositioning the writing position.

As only one GMR segment can be open at any one time, this must be the segment associated with the current output stream (so long as this is a special stream). We decided to call this special stream the 'selected stream', and if the current output stream is not a special stream then we have no selected stream. The routines

ssoutbegin() and **ssoutend()** deal with this stream selection.

There are four control operations in the example source, **sscontrol()** differentiates between them by examining the first input argument (which is an integer which we therefore expect to be in the range 0 to 3).

The initialisation operation (operation 3) is of particular note, this creates the pad (with given name), performs GMR initialisation and initialises all elements of the stream array to 'unused'. Because this is a general initialisation operation, independent of any particular special stream (indeed it should be called before any special gmr stream is created at all) it is called from Prolog with the stream name **none** and no attempt is made to use the handles (which will be passed by null pointers anyway) for this particular control operation.

Technical note: A first viewport is automatically created when GMR is initialised, before any stream is created, which forces us to complicate the example. We call this viewport the 'protected stream', allocate it to first special stream that gets opened and do not allow it to be closed. Note also that the supplied font family file, "ssexa.ff", uses /sys/dm/fonts/f7x13.b .

GMR errors are handled by passing the DOMAIN error status they return to **ssostext()** and using this as the return value.

23.3.7.3.2 Using the example

Having created the source file "ssexac.c" we then compile it into the object file "ssexac.o" and link it into a new Prolog-2 interpreter (called "ssexa.exe") by the UNIX command

    make ssexac

which uses the supplied "makefile". This executable file should be run just like the standard interpreter "prolog2.exe".

You will find it useful to define the separate control functions as separate predicates. In our example we add the following Prolog rules (from "ssexa.pro"):

```
gmr_at(Stream,X,Y) :-
    special_stream_control(Stream,[0],[X,Y]).

gmr_seek(Stream,X,Y) :-
    special_stream_control(Stream,[1,X,Y],[]).

gmr_polyline_curve(Stream,List,Flag) :-
    special_stream_control(Stream,[2,Flag|List],[]).

gmr_initialisation(Pad_Name) :-
    special_stream_control(none,[3,Pad_Name],[]).
```

The Prolog-2 User Guide

Some higher level abstraction may be useful as well, for instance defining a curve drawing function in terms of the general figure drawing one;

```
gmr_curve(Stream,List) :-
    gmr_polyline_curve(Stream,List,1).
```

Adding further functions entirely at the Prolog level is also possible, for example a predicate which moves the write position relative to its current position (instead of the absolute move that **gmr_seek**/2 does);

```
gmr_move(Stream,X,Y) :-
    gmr_at(Stream,OldX,OldY),
    NewX is OldX + X,
    NewY is OldY + Y,
    gmr_seek(Stream,NewX,NewY).
```

We have put these rules and more besides into "ssexa.pro" so that with this file consulted into your adapted Prolog-2 interpreter ("ssexac.exe") you can perform the following sequence of goals:

```
/* Initialise and name created pad */
?- gmr_initialisation("Demo").

/* Create and open the first special stream */
?- create_stream(first,write,byte,special(gmr)),
   open(first,write).

/* Draw some text in the first stream */
?- demo_text(first).

/* Create and open the second special stream */
?- create_stream(first,write,byte,special(gmr)),
   open(second,write).

/* Draw a graph in the second stream */
?- demo_graph(second).
```

23.3.7.3.3 C, Pascal and Fortran example differences

The C example takes pains to generate a unique file name (using the BSD 4.2 function mktemp()) for use as its graphics metafile and uses the UNIX error function **ssunixtext()** to report any error in doing this. The other examples take the shortcut of always using a file named "p2temp".

The Fortran example uses a second source file, "ssexaf.h", as this is the most convenient way of repeating definitions within a function subprogram ("ssexaf.f").

The Fortran and Pascal examples use **ssretval()** as explained in §23.3.6.1.

23.4 The system call compiler

This manual describes the System Call Compiler which is a utility for generating External Code which calls the VMS system functions that were specified to the compiler.

Using the compiler you will be able to call VMS functions directly from Prolog, in effect augmenting the Prolog-2 language with the VMS functions that you wish and giving you the opportunity to call VMS functions interactively.

The manual starts with an Overview which outlines the processes involved in using the compiler and is followed by two sections which explain its workings in complete detail.

An Example section is included which takes you through one complete example (the source file for which is distributed as part of Prolog-2). Read this section to see how easy it all is!

For details of the External Code interface see §23.2.

23.4.1 Overview

The compiler takes simple interface definitions of VMS system calls and produces external code (in 'C') to perform these calls and Prolog code to interface to this external code.

The generated 'C' code automatically performs all the necessary type checking and range validation (these checks are derived from the system call specifications). The generated Prolog code provides a means of calling the generated external code functions by their function name from within Prolog, and traps any runtime errors (it reports any Prolog or VMS errors through **force_error/4**).

The generated 'C' code forms part of a complete 'C' source file. This file forms a complete External Code source program, and you compile it (using the VMS C compiler) and link it into your Prolog-2 interpreter (exactly like any other external code you use).

When you want to use the VMS functions that you have incorporated into your Prolog-2 interpreter, simply load their interface calls (e.g. by consulting the generated Prolog code) first and you will be able to call the defined functions.

To use the compiler and its output you don't have to understand the files it generates. You can simply compile and link the 'C' code and consult the Prolog code in order to be able to call the VMS functions that you have defined.

For example a system function specification could be:

'lib$something'(+sinteger,-string,[+ubyte],-uword,-string -> 4).

When you've compiled this source and performed the necessary steps you will then be able to make calls to this VMS function simply by using Prolog goals like:

The Prolog-2 User Guide

'lib$something'(21,First_String,[],Word,Next_String).

The more ambitious user may wish to modify the generated code to provide enhanced functionality, or to use other external code that they have written alongside the generated external code. §23.4.5 covers how you do this, but here is a rough outline of the code that will be generated for our simple example:

'C' calling code (part of the complete 'C' source provided):

```
case 123:
    ... validate input arguments (checking types and ranges) ...
    status = lib$something(a1,a2,a3,a4,a5);
    ... check status ...
    ... validate & set output arguments ...
    return;
```

And Prolog interface code:

```
'lib$something'(In1,Out1,In2,Out2,Out3) :-
    external_code(123,[In1,In2],[Out1,Out2,Out3],[Err,H,L]),
    ( Err == none ;
    handle_error(Err,H,L,'lib$something'(In1,Out1,In2,Out2,Out3))
    ).
```

23.4.2 Format of compiler source files

The System Call Compiler uses a simple form of source code, consisting of one Prolog clause for each system call. The clause functor is the name of the system call in question and its arguments specify the types of data that are passed in the argument positions and in what directions (i.e. input or output).

To return to the example:

'lib$something'(+sinteger,-string,[+ubyte],-uword,-string -> 4)

This describes a VMS function called 'lib$something' with five arguments. The first argument is a read only signed longword, the second is a write only character string, passed by descriptor. The third argument is a read only unsigned byte which may take a default value.

The basic form of specification of an argument is **+atom**, where the data type is indicated by **atom** and the direction by — or +. In addition input arguments may also take a default value, if this is permitted for a given argument then the argument specification should be enclosed in square brackets, e.g. [+atom].

The data types supported by the System Call compiler include all the simple, common VMS data types. These are tabulated below:

The Prolog-2 User Guide

SCC type	VMS type	C type	Prolog-2 type
ubyte	unsigned byte	unsigned char	integer
sbyte	signed byte	char	integer
uword	unsigned word	unsigned short	integer
sword	signed word	short	integer
uinteger	unsigned longword	unsigned int	integer[1]
sinteger	signed longword	int	integer[1]
ulong	unsigned longword	unsigned int	'$int_pair'(H,L)
slong	signed longword	int	'$int_pair'(H,L)
real	floating point	double	real
string	character string	desc char	string

Note 1 : The Prolog-2 integer range is less than the range of a VMS longword/integer, so the data types **sinteger** and **uinteger** should only be used for longword data if you are confident that the values which will be passed will in practise fall with the Prolog-2 range (67108863 to -67108864). If in doubt use **slong** or **ulong** respectively. The generated code handles the unpacking and packing of the '**$int_pair**'(H,L) form for passing to the system function as one longword.

When using a system call that has an output string argument you may find by examining the other arguments that one of the numeric output arguments holds the returned length of the string. If so, you should specify this by following the **-string** data type with **-> n** where **n** is a number indicating the argument which holds the returned length. Thus in the above example the value of the fourth argument is the returned length of the string in the fifth.

We can summarise all the symbols that have meaning to the System Call compiler as follows:

SCC Symbol	Meaning
+	Input argument (ie 'read only' access)
-	Output argument (ie 'write only' access)
[]	Default value allowed for this input argument
-> n	The output string in this argument has its return length specified by the nth argument

23.4.3 Running the compiler and using its output

Given a source file specifying the system calls wanted one proceeds to build a Prolog system which can perform these calls as follows:

23.4.3.1 Run the System Call Compiler

Open the module called "scc.prm" with access **none** as an **actual** module (e.g. **open_module(_,"scc.prm",none,actual)**). Having done this the System Call compiler is now available, to run it use the goal **scc_go**.

You will be prompted to enter the name of the source file containing the system call specifications. If you have a number of sources that you wish to use then you can get the compiler to compile them altogether by creating a file (e.g. **list.pro**) which contains a list of the source file names (e.g. ['**smg.spec**', '**lib.spec**']) and giving the file name in list notation to the compiler (e.g. [**list**]).

The compiler then prompts you for an integer which specifies the external code function number at which the system functions should start (the default is 0). This feature is useful if you are combining external code that you have written yourself with generated system calls (see §23.4.5).

The System Call Compiler will then generate a 'C' source file (called "sccinc.c01") and a Prolog interface file (called "sccintf.p01").

23.4.3.2 Incorporating the external code into a Prolog-2 interpreter

Use the VMS C compiler to compile the supplied file "scc.c01" (this file automatically includes the generated 'C' source file "sccinc.c01"). We recommend that you direct the compiler to produce an object called "external.obj", because then the supplied External Code building files can be used (see §23.2 for more details of these). The rest of this section assumes this. To perform this compilation at the DCL level type:

cc scc.c01 /nodebug/object=external

Now link this object in with the rest of the Prolog-2 system:

@buserc

You now have a new Prolog-2 interpreter called "userc.exe" which includes the external code which can call the system functions.

23.4.3.3 Running the new Prolog system and calling system functions

The new interpreter can be run (if it is in the current directory) by typing (at the DCL level):

run userc

Once the interpreter has loaded, if you wish to make calls to the system functions you should first consult the generated Prolog file that defines the interface for you:

?- consult('sccintf.p01').

You are now ready to call the system functions directly, taking the example of the previous section you will be able to give the goal:

?- 'lib$something'(21,First_String,[],Word,Next_String).

As the above example shows, if you defined an input argument of a system function as being one that could take a default value (e.g. [+ubyte]) then you specify that the default is to be used when the goal is called by using [] as the input (though you can equally well supply a value). Note that this applies to input arguments only; if you're not interested in the value of a output argument then just ignore it by giving it '_'.

Technical Note: Input arguments declared as [+ulong] and [+slong] can be passed default input values either in the form '$int_pair'([],[]) or as just []. The high integer of the pair determines if the default is used or not — thus '$int_pair'([],3) is treated as if it was '$int_pair'([],[]) whilst '$int_pair'(3,[]) gives a runtime error).

23.4.3.4 Example

This section takes you through a complete example. The first step is to create a file of declarations of the VMS system functions we wish to be able to call. Our example uses Screen Management Guidelines (SMG) functions, whose declarations we have written by consulting the VAX Run-time Library Manual (Volume 8C, Part II, pages RTL-538 to RTL-759).

The source file of the function declarations in this example is included as part of the released Prolog-2 files (it is called "sccexa.p01"). The declarations are as follows:

```
'smg$create_pasteboard'(-ulong,[+string],-sinteger,
-sinteger,[+uinteger]).

'smg$create_virtual_display'(+sinteger,+sinteger,-ulong,
[+uinteger],[+uinteger],[+uinteger]).

'smg$paste_virtual_display'(+ulong,+ulong,+sinteger,
        +sinteger,[+ulong]).

'smg$put_line'(+ulong,+string,[+sinteger],[+uinteger],
        [+uinteger],[+uinteger],[+uinteger],[+uinteger]).

'smg$erase_line'(+ulong,[+sinteger],[+sinteger]).

'smg$get_broadcast_message'(+ulong,-string -> 3,-sword).
```

If you read the SMG function definitions in the VAX Run-time Library documentation you will be able to see how the VMS definitions translate into these function declarations.

We translate each argument definition into a source declaration by first examining the **VMS type** of the argument. We lookup the source type which corresponds to the VMS type (see table in §23.4.2), for instance in the third argument to smg$get_broadcast_message **sword** corresponds to **word integer (signed)**. Then examine the **VMS access** for the argument, and lookup the source symbol which corresponds to the VMS access (see table in §23.4.2), for instance + corresponds to **read only**. By this process you will derive argument declarations like **+sword**.

You may also see that the **VMS format** definition for the function specifies that an argument may be defaulted (the argument appears within square brackets). If this is the case for an input argument (i.e. **read only** access) then you can put this information in the declaration as well, to give declarations like **[+sword]**.

For a **character string** argument that is **write only** you may find by examination of the other output arguments that one of these holds the returned length of the string. If this is the case then you can put this information in the declaration of the string as well, to give declarations like **-string -> 3** (see declaration for smg$get_broadcast_message).

We now suggest that you work through the declarations given already in the example to check your understanding. The main thing that you will notice is that most of the arguments which are of **VMS type longword** have been declared as **integer** not as **long**. This is because examination of the meaning and usage of these arguments has revealed that they will in practise hold values which are within the Prolog-2 integer range. The only arguments that this does not apply to in the given example are the pasteboard and virtual display identifiers, as these are set by VMS and we have no prior knowledge that they won't use the full 32 bit longword range, as a consequence we treat these as **long**. (Do be careful to treat all **longword** arguments consistently, it would be no good treating such an identifier as **long** for one function if you also pass the same value as **integer** to another.)

We can now use the System Call compiler on this file of declarations. The Prolog-2 session to do this looks as follows (with output from the System Call compiler in bold type and your responses in normal type, assuming all files are in the current directory):

```
?- open_module(_,"scc.prm",none,actual).
```

** System Call Compiler **

To use this type scc_go.

This utility produces a file SCCINTF.P01 which contains the
Prolog-2 external code declarations for the system functions
and a file SCCINC.C01 which contains the core of the C calls
to perform the indicated functions.

To use the system calls you should compile the C file
SCC.C01 and link this into your Prolog-2 interpreter
as the external object. (This
C file automatically includes the generated file SCCINC.C01).
Then run this new interpreter and consult SCCINC.C01, and this
gives you use of all the system functions without further ado.

yes

```
?- scc_go.
```

SYSTEM CALL COMPILER

Give either single file name eg a.pro
Or the name of a file containing a list of names
eg [list], where list.pro has the text ['smg.pro','lib.pro'].

Enter file name: sccexa.p01
Enter the function number to start the output at
                         (<RETURN> for 0): 1

      ANALYSING ...

      COMPILING ...

      SC COMPILER COMPLETED

Then compile the 'C' code generated and link it into a new Prolog interpreter called "userc.exe" by typing the following commands at the DCL level:

    cc scc.c01 /nodebug/object=external
    @buserc

Now run the new interpreter (which can make the function calls):

    run userc

Within this new interpreter you should now load the interface code:

    ?- consult('sccintf.p01').

Then you can make calls to the declared functions. The following series of Prolog goals will create a window on your screen, write two lines of text to it, and erase part of the second line:

    ?- 'smg$create_pasteboard'(PID,[],_,_,[]),
       'smg$create_virtual_display'(10,30,VID,1,7,[]),
       'smg$paste_virtual_display'(VID,PID,2,20,[]),
       'smg$put_line'(VID,"Hello display",[],[],[],[],[],[]),
       'smg$put_line'(VID,"Some text that will be erased",[],[],[],[],[],[])
       'smg$erase_line'(VID,2,3).

23.4.4 Assumptions and limitations

Below are detailed some of the assumptions and implicit limitations of the System Call interface.

(1) The **VMS mechanism** for argument passing is assumed to be **'by reference'** for numeric arguments and **'by descriptor'** for strings.

(2) All character strings are passed in fixed length string descriptors. The buffer length used is 256, (one extra byte is used internally for the null terminating byte needed by

The Prolog-2 User Guide

'C'). Input strings are expected to fit into such a buffer (if they don't a runtime error is signalled) and the length (as set in the descriptor) is the number of bytes passed from Prolog (up to a max of 256). When an output string is written to one of these buffers we need to determine the number of bytes that have been written. Often there is another output argument that holds the returned length, if there is then you should indicate this in the source (use operator -›) and that value will be used. In all other cases we assume that the end of the output string is represented by the first null byte encountered in it (and to this end we initialise the output buffer with nulls before calling the system function).

(3) All system calls are assumed to return by value a status value (also called a 'condition value' in VMS) and that we can safely interpret success/error by interrogating the success bit of this value. If errors are detected then the error information will be passed back to the calling Prolog for processing.

(4) We assume that all argument positions are fixed as one of the **VMS types** that we recognise (see table in §23.4.2) and one-way (i.e. the **VMS access** is just **read only** or **write only**).

(5) We assume that the Prolog generated interface file is the only route via which the external code routines that apply to the system functions will be called. By relying on this we can dispense (in the 'C' code) with checking the number of input arguments (as we know that the interface code constructs correct arguments). If you intend on calling the functions directly (i.e. using **external_code**/4 directly) then you should check the number of input arguments within the 'C' code.

(6) Note that real numbers (floating point) are always D_floating in Prolog-2.

(7) You ARE allowed to declare functions which have no arguments, their declaration is of the form '**lib$something**'.

23.4.5 Extending the generated code

The System Call interface is designed to complement, not replace, the usual external code interface. You can incorporate the 'C' and Prolog files produced into any existing set of external code routines you have. To facilitate this the System Call compiler allows you to specify the external code function number at which the system calls should start, thus helping you to avoid clashes with your existing external code routines.

One way to get around the System Call limitations is to use the System Call compiler to generate code templates and to modify these to get around the restrictions you find awkward.

The main limitation that you will wish to work around (other than the restrictions on the types of arguments recognised) is the success/error detection; some VMS functions return status values which indicate a qualified success and depending on the circumstances you may wish to trap such qualifications. An example of this is '**smg$create_pasteboard**' which returns the success code SMG$_PASALREXI if the pasteboard already exists, in which case you should not delete the pasteboard with 'smg$delete_pasteboard' although all other uses of the returned pasteboard identifier are valid ones.

You can use the System Call compiler to generate calling code for non-VMS functions.

As Prolog allows predicates with the same functor, one can assert some predicates like the following to make the system calls even easier to use:

```
/* A simplified put_line which requires just virtual display
identifier and string to be output */
'smg$put_line'(VID,Line) :-
    'smg$put_line'(VID,Line,[],[],[],[],[],[]).

/* A version of get_broadcast_message which fails if there
is no message */
'smg$get_broadcast_message'(PID,Message) :-
    'smg$get_broadcast_message'(PID,Message,Length),
    Length \== 0.
```

It is worth noting that you can convert between integers and the '$int_pair'/2 form by means of the following predicate:

```
converter('$int_pair'(H,L),I) :-
    ( integer(H), integer(L), I is H * 65536 + L ;
      integer(I), H is INT // 65536, L is INT mod 65536 ).
```

23.4.6 Compiler errors

Argument in call declaration is in bad form

An argument is not in the recognised syntax, ie not +/-**atom** with optional [] and -> **n** additions, where **atom** is one of the 'SCC types' in the table in §14.4.2.

Argument providing string return length is not a numeric output argument

A string output argument has been declared as **-string -> n** where **n** is NOT the number of a numeric output argument in the function declaration.

Output arguments cannot be defaulted

Output arguments cannot be declared as having defaults permitted (ie **[-real]** is not allowed, use **-real** instead).

System function cannot be defined twice

System functions have unique names so a function name can only appear once in the

The Prolog-2 User Guide

source.

24. Windowing facilities (P only)

24.1 Introduction

This Section introduces the Prolog-2 window system, defines its terminology, and explains how its various components fit together. Later sections will give more details on the different parts.

24.1.1 Components of the windowing system

The window system consists of three 'levels':

(1) the core windowing system,
(2) an interface between the windows and the Prolog stream I/O predicates,
(3) a high-level library of predicates.

(1) the core windowing system is available through the BIPs **window/2**, **screen/2** and **viewport/2**. This is the fastest but most difficult way into the windowing system,

(2) there is an interface between the windows and the Prolog stream I/O predicates such as **get** and **put**. This allows windows to be treated as any other stream, and is central to the use of the windowing system in the PDE,

(3) the high-level library of predicates may be used to carry out certain input and output tasks such as menu selection, editing and error display. These are heavily used in the PDE menu system.

24.1.2 Window system terminology

It is important to understand some terminology before trying to read the detailed descriptions of predicates in this manual.

A **window** is a rectangular text area that has attributes:

- height
- width
- attribute.

We put height before width intentionally; in Prolog-2 predicates the Y screen coordinate ALWAYS precedes the X screen coordinates. Coordinates are measured in character units. The attribute will be described in detail in due course.

Windows and viewports

We have deliberately said nothing about the screen. A window is not necessarily displayed on the screen — it may even be too large to fit on the screen. Windows may be viewed through **viewports**, which are rectangular subsets of windows mapped onto the screen. However, and this is an important point, unless you create a viewport over

The Prolog-2 User Guide

a window it will not be visible.

Viewport parameters

Viewports are ways of looking at windows. A viewport is associated with a single window, but a window may have several viewports over it, and may even have two over the same part of the window. A viewport has a large number of parameters needed for its definition:

- Position on the screen
- Associated window
- Position on window
- Depth in the stack of viewports
- Sides on which there is a margin
- Margin attribute
- Size
- Whether revealed or hidden

Some of these are not self-explanatory. Depth in the stack of viewports is used to control the placement of viewports on the screen; a viewport of lower depth will obscure any parts of one of higher depth with which it overlaps. This is just what you would expect, and normally you create viewports with depth 0 and let other viewports cover them as they need, then pull them up when they are wanted again. You have to know what you're doing to create viewports other than at the top of the stack.

The *Sides on which there is a margin* parameter is straightforward. Usually you will say **all** or **none** but sometimes you may want to use other combinations when two viewports make up one (look at the help viewport; it's actually two viewports with partial margins joined together) or when a viewport abuts the edge of the screen.

A viewport can be hidden even if it is low in the pile; it retains its place in the stack of viewports but cannot be seen. During normal operations the window **pde_debug** is hidden, and you'd be upset if it wasn't, because it gets in the way.

24.1.3 The window manager and viewport manager

So we have windows and viewports. The window manager (**window/2**) allows you to put text into a window and defines a cursor which you can move around; you can also change the attribute to create pretty colour effects, tube diagrams, maps of Australia and so on. You have the same sort of access to a window as you do to the screen of your computer addressed as CON:, and that includes the ability to get the effects obtainable from escape sequences such as cursor addressing.

The viewport manager (**screen/2**) on the other hand only allows the various parameters for a viewport to be set, read or changed; you cannot send text to a viewport.

24.1.4 Edit manager: the lowest level

So far we have said nothing of input.

Windows and viewports have nothing at all to do with input and know nothing of the keyboard.

If you want to hit a key and have that key (or at least the letter printed on it) appear on the screen there are predicates available to allow you to get a keystroke and to put a character on the screen.

(Remember, if it seems onerous doing all this for yourself, that these are low level facilities; there are predicates that automatically echo keystrokes, written in terms of these primitives, and if you are happy with them you need never look into the low-level system.)

To make it easier to carry out these functions there is an edit manager (**edit/2**) that carries out certain low-level editing features on a window or a part of it (you may not want to edit the entire window; in the notepad, for example, you can't get into the scroll bar and edit the arrows, and in the top-level interpreter you aren't allowed to edit the prompt). Such an area is called an edit region.

There can be at most one edit region in a window, and it has to be called by the same name as the window. The edit manager will allow you to insert a character in the edit region, a desperately tedious process if you try to do it yourself just using **window/2**. Having edited the region there are all sorts of interesting ways to get the edited text out, but the approved one is to 'commit' the text and then get from the window as a Prolog stream.

Here we see the flexibility achieved by not tying keys to edit actions; the key that means 'commit all this stuff' can differ from window to window. In the top-level interpreter carriage return causes the input to be committed, but in the editor that would be irritating to say the least, and you commit the text by selecting one of the consult options from the predicate menu.

An example of a low-level editor

Almost any editor written using low-level facilities will look like this:

```
myedit(Window) :-
        repeat,
        get_key(Key),
        keytran(Key,Newkey),
        myedtable(Newkey,Action),
        edit(Window,Action),
        is_that_the_lot(Newkey),
        !.
```

Usually **is_that_the_lot(Newkey)** will fail so that another key will be obtained, but whichever key stops editing (presumably you want to allow the user some way to stop editing) will make it succeed. **myedtable** will have to allow for ASCII characters to be echoed or inserted:

myedtable(ascii(Char),insert(Char)).

to insert them, or (like the PDE) you can implement an insert/overwrite toggle.

There will also be more or less obvious actions for some of the keys:

myedtable(delete,delete).

and some function key assignments

myedtable(function(1),help).

More complex operations — page up and page down, say — you have to look after in Prolog.

Window exceptions

The only other thing to be said here about the lowest level is that there are things called window exceptions. These should not be taken lightly; they are the key to using the system efficiently. An exception may be an error or it may be a condition you want to intercept and control. For example the window editor traps the exception generated when the cursor moves out of the viewport and realigns the viewport so that the cursor can be seen. This is much more efficient than having to keep checking in the program because when the cursor has not moved off the viewport there is no overhead. You can write your own window exception handler — if you are using the low-level facilities you definitely should. If you are lazy and just write one that always succeeds you will find the window system doing some very odd things.

So much for the lowest level; we have seen a few of the sundry extra predicates (**keytran/2** for example) and there are a few more.

24.1.5 Intermediate level: using normal Prolog I/O with windows

At the next level there are no extra predicates because we use the normal Prolog I/O. Thus to get output into a window you make it the current output stream and then write to it, just as you would a file.

To get input "from" a window (i.e. from the keyboard with echo to the window) make the window the current input stream and get from it. This invokes a thing called the system editor which is not as flexible as the primitives from which it is built but allows some key reassignment and also is easier to use; for example, if you haven't set up an edit region in the window it will create one for you rather than complaining. The system editor handles its own exceptions in these circumstances.

24.1.6 Window library: the highest level

At the highest level the window library has all the blocks used to build the PDE in it, so that you can use these without having to write a lot of complex code. If you don't like them, of course, you will have to write your own; because the library routines are simpler to use than the low-level system they are less general and may not be quite what you want.

A worked example

To conclude this quick trip round the system we give a little example to allow you to set up a window; you can play around with the arguments and see how they cause what happens to vary.

We want a red on blue window in the top left hand corner of the screen with the words "Hello windows!" in it.

First create a suitably sized window:

?- **create_stream(hello,readwrite,byte,**
         window(3,16,red on blue)).

The window is created through the Prolog stream system; always use **readwrite** and **byte** as arguments.

Nothing can be done with this window until it is opened.

?- **open(hello,readwrite).**

We aren't going to read from it, of course, but there's no point in denying ourself access; it's not like a file that someone else might be trying to use or a printer where reading would be silly.

Now we want to display it:

?- **screen(hello,create(1,1,hello,0,0,0,all,**
         red on blue,3,16,revealed)).

A bit of a mouthful! In order, we have the screen position (1,1 and not 0,0 because this is the position of the text area and we want to leave room for the margin), the window (it's usually a good idea to give the viewport the same name as the window), the window position (we want to see all the window), the margin and its attribute, the size (same as the window) and revealed — show it at once. If there were to be something more elaborate in it we might create it hidden, paint it and then — WHAM! — reveal it.

The Prolog-2 User Guide

To get the text into the window we can write it or we can use the window manager directly. Let's do the latter. To leave some spaces around it we start by cursor addressing:

```
?- window(hello,cursor_address(1,1)).
?- window(hello,text("Hello windows!")).
```

And there it is. To get rid of it all

```
?- screen(hello,delete).
?- close(hello).
```

Most of the memory used has already been reclaimed, but for the sake of tidiness:

```
?- delete_stream(hello).
```

In the next three sections we shall look in detail at the three manager predicates.

24.2 The window manager

Recall that windows are rectangular text buffers and not bits of screen.

In §24.1 we said that you have the same sort of access to one of these windows as you would to the screen of your computer, including functions for which you would use escape sequences. In other words, you can paint a window in any way you like.

This section covers the functions of the window manager, which handles this painting, but first discusses how to create and open windows.

24.2.1 Creating windows

Creating windows

Windows are created through the Prolog-2 stream system, even though they may perhaps never be used as Prolog streams. The predicates associated with the stream system are discussed in Chapter 18, where it is vaguely suggested that the stream descriptor may be a window.

In creating a window you have to specify the first three arguments to **create_stream/4** and as the fourth you have to supply a window description.

You should specify the access argument as **readwrite** and the type as **byte**. The window description is a structure whose functor is **window/3** and whose arguments are:

(1) the number of rows
(2) the number of columns
(3) the attribute.

The number of rows and columns must not exceed 65535 (in practice the amount of

250

memory available will impose a stricter limit; a window of X rows and Y columns occupies approximately 2*X*Y bytes of heap space).

An attribute is a structure that specifies the colour of a window and also whether it is bright and whether it flashes. A colour is specified in the form **Foreground on Background** (**on** is an infix operator) where **Foreground** and **Background** are colour names from the following list:

black
magenta
red
yellow
green
blue
cyan
white.

Some systems will not have all these colours available, in which case the non-existent ones will be mapped into the closest approximation available. Unfortunately there are no combinations other than white on black and black on white that will look reasonable on all systems, so writing portable code that may use colours is a problem. The best solution is to use the system colours as described in §25.2.1.

As well as colour you can specify the attribute **flashing** and/or **bright** (these are prefix operators). For example

bright cyan on yellow

is a legal attribute. It doesn't matter which order the prefix attribures are supplied in. Note that the **bright** attribute affects the foreground colour only.

Example: A small window using the colour scheme of the menu front end could be created by:

create_stream(small,readwrite,byte,window(10,20,bright yellow on blue)).

The name **small** will be used to refer to this window in all subsequent operations.

It is as important to note what is not specified here: we give no indication of where (or whether) the window is to be displayed. Indeed it is possible to have a window that is larger than the screen (the **pde_notes** window is 100 lines deep, for example). The PROLOG2.MNU file supplied has lots of examples of window creations.

Opening, closing and deleting windows

The Prolog-2 User Guide

Before doing anything to a window it must be opened. Note that space will not be allocated to the window until it is opened, so if you are short of memory there is no need to keep deleting windows; just open and close them. Always open windows in **readwrite** mode.

?- open(small,readwrite).

When you have finished with a window you can close it:

?- close(small).

and free the space it occupied (of course, the contents will be lost). You can tidy up by deleting the window altogether:

?- delete_stream(small).

and this is sensible because although stream entries aren't very big, when there are lots of streams it takes longer to find the one you want.

Inspecting streams

The other predicate from the stream system that is relevant here is **stream/5** which tells you what streams there are. The fourth argument is matched with a structure which, in the case of a window, is the structure you used to set the window up (the attribute may have got changed a little).

24.2.2 window/2

The window manager maintains a cursor, called the window cursor; this prescribes where the next window output is to go.

The cursor can have as value the co-ordinates of any point in the window (Y first, as usual) or may be undefined. The top left hand corner is the origin of co-ordinates and the Y axis grows downwards; the unit is a single character position. The cursor is initialised to (0,0) when the window is opened. Of course, this cursor has nothing to do with the flashing underline or whatever that you may see on the screen.

All calls to **window/2** take the form

window(W,Op)

where **Op** is an allowed window operation. There is a list of legal operations in the entry **window/2** in the Prolog-2 Encyclopaedia.

24.2.3 Windows as Prolog streams

A window is a Prolog stream and can, like any other stream open for writing, be made the current output stream. When this is done the **put** predicate will cause output to the window.

In fact quite a lot of predicates use this interface; for example **write/1**. You can deduce what **write** will do from the description of **put** that follows. Do not make the mistake of thinking that the system will be clever enough to optimise, say

?- write("Tityrus").

into

?- window(COS,text("Tityrus")).

where **COS** is the current output stream. All output through **write** is turned into single character output and sent through **put**; for this reason the handling of strings that are too long for the window is unintelligent.

When outputting to a window **put(Char)** behaves like

list([Char],S),window(COS,text(S))

except in the handling of exceptions. No window exceptions at all are generated. Single character output can never generate **line_no_room** but we could well get **cursor_undefined** after a previous **put** had filled the window. In fact what happens is that when **put** finds the cursor undefined it calls **scroll_up** to make more room in the window and define the cursor. Hence if you use ordinary stream output to fill a window it will automatically scroll when full. (If you're interested, that's not quite right. It will not scroll until you try to put a character with the cursor undefined. You can therefore fill a window without scrolling it — this is useful if you want a one-line window completely filled with text.)

Note that the **amend_out_of_viewport** exception is also disabled during **put**.

You can also **get** from a window, but that uses the edit manager, which we shall discuss in §24.4.

24.3 The screen manager

The screen manager enables the programmer to set up and manage viewports. A viewport is a rectangular area of the screen that lies over part of a window (see §24.1). The screen manager ensures that whenever the window is changed the screen changes as necessary.

The viewports form a stack with shallower members obscuring deeper ones where they overlap. The deepest viewport is set up by the system and is called **background**. Every viewport has a depth in the stack.

The Prolog-2 User Guide

There are a number of properties of viewports that we shall enumerate in a moment. They have to be specified when the viewport is created. Some of them can be changed by special calls and others through an all-purpose change routine. One of them (the associated window) cannot be changed at all.

24.3.1 Properties of viewports

A viewport has the following properties:

- Position of the top left corner on the screen (SY,SX)

- Associated window (Win).

It is permissible for a viewport to have the same name as a window, and it is a good idea to give it the same name as the associated window.

- Position of the top left corner over the window (WY,WX)

A viewport must fit completely within the screen area and also within its associated window. Attempts to run over the edge will give the **viewport_too_big** exception, and, if ignored, pretty graphics characters not of your choosing.

- Depth (D)

Normally viewports are created at depth 0 and their depth gets increased as more viewports are created or pulled up. A viewport may be restored to depth 0 by pulling it up. There is no converse **thrust_down** operation on viewports; the thing to do if you want to get rid of a viewport is to hide it.

- Margin (M)

This is to specify which sides of the viewport have margins. Normally **all** or **none** are used, but you can create margins on some sides but not others using atoms made up of the letters **l r b t** (left right bottom top) in that order. For example to get a margin at the top and on the left use **lt** (not tl).

- Margin Attribute (Matt)

This is the attribute of the margin; very often this will be the same as that of the window. Attributes are described in §24.2.1. If there is no margin you can use an anonymous variable for this argument when creating the viewport — indeed, if you try to specify an attribute it will be ignored. The info call always returns attribute **black on black** when there is no margin.

- Size (H,W)

H is the height in rows and W the width in columns.

- Revealed (R)

This must be one of the atoms **hidden** or **revealed**.

Irrespective of its depth a viewport can be hidden or revealed. A hidden viewport maintains its position in the stack but is not seen. Therefore it is possible for a top level hidden viewport to get 'covered up' just as a visible one can. In general, to display a viewport you should both unhide it and pull it up.

The variable names in the above will be used without further explanation in the list of calls.

24.3.2 Calls to the screen manager

As with the window manager calls take the form **screen(Name,Op)** where Name is the viewport and Op an atom or structure prescribing the operation desired. A complete list of operations will be found under **screen/2** in the Prolog-2 Encyclopaedia.

The main work of the screen manager is not responding to explicit calls but keeping the screen up-to-date. The **amend_out_of_viewport** exception will be generated when a window is changed outside the area under a viewport. The programmer may trap this exception and move the viewport or pull it up, but usually it is best to ignore it. For input the editor's exception **edit_cursor_invisible** is more useful.

The precise rule for generating this exception is as follows:

When a window is changed, see whether any viewport is over the changed cell; if not give the exception.

If there is a hidden viewport then do not give the exception even if the viewport would be obscured if it were not hidden.

If all viewports are revealed and none of the parts currently on the screen contains the changed cell then give the exception.

24.4 The edit manager

The edit manager allows the programmer to use a region of a window, called an edit region, for editing. This is possible but cumbersome using the window manager. The edit manager knows nothing of the keyboard, however, and can better be thought of as a series of routines for doing output to a window of a more elaborate kind than the window manager supports. The edit manager in fact keeps a second copy of the edited text with carriage returns and the like intact, and ensures that the window displays this text. By pairing the edit manager with the keyboard routines an editor may easily be produced; and the system editor is one such tool. This is the editor invoked by **getting** from a window.

The Prolog-2 User Guide

24.4.1 Terminology

There may be at most one edit region in a window, and it must be rectangular. The edit region will be referred to by the name of its window.

You should not do direct window output to an edit region; this will confuse the display. Because the edit manager keeps a second copy of the text rather than reading it from the window you will not corrupt (or affect) the edit. This point must be borne in mind all the time; for example, you cannot set up a piece of text to be edited using the window manager's text function because the edit manager knows nothing of this; you must use the edit manager text function.

You can think of the edit manager as maintaining and amending a text buffer which, as a side effect, it displays in the window.

Unlike the window manager, the edit manager knows about lines, that is, strings terminated by carriage returns. These are not the same as window rows; a line may run over several rows by wrapping.

Text: committed and uncommitted

At any time the text the edit manager knows about may be in one of two conditions: committed or uncommitted. The programmer determines which text is in which state by sending a commit instruction to the edit manager. Committed text cannot be edited; the cursor will not move back over it. Uncommitted text can still be edited. On the other hand, uncommitted text cannot be removed from the edit region by get. The text in the edit region that is committed must come before the uncommitted text.

The read limit and the write limit

The boundary between committed and uncommitted text is called the read limit because it is as far as reading from the edit region is allowed to go. The editor also remembers the write limit, which is as far as the text in the window has been written; it is not normally the same as the end of the edit region.

The read cursor and the write cursor

There are two cursors maintained as well: a read cursor and a write cursor. The read cursor is between the start of the edit region and the read limit and marks the position where the next character will be got from (you can't see it). The write cursor is the window's own cursor and lies between the read limit and the write limit; it determines where the next character inserted or echoed can go. It is represented, under certain circumstances, by a physical cursor.

```
|─────────────────^─────────────────|─────────────────^─────────────────|
            read cursor        read limit    write cursor        write limit
```

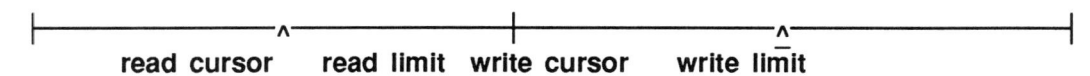

An illustrative example

Before we get to the details of different calls let us look at an example to clarify the terminology.

Suppose I start with a clean edit region and use the system editor to input to it; someone in there is doing **gets** from the window and I am sitting at the keyboard pressing keys. I want to type in the second clause of append.

At the start the read cursor, read limit, write cursor and write limit are all at the start of the edit region. A **get** is suspended waiting for a character from the edit region. I type lower case **a**. The write limit and the write cursor advance, but not their read equivalents. As I type

> **append([H,T],A,[H|T1]) :-**

the write cursor and limit move across the window. Then I notice that I typed [H,T] instead of [H|T] so I go back and edit it. The write cursor moves back, the write limit stays put. Then, happy with this line, I type carriage return, which, given the way the PDE sets up the keys means 'add a carriage return and commit'. The carriage return moves my cursor to a new line, the commit advances the read limit to what was the write limit, that is, the start of line 2. The read cursor is still at start of edit, and the write cursor and limit are at the start of line 2. But as soon as the read cursor and the read limit differ the suspended **get** succeeds, returning the **a** of append and advancing the read cursor one place. This will continue until all the line is processed and the read cursor has reached the start of line 2. It is now equal to the read limit and therefore the next **get** will suspend.

I can now type in my second line

> **append(T,A,T1).**

advancing the write cursor and limit and then key carriage return to commit. While doing this I cannot go back and edit line 1 because I committed it and it has already been processed. When I commit the read limit moves to the start of line 3 and the read cursor is free to move through the second line.

As there is a Prolog terminator after the clause, it is probably the case that there will be no more **gets** and no more chance to advance the write limit. (This assumes that the edit manager can only be invoked while a **get** is suspended, which is not true; the notepad editor, for example, does not contain a single **get** call. Editing in a suspended **get** is the most usual practice though, and the only one supported by the system editor.)

24.4.2 Edit manager functions

The Prolog-2 User Guide

Format of edit manager functions

Edit manager calls take the form

edit(W,Op)

and a list of allowed operations will be found under **edit/2** in the Prolog-2 Encyclopaedia.

Most of the editor functions are concerned with editing proper. These take a fixed form: the string of characters from the read limit to the write limit is transformed in some way and then replaces the existing string in the window. The operation defines where the write cursor goes; the write limit is the end of the new string. The read cursor and read limit are not involved in these operations.

Editable area: definition

In order to understand some of the descriptions that follow it is necessary to know what the term 'editable area' means. The editable area is a subset of the edit region.

The editable area consists of all the places where part of the edit string would be written if it were output using the text routine. For example, if the single line **foo** has been typed then the editable area consists of the first three positions in the first row of the window. If two lines

        foo
        bar

have been typed then the region includes them both as well as the position to their right (this is viewed as holding the carriage return) but no more. If the first line was too long to fit in the window and had to be wrapped then the entire first row of the window and the second up to the end of the string are the editable area.

Briefly, the editable area is the edit region from the read limit up to the write limit less the ends of rows that follow carriage returns. The reason for defining this is that the cursor is not allowed to move outside the editable area.

24.4.3 Handling of tabs and control characters

The handling of tabs and control characters is different in the edit manager. The tabs and control characters are kept in the edit manager's copy of the region, but when the edit manager writes them in the window it expands control characters into the form caret-followed-by-letter used by DOS (for example, control-D is printed as ^D) and tabs into spaces. However it remembers that these are composite characters and only counts the first of them as part of the editable area. Therefore if as a result of (say) a **cursor(Y,X)** the cursor ends up in the middle of an expanded control character then it is spaced left so that it is on the caret. Also **backspace** and **delete** delete whole control characters and tabs, and in overwrite mode replacing a composite character by a simple one appears to shorten the line.

24.4.4 Exceptions

The generation of exceptions by the edit manager is considerably more complex than by the window manager. The following exceptions can in principle be generated:

amend_out_of_viewport
edit_cursor_invisible
edit_cursor_moved
edit_too_big
edit_region_not_found
edit_out_of_range

Buffered and programmable windows

However, not all windows generate all exceptions. There are two kinds of window from this point of view: buffered and programmable.

These differ in the handling of the case where the write limit wants to move beyond the end of the edit region. In a programmable window the exception **edit_out_of_range** is generated in these circumstances. In a buffered window the top row of the edit region is committed and the edit region is scrolled so that there will be room for the extra text. It is still possible for a buffered window to generate the **edit_out_of_range** exception, but only on cursor moves.

Handling of exceptions is discussed in §24.5.

24.4.5 The system editor

Consequences of calling get

In §24.2 we finished with an account of **put**; here we conclude by discussing **get**. It should be stressed that all traditional Prolog input goes through the same interface as **get/1** so that we could as well be speaking here of **get0/1** or **read/1**.

When the current input stream is a window and **get** is called the following actions are taken:

- if there is an edit region and its status is **ready** then a character is taken from the read cursor position and the read cursor is advanced

- if there is an edit region and its status is **not ready** then the system editor is invoked to **get** characters for the edit region until the status changes

- if there is no edit region then one is initialised automatically. These automatically initialised regions are called TTY regions and behave differently in some respects; principally in that they have their own exception handler so that the user never sees exceptions from them. Once the region is initialised characters are got using the system

The Prolog-2 User Guide

editor as before.

Note that the system editor is never invoked unless **get** is called when the edit region is not ready. The system editor differs from the rest of the edit manager in knowing about the keyboard, and this is not what you want if you have decided, say, to make the user select characters from a picture of the keyboard using a mouse. In this case you will have to do more work yourself.

The system editor is the following rather trivial little program:

sysed :-
    get_key(X),
    keytran(X,Y),
    state(edit_key(Y),Op,Op),
    perform **Op.**

perform **Op** usually, but not always, means **edit(Window,Op)**.

Thus the user can determine the significance of keys to the system editor by setting the system state **edit_key**. The routines referred to will be described in full in §24.6 (Other Windowing Predicates). **sysed** is called repeatedly until the status of the window becomes ready. (A perverse setting of the keys may lead the editor to place keys in a window other than the one waiting for input. There is nothing illegal about this, but it is not recommended.)

There is another context in which the system editor is called. If **user polling** is switched on then every time the Prolog interpreter calls a goal it checks whether there is a key ready, and if there is then it calls the system editor. It terminates after one call whether or not any window has become ready as a result.

More details about setting the keys using **edit_key** are given in §24.6.

24.4.6 TTY windows

We conclude §24.4 with an account of TTY windows.

TTY windows can be created by initialise/0 calls to edit and by **get** when it discovers that there is no edit region. They differ in the following respects from other edit regions:

• A TTY window never generates exceptions. It handles all exceptions for itself. The only exception it takes any notice of is **edit_out_of_range** when the write limit tries to pass the end of the edit region. In this case it scrolls the entire window (not just the edit region). The co-ordinates of the edit region are altered so that it scrolls up in the window. If as a result any of the edit region is lost from the window then the characters in that row are committed. The edit region is extended by adding the new row scrolled in to it.

• When a TTY window has status **not ready** then before calling the system editor **get** reinitialises the edit region so that it runs from the window cursor to the end of the window (this is maybe not a rectangle, but it gets round that). The attribute given is the same as that of the window.

- When a TTY window is committed the window cursor is moved to the write limit.

The purpose of the latter two features is to allow mixed input and output as a teletype does. Typically the system tries to read a question or command; this causes an edit region to be initialised from the end of the prompt (the current window cursor) to the end of the window. The user therefore can type in at the natural place. At the end the window cursor moves to the end of the input term so that the answer follows the user's question. The prompt is then repeated and the user types into a new region (it would be unnatural to expect the last one to be used).

If this all seems rather complicated, look at the **pde_main** window in the development environment; this is a TTY window. Each time you type a query you are typing in a new edit region, and input and output interleave properly. The window also scrolls as you would expect.

Once a window has acquired a TTY edit region the only way to change it back to an explicitly declared region is to close the existing region. This causes the TTY status to be cleared.

24.5 Window exceptions

When the window handler detects a condition that it cannot handle — or where its handling might not be what the user wants — it generates a window exception. The exceptions that can be generated have been discussed in §15.2 to 4 of this Manual and are summarised under the entry **window exception** in the Prolog-2 Encyclopaedia..

First, though, we want to discuss how the user can handle exceptions.

Types of window exception

There will normally be three groups of exceptions:

(1) exceptions to be regarded as errors and handed to the error handler

(2) exceptions to be treated specially

(3) exceptions to be ignored.

Prolog-2 is configured with an exception handler called **sys_exception** which either treats exceptions as errors or else ignores them; in other words there are no errors in group (2).

Generally, a window exception handler is a predicate with two arguments which the window system will call after a window exception occurs. The system state

window_exception takes as its value the name of this predicate (there is no need to specify the arity as it is always 2).

When the predicate is called the window system passes two arguments to it:

(1) the atom rep of the exception

(2) the goal which caused the exception. From this the call and its parameters can be determined.

Exception handling — the general case

The handling of exceptions normally involves a transfer of control to the exception handler after some tidying up; if the handler succeeds then the call succeeds and if it fails then the call fails.

Exception handling in the system editor

There is an exception to this: in the system editor, the exception is processed and control is transferred back to the editor whether the handler succeeded or failed; in this case the only way out is to have the handler abort. (Of course, if the system editor found no edit region and set one up, there will be no exceptions anyway; the last remark is only relevant where get finds an edit region set up.)

When you install an exception handler, you should bear in mind that there may be one in use that is needed by some windows already existing. The P.D.E. is quite good-natured about having its exception handler changed, but under some circumstances it can get confused. Unless you are packaging an application where you know that all the windows are your own it is better to chain your window handler onto the front of the existing one thus:

```
install_we(Goal) :-
       state(window_exception,Oldwe,Oldwe),
       assert((new_exception(A,B) :-
              G =.. [Goal,A,B],
              G,
              !)),
       assert((new_exception(A,B) :-
              G =.. [Oldwe,A,B],
              G)),
       state(window_exception,_,new_exception).
```

If your new handler fails control passes to the old one. Then write your handler so that it only applies to your own windows:

```
my_exception(Ex,window(Win,Call)) :-
       mine(Win),!,...
```

and so on.

More simply, if you know that a piece of code will only use your own windows, install your exception handler at the start and restore the old one at the end. Beware of the interrupt handler, though!

Window exception handlers must be public.

Example code

Here is an example bit of code from an exception handler that detects lines that will not fit in a window and wraps them without breaking words.

The advantage of this style of coding is that there is no need for an explicit check each time a string is output; the exception can be relied upon to handle the output. You can therefore build windows with quite sophisticated properties and ignore the complexities in the rest of the code.

```
/* There are several problems with this bit of code.

(i) What to do if there are no blanks in the string?

(ii) What if the line is too long only because of trailing blanks?

The reader is invited to improve the code. */

wrap_exception(line_no_room,window(mywindow,text(Text))) :-
        stream(mywindow,_,_,window(_,Width,_),_),
        divide_line(Text,Width,Start,Finish),
        window(mywindow,text(Start)),
        window(mywindow,text(Finish)).

/* If the line is very long the second call may generate a second exception, but
there is nothing illegal about this. Of course, if you keep generating the same
exception from the same call you get a closed loop */

divide_line(Text,Width,Start,Finish) :-
        get_last_blank(Text,Width,Pos,0),
        blank_line(Bl),
        Start is_string
                substring(substring(Text,0,Pos)&Bl,0,Width),
/* a handy trick for padding a line with blanks */
        Finish is_string delete(Text,0,Pos+1).

get_last_blank(Text,End,Pos,K) :-
```

The Prolog-2 User Guide

```
        I is index(Text," ",K),
        I < End,
        !,
        I1 is I+1,
        get_last_blank(Text,End,Pos,I1
).
get_last_blank(Text,End,K,K).
```

/* blank_line(X) instantiates X to a string of 80 spaces */

blank_line("   ").

24.6 Other windowing facilities

The windowing system uses a number of predicates and system states that have not yet been discussed; their descriptions are gathered here.

24.6.1 The keyboard

The largest group of these predicates is concerned with getting keystrokes from the keyboard. It should be noted that none of these predicates echoes to the screen; we are at a lower level than **get0** and family. Note also that these predicates access the keyboard regardless of the current input stream.

Raw and translated keystrokes

Before we start we should be explain that there is a distinction between 'raw' and 'translated' keystrokes.

Raw keystrokes are integers representing the key pressed. The representation is not documented, though a little experiment will enable you to work it out.

Translated keystrokes are atoms or structures that specify which key was pressed in a portable way. This is not to say that they are restricted to ASCII values; for example, the cursor keys have special non-ASCII representations.

Subdivision of keyboard

Most keyboards can be divided into a number of groups as keys:

(1) ASCII keys

These are keys that have an ASCII value associated with them. This does not include 'extended ASCII' — it must be a single byte value. "A" is such a key and so is the space bar. Ins is definitely not. Backspace is a borderline case — some would call it ASCII 8 — but in Prolog-2 backspace and other 'special keys' are treated differently and send special values, although holding control and pressing H sends **ascii(8)**.

(2) Function keys

There are forty function keys, representing the unshifted and shifted versions of the 10 function keys on the keyboard. Thus:

1-10	F1-F10
11-20	Shifted F1-F10
21-30	Ctrl F1-F10
31-40	Alt F1-F10

Note that F11 and F12 cannot be obtained by pressing the keys so marked on newer keyboards.

(3) Special keys

Function keys are keys that are detectable (unlike the shift keys, say) but have non-ASCII values. The cursor movement keys are such; they have special symbols rather than ASCII characters written on them.

(4) Scan keys

This group covers keys that do not fall into any other category, such as **control cursor_right**.

Names used for keys in this documentation

Throughout this documentation the symbolic names returned from **keytran** have been used to name keys.

The allowed structures for translated keys may be any of the following:

- **ascii(N)** where N is an integer between 0 and 255 inclusive

- **function(N)** where N is an integer between 1 and 40

- **scan(N)** where N is the scan code; this is used for keys that have no useful translation

- one of a number of atoms representing particular keys, that is:

esc, cr, backspace, delete, insert, cursor_up, cursor_down, cursor_left, cursor_right, cursor_home, cursor_end, page_up, page_down

The following predicates access the keyboard:

get_key/1

265

The Prolog-2 User Guide

last_key/1
key_ready/0
keytran/2

24.6.2 Configuring the system editor

The system editor was discussed at length in §24.4. The following system states that configure it.

edit_key(Key)
user_polling
edit

24.6.3 Miscellaneous windowing predicates

The following predicates are also part of the windowing system:

redraw_screen/0
clear_screen/0
viewport/1
where/5

24.7 The window library

The window library contains a number of utility predicates to make the windowing system easier to use. A list of all predicates in the library will be found under the item **window** in the Prolog-2 Encyclopaedia.

24.8 Using a mouse

You may use a MicroSoft mouse with Prolog-2. The simplest way to use it is to keep it for the parts of the PDE that use a mouse. If you want to write code of your own that uses a mouse then you have two options: you can either use the predicates in the window library ; or you can interface directly to the mouse using the built-in predicate **mouse/3** (described in §24.8.3). These three approaches are described in that order in this chapter.

24.8.1 Installing and using a mouse

You have to tell Prolog-2 that you intend to use a mouse. Your Prolog system can be set up to examine an interrupt vector and see whether the mouse driver is there; if it is then it will be used.

This mouse initialisation can safely be put in your MNU file provided that you are not going to run on a machine that uses the interrupt in question for some other purpose; this can lead to fatal errors. Therefore, if you have a mouse or believe that a mouse could be installed, you should look at the MNU file supplied where you will find the line

/* mouse(-1,[55],_). */

This, you will have observed, is a comment. If you remove the comment characters /* and */ the system will look for a mouse at interrupt 51 (the usual place) on startup. If one is not found then the system will run as before. This approach will work, for example, on all IBM PC family machines. However, if the system crashes during start-up, recomment the line; mouse support is not available on your machine.

Once you have attached a mouse and installed the driver you will find that when a menu selection is offered, for example, a character size block appears in the window; the character attribute changes in a subtle way underneath (to be precise, whichever of Red, Green and Blue used to be absent is now present and vice versa). The block moves around in response to your moving the mouse. Generally you click with the left button to select an item and with the right button to get out of the menu. The precise rules are given under the entry **menu/5** in the Prolog-2 Encyclopaedia.

24.8.2 The mouse library functions

The following predicates in the window library are likely to be of interest:

get_key_click/1	Reads the keyboard or mouse clicks
mouse_installed/0	Succeeds if there is a mouse
mouse_off/0	Switch off mouse cursor
mouse_on/2	Switch on mouse cursor
restrict_mouse/1	Keep mouse in a viewport
wait_key_click/1	Waits for keyboard or mouse click

You should note that these predicates may not behave as expected if mixed with low-level **mouse/3** calls; for example, the low-level call that swaps the mouse buttons will mean that you have to read 'left' for 'right' and vice versa throughout.

24.8.3 Microsoft mouse-manipulating functions and mouse/3

mouse/3

The predicate **mouse/3** is a Prolog language binding for the mouse function described in Appendix A to the MicroSoft Mouse User's Guide. That guide should be consulted for full details of the different calls.

The language binding works as follows: the first argument to **mouse/3** must be an integer and is the function number. The second is the list of input arguments and the third will be matched with the list of output arguments.

Switching off mouse use with -1

The Prolog-2 User Guide

In addition to the calls listed in Microsoft's Appendix A there is one extra function, numbered -1. This has one input argument, which should be the number of the interrupt vector used for the mouse. There are no output arguments. Until this call has been made all other calls to **mouse/3** will succeed and match the output argument with []. This means that you can switch off mouse use in a system simply by removing the -1 call, and you are then safe from the possible difficulties caused by uninitialised interrupts.

24.8.4 Reference list of mouse functions

The functions from Appendix A of the *Microsoft Mouse User's Guide* are described briefly here for reference.

Mouse co-ordinates

In what follows positions are always in mouse co-ordinates, which are 8 times cursor co-ordinates. To get the screen position you must divide each by 8:

SY is Y//8, SX is X//8.

The origin of co-ordinates is the top left corner in both systems.

Mouse error-handling

Error handling is restricted to type checking; no check is made by Prolog-2 that, for example, co-ordinates are in range. Error **graphics** is given for all incorrect arguments types that Prolog-2 detects.

0. Mouse Reset

Call:
　　mouse(0,[],Output).

Arguments:
　　Output will be set to [-1,N] if an N-button mouse is installed

Purpose:
　　Reset mouse parameters to defaults

1. Show cursor

Call:
　　mouse(1,[],_).

Arguments:
   None

Purpose:
   Switch on cursor

2. Hide cursor

Call:
   mouse(2,[],_).

Arguments:
   None

Purpose:
   Switch off cursor

3. Get position and button status

Call:
   mouse(3,[],[Stat,Y,X]).

Arguments:
   Stat   0 no buttons down
               1 left down
               2 right down
               3 both down
   (Y,X) mouse cursor position

Purpose:
   See which buttons are down and where mouse is

4. Set mouse cursor position

Call:
   mouse(4,[Y,X],_).

Arguments:
   (Y,X) Desired cursor position

Purpose:
   Move mouse cursor

5. Get button press information

The Prolog-2 User Guide

Call:
   mouse(5,[Button],[Stat,No,Y,X]).

Arguments:
Button	0 for left, 1 for right
Stat	0 for up, 1 for down
No	Number of presses since last call or reset
(Y,X)	Mouse cursor position at last press

Purpose:
   See if button pressed and if so where

6. Get button release information

Call:
   mouse(6,[Button],[Stat,No,Y,X]).

Arguments:
Button	0 for left, 1 for right
Stat	0 for up, 1 for down
No	Number of releases since last call or reset
(Y,X)	Mouse cursor position at last release

Purpose:
   See if button released and if so where

7. Set min and max horizontal position

Call:
   mouse(7,[Min,Max],_).

Arguments:

Min	Minimum allowed Y co-ordinate
Max	Maximum allowed Y co-ordinate

Purpose:
Restrict mouse to horizontal bar

8. Set min and max horizontal position

Call:
   mouse(8,[Min,Max],_).

Arguments:
Min	Minimum allowed X co-ordinate
Max	Maximum allowed X co-ordinate

Purpose:
Restrict mouse to vertical bar.

9. Set graphics cursor block

This function is not available from Prolog-2

10. Set text cursor

Call:
mouse(10,[Type,Start,End],_).

Arguments:
Type   0 for software, 1 for hardware cursor
Start   Screen mask (software) or start scan line (hardware)
End   Cursor mask (software) or end scan line (hardware)

Purpose:
Configure cursor appearance

See Microsoft mouse manual for details

11. Read mouse motion counters

Call:
mouse(11,[],[Horiz,Ver]).

Arguments:
Horiz   Net horizontal motion in mickies
Ver   Net vertical motion in mickies

Purpose:
Get mouse net motion (There are 200 mickies in an inch.)

12. Set user-defined subroutine mask

Not available from Prolog-2

13. Light pen emulation mode on

Call:
mouse(13,[],_).

Arguments:

The Prolog-2 User Guide

None

Purpose:
Allows mouse to be read as though it were a light pen

14. Light pen emulation mode off

Call:
mouse(14,[],_).

Arguments:
None

Purpose:
Switches off function 13

15. Set Mickey/pixel ratio

Call:
mouse(15,[Horiz,Ver],_).

Arguments:
Horiz	Mickeys/pixel horizontally
Ver	Mickeys/pixel vertically

Purpose:
Makes mouse more or less sensitive

16. Conditional off

Call:
mouse(16,[TopX,TopY,BottX,BottY],_).

Arguments:
(TopX,TopY)	Top left of off rectangle
(BottX,BottY)	Bottom right of off rectangle

Purpose:
Switch off mouse if in off rectangle

19. Set double speed threshold

Call:
mouse(19,[Thresh],_)

Arguments:
   Thresh   Speed in mickeys/sec at which screen cursorspeed doubles

Purpose:
   Speed up long mouse movements for those with big desks

25. The program development environment

25.1 Structure of the Program Development Environment

The Prolog-2 Program Development Environment (PDE) is a collection of tools that enable the programmer to use the Prolog-2 interpreter/compiler as a development system. These capabilities include:

(1) quick testing of goals by entering a query,
(2) error handling,
(3) interrupt handling,
(4) information formatting routines,
(5) debug interaction,
(6) environment management,
(7) editing.

None of these features are likely to be wanted in finished applications; the programmer will supply routines to take over the functions of those in the PDE when development is complete.

If you are familiar with systems other than Prolog-2, you may be accustomed to regarding some or all of these features as 'built in'. Because Prolog-2 is designed for the production of packaged applications, it is divided into a core program — the logical theorem prover with the library of built-in predicates — and a development environment suitable for testing applications. It is your responsibility to provide run-time error facilities, for example, for your packaged application.

The Prolog-2 program has no facilities for interaction built into it. It can be regarded as a tool that takes and evaluates goals with no procedure specified as to where the goals come from. In fact the Prolog-2 system on startup performs some initialisation and then jumps into the theorem prover with the name of a fixed goal that it will either be $boot or the start goal of a packaged application. $boot causes the appropriate MNU file to be consulted. In the PDE the MNU file loads the PDE files and then executes the 'top level interpreter' program, a query system that reads goals and reports to the user whether they can be proved or not. But without the PDE there would be no query interface to the core system.

Breaks: error, interrupt, debug

This is not the core system's only deficiency. In the course of proving a goal a number of conditions may arise that can be regarded as abnormal — these are called 'breaks' in execution.

Breaks arise from several sources:

(1)   some built-in predicates regard certain arguments in certain circumstances as **errors**

(2)   the user can cause a break in execution by holding down the break key on the keyboard

(3)   in debug mode the interpreter generates a break every time a port of a user goal is passed

Prolog-2 services these three kinds of breaks (errors, interrupts, debug) by calling a goal that has been specified to it; the PDE supplies goals suitable for development of programs.

Formatted printing

As well as breaks in execution, there are other interfaces between the core system and the PDE. An example is the **listing** BIP, which calls a pretty printing routine to output the clauses in appropriate format. In the PDE an elaborate pretty-printer is supplied; in a packaged application it is unlikely that listing will be used, and so no print routine is needed.

Development tools

So far we have seen two ways in which the PDE supplies an interface between the user and the core system: it supplies a start-up goal and it handles conditions that arise in the system either because of breaks or because of the use of certain BIPs. It has, however, a third function, unrelated to interfacing with the core system. This is to supply development tools to make the programmer's task easier. Unlike the other features discussed these are directly under programmer control. The help and menu systems and the editor are the major such tools supplied.

The windowed and TTY PDEs

In P the PDE uses a number of windows to enable the user, for example, to watch debugging output without disturbing program output. In UV all parts of the PDE share a single output stream to the user terminal. Where it is necessary to take account of these differences we shall refer to the windowed and the TTY PDEs, respectively.

The PDE and the rest of the system

To conclude this section, it should be noted that the distinction between the PDE and the rest of the system is not absolutely clear cut. The windowed PDE will not work without the window library, and some of the facilities in that library (the calculator, for example) are designed specifically for the PDE. Moreover, there are development tools that are not described in this chapter, such as the lint checker, the compiler and the token compiler. These function as application programs running from the top-level interpreter and differ from the PDE in that they take full control of the system and carry out a specific task, then terminate. They are described in their own chapters.

25.2 Setting up and terminating the windowed PDE

Setting up the PDE

The job of setting up the PDE is done jointly by code in the MNU file and by the module **systed**.

The reason for so dividing the initialisation code is simply that it is expected that many users will want to alter the number of modules loaded or the colours and positions of windows opened, whereas it is less likely that users will want to reconfigure the status line or the keyboard setup.

The internal design of **systed** is not discussed here because the source is heavily commented. Users who are keen to get on using the PDE can skip most of this chapter at first reading and return to it when they find aspects of the system they want to reconfigure. They will however probably want to read the Section on what the various keys do (§25.2.7.1 below).

Users of 12 have no access to the MNU file and cannot reconfigure the start-up procedure.

Initialisation

The initialisation code has the following tasks:

- Program keys
- Set the system colours
- Establish a window exception handler
- Create various windows
- Print the sign-on message
- Open various modules

This is roughly the order in which these tasks should be performed. The module **systed** carries out the first three, the MNU file the rest.

The module **systed** exports a predicate **setup_system_editor/1** that causes the initialisation code in **systed** to be evaluated. The first statements in the MNU file that opens the PDE must open **systed** and call **setup_system_editor**; other windows cannot be opened unless this is done (this is because **systed** establishes the screen layout and system colours). The argument to **setup_system_editor** is a string to be displayed during start-up.

Closing down

The PDE halt goal is also stored in **systed**. **systed** is a program module and therefore is not resident in memory other than at startup and closedown.

25.2.1 The system colours

The first part of PROLOG2.MNU establishes the system colours. To do this it has to open the **systed** module.

/* 1. Starting the system editor */

/* The system editor module contains key settings and other things essential to the operation of the P.D.E. If it is omitted the user must supply alternative settings. The system editor also processes the colours for the P.D.E. window. Any clauses for user_col, used to reconfigure the colours of system windows should be inserted immediately after this comment. */

?- default_name_p2("SYSTED","PRM",Y),
      open_module(_,Y,none,actual).

?- setup_system_colours.

Different colours look better on different systems; **systed** examines the hardware configuration and sets colours suitable for the PDE windows. These can be retrieved using the predicate **system_col/2** (you can see this being done in the MNU file). **system_col/2** takes as its first argument an atom and returns an attribute as its second. The atoms are listed in the article **system colours** in the Prolog-2 Encyclopaedia.

Example: To make the help window come out black on yellow:

user_col(help,black on yellow).

?- default_name_sys("SYSTED","PRM",F),
      open_module(_,F,none,actual).

?- setup_system_colours.

... rest of MNU file as supplied.

25.2.2 The PDE windows

The next part of the PROLOG2.MNU file sets up the PDE windows.

There are a few fixed windows associated with the PDE which are set up by the MNU file.

These windows are:

pde_main   The main top-level interpreter window, used by **top**.

pde_status   The status line, used by anyone. The routines that maintain the status line are in **systed**.

The Prolog-2 User Guide

pde_help The help display. **pde_help** is used exclusively by the module **help**.

pde_break The break window is used by the top-level interpreter when in a break state. All break levels use the same window.

pde_debug The debug window is used by Prolog-2 to display the trace interaction. Unless you select the debug menu you will also select debug options by typing in **pde_debug**.

pde_menu Used for the interrupt and error menus.

pde_info Used for various information displays, principally for error messages. If you correct a syntax error you will also use this as an input window.

Note:

(1) You can tell from the above which windows it is safe to leave out in which circumstances.

(2) The PDE uses the explicit names of these streams on occasion. Although the system state debug is set to **pde_debug**, for example, that does not mean that the module debug will look at the state to decide which stream to use. You must not change the names of these streams. In addition they must be windows. If you make them, say, files the behaviour of the PDE will be unpredictable.

(3) It is good practice to use the system colours to set up these windows, but of course you can set the colours explicitly if you like. If you do this, though, you take responsibility for portability between different displays; blue on some colour systems comes out underlined on some mono ones. If you use the system colours you will avoid this problem.

(4) Although you are free to change the size and position of windows, you should bear in mind their purpose. A very small **pde_main** window may make input very difficult. A **pde_menu** that is too short to hold the error and interrupt menus will cause problems.

25.2.3 Standard streams

Some of the windows just set up have to be used as values of system states.

/* 3. The standard streams */

/* The following assignments should not be changed if the supplied
  program development environment is being used */

```
?-      state(stdio,_,pde_main),
        state(error,_,pde_menu),
        state(debug,_,pde_debug),
        state(help,_,pde_help).
```

25.2.4 The virtual drive

The virtal drive is not set in the PROLOG2.MNU file because not all systems have the same names for drives. The virtual drive must be able to accommodate any Prolog-2 temporary files (the largest of these will be the image of Prolog-2 written when **command/?** is used), and, subject to this constraint, should be the fastest drive available. For most hard-disk users uncommenting the directive in the MNU file will be the best solution.

/* 4. Setting the virtual drive */

/* As configured the system will always use the root directory of the default drive for virtual files and saved images. If you have a hard disk C you can uncomment the following line and make sure that is used. If you have a RAM disk with enough space on it you can speed up the command BIPs spectacularly by using that. */

/* ?- state(virtual_drive,_,"C").*/

25.2.5 The mouse

The mouse is initialised next. If there is a mouse but you don't want to use it the directive may be removed.

/* 5. The mouse */

/* Initialise the mouse. On systems which (contrary to the indication that this is reserved for DOS) use interrupt 33H for something else you must comment out this directive, or unpredictable behaviour will result. */

?- mouse(-1,[51],_).   /* INT 33H */

25.2.6 External editor

The external editor is available from the menu system provided its command path has been specified. The PROLOG2.MNU file installs WordStar, but may easily be edited.

/* 6. Installation of an editor */

/* This assertion can be used to install the user's own editor in the menu system for fast access. Replace the string "C:\\WS4\\WS" with the path for your editor and replace max by the amount of memory it needs. Then uncomment the statement. The relevant option is on the system menu */

The Prolog-2 User Guide

?- '$sys'(assert(param(user_editor,"C:\\WS4\\WS"+max))).

25.2.7 Setting up the system editor

Next the system makes an initialisation call to systed.

/* 7. Setting up the system editor */

/* setup_system_editor is exported by SYSTED and sets up the edit keys. It also prints the sign on message, which is the address below. This is not the copyright message and the user is free to change it, but if you have a dealer address and telephone number there you will find it a quick way of remembering who to ring in case of difficulties! Don't make it more than five lines. */

?- setup_system_editor(
"   Name of Prolog-2 vendor").

25.2.7.1 Setting system keys

PDE modules use a common convention about the significance of keys that is an extension of the conventions used by the window library. For convenience that whole set of conventions is listed here. You should note, however, that some of the keys will not always be active. For example, there would be little point in using <F3> to recall a command when selecting from a menu or using the calculator. It *is* the case that the same key always does the same thing when it is active.

<Esc>   Escape from what you're doing. This may mean abandoning an edit or selecting a default from a menu. The same effect can be obtained by clicking the right mouse button if you have an appropriate mouse. Because the top level interpreter is the lowest level, <Esc> has no effect on it.

Backspace   Delete a character to the left.

                All these have the obvious cursor movement effects.

<Enter>   Accept the current edit, selection or whatever.

<Delete>   Delete the character at the cursor

<Insert>	Toggle between insert and replace mode. Note that this is a global toggle; if you change it in the editor it stays changed in the top level interpreter. The current setting is displayed on the status line.
<F1>	Help. Help will try to reconstruct a help context based on what you are doing; if it is unable to it will enter the help system at the root instead.
<F2>	Menus. From the top level interpreter this enters menus at the top; in other places it may enter a local menu system.
<F3>	Back through command stack. The command stack is maintained by the top level interpreter and is only available there; see §25.10 for details.
<F4>	Forward through command stack.
<F5>	Clear.
<F6>	Show function keys. A table of function keys that are currently available will be displayed.
<F7>	Hide all PDE windows. They remain hidden until a key is pressed.
<F8>	Hide debug window until needed. The debugger normally leaves its output on the screen between goals. If this gets in the way you can use this key to hide it.
<F9>	Hide the current window until a key is pressed. The current window is the one in which you are working. In this context it should be remarked that the PDE is strictly modal in its handling of windows, and there is only one that you can work in at any one time.
<F10>	Reveal the debug window. This is only needed in exceptional circumstances; it is usually revealed when needed.

25.2.7.2 Signing on

The sign-on message is printed by **systed**. This is not a copyright message and you may change it as you please, or omit it. It will be written to the stream **pde_main**. It will be cleared by **top** when it is loaded.

The other startup output goes to the status line and is only there to alleviate the boredom of waiting for the PDE to load. As soon as the status line is available the PDE writes the name of the system directory on it; this can be helpful if you have several MNU files on a disk in different directories and are not sure which you are using.

25.2.7.3 Setting the default window exception

Finally **setup_system_editor** establishes a window exception handler for all PDE

The Prolog-2 User Guide

windows. This is called **pde_exception/2**. Exceptions that are not generated by PDE windows will fall through this and succeed.

If you need to establish your own window exception handler, the correct way to proceed is to chain it onto the start of the existing one, and to code it so that it only affects your own windows. For example, suppose I have a window called **sensitive** in which all window exceptions are to fail. To install a handler say:

my_exception(Excode,window(sensitive,_)) :- !,fail.

```
?-  state(window_exception,Oldwe,Oldwe),
    Goal =.. [Oldwe,A,B],
    assert((my_exception(A,B) :- Goal)).
```

The directive constructs a call to the old handler if the new one isn't used. You should always do this rather than simply switching off all window exceptions; parts of the system you don't know about may be relying on trapping some of them!

25.2.8 Registering system windows

Registering windows ensures that they are tidied neatly in the case of an abort. Windows are classified according to their desired status after a system restart:

p	Window exists and is displayed
h	Window exists but is hidden
t	Window does not exist

Naturally none of the windows created here will be of type t.

/* 8. Registering the system windows */

/* Registering a window is a way of specifying what should happen to it when an abort occurs. p means permanent, h means permanent but hidden and t means temporary */

```
?-      register(pde_main,p),
        register(pde_status,p),
        register(pde_notes,h),
        register(pde_help,h),
        register(pde_help_menu,h),
        register(pde_break,h),
        register(pde_debug,h),
        register(pde_menu,h),
        register(pde_info,h).
```

25.2.9 Loading the PDE modules

The supplied MNU opens modules in the following order:

syted
window
pretty
sysmess
grules
dec10
int
debug
error
efile
help
htext
edit
top

In other words **systed**, then core facilities, then the PDE.

If you want to leave parts of the PDE out you should observe the following rules:

(1)   You must load **window**; the PDE uses routines from it.

(2)   If you load **error** you must load **efile**; if **help**, **htext**; if **menus**, **menudata** and **menuinfo**.

(3)   Although the final statistics display is called from **systed**, you will not see it unless **sysmess** is loaded.

The menu system — that is, the modules **menus**, **menudata** and **menuinfo** — is not loaded from PROLOG2.MNU. Instead it will be loaded the first time the <F2> function key is pressed, and will then remain in memory unless removed.

You may also want to add things to the file: **syslib**, **gemlib** or **pr1ops**. Such additions should come as near to the start as possible, but not before **systed**.

Do not try to open the compiler, the lint checker or the token compiler from PROLOG2.MNU; these are opened when needed by the system. You should ensure that they are available in the Prolog directory.

Note the use of **default_name_p2** to open the system modules. This means that the files should be in the same directory as the Prolog-2 executable file, irrespective of the location of the MNU file.

25.2.10 Starting the top-level interpreter

The last thing in PROLOG2.MNU is the code that starts the top-level interpreter. This

The Prolog-2 User Guide

may vary from time to time but will be roughly as follows:

/* 10. Starting the system */

/* The following code sets up the top-level interpreter and prints the initial help message - you can suppress or amend the message if you don't like it. */

```
?-      state(stdio,Window,Window),
        state(halt_goal,_,prolog_halt_goal),
        state(interrupt_goal,_,interrupt),
        state(error_goal,_,error),
        state(error_break,_,on),
        state(type_class,_,prolog),
        state(token_class,_,prolog),
        state(window_exception,_,sys_exception),
        state(global(12),_,0),
        window(Window,clear),
        tell(Window),
        write("Press F1 to get help at any time"),nl,
        write("Press F2 to get a menu of facilities"),nl,
        write(
        "To enter a program select \"Notepad\" from this menu"),
        nl,
        write("To enter a query type it at the ?- prompt"),nl,
        write("F6 gives a summary of function key actions"),
        nl,nl,
        window(pde_status,clear),
        status_line(other,_,"Insert"),
        state(abort_goal,_,prolog),
        restart.
```

You can delete the **write** statements if you want.

25.2.11 Closing down

systed also contains the PDE closedown procedure. This allows the editor to prompt for changed files to be saved and prints the closedown statistics. It than transfers to the system close down, which flushes all buffers and goes to the operating system terminate procedure.

If you are using the PDE and want to add your own closedown traps you should chain them onto the start of the existing trap rather than overwriting it (see §25.2.7.3).

25.2.12 How to select from a menu

Items in parentheses

When the menu is displayed items may be in parentheses; this means that these items

The Prolog-2 User Guide

are not available on this occasion, but will be under the right circumstances. Such items will be called disabled; the rest are enabled.

A bar is placed over a menu item — usually the first enabled item. The bar responds to the cursor keys (<home>, <end>, <page_up>, <page_down>, <cursor_up>, <cursor_down>). In a small menu such as the interrupt menu only <cursor_up> and <cursor_down> will be needed. In larger menus the paging keys can be used to move up and down in larger steps. To select an item, move the bar there and press <Enter>. In addition each option may be selected by keying the first (usually the only) upper case letter in the item (either case will do).

The escape and function keys

Other keys active in menus include:

<esc>   As usual, <esc> means leave the menu. In this case a default action will be selected.

<F1>   As usual, <F1> means help. If you press <F1> you will get help on the option on which the bar is sitting; if you select help from a menu you will get into the help system at some appropriate place as described with individual menus.

<F7>   As usual, <F7> means conceal all PDE windows.

<F9>   As usual, <F9> means conceal the menu. This is hardly necessary in small menus unless you are very unlucky.

Of mice and menus

If you have a compatible mouse installed you can use it for selecting from menus.

An inverse video square will appear in the menu window and can be moved around within the window; it attracts the bar towards itself. If you click the left button you select the item where the mouse cursor is (unless it is disabled. Note this carefully; you do NOT select the item where the bar is, though these will very often be the same). Pressing the right hand button on the mouse has the same effect as pressing the <esc> key.

If there is a mouse installed then it will not be possible to select from a menu using the cursor keys. If you prefer to use the cursor keys, uninstall the mouse.

Pre-empting a menu

You can type ahead to a menu by typing an appropriate letter, and the menu will then not appear; but you cannot cursor-ahead or click-ahead.

The Prolog-2 User Guide

25.3 Setting up and terminating the TTY PDE

The setup procedure for the TTY PDE is much simpler. First of all there is a standard utility predicate for loading a system module:

```
'$load_system_prm'(N,X,ACCESS)
    :-
    write(" Loading module "),
    default_name_sys(X,"prm",SYSTEM_NAME),
    write(X),
    write(" --> "),
    write(N),
    open_module(Name,SYSTEM_NAME,ACCESS,actual),
    write(" ("),
    write(Name),
    write(")"),
    nl.
```

25.3.1 Signing on

The sign-on message is printed as follows (example from V):

```
?-      write("Prolog-2/VAX    Version v"),
        version(High,Low),
        write(High),write("."),write(Low),nl,nl.
```

25.3.2 Loading standard modules

The modules are then loaded as follows:

```
?- '$load_system_prm'(int,     "int",none).
?- '$load_system_prm'(error,   "error",none).
?- '$load_system_prm'(efile,   "efile",none).
?- '$load_system_prm'(help,    "help",none).
?- '$load_system_prm'(biphelp,"biphelp",none).
?- '$load_system_prm'(debug,   "debug",none).
?- '$load_system_prm'(dec10,   "dec10",none).
?- '$load_system_prm'(sysmess,"sysmess",none).
?- '$load_system_prm'(pretty,  "pretty",none).
?- '$load_system_prm'(compiler,"compiler",none).
?- '$load_system_prm'(subproc,"subproc",none).
?- '$load_system_prm'(lint,"lint",none).
?- '$load_system_prm'(grules,"grules",none).
?- '$load_system_prm'(config,"config",none).
?- '$load_system_prm'(pde,     "pde",none).
```

Most of these modules are similar to those loaded in the windowed PDE. **pde** is a variant of **systed**.

25.3.3 Loading I/O routines

In V it is possible to load code to display the PDE in windows; we call this the SMG PDE because it uses the SMG window package. This interface will be described below. Which of the two interfaces is loaded depends on which I/O module is opened. In U only the TTY interface is available.

```
/*
        Load chosen io module
        ---------------------
        (note that these are strictly alternatives, DO NOT LOAD BOTH)
*/
```

/* If Prolog-2 is being run interactively then load the window module, otherwise load the tty module */

?- interactive -> '$load_system_prm'(iowindow,"iowindow",none) ;
                  '$load_system_prm'(iotty,   "iotty",none).

25.3.4 Loading the top-level interpreter

Lastly the top-level interpreter is loaded, the temporary load predicate removed and the top-level interpreter started.

?- '$load_system_prm'(top,   "top",none).

?- retractall('$load_system_prm'/3).

?- prolog_start_goal.

25.3.5 The SMG PDE

The SMG PDE is a variant of the TTY PDE that distributes input/output between windows. It differs from the TTY PDE in using **iowindow** rather than **iotty** for I/O calls; all other modules are the same. The small module **config** contains code to switch between SMG and TTY modes. The predicates used for this are called **tty_mode** and **window_mode**.

25.4 System message facilities

The Prolog-2 system rarely speaks to you. Its built-in message routine is used only for

(1) the banner

(2) fatal error messages.

In the first case it is not thought desirable that the environment should be left to supply the message; in the second, the state of the system is so seriously affected that the environment cannot be trusted to output a message. A special case of this occurs when

The Prolog-2 User Guide

an error occurs before the environment has signalled that it is capable of handling errors by setting an abort goal.

All other output is passed through the environment. The following system predicates will produce no output unless appropriate routines are loaded:

statistics/0 Requires **stats_mess/0**.

core/0 Requires **core_mess/0**.

debugging/0 Requires **debug_mess/0**.

backtrace/0,1 Requires **back_mess/1** (the argument being the number of ancestors wanted, as in **backtrace/1**. **backtrace/0** calls **back_msg/1** with argument 10).

listing/? All forms require **pretty_clause/2**, which takes as arguments firstly the clause and secondly a variable name structure for it. The forms of listing that can list several predicates also use **pretty_pred/1** to print a comment with the predicate name and arity in it.

command/? The forms of **command** that print a message prompting the user to press a key to return to Prolog-2 use the predicate **command_msg/0** to print the message *and to wait for the key*. Therefore omission of this predicate will suppress not only the message but also the wait.

Further details of these predicates will be found in the Prolog-2 Encyclopaedia.

25.5 Interrupts and the interrupt menu

The conditions that generate a keyboard interrupt are described elsewhere; the PDE supplies a predicate, **interrupt/0** in the module interrupt, which handles interaction with the user on detection of this interrupt.

The BIP **interrupt/0** displays a menu in the window **pde_menu** and allows the user to select an option.

25.5.1 Interrupt menu options

The options available on the interrupt menu are summarised below.

Abort Abort execution. This is the traditional way of breaking out of a closed loop. The existing evaluation is cleared and the abort goal is executed. If you are using **top** from the PDE the abort goal restarts the query system at break level 0 (see §25.11).

Break Enter break state. The goal **break/0** is evaluated. If you are using **top**

The Prolog-2 User Guide

from the PDE this gives a new invocation of the query system in the **pde_break** window with a number identifying the break level to the left of the **?-** prompt (see §25.11). When you leave break, the interrupt menu is redisplayed.

Continue Continue execution. The application continues as though it had not been interrupted.

Exit Exit from Prolog. The confirmation menu is displayed to check that you did not select this by accident. The confirmation menu is a query box from the window library. If you cancel, the interrupt menu is redisplayed; if you select OK then the halt procedure is executed (see §25.2-3).

Notrace Like continue, but if tracing was on it is switched off first.

Trace Like continue but tracing is switched on. As usual this means that the common module is debugged if no other module has been selected. To debug a different module you have to enter a break state and use the **debug/1** BIP.

Help Enter the help system at the root (see §25.8). On leaving help, the interrupt menu is redisplayed.

25.6 Debugging

The next kind of break that the PDE traps is the debug break.

Chapter 21 explains how the Prolog-2 system contains code to output the trace messages at each port to the debug stream; on the other hand, the code that handles the user interaction at the debug prompt is not part of the core system.

The user can specify interaction at a port either by switching tracing on or by spying; and can also adjust which ports are leashed for interaction.

The Prolog-2 system contains a number of system predicates that can be called from a debug break to affect the course of execution or the degree of reporting, but provides no way to access them.

The PDE supplements this deficiency by allowing the user either to select an option by typing a letter (as in DECsystem-10 Prolog) or to call up a menu and select from that as described in §25.2-3 of this Manual.

Although strictly speaking there are no restraints on the way that interaction at a leashed port can take place, there is a recommended set of abbreviations for the various possible options. The PDE keeps strictly to these conventions, adding a few window-related options; there is therefore little to be said here about the list of options available. A full list of options is given in the Prolog-2 Encyclopaedia under **debug_menu**.

The Prolog-2 User Guide

25.6.1 Goal annotations

Annotations appear in [] after the goal. They are produced by the debugger and will therefore only be printed at call ports where interaction takes place.

Undefined predicates are marked [**Undefined**]. Predicates exported by modules other than the debug module are annotated with the name of that module; system predicates are marked [**system**].

The other annotation that is sometimes printed is an exclamation mark ! used to indicate possible circularities. The mark is printed when the current goal is a special case of its ancestor of half depth (being equal is a special case of being a special case).

25.6.2 Debugging in the windowed PDE

pde_debug is a TTY style window, as are **pde_main** and **pde_break**. This means that is designed for both system output and user input, with the two interleaved. It indicates that it is awaiting input by outputting a ?.

pde_debug as set up in the distributed PROLOG2.MNU is larger than the viewport with the same name. It is possible to change **pde_debug** to a view window (defined in §24.1; see also §25.9 of this Manual) and page up and down over it to see debugging output that has scrolled off the screen; but in this mode it will not accept input. When you have finished viewing it returns to the original position so that you can see the input you type.

pde_debug is revealed when debugging is switched on and is hidden when it is switched off. If you are not tracing then its presence on the screen may be a nuisance; while you are in **pde_main** or **pde_break** <F8> will hide it until it is needed.

pde_debug obeys the usual conventions for input to TTY windows (see §25.2). The following function keys are active:

<F1>	Help. Enters help at the 'debug options' node
<F2>	Menu. Invokes the menu of debug options
<F5>	Clear editing
<F6>	Show keys
<F7>	Temporarily hide all PDE windows
<F9>	Hide **pde_debug** temporarily

The module debug also exports a predicate **debug_streams/2** which is called by the Prolog-2 interpreter every time the debug module is changed. It pulls up the debug window and unhides it if debugging is switched on; and it updates the status line display.

It should be noted that the debug window appears when:

(1) debugging is switched on or switched to a new module

(2) any interaction with the user is to take place
(3) <F10> is used during input to a PDE window.

or to any TTY window that has not reconfigured the system editor. Under these circumstances **pde_debug** will also be pulled up.

It disappears when

(1) debugging is switched off
(2) <F8> is used to hide it
(3) option i on the debug menu is selected.

It may also get covered up by other windows. It is usually the case that the window is there when you don't want it, rather than the other way round. However, if you have leashing set to **none** and you hide the window then unless you get an opportunity to press <F10>, say because your program is demanding input, you will not see the trace.

25.7 Error handling

In debugging the Prolog-2 system takes responsibility for the display and the PDE deals with interaction; but when an error occurs the PDE is responsible for all error handling — all the system's built in error handler can do is print a numeric message and terminate. Only one predicate, **error/4**, is exported by the module **error**, and this is invoked whenever an error occurs and error breaks are enabled.

25.7.1 The BIP error/4

The format of the call to **error/4** is described in Chapter 20.

The arguments to error/4

To recap, the four arguments to **error/4** are:

(1) Error class: indicates the seriousness of the error

0	Syntax
1	Normal
2	Serious: the current evaluation is lost and the error must eventually be aborted
3	Fatal: fatal errors are not passed to the error handler.

(2) Error number.

(3) Error goal: this is an attempt by the system to reconstruct the goal that caused the error; it will not always be successful, because some Prolog-2 predicates are defined in terms of internal predicates that will be displayed instead.

In compiled code the error handler displays the compiled module where the error occurred and the offset in the module. This may be used with a symbol table to locate the approximate cause of the error.

The Prolog-2 User Guide

(4) Supplementary information: this depends on the error. For example, if the error number is **system** (system error) this returns the system error code.

25.7.2 Displaying the error message

Error messages are stored in the module **efile**. The user may replace **efile** with a different file of messages, provided the appropriate form of predicate is used.

The module errfile exports a predicate **error_file/3** whose arguments are as follows:

(1) The error number (normally an input argument).

(2) The error message, stored as a string (normally an output argument).

(3) The symbolic name of the error. This is displayed in brackets after the error number, and may be looked up in the Prolog-2 Encyclopaedia. It is also used to find the relevant help for the error in the help system.

The error message is displayed in the window **pde_info**. A syntax error will also display the context, that is, the term being read when the error occurred with the message **[here]** at the point where parsing was abandoned.

The context buffer

As explained in the Prolog-2 Tokeniser Manual, there is a fixed size buffer used for storing terms being parsed. If this fixed size buffer fills up characters are moved along and earlier ones are lost as a result. If this has happened three dots will occur at the start of the context.

When a syntax error occurs Prolog-2 tries to reach the end of the term, firstly so as to report the context fully and secondly to start the next term at the right place.

If it has not reached the end of the term by the time the buffer is full it will not scroll the buffer (it doesn't want to lose the point where the error occurred) but it will continue looking for a terminator without storing characters. If this happens three dots will appear at the end of the error context.

In either case the context is said to be incomplete.

Sometimes an incomplete context will be reported erroneously because of the syntax error. For example, the term

a('$foo) - b('$bar').

would fit easily in the buffer. However the missing ' after foo, which is reported as 'Missing comma or operator' after the $ of $bar is read, will also prevent the terminator from being detected (it still thinks that '). starts a quoted atom). The input stream will continue to be scanned for terminators and will probably overflow the buffer.

If an error message cannot be found (**error_file/3** fails) then the message **???** is displayed. This should not happen unless you have changed **efile** or are using one from the wrong version of Prolog-2.

25.7.3 Error options

The error menu is displayed immediately after **pde_info**. Some items will always be disabled: the options available depend on the seriousness of the error:

Syntax(0)   a b e f h r

Normal(1)   a b e f h t

Serious(2)   a e h

Selection from the menu is made as described in §25.2-3 of this Manual (Interrupts). The options are as follows:

Abort   Abort execution

The evaluation is cleared and the abort goal is executed. If top is loaded this causes the top-level query system to be restarted at break level 0

Break   Break

The goal **break** is evaluated. If top is loaded this causes the top-level query system to be invoked at another level. After the break the menu is redisplayed

Exit   Leave Prolog

The usual query window is displayed first. If the user cancels that exit the menu is redisplayed

Fail   Fail the goal

The Prolog-2 User Guide

This is the usual response to normal errors and allows execution to carry on. If you are debugging this is a sensible option to use because it causes the FAIL port of the error goal to be leashed as though it had been skipped to, and therefore you get a chance to interact through the debugger, where many more options are available

Help   Help

Enter the help system at the point indicated by the error file. After the help session is over the error menu is redisplayed

coRrect   Correct syntax

This is only allowed for syntax errors where the context is complete; if it is incomplete the correct option will be disabled. When correct is selected the window **pde_info** is redrawn with only the incorrect term in it. It can then be edited using the edit conventions appropriate for a TTY window

Trace   Trace execution

Trace is switched on and the goal is failed. As usual, if debugging was off it will be switched on for the common module. This is not usually a very helpful option. Tracing only affects goals whose call ports have not yet been reached, so that the goals that caused the error will not be reported, even though some of their ports have yet to be traversed.

25.8 The help system

25.8.1 The help system in P

The help system is a completely optional part of the PDE; everything else will work without it. It is useful to have it available, especially for help on system predicates if you forget the order of arguments, and if you use the menu system, for which it provides the documentation.

A help system that requires a manual of its own has failed in its purpose, and there should be no need to refer to this chapter before using help. Pressing <F1> and looking around is the best way to learn about help. Having said that, we proceed to give details of how it works.

Structure of the help system

The help system is a network of nodes associated with each of which there is a string of text. Each node has an ID which is a string which is used to identify the node. It is never necessary or useful to remember these IDs.

The help system is divided into 'chapters' for indexing purposes. The only node that is not in any chapter is the root; this is available from every node.

This Chapter of the Manual will describe the organisation of help down to the help system chapter level; beyond that the user can discover the help system's chapter structure by turning to its index page.

25.8.1.1 Using help

The help predicates

The module help exports two predicates, **help/0** and **help/1**.

help/0 enters the help system at the root. It is possible to get into help from the top-level interpreter by typing

?- help.

but more usually you will select help from a menu or press <F1>.

When you are in help, the text for the active node will be displayed in the window **pde_help** and the help menu will contain a menu of possible actions from which you select in the usual way.

The first item on the menu is always \. The other fixed items are:

- Last, which returns to the previous item

- Enter, which allows you to type the name of a help node.

The root node has a number of useful nodes available from it:

(1) Instructions

A concise resume of these instructions

(2) Indexes to all help chapters

From the root node you can get to the index for any chapter.

The index nodes are like other nodes but contain a list of menu entries and in some chapters a brief account of the contents of that node. Using the index you can get quite deep in the help network quickly, but not every node is on the index. The less you know, the earlier on the index should be your selection.

25.8.1.2 Chapters in the help system

Help system chapter numbers are given here for reference but have no other significance.

The Help system chapters are:

0	Indexes and instructions
1	System predicates and states, expressions etc
2	The PDE
3	How to ...?
4	Menu help
5	Error help
6	Glossary

You will not normally enter 4 and 5 from the index; they are designed for help with the menu and error systems respectively.

Chapter 0: Indexes and instructions

Chapter 0 is one flat level hanging off the root node; it consists of the instructions and the five other indexes.

Chapter 1: System predicates and states

Chapter 1 contains most of the detailed information in the system; its nodes are used as leaves by other chapters. The highest level, that immediately below the index, is a menu of predicate names.

A few predicates have deeper structures:

- All predicates that evaluate expressions have an entry into the expressions help nodes

- **state**/3 has a menu of all system states

- Multi-function predicates like **window**/2 have a menu of possible arguments

Chapter 1 name entries are used by the help system when the <F1> key is pressed while editing; if a predicate name is to the immediate left of the cursor that is used as the entry node.

Chapter 2: The PDE

Chapter 2 is a condensed version of this Manual.

Chapter 3: How to ...?

Chapter 3 is only accessible through its root; its structure corresponds roughly to the divisions of the Prolog-2 Language Reference Manual and allows you to get help about particular tasks when you don't know the names of the necessary predicates.

Chapter 4: Menu help

Chapter 4 contains entries for all the help items obtainable by pressing <F1> in a menu. The chapter is divided at the top level according to the different menu systems (menus itself, error, interrupt, debug and the editor) and each subdivision is structured like the appropriate menu system.

Chapter 5: Error help

Chapter 5 contains the help items for error conditions used when the user selects help from the error menu.

Chapter 6: Glossary

The glossary is used on other help screens to explain non-standard terminology.

25.8.1.3 Adding help

It is possible for the programmer to add help to the system by defining extra chapters. Some chapters are reserved for extra Prolog-2 utilities (e.g. PTANG).

The procedure for adding help is as follows:

(1) Select a predicate name that is not being used elsewhere (e.g. **lizard_help**).

(2) Select an integer chapter number. Numbers up to 100 are reserved for Prolog.

(3) For each help screen you need to specify:

>(a) a help token. This must be of the form "**N_token**" where N is your selected chapter number and token a unique identifier within the chapter ("**101_salamanders**").

>(b) the text. Supply a list of strings and make sure it fits because nobody else will.

>(c) the menu. The part above the bar is generated automatically — leave it out. The menu items are of the form

Token-Title

where **Token** is one of the help tokens ("**101_salamanders**", say) and **Title** is the string to appear "**Salamanders**").

Specify this information by supplying clauses for your predicate name:

The Prolog-2 User Guide

lizard_help(Token,Text,Menu).

Remember to make this a public predicate.

(4) Tell Prolog-2 to use your chapter for that help chapter by saying, e.g.

?- '$sys'(assert(param(help_chapter(101),lizard_help))).

(5) You cannot get into your own help from the help Enter option. To invoke help with your own screen as start page use

help(101,"salamanders").

You can also add your help to a menu by specifying the help menu item in the form 101*"salamanders". If you omit the override 101* **chapter** 4, the system menu help chapter, will be used.

25.8.1.4 The predicates help_text/3 and help_alias/3

The **help_text/3** predicate is used by the help system to retrieve nodes of the help system. **help_text/3** is stored in the file HTEXT1.PRM.

The arguments of **help_text/3** are as follows:

(1) The node ID

(2) A list of strings of text associated with the node

(3) A list of nodes to be added to the help menu when this node is selected. Each node takes the form.

Token-Title

where Token is the node ID and Title the description of it to be displayed on the menu.

The menu system automatically generates accelerator keys for its menus; so Title should usually be a lower-case string.

help_alias/3 is identical in format but is used for Chapters 2-6 of help and is stored in HTEXT2.PRM.[2]

25.8.1.5 Help in 4

The help system in 4 uses a different data representation. The two predicates described in §25.8.4 are stored in files HTEXT1.PRO and HTEXT2.PRO, and a predicate

---

[2] The exact arrangement of help text is influenced by the need to ship software on 360K diskettes, and may change in the future.

help_index/2, exported by the module hindex stores the offset of each clause in the file. This representation is used because there is no virtual memory in 4.

25.8.2 The help system in UV

Prolog2 provides help on all its built-in predicates. The help system is intended to augment, not replace, the manuals: the descriptions of bips are concise summaries of the full information contained in the written documentation.

?- help(token).

Prolog searches its library for all help items which contain the string "token" and displays them in alphabetical order. If, however, you specify an exact match like help(get_token) then that item is displayed first, all the succeeding matches are then displayed in alphabetical order.

To exit the help facility, press the "n" key in response to the "Another entry (y/n) ?" prompt.

After help has finished it returns you to the top level interpreter ("?-" prompt) and you may enter goals in the usual way. However, if you are running the SMG PDE the help screen will remain on the screen, enabling you to read it while you type a goal. With the help window on the screen you will only be able to see a few lines of output from the TLI. The help window may be hidden by calling the "hide" menu ("GOLD-1" on the keypad) and selecting the "Help" option, or by calling "hi(help)" which is bound to "GOLD-PF3" on the keypad.

The Prolog interpreter also provides another entry into the help system via a Unix-style "apropos" call.

?- apropos(get).

This displays the names of all the Prolog2 bips which contain the string "get" (get,get0,ttyget etc.,).

Help is available from all areas of VMS where you are likely to be doing Prolog development work, namely the DCL command line, the TPU editor and the Prolog interpreter itself.

The method of access to help varies slightly depending on the environment from which you call it. Examples of access are given below:

(1) From the DCL Command line

$ PHELP get_token

Invokes the VAX/VMS interactive help system and displays the description of the Prolog2 built-in predicate "get_token". You are prompted by VMS for further items. Hitting a Carriage return at the "Topic? " prompt will terminate help.

The Prolog-2 User Guide

    $ HELP get_token

Similarly invokes the VAX help facility, but you may mix requests for help on DCL topics with Prolog topics.

(2) From Prolog:

?- help.

(3) From the Prolog Editor:

Using the extension to Digital's EVE editor which is provided with this release allows access to Prolog help from an edit session. You may invoke the VAX/VMS help system within a special editor buffer during the edit session by pressing "CTRL/H". To get help on an item, enter its name or an abbreviation as if you were in DCL and hit carriage return when finished.

After you have finished the editor automatically removes the help window and returns you to your old editing context including repositioning the cursor. This is useful if you have forgotten, for instance, what the fifth argument to module/6 does. Type as much as you can remember, invoke help on "module" and immediately continue typing.

25.9 The menu system

The menu system is only present in the windowed PDE. Like help this is part of the system which can happily be left out.

Purpose of the menu system

The menu system provides a convenient way of carrying out common Prolog-2 tasks. Although anything you want to do in Prolog-2 can be done by queries entered at the top-level interpreter prompt, this requires you to know the name of the predicate and the order of argument. The menu system relieves you of this burden; it prompts for the necessary inputs. (It is also possible to have the menu system log the commands it uses so that you can store them and use them in programs.)

Using the menu system

Like the help system the menu system is supposed to be self-explanatory, so full documentation is not given here. Only the top level menu is discussed in detail.

Often (but not always) it is helpful to think of tasks in terms of the things they operate on. For example, suppose you want to consult a file. Look not for consult but for file; this is (naturally enough) attached to the I/O section of the main menu. On the file menu you will find a list of things you can do to files; consulting is one of them.

The usual way to get into the menu system is to press the key <F2>. In the debugger and the editor this displays a local menu, but elsewhere it displays the top-level menu of the menu system.

Menus uses the **menu** predicate in the window library, and the description in the Prolog-2 Encyclopaedia gives a full account of how to build a menu from the programmer's point of view.

Organisation of the menu system

The menu system is organised as a tree, with child nodes appearing to the right of, and further down the screen than, the parent menu. When a child menu is active the parent menu loses its title and is lowlighted.

Command menus and parameter menus

Menus in the menu system can be divided into two kinds:

(1) command menus
(2) parameter menus.

(1) Command menus

A command menu is a list of possible actions, which may be to carry out some task or to display another menu. For a complex task a child menu may be displayed with a number of parameters and a "Go" option on it; when Go is enabled there is enough information to carry out the command and the user may select it. Sometimes (typically after sending a command to Prolog-2 to carry out a task) a menu automatically disappears; sometimes a menu is displayed until the user keys <esc>. These actions are designed to be what is normally wanted, but will sometimes be wrong.

(2) Parameter menus

Parameter menus are a list of possible values for a parameter; they are one of a number of ways in which the menu system establishes the value of a parameter. The other devices are all in the window library and are therefore documented from the programmer's point of view in The Prolog-2 Encyclopaedia; the descriptions that follow are intended rather for the user.

Menus

Menus are the most important form of input selector in the system.

The procedure for selecting from a menu was described in §25.2.12.

Check menus

These provide several options, more than one of which can be selected. For example, when selecting leashing ports the user is presented with the menu:

>   Call
>   Exit
>   Redo
>   Fail

which are the four ports of the box model. Selecting one of them does not cause the box to disappear but instead makes a tick appear alongside it. Selecting it again makes the tick disappear. When all the selected items are ticked the user keys <esc> to cause the selection to take effect.

String box

A string box is a one-line window in which the user can type a string. A default may be displayed; if the first key pressed is not an edit key the window will be cleared. The edit keys work as usual and <Enter> commits the typing. <esc> leaves the window but causes the default to be used even if it has been overtyped.

String box with menu

A string box with a menu is just like a string box except that a menu of options is also available. This fact is indicated by the presence of an inverse video M at the left of the window. At any point you may press <F2> to see the menu. If you then select from the menu that selection will be used and the menu and box will disappear. If you escape from the menu you return to editing in the string box. Typically this combination is used for potentially very long menus where it may be easier to type the desired option than find it on the menu.

Valuator box

A valuator box is like a string box but will only accept digits and the minus sign. In addition it cannot be committed if the value is outside a certain range.

Locator

The locator is used to select a position on the screen. If a mouse is attached the locator uses that and the cursor keys are disabled; click at the required position on the left button. If there is no mouse the cursor keys will steer the 'mouse cursor' around and selection is made by pressing <Enter>.

Attribute box

An attribute box allows the user to enter a video attribute and to see an example of it. There are five windows, four used for foreground, background, bright and flashing;

select the part of the attribute you want to change with the up and down cursor keys and change it with the left and right cursor keys. The fifth window, marked Go, shows the complete attribute. Move the cursor to this and press <Enter> when you are finished. The mouse can also be used in an attribute box if attached; clicking in one of the top four lines changes that attribute, clicking Go selects that attribute.

Alarm box

An alarm box appears to indicate an error; the bell is sounded. After you have read the message press <esc> to clear the box.

Query box

A query box is a special menu whose options are 'OK' and 'Cancel'. It allows you to think twice about irreversible actions like deleting files.

Error handling in the menu system

Error handling in the menu system works as follows:

- As far as possible, errors are prevented by disabling options that would cause them.

- Where this is not possible (for example, where input is from a string box and, say, the user while creating a module types the name of one that already exists) an alarm box is used to inform the user of the error.

- In some cases errors will escape the menu system and fall into the Prolog error handler. In the case of space errors (unlikely unless you entered menus from a break window) you have to select **abort**, and the menu system will be cleared away. Otherwise selecting **Fail** keeps you in the menu system.

Other points are described in the sections on different parts of the system to which the rest of this chapter is devoted. The simplest way to find out what an option does is to move the bar onto it and press the help key, <F1>.

25.10 The editor

The Prolog-2 editor is a part of the windowed PDE, although it can be used as well in packaged applications. It makes available a predicate that allows the user to edit a window using a specified viewport — this is called **edit_window**/1. This makes available to the user the features of **edit**/2 as well as a number of extra Prolog-specific utilities.

As we have seen, the PDE establishes a notepad window, **pde_notes** at startup and the user can edit this window by selecting **Notepad** on the tools menu. The [option on the debug menu has the same effect.

The Prolog-2 User Guide

There is also a predicate **edit_window/0** that displays a menu of options that allow the selection of windows for editing and from which **edit_window/1** can be invoked once a window is selected. The user who wants to split a window between two viewports or edit several windows at the same time should use this; it is available as the **Edit** option on the tools menu.

Editor limitations

The editor is designed for use in debugging. It is not supposed to be used as a full-scale program editor, still less as a word processor. Options to load and save files have been incorporated so that the user can debug small programs without losing the source form, but it cannot be expected that a full-scale application will fit into the window.

There are a number of restrictions that should be noted:

(1) the window **pde_notes** is only 100 lines deep. Loading a longer file will give a 'File too large' error and cause the window to be cleared;

(2) you can expand the notepad window or edit a different one, but certain operations require that the whole text string in the window may be stored on the global stack. There is, therefore, an upper limit on window size in the editor that depends on your INI file; but under no circumstances would a file whose size exceeded 64K bytes be acceptable in 123;

(3) with big windows certain options that require global processing of the window (Goto on the Search menu for example) become very slow. After a few hundred lines even the marking of a block becomes slowish;

This warning is not supposed to put you off using the editor for appropriate files; merely to prevent you from throwing away your favourite word processor before you have discovered the Prolog-2 editor's limitations. §25.2.6 explains how you can install your normal editor to edit files from Prolog.

As most users will only need the notepad editor it is described first. The full features supplied by **edit_window/0** are described later.

25.10.1 Simple editing

When the editor is invoked the notepad is unhidden and pulled-up and the cursor appears in the edit window. If a mouse is available the mouse cursor appears as well. When the editor is reinvoked the cursor will be in the same place as before, but the mouse cursor will always be in the top left hand corner.

The user may type into the window using the alphabetic keypad and may use all the edit keys. The edit mode (inserting or replacing) is independent of the mode used in the top level interpreter; that mode replaces the TLI mode on the status line when the editor is invoked, together with certain other status information as described below.

Keys to note

The following keys warrant special mention:

<F1> As in the top-level interpreter this tries to find a built-in predicate name to the left of the cursor in the window and give help on that. Otherwise the help system is entered at the root.

<F2> The edit menu is displayed in the top left hand corner of the edit window. The more advanced edit options are available from this menu, and will be described in subsequent sections of this chapter.

<F5> This clears the line on which the cursor is positioned. It does not clear the whole edit (that would be dangerous!); to do this, select **New** from the file menu.

<F6> This gives the display of active function keys.

<F7> As usual this hides the edit window until <esc> is keyed.

<F9> Hides the complete PDE with the exception of the permanent windows **pde_main** and **pde_status**.

<esc> This key ends the editor session, but without destroying any work; next time you select the notepad everything will be as you left it.

The left hand column of the edit window is not used for editing but instead displays a 'scroll bar' (you need to watch for this if you set up your own window for editing; see below). The scroll bar may have arrows at the top and/or the bottom if the edit area extends beyond the viewport in that direction. These are merely for information unless you have a mouse, in which case you can click them instead of keying PageUp and Page Down. An inverse video M will appear near the top of the bar; clicking this is equivalent to pressing <F2>.

25.10.2 The file menu

The file menu allows you to load and save files from the editor.

The file menu options are:

Load
New
Save
save As
Template

25.10.3 The predicate menu

The predicate menu allows the user to consult or reconsult some or all of a window into the database or to list a predicate into a window.

The options are:

Module
Predicate listing
Consult
Reconsult

25.10.4 The form menu

The form menu allows you to try various tests on all or part of the window. In each case the whole window will be tested unless a block is marked, in which case the highlighted area will be tested.

The options on the form menu are:

Brackets
Syntax
Pretty
Eval

Although you can edit anything you want in a window, it usually only makes sense to apply these options to Prolog code.

25.10.5 The block menu

The block menu allows you to define a block and to Cut, Copy and Paste. Certain other menu options behave differently depending on whether a block is defined.

If you have a mouse you may establish a block by pressing the left button at the start of the block and dragging (moving the mouse with the button held down) to the desired end position, where the button should be released. You may also move the cursor to a position by clicking there without dragging.

The options on the block menu are:

Start
End
Cut
Paste
Copy

25.10.6 The search menu

The search menu allows you to search for a string in the window and (optionally) replace it by another one.

The options are:

Find
Again
Find/replace
Options
Goto

25.10.7 Details

The details option displays a window telling you:

- which file, if any, you are editing

- what the edit module is

If you use the editor from the top-level interpreter this information will be displayed on the status line; you only need details when you are using the editor without loading the rest of the PDE.

25.10.8 The multi-window editor

The full editor may be invoked from the tools menu or by the Prolog call

?- edit_window.

The full editor has a selected viewport which will be used if you select the Edit option. You may use the menu to change the selected viewport or to split it into two. You may also create and delete viewports. (In all these discussions we refer merely to viewports. This is because it is possible to deduce the window from the viewport but not vice versa.) When the selected viewport is edited it is pulled to the top and unhidden, but at the end of the edit it is not hidden (as the notepad would be) unless you explicitly select hide; thus it is possible to have several editor viewports on the screen at the same time.

In editing multiple windows you should note that the find options, last search and replace strings and edit mode are common to all edit viewports whereas the other parameters differ from window to window. The viewport being edited, if any, has its parameters on the status line.

When the full editor is invoked a menu appears with the following options:

New
Move
Select
Delete
Edit

The Prolog-2 User Guide

sPlit
Join
sWitch
deFaults

These will be described in a moment. The windows are displayed as they were last time you were in the editor. To finish a session with the editor type <esc> at this menu; all the editor windows will be hidden.

New

New creates a new window with the default parameters. Unless you have changed these it will lie over any other windows you have created; if you want to see several windows at a time you have to move them about.

The default parameters are not checked for consistency until a window is created. If at this point you get an error you will have to go and change them.

The new window is selected.

Move

Move allows you to move the selected window around. The cursor keys move the window until <esc> is pressed.

If a window is split it will be joined for the move and split again at the end. You cannot move the two halves of a split window to different places.

Select

Select selects the next window. The windows are selected cyclically, the selected one being pulled up.

Delete

Delete the selected window. If it contains a changed edit you will be prompted to save it.

Edit

Edit allows you to edit a window. You can see which one you are editing because the scroll bar appears in it (unless you have moved it over to the left margin). Editing a window is just like editing the notepad; but when you finish and press <esc> the window remains displayed and the editor menu appears.

sPlit

This divides a viewport into two, both over the same window. If you then select Edit you will edit the top half; if you manage to move this over the same area as the bottom half you will see changes in both halves. If you want to edit the bottom half you must select sWitch from the editor menu.

Join

This rejoins two split viewports.

sWitch

sWitch toggles between the two halves of a split window.

deFaults

The default settings for new windows determine the size of the window, the size and position of the viewport and the attribute.

The initial defaults are set to be the same as those of the window pde_notes if that can be found, otherwise to apparently sensible figures.

You can edit the defaults from the default menu. You should not try to make the viewport narrower than 20 columns or shallower than 3 rows because there will then be no room for the other boxes the editor tries to display over the viewport. You can, on the other hand, make the attribute as ridiculous as you like.

25.11 The top-level interpreter

The top-level interpreter is the last module to be opened by the PDE and also one of the simplest. It supplies a simple query system allowing the user to type questions and see whether they can be proved. It is in the nature of Prolog that this apparently limited facility in fact makes available all the features of the system.

25.11.1 Initialisation and break levels

Initialisation

We saw in §25.2 that after the initialisation of the PDE the MNU file calls the goal

The Prolog-2 User Guide

prolog in top[3].

After this it enters what we shall call the query loop; this is described in §25.11.2 below. If it ever leaves the query loop (and the only way of doing this is by reading an end_of_file character) then the optional halt procedure is entered; if the user decides not to halt the query loop is reentered.

The break predicate

The predicate **break** is similar but enters the system at break level one higher than the present. When the break level is greater than 0 a number of things behave differently: the break level appears to the left of the ?- prompt and also on the status line and the break window, pde_break, is used as standard I/O instead of pde_main. Increasing the break level beyond 1 does not cause another window to appear though.

When break leaves the query loop (again because the user has typed EOF) the break level is decremented. If it becomes 0 then the window pde_break is hidden.

25.11.2 The query loop

The query loop consists of four statements in the tail of the predicates prolog and break:

```
...,
repeat,
state(input,_,user),
state(output,_,user),
top ...
```

where top processes a single query in a way to be described. top always fails unless it reads an end of file.

Note carefully the two **state** statements; they have the effect of switching the current input and output streams to user before the next query. This enables the user to see the prompt and type the question, and is therefore a good thing, but can lead to misunderstandings. If you type:

?- tell(myfile).

?- write("Hello myfile").

as successive lines the message will be sent not to myfile but to the pde_main or pde_break window.

The effect of this **tell** is undone at the end of the query (otherwise the reply 'yes' would

---

[3] To be precise, it makes **prolog** the abort goal and then restarts.

be sent to the file!). You have to say:

?- tell(myfile),write("Hello myfile").

to get the message into the file.

25.11.3 How a single query is entered and processed

Next we look at how a single query is entered and processed.

The following steps are performed in this order:

- the break level is written if greater than 0
- in the windowed PDE the break window is pulled-up in case the last query caused it to be obscured (not relevant at break level 0)
- the ? part of the prompt is written
- a full garbage collection takes place
- the debugging invocation counter is set to 0
- the read prompt is set to -
- a term is read with variable names retained; even if there is an error the read is forced to succeed
- the term is placed in the command buffer
- if there was a syntax error then the cycle stops
- the read prompt is set to the empty atom
- the term read is processed in a way to be described.

This sequence associated with reading a query is not likely to be of great interest, but you can draw a few conclusions from it.

- there is no point in just typing

?- trimatoms.

to cause garbage collection.

- if there is a long pause between the ? and the - it is because garbage collection is taking time: be patient!
- if there is a syntax error the read fails and the cycle is restarted at its second step.

The Prolog-2 User Guide

Therefore after processing the error there is no reply, merely another prompt. Provided you fail the syntax error the erroneous term will be put in the command buffer so that you can edit it next time. If you abort the error the whole system goes back to the goal prolog and the erroneous term is lost.

What happens when a query is processed

- If the query was a variable then an error is signalled.

- If the query was end_of_file then the query predicate succeeds, with effects already described. All other inputs cause the predicate to fail and therefore to return for another query.

- If the query was a list it is handed to the **conlist**/1 BIP for processing.

- Otherwise the query is a question to be evaluated. It is called (using **call**/2 with second argument common, so that queries will use private predicates in the common module).

If it fails the reply **no** is printed and that concludes the cycle.

If it succeeds then the action taken depends on whether there are any named variables in the query, that is, variables other than _. If there are, then the instantiations of these variables after the call are printed. If the variables did not get instantiated then they will be printed as _N for some integer N. The writeq predicate is used so that strings are output quoted. The user is then asked

More (y/n)?

and may reply y to see further solutions and n to ignore them. y causes the system to backtrack into the query and try to resatisfy it.

If there are no variables then the answer "yes" is printed and there is no option to backtrack. Occasionally this may annoy you; a goal with no variables may usefully be resatisfiable because of its side effects. If you like music you can type

?- repeat,bell.

and you will hear the bell; you will then see the message **yes** and be prompted for another query. The repeat had no effect.

The only way round this is to include a dummy variable in the query:

?- repeat,bell,X=X.

say; then you can hear the bell as often as you want (but also you will see a meaningless instantiation of X each time). Remember that not resatisfying variable-free goals is a feature of the top-level interpreter; the Prolog-2 system itself will resatisfy them without difficulty.

25.11.4 The top-level interpreter in the windowed PDE

The windowed PDE has extra command and variable buffers.

The command buffer has room for 10 terms; once it is full the oldest ones are lost. You can examine the buffer by pressing <F3> to move up and <F4> to move down.

The function key <F11> (press shift and <F1>) displays a window showing the contents of the command buffer.

When a query succeeds and binds variables the values of the variables are remembered. They may be accessed in subsequent queries by using the same variable name preceded by an underscore. The values remain until another query succeeds and binds variables. Thus

?- open_module(X,"foo",readwrite,actual).

X = 'Some ludicrously long name you don't want to retype'

More (y/n)?n

?- state(output_module,_,_X).

yes

?- write(_X).

Some ludicrously long name you don't want to retype
yes

The <F11> window also shows the variable settings remembered.

25.12 The enhanced environment in V

By installing Prolog-2 properly in V it is possible to secure easy access to the TPU editor.

The following diagram gives an overview of the system:

The Prolog-2 User Guide

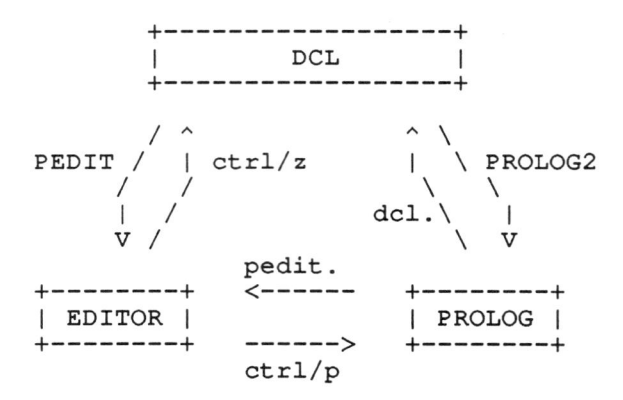

```
                    +------------------+
                    |       DCL        |
                    +------------------+
                   / ^              ^ \
         PEDIT    /  | ctrl/z       |  \  PROLOG2
                 /   /              \   \
                |   /           dcl. \   |
                v  /                  \  v
          +--------+   pedit.       +--------+
          | EDITOR |   <------      | PROLOG |
          +--------+   ------>      +--------+
                       ctrl/p
```

The arrows are annotated with the commands to be typed to move from tail to head.

25.12.1 Invoking Prolog-2

Typing "PROLOG2" at the DCL prompt invokes the Prolog2 interpreter.

Prolog is spawned as a subprocess of your default process, and is given the name "USERNAME_PRO". The Prolog process will not close down until you type "halt." at the "?-" prompt, but you can leave it temporarily in two ways:

25.12.1.1 Attaching back to your default process

Typing "dcl." at the Prolog prompt hibernates the Prolog process and saves its context for future use. All the files you have consulted will still be there - you will even stay in a break state if you attach to your default parent process from a "1?-" prompt.

In order to resume your Prolog process from the DCL level, type "PROLOG2" again at the DCL prompt. This time, control will be passed back to your Prolog process and you can continue where you left off.

25.12.1.2 Attaching to a Prolog Editor Session

If you have previously invoked a Prolog editor session (see §25.12.2) you may attach directly to it with "pedit." from Prolog. The Prolog context is saved and you will enter the editor in exactly the same place that it was left.

25.12.2 The Prolog editor

Version 4 of VAX/VMS provided a new text processing facility called VAXTPU. This facility enables powerful customised editors to be written; we have provided a simple customised editor.The current Prolog editor allows you to keep an editor process and a Prolog process running together and to easily switch between the two. It also allows easy access to the Prolog2 help facility whilst in the editor.

In order to use the editor and the Prolog session properly you must have the privileges to spawn two VMS subprocess — the DCL command "SHOW PROCESS/QUOTA" reveals your subprocess quota. If it is less than two your system manager will have to change it.

25.12.2.1 Invoking the Editor

Edit a new file, say "foo.pro" with "PEDIT FOO.PRO". The system spawns a process for the editor and calls it "USERNAME_PRO".

25.12.2.2 Extra Commands from the Editor

You are now in the default eve editor and can edit the file in the normal way. However pressing "CTRL-P" will write out the file if it has been modified and attach you to your previously spawned Prolog process. If you don't yet have a Prolog process, a warning message is issued and attaching fails.

Pressing "CTRL-Z" will, as usual, write out your file but instead of closing the editor down it is hibernated for future use. The whole of your editing context will be remembered and can be quickly recovered by typing "PEDIT" at the DCL prompt.

Now you can spawn a Prolog process (see §25.12.1) and attach to the editor from Prolog or DCL.

"CTRL-H" from the editor enters a DCL style help facility, but the information is displayed in an edit buffer.

25.12.3 Accessing help on Prolog from DCL and the editor

25.12.3.1 From the DCL Command line

$ PHELP get_token
Invokes the VAX/VMS interactive help system and displays the description of the Prolog-2 built-in predicate "get_token". You are prompted by VMS for further items. Hitting a Carriage return at the "Topic? " prompt will terminate help.

$ HELP get_token
Similarly invokes the VAX help facility, but you may mix requests for help on DCL topics with Prolog topics.

25.12.3.2 From the Prolog Editor

You may invoke the VAX/VMS help system within a special editor buffer during the edit session by pressing "CTRL-H". To get help on an item, enter its name or an abbreviation as if you were in DCL and hit carriage return when finished.

After you have finished the editor automatically removes the help window and returns you to your old editing context including repositioning the cursor. This is useful if you have forgotten, for instance, what the fifth argument to module/6 does. Type as much

The Prolog-2 User Guide

as you can remember, invoke help on "module" and immediately continue typing.

25.12.4 Installation procedure

Installing Prolog2 is simple: after the tape has been loaded into a separate Prolog directory, execute the supplied command file $setup.com by typing

$ @$setup

at the DCL prompt.

The command file generates some symbols and logical names to enable Prolog and the editor to know about their environment. Each user who wishes to run Prolog should execute this procedure in their own "LOGIN.COM" command file as the symbols generated depend on the user's VAX username. This is because names unique to the system are given to the spawned editor process and the spawned Prolog process.

The setup file generates the following DCL global symbols:

1. PROLOG2   The main symbol used to invoke the Prolog2 interpreter in spawned mode. The same symbol is used to reattach to a spawned Prolog-2 session.

2. PEDIT   This invokes a spawned edit process and may take a file as an argument. If a spawned edit session exists already, the argument is ignored and you are attached to the edit process.

3. PHELP   Invokes the VMS help facility using the Prolog2 help library. This symbol takes an optional help item as argument.

4. PROLOG2$ This allows you to invoke Prolog-2 without spawning it.

5. PEDIT$ Similarly, allows the Prolog Editor to be invoked without spawning. This symbol takes an optional file as argument.

The setup file also defines a logical name called PROLOG2$BASE which points to the Prolog directory. It is good practice to use this logical name to refer to files in this directory as it reduces maintenance when moving to a new release of Prolog-2.

25.12.5 An example session

A complete session using the environment is given below. We are developing a short program to reverse lists, the code for which is:

```
nrev([],[]).
nrev([X|Rest],Ans) :-
        nrev(Rest,New),
        append(New,[X],Ans).
```

```
append([],L,L).
append([X|L1],L2,[X|L3]) : append(L1,L2,L3).
```

(There is a syntax error in the last line)

25.12.5.1 Enter the editor

$ PEDIT nrev.pro

The editor is invoked as a spawned process. Enter the example code above.

25.12.5.2 Back to DCL

CTRL-Z

The file is written and control passed to DCL. The edit session still exists.

25.12.5.3 Invoke Prolog-2

$ PROLOG2

Prolog-2 is invoked as a spawned process; by default the PDE is in SMG mode.

25.12.5.4 Consult the source file

But, we've forgotten the name of the file so we'd like to get back into the editor to see this. First we find what the keypad definitions are by pressing PF2, and seeing that "5" corresponds to pedit ...

25.12.5.5 Enter the editor.

Press "5" on the keypad.

25.12.5.6 View file name

The file name is shown at the bottom of the screen. Now

25.12.5.7 Attach back to Prolog-2

Press CTRL-P

The buffer is not written since it has not been modified, but control is passed immediately back to the Prolog process.

25.12.5.8 Consult the source file

?- [nrev].

Consults the file in the normal way ... but there is a syntax error, select "abort" from the

The Prolog-2 User Guide

error menu, and

25.12.5.9 Reattach to the editor

Press "5" on the keypad.

The edit session is resumed. Correct the syntax error and press CTRL-P to return to Prolog. The buffer is written.

25.12.5.10 Repeat cycle

The file may now be reconsulted and the cycle repeated until the code is working satisfactorily. You may find it convenient to use an extra rule like

ed :- pedit,reconsult(nrev).

whilst debugging.

25.12.5.11 Temporary exit to DCL

The screen is disturbed by a "NEW MAIL" message. To read it press "4" on the keypad, Prolog-2 is suspended and control passed to DCL. After reading your mail attach back to Prolog with "PROLOG2".

25.12.5.12 Shutdown system

?- halt.

Terminates Prolog in the usual way.

$ PEDIT

Attaches to the Prolog editor, then pressing the "DO" key (on a VT200 series terminal) or "PF4" (on a VT100 series terminal) and entering "exit" will write out modified buffers and terminate the edit session.

26. Operating system interfaces

26.1 The DOS interface

26.1.1 The DOS file system

This Chapter is only a brief summary of how DOS handles files. More details can be found in the DOS Manual supplied by the manufacturer of your DOS. Readers already familiar with DOS file handling may skip straight to §26.1.2.

Units and drives

DOS has available to it a number of units. By rights a unit is a disk drive, either fixed or removable, but in successive versions of DOS so many new ways of creating units have been introduced that most machines will now have more units available than they have physical disk drives.

The following summary may be useful:

(1) On a machine with only one floppy drive A may also be called B. The system will remember which it is and when the other is wanted it will prompt the user to change disk.

(2) ASSIGN allows the user to change the name of a drive.

(3) The user can install a device driver that behaves like a disk by using a DEVICE= statement in the CONFIG.SYS file. The most commonly used of these is VDISK, which can be used to make a piece of RAM look like a disk. In DOS 3.20 and above there is also a driver called DRIVER.SYS which can be used to refer to the same physical drive by another name, as A: and B: are used under old versions of DOS; the system prompts for change of diskette when a different name is used.

(4) The user can also set up some extra names just for the pleasure of having them using the LASTDRIVE= statement in CONFIG.SYS. These do not refer to any unit to start with but can be used in renaming commands.

(5) The SUBST command allows a directory on one unit to be referred to as though it were a separate unit. Normally the new unit name will be one of the free ones created by LASTDRIVE=.

(6) Then there are network drives ...

What this demonstrates is that unit is a better term than drive.

The default drive

Units are referred to by letters A, B, ... At any time there is a default drive which is the one you (probably) see to the left of the > in the prompt and which is used for files where no explicit drive is specified.

The Prolog-2 User Guide

Units and volumes

A unit can be removable or non-removable. Removable means you can take the disk out and put another one in. Hard disks are normally non-removable, as are RAM disks; floppy diskettes are removable.

The thing that gets removed is called a volume. In non-removable units the volume is the same as the unit.

Volumes and directories

Each volume is partitioned into directories.

A directory is a collection of files each of which has a different name. There may be two files with the same name in a volume provided they are in different directories. Every file on the volume is in precisely one directory. At any time there is a current directory, which is the one used when no directory is specified.

Directories can themselves belong to directories in the same way as files. The same naming convention applies; that is, two directories can have the same name provided they are in different directories. With one exception every directory is a member of exactly one directory, called its parent. The exception is the root directory, which cannot be a member of any other directory.

Paths

A path is a way of describing a directory. As the name path implies it tells you how to get from somewhere to the directory. It consists of a number of directory names each followed by the character \. For example

tony\prolog2\prog

is a path. It describes the directory obtained by starting in the current directory and descending to the subdirectory tony, from there to prolog2 and from there to prog. Note that even if several descendants of the current directory are called prog, the path described a unique one.

The special name .. in a path denotes the parent. Thus

..\lisp

goes from the current directory and from there to one called lisp.

A path that begins with the character \ is taken to start not from the current but from the root directory.

Files

A file is a collection of bytes on the volume. It is referred to by a filename of up to eight characters and an extension of up to 3.

26.1.2 File streams

In Chapter 18 the stream-handling predicates

create_stream/4
open/2

are described. Both these have arguments which depend on the operating system.

The function of this section is to describe those arguments allowed under DOS.

create_stream/4

The device specification for a file in **create_stream/4** has the form:

file(Filespec).

A file spec in Prolog-2 is a string made up as a DOS file spec, that is:

Drive:Path Name.Ext

where all but Name are optional. For example

"C:PROG.PRO"

refers to the file PROG.PRO in the current directory.

Remember that to represent \ in a string you must write \\. So the file GARY.PRO in the root directory has file spec

"\\PROG.PRO".

open/2

The arguments to **open/2** are the stream name and an open access specifier.

Usually the access specifier will be simply read, write or readwrite. For certain networking applications, however, extra modes are provided to allow file sharing. Read on only if the usual attributes are not sufficient for what you need to do and if you have DOS 3.00 or above.

The full form of the open mode is a list with up to three elements. These are:

- an access specifier: **read, write** or **readwrite**

The Prolog-2 User Guide

- a sharing specifier: one of the atoms **compat**, **deny_rw**, **deny_r**, **deny_w** and **deny_none**

- an inheritance specifier: **private** or **inherit**

The access specifier must be present. If the sharing specifier is omitted, compat is assumed; if the inheritance specifier is omitted, inherit is assumed.

The meanings of these terms will be found precisely specified in the DOS Technical Reference Manual supplied with your DOS software.

Broadly speaking, compatibility mode is just as in DOS 2.10; the deny modes deny other users that particular access to the file. A file is inherited by a child process if inherit is specified.

The following additional predicates are provided for access to the file system:

chdir/1
default_drive/1
default_name/3
default_name_sys/3
disk_free_space/4
file_date/4
file_time/4
login/1
mkdir/1
rmdir/1
size/2

26.1.3 The command processor

This chapter discusses firstly how the command processor loads Prolog-2 and secondly how Prolog-2 loads the command processor.

The account here amplifies the account of start-up in Chapter 22.

26.1.3.1 Starting Prolog-2

When the command processor loads Prolog-2 it looks for the file PROLOG2.EXE first in the current directory and then in the 'path' set by the PATH statement. When it finds PROLOG2.EXE it loads it and builds a Program segment prefix for it including a copy of the command line and a pointer to the environment. This information can be recovered by the programmer, as we shall see.

When Prolog-2 gets control it looks at the command line for a file name and treats that as the name of a file with default extension INI; if the command line is empty it uses PROLOG2.INI. What happens next depends on the version of DOS being used. In version 2.10 PROLOG2.INI will be converted into a complete file name by adding the current directory on the front, but in DOS 3.00 and above the directory where PROLOG2.EXE was found is used. The reason for this discrepancy is that the latter behaviour is more useful but in DOS 2.10 there is no way of finding where PROLOG2.EXE was. Of course if the file on the command line had a path beginning with \ then no extra processing is necessary.

If the INI file is not found then standard defaults are used and the name supplied is treated as the name of the MNU file. Otherwise the directory where the INI file was found is called the system directory. Prolog-2 reads the memory allocation parameters from the INI file and sets up memory accordingly. It then reads the name of the MNU file and parses it using the system directory.

In the course of configuration the system checks to see whether an 8087 or related co-processor is available. If it is then it looks in the system directory for a file called PROL8087.BIN. If it finds one it will load it as an interface to the 8087 and use that instead of the emulator for arithmetic.

Finally it consults the MNU file.

26.1.3.2 Retrieving start-up information

The following predicates retrieve start-up information:

co_8087/0
command_line/1
get_string/2
set_string/2

26.1.3.3 Start up procedure for EXE files

The above account describes the normal start-up procedure of Prolog-2. We turn now to the start-up procedure for EXE files created by the predicate **save_exe/2**. These are packaged EXE files produced by the Prolog-2 system. They use slightly different start-up code.

When a packaged application is loaded it does not look for an INI file; it uses the memory allocation parameters that were used for the system that packaged it. Therefore the whole command line (other than the application name) can be retrieved through the **command_line/1** predicate.

The rest of the start procedure is similar to the unpackaged start procedure. Note that the 8087 load procedure is the same: therefore you can package an application and have it use an 8087 if present. If you do not want users to be able to use an 8087 leave out the file PROL8087.BIN.

At the end of the start procedure, instead of consulting the MNU file the system executes the start goal specified in the save_exe goal.

26.1.3.4 Loading the command processor

You can also load the command processor from Prolog-2. The command processor can be invoked interactively, so that you can type in a number of DOS commands, or it can be invoked to execute a particular command.

When loading a command processor you have the option to free some memory for it. If you load it often, you may decide to leave some free space all the time, in which case no extra memory would have to be freed. Memory can be left free by specifying a max-Free value for the init_alloc(heapseg) system state. Normally you will take all memory for Prolog and free just what you need. What you need depends on what applications you intend to load in the command session.

The predicates

**command/0,
command/1
command/2**

access the command processor.

26.1.4 System errors

Prolog-2 handles system errors through error **system**. It passes as an extra argument the error number passed to it by DOS, and this is used in some cases by the error handler to generate an error message.

The reason for this approach is as follows: successive versions of DOS have introduced more and more errors, some of them very obscure ('Network device no longer exists'...) and it seems futile to try to keep up with them in Prolog-2. At the same time it is unreasonable to cut the user off from what may be crucial error information. The solution is adopted is to supply messages for the most common errors and leave the network user to consult the documentation for the more obscure ones.

26.2 The UNIX interface

26.2.1 Review of UNIX terms and concepts

This section reviews important UNIX terminology for users who may be rusty.

It also describes important conventions regarding filespecs in Prolog-2: even fluent UNIX speakers should read the sections on filespecs and defaulting components of filespecs.

File specification

A UNIX file specification is a name which uniquely identifies a file.

A file specification as far as Prolog-2 is concerned (henceforth abbreviated to filespec) consists of the following components:

(Apollo machines)
> //**node_name**/**path**/**filename**.**extension**

or

(SUN machines)
> /**path**/**filename**.**extension**

Note that there is no natural concept of a file extension under UNIX: Prolog-2 imposes this convention on the UNIX file system as an aid to portability. This leads to some minor complications discussed below.

File Specification components

node_name or system_name: (important only if you want to access a file held on other computers in a network); if no node is specified the system assumes that the file is held on your local computer. The precise syntax of the node component is machine-dependent, and indeed there may be no node name at all under some implementations of UNIX (such as SunOS).

path: A path in UNIX is a specification of the directories in the file tree which must be traversed in order to reach a particular directory in that tree. Prolog-2 treats everything between the node or system name and the final '/' character in the filespec as the path component of a filespec. In some UNIX implementations a path may be null i.e. a file may appear directly under the node (which itself appears as a pseudo-directory).

There are four special character sequences which may be used in pathnames:

(i) .

Where the . character appears in a pathname it stands for the **current directory**. If the current default directory is /user/me, then the path ./mysub stands for the path /user/me/mysub. The path **mysub/./a** stands for user/me/mysub/a, as the . component of the path stands for the path **so far** i.e. it is a kind of no-op in pathnames.

(ii) ..

Where the .. sequence appears in a pathname it stands for the directory above the current one. It may be used more than once in a pathname to move up to the parent of the preceding directory.

Examples:

If the current default directory is /user/me, then

> ../**someoneelse**

The Prolog-2 User Guide

points to /user/someoneelse, while

../../sys/ins

points to the directory /sys/ins

(iii) /

The pathname / is the root directory on the node where your default directory is.

Example:

If your default directory is //**master/user/me**, then the pathname /**user/foo** stands for //**master/user/foo** i.e. it is not interpreted relative to your default directory.

(iv) //

On APOLLO machines only, this path stands for the root wherein all nodes' file systems appear (where the machines are networked).
As in the case of /, a path which starts with // is not interpreted relative to the default directory.

filename: names the file: Prolog-2 treats everything between the path and the first '.' character in the filespec as the file name.

extension: Some extensions have special significance to the Prolog-2 system (much as the '.c' extension has special significance to the C compiler in UNIX systems). Prolog-2 treats everything beyond the first '.' character after the file name as an extension: under UNIX there need not necessarily be an extension.

Note: an extension itself containing '.' characters is valid under UNIX, so filespecs like: **myfile.pro.1** are valid, and can be handled by the Prolog-2 defaulting system. This is not the case under other operating systems such as VAX/VMS or MS-DOS, so do not use extensions like this if you want your code to be portable.

Under VAX/VMS and MS-DOS, there must always be an extension but it may be null i.e. just '.'. Under UNIX, unfortunately, the extension may be null or simply not exist at all. This causes slight problems for the Prolog-2 extension defaulting mechanism which we shall discuss next.

Default filespec components under UNIX

UNIX Prolog-2 will assume defaults for various components of a filename: all components except the file name itself may be defaulted.

This defaulting mechanism is available to the user via the BIPs **default_name/3** and **default_name_sys/3**, but is also operated by various other BIPs which expect a filename as an argument.

Remember that a filespec consists of the following components:

node/path/filename.extension.

The precise defaults used vary from BIP to BIP, but are documented with that BIP in the Prolog-2 Encyclopaedia.

For instance, the BIPs **see/1** and **tell/1** expect filenames as their arguments: if no file extension is specified then the extension defaults to **.pro**. If no path is specified then it defaults to the current default directory.

For example, if you **tell** a file called **myfile** and omit the remaining filespec components, the system will insert defaults for the missing elements as follows:

node:	your local computer
path:	your current default directory
extension:	.pro

How to specify no extension when defaults are applied

In other Prolog-2 implementations, the extension '.' is used to denote no extension (as files with no extension appear in the file systems as <filename>.). Under UNIX, unfortunately, a file with no extension appears as just <filename>, and is therefore indistinguishable from a filename where the extension is expected to default. For this reason, BIPs which apply default extensions (such as **default_name/3**, **consult/1**, **see/1** and **tell/1**) treat a filename ending with the '.' character as a file with a null extension. This enables people both to write reasonably portable file-handling code, and to handle files which under UNIX may have no extension whatsoever (as opposed to the null extension allowed under VAX/VMS and MS-DOS) at a small cost in intuitiveness.

Examples of null and non-existent extension defaulting

The following examples apply where a ".pro" extension is the default (as in **see/1**, **tell/1**, **consult/1** etc):

The Prolog-2 User Guide

Filename	Filename which will be used	
myfile	myfile.pro	(default applied)
myfile.pl	myfile.pl	(extension ".pl")
myfile.	myfile	(no extension)
myfile..	myfile.	(null extension ".")
myfile...	myfile..	(extension "..")
myfile.pro.2	myfile.pro.2	(extension ".pro.2")
myfile.p.	myfile.p	(extension loses '.')

Note that it is only in the first case that the default extension is actually applied.

Note also that when Prolog-2 actually goes to open or use a file whose extension contains a **trailing** '.' then this '.' is effectively removed from the filename. Thus to consult a file **myfile** in the default directory use **consult('myfile.')**. Watch out for this.

This removal of the trailing '.' applies **only at the time the filespec is passed to the operating system,** so you will find that **default_name/3** and **default_name_sys/3** do not do it. This is so that on those occasions when a filespec is passed through the defaulting procedure twice the effect is the same as if it had been only performed once. (This sounds unlikely but in fact happens when programmers write code like:

    default_name(FILE,".pro",FULLFILE),
    create(FULLFILE).

as **create**/1 applies defaults itself).

The best way to avoid these complications is to adopt the Prolog-2 file extension discipline where files have three-character extensions: this will also give you portability to VAX/VMS and MS-DOS implementations.

Wildcard characters in UNIX filespecs

Some Prolog-2 BIPs accept filenames containing wildcard characters. The UNIX wildcarding features are rather more powerful than those provided under other operating systems. Their syntax and meanings are summarized here.

NOTE: APOLLO users running under AEGIS will get this set of wildcard conventions rather than the AEGIS conventions.

(i) *

Matches with any string (including the null string).

(ii) ?

Matches any single character.

(iii) [ac.]

Matches the characters a, c or . and no others.

(iv) [a-z]

Matches a single character in the range a to z.

(v) Single quotes

Single quotes escape a special character (e.g. [or *). To escape a character means that it will be treated as an ordinary character rather than a special (or "control") character. Only special characters may be quoted, including '. Within square brackets no characters have special meanings, and a string of characters is interpreted 'raw'.

Note that only one special character may appear between a pair of quotes, so in order to specify a string consisting of the characters [and * you must type '['*', not '[*'.

(vi) [^ac]

Stands for any character not in the string following the ^.

(vii) [^a-z]

Stands for any character not in the range a to z.

NOTE: if a] character occurs within a square-bracketted list then it must occur as the first character in the list after the [, or after the ^ character if used.

EXAMPLES

Suppose you have three files:

      abcd.p00
      abcf.p01
      abc0.p01

then the following wildcarded filespecs will match different subsets of the three files:

[d0].   matches abcd.p00 and abc0.p01

The Prolog-2 User Guide

abc[a-z].p*	matches abcd.p00 and abcf.p01
abc[^a-z].p0*	matches abc0.p01 only
abc?.??1	matches abcf.p01 and abc0.p01
*[a-z].*1	matches abcf.p01 only

The wildcards accepted are similar to the shell conventions, in that * and ? have their normal meanings, but additionally some of the square-bracket notations used in regular expressions are also supported. The \ escape convention is not used: instead we use single quotes to escape special characters.

The following csh and sh conventions are not supported:

(i) ~ : csh convention for login directory pathname
(ii) a{b,c} to mean the two file names ab and ac
(iii) [a\z] APOLLO csh convention for [a-z]
(iv) [!a] SUN sh convention for [^a]

As you can see, filename wildcard conventions under UNIX are pretty chaotic, varying between shells and between implementations. We hope we have provided a reasonably common subset of the most useful ones.

Case sensitivity

In UNIX, case is significant. Whenever Prolog-2 supplies default parts of filenames (such as a .pro extension) they are lower case. Filespec components supplied by the user may be in any case, but because Prolog-2 supplies defaults in lower case then it is best to stick to lower case.

Note: if lower case filespecs are used under MS-DOS or VAX/VMS, then they are treated as upper case anyway, so using lower case filespec components does not compromise portability.

Standard input, output and error streams

Whenever a UNIX program runs, it inherits a number of 'standard' I/O streams: input, output and error. The standard input is where it expects to be able to read its input from; the standard output is where it should write its output unless told otherwise, and the standard error is where any error messages should be displayed.

With the glass_tty type interface initially supplied with UNIX Prolog-2, these three streams correspond to the Prolog-2 standard input, output and error streams.

The Shell

UNIX systems generally interact with the user via a class of programs known as shells.

These are programs which accept commands from the standard input, interpret them in various ways and occasionally run other programs as a result.

There are two common shell programs supplied with UNIX systems: the Bourne shell and the C shell. Under some systems it is configurable as to which shell is run by default.

Prolog-2 has features which allow access to shells and shell commands without leaving Prolog-2. These are detailed in §26.2.6.

26.2.2 Default and system directories

The Default Directory

Your default directory on startup is the directory you were in (your current directory) when you first invoked the Prolog-2 system. It is the directory shown when you type 'pwd' at the shell (or 'wd' under AEGIS).

You can find out what your default directory is, and change the default, from within Prolog-2. (See §26.2.4)

Note that this default is inherited by processes you spawn, but will **not** be changed in your parent shell (the one from which you ran Prolog-2 in the first place).

The System Directory

The system directory is the directory within which the Prolog system expects to find its own modules (such as the compiler modules or the lint checker).

There is an elaborate system for determining where this directory is, but in the simplest case it will be the directory where the **prolog2.exe** file is kept. See §26.2.3 for complete details of how the system directory pathname is determined.

The reason for having a system directory is so that the Prolog-2 package can be used by many users from a single directory: this saves disk space and allows transparent product updates.

The overall strategy is for each user to create his own Prolog development directory (which will generally be his default directory) and edit all his Prolog-2 source files from within this directory. He then uses the Prolog-2 system from the system directory.

26.2.3 Starting and stopping

Chapter 22 gives general information about starting and stopping Prolog-2 which applies to all implementations. The information in the present section is specific to UNIX Prolog-2; it supplements the information given in Chapter 22.

The Prolog-2 User Guide

Node names

In most places where a system or node name features in a filespec, the APOLLO form is used. SUN users should ignore node names.

26.2.3.1 Starting Prolog-2: the normal startup procedure

In the simplest case, Prolog-2 may be run from a central directory where all the distribution files are stored. If the name of that directory is:

//master/prolog2   (APOLLO machines)
/prolog2   (other machines)

then Prolog-2 may be run by simply typing:

//master/prolog2/prolog2.exe (APOLLO machines)
/prolog2/prolog2.exe   (other machines)

at a shell.

The Prolog-2 startup procedure moves through a number of stages, as follows:

(i) The **prolog2.exe** file is loaded and run by the operating system

(ii) The Prolog-2 system looks for a **.ini** file (by default called **prolog2.ini**) which contains various system parameters. This file is read, and the various memory allocations required by the system are performed. A default **prolog2.ini** is supplied with Prolog-2. In the simplest case, Prolog-2 looks for its **.ini** file in the directory specified for the **.exe** file.

(iii) The system consults a file (by default called **prolog2.mnu**). This file should contain directives to load up the Prolog-2 modules required by the application, and to execute a start goal exported by one of those modules. A default **prolog2.mnu** is provided with the system, but the user may write his own. In the simplest case, Prolog-2 looks for the **.mnu** file in the same directory as it finds the **.ini** file.

Steps (ii) and (iii) are user-configurable, and the ways in which this can be done are discussed in §26.2.3.2.

Simplifying the startup procedure

Typically, the Prolog-2 system will be installed in one directory on the system. Let us suppose for the moment that this directory has the node and path **//master/prolog2** (or **/prolog2** on other systems). The simplest way for individual users to run the system is for each user to create a shell script called **prolog2** in his home directory which looks like this:

(SUN systems)

```
#
/prolog2/prolog2.exe $*
```

(APOLLO UNIX systems)

```
#
//master/prolog2/prolog2.exe $*
```

(APOLLO AEGIS systems)

```
#
//master/prolog2/prolog2.exe ^*
```

The funny characters after the **prolog2.exe** filespec allow command line parameters to be passed through to the prolog2.exe when it executes. We shall see that you may want to do this for a number of reasons.

The system-installed copy of Prolog-2 can then be run by simply typing **prolog2** at the shell.

More sophisticated startup routines are possible: §26.2.3.2 outlines how to go about creating these.

How the system directory is determined

This sub-section discusses in detail how the location of the system directory is determined. It is only necessary to understand this if you wish to start modifying the startup procedure. There are some minor differences between machines.

Stage (i)

The first default for the system directory is the directory associated with the **prolog2.exe**. This is the user's current default directory UNLESS a pathname is explicitly attached to the prolog2.exe filespec, when it will be that pathname. Such a pathname is interpreted relative to the user's current default directory.

For example, if Prolog-2 is invoked by typing:

foo/prolog2.exe

and the user's current working directory is

/me

then the initial system directory will be:

The Prolog-2 User Guide

/me/foo

Stage (ii)

Prolog-2 expects to find by default a **prolog2.ini** file in the initial system directory (established during stage (i) of the startup). If, however, a .ini filespec is specified on the command line as e.g.:

/prolog2/prolog2.exe myprolog2.ini<CR>

then the default .ini filespec is overridden. Furthermore, if the .ini filespec includes an explicit path, then the directory where the .ini file is found then **becomes the system directory**.

The .ini file may itself contain a line of the form:

SYSDIR   <directory spec>

The directory spec may optionally include a node e.g.:

SYSDIR   //master/prolog2   (APOLLO machines)
SYSDIR   /prolog2   (other machines)

If so, then the system directory **becomes the directory specified on this line**. Otherwise it remains as the directory where the .ini file was found.

Stage (iii)

Lastly, the .ini file will contain a line of the form:

MNUFILE   filespec

Prolog-2 looks for its **.mnu** file at filespec. Normally the user will either use the system default .mnu file (provided with the system, called **prolog2.mnu**), or specify a customized .mnu file in his/her local directory.

Once the .ini file has been processed then the system directory is fixed for the remainder of this run of Prolog-2. The default directory, on the other hand, may be modified dynamically.

Note that the order of SYSDIR and MNUFILE parameters in the .ini file is significant: if an MNUFILE parameter is preceded by a SYSDIR parameter, then the default directory applied to the MNUFILE filespec will be the one specified in the SYSDIR parameter: otherwise it will be the directory where the .ini file was found.

The following section contains examples of the most commonly required ways to modify the startup procedure.

26.2.3.2 Modifying the startup procedure

In the following examples, node or system names have been omitted for clarity. **Any path or directory name used may have a node or system name prepended to it**, so that, for instance, the system directory may be on a different node in the network to your own local directories.

Modifying the default .ini file memory sizes

The simplest modification you may wish to do is to change the default sizes of workspace, heap etc for running your own applications.

This is simply achieved by copying the system-supplied **prolog2.ini** file into your home directory, renaming it to, say, **myfile.ini**, and then modifying the various initial memory allocation parameters.

In order to use the normal **prolog2.mnu** and system-supplied modules you should also insert a SYSDIR parameter line to point Prolog-2's system directory back to the central directory where the system has been installed.

Example

Directory where system installed: /prolog2

Home directory: /user/me
Current default directory: /user/me

/user/me/my.ini contents:

```
SERIAL              nnnnnnnnnnnn
WORKSPACE           500000
HEAP                2000000
ATOMS               60000
TRAIL               20000
CONTEXT_BUFFER      1024
SYSDIR              /prolog2
MNUFILE             prolog2.mnu
END
```

The Prolog-2 User Guide

Command line:

/prolog2/prolog2 /user/me/my.ini<CR>

When this command is executed, the local **.ini** file /user/me/my.ini will be used during stage (ii) of the startup, but the standard **.mnu** file in /prolog2 will be used during stage (iii). After startup, the system directory will be /prolog2, and this is where system-provided modules such as the compiler will be loaded from.

Note that the command line may be contained in a shell script as recommended in §26.2.3.1.

Using your own .ini and .mnu files, but using the supplied system modules

This is the next stage of customising your startup procedure. All that is necessary is

(a) to edit and specify your own local **.ini** file as in the first example

(b) specify additionally in your **.ini** file a **.mnu** filespec which points to your own customized **.mnu** file.

Example

Directory where system installed: **/prolog2**

Home directory: **/user/me**
Current default directory: **/user/me**

/user/me/my.ini contents:

```
WORKSPACE         500000
HEAP              2000000
ATOMS             60000
TRAIL             20000
CONTEXT_BUFFER    1024
MNUFILE           mystartup.mnu
SYSDIR            /prolog2
END
```

Command line:

/prolog2/prolog2 /user/me/my.ini<CR>

(assuming you have set up the simple script **prolog2** as advised earlier)

When this command is executed, the local **.ini** file /**user/me/my.ini** will be used during stage (ii) of the startup, and the **.mnu** file used during stage (iii) will be the file /**user/me/mystartup.mnu**. The default system directory is set to /**prolog2**, so that system modules like the compiler and lint checker are still picked up from the central directory.

By copying **/prolog2/prolog2.mnu** to **/user/me/mystartup.mnu** and then editing it, the user can alter which system modules are loaded, and can execute directives of his/her own when Prolog-2 is run.

Again, the command line may be contained in a shell script as recommended in §26.2.3.1.

Note that because the MNUFILE parameter precedes the SYSDIR parameter, the MNUFILE filespec will be interpreted relative to the directory where the **.ini** file was found: this allows multiple users to use similar .ini files which will then pick up a .mnu file from their own local directories, while leaving the system directory set to the central one used by everyone on the system.

Full customization of the system

Advanced users may want to start replacing system modules with modules of their own. They may wish either to customize the development environment or to package up applications for distribution to other users.

In such case the approach should be to copy those supplied system modules which they still require into a new directory where their customized version of Prolog-2 will reside. At the same time the files **prolog2.exe** and **system.prm** should be copied over. This new directory must become the default system directory, so must have a customized **prolog2.ini** and **prolog2.mnu** in it.

If the application directory is called:

/user/applic

then the system may be run by typing the command line:

/user/applic/prolog2<CR>

Once such an application is set up, then individual users can do the same minor customizations illustrated above.

Customizing the .mnu file

Alterations which you may want to make to the **.mnu** file range from trivial ones to major re-writes of the startup code.

A trivial example is the addition of your own default settings for system states. For instance you may wish to insert the following directives:

```
?- state(gcguide(cost),_,50).         /* Allow GC for up to 50% of cpu time */
?- state(gcguide(margin),_,64000).    /* Trigger auto heap GC when free heap falls
                                         below 64000 bytes */
```

```
?- state(gc,_,full).            /* Enable all auto GC */
```

to alter the default configuration of the automatic garbage collector when you run Prolog-2. Note that any such directives should be inserted into your customized .mnu file **before** the directive **?- prolog_start_goal** as this effectively terminates the consulting of the .mnu file.

If you wish to do away with some of the system modules (such as 'grules', the grammar rules parser) on startup, then it is sufficient to simply comment out the relevant **default_name_sys/3** and **open_module/4** directives.

If, however, you wish to open modules of your own at startup, then you must think carefully about whether they reside in your local directory or within what you have defined to be the system directory. In the former case you will need to use **default_name/3** to expand the filename of the module; in the latter you will want to use **default_name_sys/3**.

These two BIPs are the means whereby the defaulting mechanism for filespecs is made available to the Prolog programmer. They differ only in whether the default node and path used are derived from the system directory or from the current default directory.

26.2.3.3 Introduction to the TLI

This section gives a brief overview of consulting files and entering goals to be proved: for further details consult Chapter 25.

When Prolog-2 has finished its startup procedure, it will be executing a module. With the default PDE supplied with the system, this will be the Top Level Interpreter or **TLI**.

The TLI prints a prompt that looks like this:

?-

Between printing the '?' and the '-' it does a heap and stacks garbage collection, which may sometimes cause a small delay.

In the following examples the prompt is shown for clarity, but should not be typed by the user. The symbol **<CR>** means that a carriage return should be typed at the point where the symbol appears. Don't forget to type the '.' terminator first, otherwise the Prolog read system will expect further input on the next line.

The user may type goals in the Prolog-2 syntax for the theorem prover to prove, such as:

?- atom(foo).<CR>

to which the TLI will reply **yes** because the goal succeeds.

If the goal succeeds, and contains one or more variables, then the TLI displays the bindings of those variables and asks the user whether he/she wants any alternative solutions by printing:

More y/n ?

to which the user should reply y<CR> or n<CR>

Consulting files

A Prolog source file is initially loaded into the database by consulting it.

A special syntax which the user may use to consult a source file is the square brackets notation. If the TLI is given a list of filenames then it will consult the files in the list. A default extension of **.pro** and the user's default directory pathname will be used if no extension or pathname is supplied.

Example

If the default directory is **/user/me**, and the user types the following directive to the TLI:

?- [source1,'/applic/main','test/source2.facts'].<CR>

then the TLI will consult the following files:

/user/me/source1.pro
/applic/main.pro
/user/me/test/source2.facts

(See §26.2.1 for a full discussion of file extension defaulting.)

26.2.3.4 Stopping Prolog-2

To stop Prolog-2 from the TLI simply type:

?- halt.<CR>

This form of **halt** ensures that a non-error status code is returned to the shell.

If you want to return a UNIX status code on exit, then use the BIP **halt/1**. This BIP takes an integer as its argument.

Example

halt(2)

this will cause Prolog-2 to exit with a status code 2 (which happens to mean "no such file or directory" under UNIX). See §26.2.6 for a full discussion of UNIX errors.

26.2.4 Predicates for file and directory manipulation

get_default_directory/1 and pwd/1
set_default_directory/1 and chdir/1
mkdir/1
rmdir/1

file/2
files/2
exists_file/1
delete_file/1
rename/2
rename_file/2
create/1

file_details/2 and /4
file_body_extension/3
file_date/4
file_time/4
size/2
set_mode/2

default_name/3
default_name_sys/3

26.2.5 Miscellaneous I/O

26.2.5.1 Introduction

This chapter contains additional information about the functioning of I/O under UNIX Prolog-2.

The various BIPs which create, delete, open, close, read and write streams, as well as those which handle file positioning, are documented in the Prolog-2 Encyclopaedia. This chapter merely points out machine-specific features where these are relevant.

For information on special streams under UNIX, refer to §26.3.

26.2.5.2 Opening files

open/2
open_read/1
open_write/1
open_readwrite/1

No matter what mode the file is opened in, the initial position (as indicated by a call to at/2) will be start of file.

Readwrite mode and UNIX

It is a feature of UNIX that files opened for readwrite access may be both read and written to, but sequences of reads must be separated chronologically from sequences of writes, and vice versa, by an intervening **seek/2** call. If this is not done, then the results are unpredictable.

On SUN machines, there is a limit of 30 on the number of open files per process under currnt releases. If you hit this limit then you are strongly advised to close some files before trying to continue, as Prolog-2 may need to open temporary files of its own under various circumstances (for instance when executing **files/2**).

26.2.5.3 Positioning in files

seek/2
seek_read/1
seek_write/1
at/2
reading_at/1
writing_at/1

Note that you can **seek** or **at** on any file stream under UNIX (this is not the case under VAX/VMS, where there are restrictions on what you can do with some types of files).

Remember that a **seek/2** call is necessary between sequences of reads from and writes to a file opened in readwrite mode. (See preceding section.)

Seeking past end_of_file in a file opened with write or readwrite access will pad the file with space characters from the current end_of_file to the position sought to, thus moving end_of_file to that position.

26.2.5.4 Getting single characters from streams

get0/1
get/1
getbyte/1
ttyget0/1
ttyget/1

26.2.5.5 Newlines

skip/1
nl/0

Under UNIX, the BIP **nl/0** puts out a single ASCII 10 character, as this is all that is necessary to force a new line under UNIX.

If you use **skip(10)** to skip input characters up to end of line then your code will not be portable to PC implementations of Prolog-2, or to future versions using different operating systems.

The Prolog-2 User Guide

26.2.5.6 End of file character, and other control characters

Generally, the end_of_file character under UNIX is Ctrl-D (ASCII 4). On SUN machines this will be the character which is recognized by Prolog-2 as end_of_file.

On Apollo machines, the default end_of_file character is Ctrl-Z (ASCII 26), although your system manager may have altered the key definitions in force to make your system look more like a pure UNIX system, in which case you will probably type Ctrl-D just as on other UNIX systems. In both cases, the end_of_file character will still be 26 when got from files.

When using the BIPs **read/N** and **getbyte/1**, end of file is always indicated by returning the atom **end_of_file**.

Terminating consult(user), break states and the TLI

Traditionally under DEC10 Prolog, an end_of_file character is typed to terminate a user consult, or to exit a **break** state. Usually this is the character Ctrl-Z in Prolog-2 implementations, or alternatively the end_of_file character recognized by the OS. For technical reasons this cannot be on SUN machines (and on most UNIX systems), so the character **Ctrl-E** is used instead. Note that the atom **end_of_file** will always terminate consults and breaks on **any** Prolog-2 implementation.

The use of control keys on SUNs and APOLLOs is as follows:

SUN machines (and most others):

Ctrl-E	Terminate consult(user) or break state
Ctrl-C	Invoke keyboard interrupt handler
Ctrl-D	Close down stdin (terminate process)
Ctrl-Z	Stop Prolog-2 process completely (may be resumed using %)
Ctrl-S	Suspend output
Ctrl-Q	Resume output

APOLLO machines:

Ctrl-Z	Terminate consult(user) or break state, and normal end of file character
Ctrl-Q	Invoke keyboard interrupt handler.

26.2.5.7 Currency character

To ensure that £ appears as the currency symbol in currency output formats use a font whose name has the .uk suffix on APOLLO machines. Prolog-2 uses character code 35 to represent the £ sign. $ appears correctly under all fonts: Prolog-2 uses character code 36 for this.

On SUN machines, the supplied fonts have no £ character, so the currency symbol will appear as #.

26.2.5.8 The printer stream

Refer to the UNIX Special Streams Manual for details of how to send output to the system printer.

26.2.5.9 TTY flushing

On Apollo machines using the Display Manager, I/O to and from a pad is line-buffered. This means that characters output using put/1 will not appear until either a newline is output or input is requested from the terminal. There is no point in applying automatic flushing in this case as the current output is obscured by the input portion of the pad.

On SUN machines one runs in tty mode by default, with no separate input window, so automatic flushing is performed on the SUN after every output BIP.

26.2.5.10 Floating-point errors on SUNs

If your SUN does not have floating-point hardware then some error conditions in FP arithmetic will not be reported as the relevant exceptions are not raised. Instead you will find that reals may contain the conventional value "Infinity" and will appear as such when written out by Prolog-2.

26.2.6 Shells, errors and environments

26.2.6.1 Running shells or shell commands

command/0
command/1
command/2
command/3
shell/0

These four BIPs allow you to run UNIX shells without leaving Prolog-2.

26.2.6.2 Operating system errors

There is a system state which allows you to retrieve the UNIX error number which caused a **system** error.

state(unix_error_number,Oldnum,Newnum)

sys_unix_error/2

This is a BIP which gives the user access to UNIX error messages (it is used by the Prolog-2 error handler to supply extra information in event of a **system** error. 160).

sys_os_error/2

This BIP takes a 32-bit status code (represented as a '$int_pair'/2 structure) as its first argument, and yields a text string which is an OS-specific error message.

26.2.6.3 Process environment

BIPs are provided under UNIX Prolog-2 to enable you to get command-line parameters, environment variables, user id, and to find out whether you are running interactively or not.

Command-line parameters

command_line/1

Environment variables

get_string/2
userid/1

Process mode

process_mode/1
interactive/0

CPU time

There is an extra **cputime** option available to the BIP **statistics/2** under UNIX.

26.3 The VMS interface

26.3.1 VMS concepts

This section reviews important VAX/VMS terminology for users who maybe rusty. Fluent users should skip ahead to §26.3.2.

File specification

A VMS specification is a name which uniquely identifies a file.

A file specification (frequently abbreviated to filespec) consists of the following components:

node::device:[directory]filename.filetype;version

File Specification components

node: (important only if you want to access a file held on other computers in a network); if no node is specified the system assumes that the file is held on your local computer

device: the name of the physical device (tape, disk) on which the file is stored. If no device is specified the system assumes the file is held on your default disk

directory: a file that catalogues other files

If no directory is specified the system assumes the file is held in your default directory. (See below for more on the default directory)

A directory name is enclosed in square brackets to delimit it from the surrounding components. A directory may be broken down into subdirectories.

(**subdirectory**: optional. Concatenated to its parent directory within the same square brackets using a period e.g. [directory.subdirectory])

filename: names the file

filetype: indicates nature of file contents; follows the filename and is preceded by a full stop (period).

version: indicates the version of the file named by filename. This is the final component of the file specification; follows filetype and is preceded by a semicolon. Version number is increased by 1 each time a file is modified.

Defaults in VMS

A default value is a value which the operating system assumes if you do not specify one; such defaults are widely used in VMS.

In the filespec context the operating system can insert defaults for all components except the filename:

node::device:[directory]filename.filetype;version

For example, if you ask for a directory listing on a file called **filename** and omit the remaining filespec components, the system will insert defaults for the missing elements as follows:

node:	your local computer
device:	your default disk
directory:	your default directory
filetype:	.LIS
version:	the highest version number in your directory

The Prolog-2 User Guide

The Default Directory

Your default directory on startup is the directory you were in (your current directory) you first invoked the Prolog-2 system. It is the directory shown when you type SHOW DEFAULT at the DCL prompt.

You can find out what your default directory is, and chamge the default, form within Prolog-2. (See §26.3.3).

Logical names in VMS

Logical names are short and meaningful names for files and devices; they are effectively abbreviations for longer and perhaps unmemorable physical names.

The System Directory

This is the directory containing the PROLOG2.EXE file and the distribution software.

The reason for having a system directory is so that the Prolog-2 package can be used by many users from a single directory: this saves disk space and allows transparent product updates.

The overall strategy is for each user to create his own Prolog development directory (which will generally be his default directory) and edit all his Prolog-2 source files from within this directory. He then uses the Prolog-2 system from the installed Prolog-2 base.

26.3.2 Starting and stopping

Chapter 22 gives general information about starting and stopping Prolog-2 which applies to all Prolog-2 implementations. The information in the present Section is specific to VAX Prolog-2; it supplements the information given in Chapter 22.

26.3.2.1 Starting Prolog-2

Simplifying the startup procedure

The naive user ought to be able invoke the Prolog-2 system without copying it into his own directory. We therefore recommend that the user or system manager set up a simple set of logical names and symbols, for example:

DEFINE PROLOG2$BASE DISK$USER:[PROLOG2]

PROLOG2 :== "RUN PROLOG2$BASE:PROLOG2"

or

PROLOG2 :== "RUN DISK$USER:[PROLOG2]PROLOG2"

This enables the naive user to call Prolog-2 simply by typing

prolog2

at the DCL prompt.

More sophisticated startup routines are possible: §26.3.2.2 outlines how to go about creating these.

26.3.2.2 Modifying the startup procedure

Startup without a .INI file specification -- the default procedure

Prolog-2 searches automatically for the PROLOG2.INI initialisation file when it is loaded.

The default system directory is searched for a .INI file called "PROLOG2.INI". (See §26.3.1 for a definition of the default system directory.)

Startup with a .INI file specification

You can specify a .INI file for Prolog to pick up by including the name of the .INI file on the command line which runs Prolog. If this .INI file specification contains a directory specification then Prolog will search there for the named .INI file; if not it will search the default system directory.

To alter the startup procedure you must change the PROLOG2.INI file (in the system directory): however this may not be possible as many users have access to this area and it is likely to be protected from modification.

Creating your own startup procedure

To create your own startup procedure you write your own .INI file and call this when starting Prolog.

The most practical approach is to take the distribution file PROLOG2.INI and modify it. You would then start Prolog by typing

PROLOG2 $HOME:MYFILE

where $HOME has been defined.

If the .INI file specified cannot be found a VMS error is reported and the Prolog loading procedure terminates.

Examples of modified startup procedures

The Prolog-2 User Guide

Below are a series of common examples showing how to modify and use the Prolog-2 system from the command language provided by the host operating system.

We first define:

PROLOG2 :== "RUN PROLOG2$BASE:PROLOG2"

or

PROLOG2 :== "$ DISK$USER:[PROLOG2]PROLOG2"

We can now call Prolog-2 in various ways:

(1) By typing

prolog2

This causes Prolog-2 to be loaded form the release directory; the system will use the .INI and .MNU files from the release directory.

(2) By typing

prolog2 Fred

This causes Prolog-2 to be loaded from the release directory and loads the file FRED.INI from the release directory.

Note that the MNU file will be located using the file name contained within the .INI file.

(3) By typing

prolog2 $HOME:APPLIC

(For this example we will assume the logical name $HOME is set to the directory in which the user is developing his application — his default working directory.)

When the Prolog-2 system is invoked in this way the file $HOME:APPLIC.INI is used for starting the application. You must also ensure that the MNUFILE field of the .INI file (see §26.3.2.3) has been modified to "$HOME:APPLIC.MNU".

We recommend you create a file called $HOME:APPLIC.MNU (copied from

PROLOG2.MNU and modified). Note that the BIP **default_name_sys**/3 will still parse file names with respect to the system directory (i.e. the directory in which the PROLOG2.EXE file was loaded).

This latter method enables you to tailor your startup procedure to your own needs. You can also define a symbol such as:

PROLOG :== "$ DISK$USER:[PROLOG2]PROLOG2 $HOME:APPLIC"

and use this to call your customised Prolog-2.

26.3.2.3 The initialisation file

Modifying the .INI file

The .INI initialisation file used by VAX Prolog-2 may be modified using an ASCII editor. However users must make sure that they are aware of the rigid formatting conventions.

Contents of the .INI file

The .INI file typically contains the following fields:

```
/*      */
/*    An Example PROLOG2.INI file*/
/**/
WORKSPACE           100000
HEAP                1000000
ATOMS               6000
TRAIL               1000
CONTEXT_BUFFER      1120
MNUFILE             prolog2.mnu
END
```

First note the following general constraints:

- blank lines cannot be used in the .INI file,
- all these lines must be present: if any are omitted the system will report this and abort,
- all the values must be legal: if any are out of range or invalid the system will abort,
- with byte values you may find that the allocation is not quite what you specified; this is because the system will align the quantity to its own internal requirements.

We shall now explain each line in the example code above:

/*

Introduces a comment line; it enables you to place comments in the INI file. Note that

The Prolog-2 User Guide

no closing */ is required — the comment finishes with the line

WORKSPACE   100000

Specifies the number of bytes to be allocated to the workspace. The workspace contains the local and global stacks

HEAP   1000000

Specifies the number of bytes to be allocated to the heap

ATOMS   6000

Specifies the number of atoms to be allocated in the atom table ie the maximum number of atoms allowed in the Prolog-2 system

TRAIL   1000

Specifies the maximum number of trail entries to allocate space for within the Prolog-2 system

CONTEXT_BUFFER   1120

Specifies the size of the context buffer to be used

The size of the context buffer is only important for correction of errors; it is this context buffer size that is edited.

MNUFILE   prolog2.mnu

Names the MNU file to read on startup.

Note that of the name needs further expansion of defaults then the file name will be expanded relative to the system directory. Thus if you are using your own file then you will have to provide the full name.

END

The final entry in the .INI file.

26.3.2.4 Stopping Prolog-2

The standard method of stopping Prolog-2 is using the BIP **halt/0**; this causes an immediate return to VMS. There is also a form **halt/1**, which takes a VMS status code as input argument. **halt/1** acts like **halt/0** in stopping Prolog-2, except that Prolog exits with the given status code.

VMS status codes are described in §26.10.3.2.

26.3.3 Accessing the directory

The following BIPs are available for directory access:

mkdir/1
chdir/1
rmdir/1
get_default_directory/1
set_default_directory/1

26.3.4 File handling predicates

The following predicates are available for file-handling:

exists_file/1
delete_file/1
rename_file/2

26.3.5 Additional opening predicate

Prolog-2 provides three predicates which explicitly open Prolog files:

open_read/1
open_write/1
open_readwrite/1

The argument is the name of a file to be opened — for reading only, writing only, or reading and writing simultaneously.

(These three predicates are fully described in the Prolog-2 Encyclopaedia)

Additional Prolog-2 predicates for VMS

Prolog-2 provides additional two-argument forms of these predicates for optional use with VMS files:

open_read/2
open_write/2
open_readwrite/2

The first argument is the name of a VMS file; the second argument is a structure defining that file's type.

open_(access)(Filename,type(T))

(VMS file types are briefly described in §26.3.1 and fully in VAX/VMS documentation.)

T must be a string or atom and is the VMS file type e.g. ".PRO".

The Prolog-2 User Guide

If no file type T is specified **type** is set to ".PRO" by default.

These variants are provided principally for compatibility with Prolog-1.

26.3.6 Random access to files

The Prolog-2 BIPs **seek/2** and **at/2**, which adjust and report the file pointer position, work slightly differently with certain types of VMS file.

This section explains these differences.

26.3.6.1 Terminology: streams in Prolog-2 and VMS

Both Prolog-2 and VAX/VMS documentation use the term "stream" in the context of files. Readers may find this less than helpful.

Streams in VMS

In VMS the term "stream" refers not to Prolog-2's input or output streams but to the format of records making up VMS files.

VMS files consist of four possible types of record:

- fixed length
- variable length
- variable length with fixed-length control
- stream

(See VAX/VMS documentation for more on VMS record types.)

Stream and non-stream

When positioning the file pointer Prolog disregards these distinctions and treats all VMS files as consisting of either stream or non-stream records.

Files created from within Prolog (e.g. by using **tell/1** or **create_file/1**) are stream files; files created outside Prolog will usually be non-stream.

Finding out about VMS file types

To find out whether a currently open Prolog stream is composed of stream or non-stream VMS records use the BIP **stream_details/4** (see §26.3.8):

stream_details(PrologFileStream,I/O,Fullspec,Kind)

which will instantiate **Kind** to stream, non-stream or unknown.

Converting between file types

You can convert VMS non-stream files to stream files (and vice versa) using the VMS CONVERT utility.

(See VAX/VMS documentation for more on the VMS CONVERT utility.)

26.3.6.2 seek/2, at/2 and VMS files

When used with VMS files composed of stream format records the BIPs **seek/2** and **at/2** work as described above.

When used with VMS files composed of records in non-stream format the BIPs **seek/2** and **at/2** are subject to the limitations described below.

seek/2

In a VMS non-stream file you cannot seek to any character position you choose. You can seek to only two positions: the start of the file (character position = 0) and the end (character position = atom **end_of_file**).

Thus

seek(PrologFileStream,0)
seek(PrologFileStream,end_of_file)

Attempts to seek anywhere else within **PrologFileStream** will fail.

at/2

In a VMS non-stream file you cannot discover how far the file pointer is (in bytes) from the start of the file: you can only discover how far the start of the current record is (in bytes) from the start of the file.

26.3.7 Character based I/O

Prolog-2 contains BIPs to read and write individual characters (from and to the Current Input and Output Streams, respectively).

26.3.7.1 Character output

Prolog-2 provides two BIPs for character output:

put/1
putbyte/1

26.3.7.2 Character input

Prolog-2 provides three BIPs for character input:

get/1
get0/1
getbyte/1

26.3.8 File and stream details

This chapter describes predicates for discovering the details of

(1) files
(2) devices
(3) streams

26.3.8.1 File details

The predicate **file_details/3** is provided to help the Prolog programmer manipulate VMS filenames.

26.3.8.2 Stream details

The predicate **stream_details/4** provides information about currently open streams.

26.3.8.3 Device details

The predicate **device_details/2** provides information about VMS devices.

26.3.9 Logical names

This Section describes predicates for creating and translating VMS logical names from within Prolog-2.

Logical names are widely used in VMS as brief and memorable abbreviations for long and distinctly unmemorable file specifications and device names.

The topic of logical names is dealt with at great length in VAX/VMS documentation; users who wish to pursue the subject should look there.

Prolog-2 provides two predicates for creating VMS logical names:

create_logical_name/2
create_logical_name/3

These predicates enable Prolog-2 to pass information to VMS.

Prolog-2 provides two BIPs for translating VMS logical names:

translate_logical_name/2
translate_logical_name/3

These two BIPs enable Prolog-2 to take information from VMS.

26.3.10 System errors and codes

This Section describes describes how Prolog-2 accesses system error messages and how these messages can be inspected or edited. It also explains how Prolog-2 represents and reports VMS status codes.

26.3.10.1 System errors

System errors are handled by the error handler **error/4**:

error(ErrorType,ErrorNumber,ErrorGoal,OtherInfo)

All system errors generate a Prolog-2 **system** error.

ErrorGoal is the goal which causes the error; **OtherInfo** is the supplementary error code for this system error.

This supplementary code corresponds to a system error detailed as **sys_error_file(OtherInfo,Text)** in efile.prm ; **Text** is the text for the error.

The reason for this approach is that successive versions of VMS have different error messages, and it is impractical to attempt to update Prolog-2 documentation in step with VAX/VMS amendments.

Inspecting the error message list

The current list of error messages is in the module **efile.prm**.

This list can be inspected by taking input from **efile**:

state(input_module,OldInput,efile).

and then applying **clause/2** to **sys_error_file/2** or **error_file/3** for system and general errors respectively.

System errors:

Repeatedly resatisfy **clause/2** for **sys_error_file/2**:

clause(sys_error_file/2,ErrorMessage).

General errors:

Repeatedly resatisfy **clause/2** for **error_file/3**:

clause(error_file/3,ErrorMessage)

The Prolog-2 User Guide

(Remember to tidy up afterwards by restoring **input_module** to its original setting)

Amending error messages

The **efile** module has **readwrite** access: this enables you to edit the error messages supplied at will.

26.3.10.2 VMS status codes

Status codes in VMS

VMS status codes are values which indicate the success, error or failure of a function.

These VMS status codes are represented as 32-bit integers. Prolog-2's integer range, however, is less than 32 bits; we therefore need a special method of representing these status codes in Prolog-2.

The Prolog structure '$int_pair'(High,Low)

Prolog-2 represents VMS status codes using the structure

'$int_pair'(High,Low)

where **High** and **Low** are Prolog-2 integers representing (respectively) the high and low 16-bit values of the full 32-bit code.

This structure is used in handling VMS system errors, outputting VMS status messages (using **vms_message/1** see below) and in reporting process completion (see **halt/1** and **call_vms/3** in §26.3.11).

state(vms_error_number,Old,New)

The Prolog-2 system state **vms_error_number** holds the VMS error code for the most recent VMS system error.

If no error has occurred since starting the present Prolog-2 session then **vms_error_number** will be set to **none**, indicating the VMS status code for no error, SS$_NORMAL.

The system state **vms_error_number** is saved in the Prolog-2 representation **'$int_pair'(High,Low)**.

It is not possible to change the value of this state except to clear the value by setting it to **none**.

vms_message/2 decodes error messages.

force_vms_error/2 simulates a VMS error.

26.3.11 Accessing the command processor

You can call the VAX command processor from Prolog-2.

The command processor can be invoked interactively; alternatively it can be invoked specifically to execute some particular command.

Invoking the command processor interactively has the effect of temporarily switching you back to VMS and so enables you to type in VMS commands until you choose to return to Prolog. To end the interactive session you type **lo** or **logout**.

Invoking the command processor for a specific DCL command causes that command to be executed and then automatically returns you to Prolog. This means you can include DCL commands within a Prolog program.

The VMS command processor is invoked by spawning a subprocess.

(1) **command/0**
(2) **command/1**
(3) **call_vms/1**
(4) **call_vms/3**

all call the VAX command processor.

26.3.11.1 Spawning limitations

In some versions of VMS the system call to spawn will not recognise incomplete logical names in lower case, for example "tt", though it will recognise upper-case names like "TT". The spawning call may also fail to recognise incomplete logical device names which end in a colon, so that "TT:" will not be translated but "TT" will.

A spawning call usually recognises fully specified logical names such as _TXA4: without trouble. The Prolog predicate **device_details** (see §17.3.8) will generate such names. If there is any doubt it is better to give goals like:

device_details('tt',[_,FullName|_]),
call_vms(Command,[input(Fullname)],Status).

rather than

call_vms(Command,[input('tt')],S).

26.3.12 VMS sub-processes

26.3.12.1 Fundamentals

26.3.12.1.1 Overview

The Prolog-2 Subprocess facility allows you to write your own BIPs in C, Fortran, Macro

The Prolog-2 User Guide

or other languages; these BIPs can then be called from Prolog just like those in Prolog-2's BIP library.

Prolog-2's Subprocess facility is particularly useful when you wish to perform some advanced function which is not available in Prolog, or to execute complete external applications. You simply write the desired code in an appropriate language and link this with the Prolog-2 subprocess interface routines. When you want to use your new routine you simply call the Prolog-2 Subprocess facilities from within Prolog-2 (using the BIPs supplied). Subprocesses allow more general and powerful functions to be integrated with Prolog than is possible using the External Code facility (detailed in §23.2).

Subprocesses also have the ability to run synchronously or asynchronously with Prolog (synchronisation is by means of event flags); there is no risk of their interfering with Prolog provided the interface conventions are observed. On the Prolog side the subprocess is accessed by means of BIPs; on the subprocess side the Prolog interpreter is accessed by means of the subprocess interface functions supplied. Broadly speaking each subprocess BIP is mirrored by a corresponding interface function, and these allow data passing (similar to that of External Code) and process synchronisation. None of these subprocess-specific BIPs is resatisfiable.

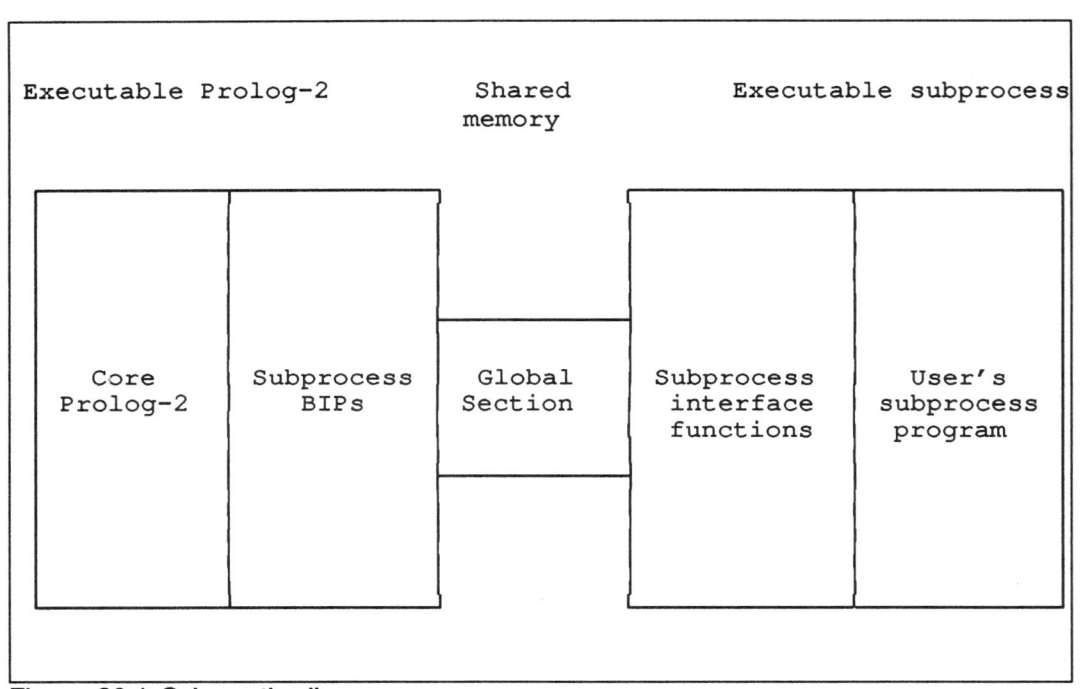

```
Executable Prolog-2        Shared           Executable subprocess
                           memory

   ┌──────────┬──────────┐  ┌──────┐  ┌──────────┬──────────┐
   │          │          │  │      │  │          │          │
   │          │          │  │      │  │          │          │
   │   Core   │Subprocess│  │Global│  │Subprocess│  User's  │
   │ Prolog-2 │   BIPs   │  │Section│ │ interface│subprocess│
   │          │          │  │      │  │ functions│ program  │
   │          │          │  └──────┘  │          │          │
   │          │          │            │          │          │
   └──────────┴──────────┘            └──────────┴──────────┘
```

Figure 26,1 Schematic diagram

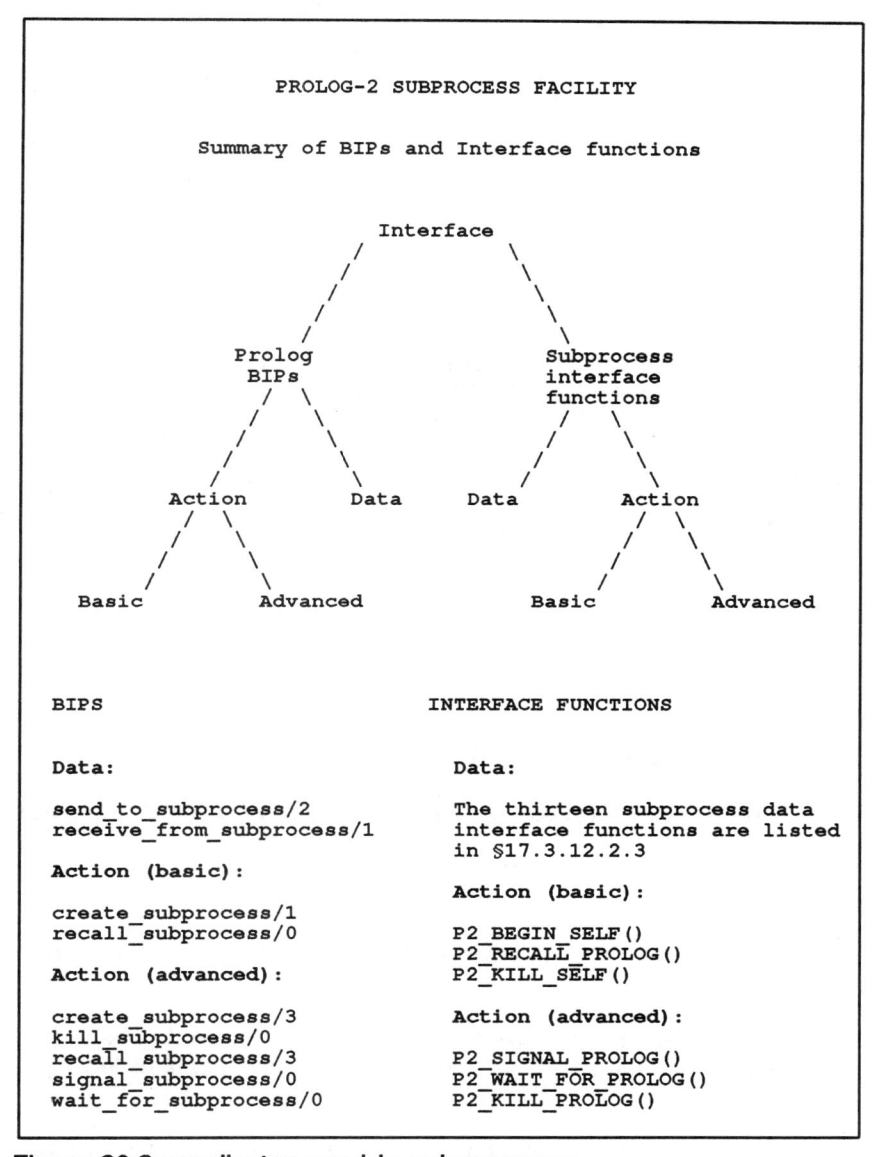

```
          PROLOG-2 SUBPROCESS FACILITY

      Summary of BIPs and Interface functions

                      Interface
                     /         \
                    /           \
                   /             \
                  /               \
               Prolog          Subprocess
               BIPs            interface
               / \             functions
              /   \             /    \
             /     \           /      \
          Action   Data     Data    Action
          / \                        / \
         /   \                      /   \
       Basic  Advanced           Basic   Advanced


 BIPS                    INTERFACE FUNCTIONS

 Data:                   Data:

 send_to_subprocess/2    The thirteen subprocess data
 receive_from_subprocess/1   interface functions are listed
                         in §17.3.12.2.3
 Action (basic):
                         Action (basic):
 create_subprocess/1
 recall_subprocess/0     P2_BEGIN_SELF()
                         P2_RECALL_PROLOG()
 Action (advanced):      P2_KILL_SELF()

 create_subprocess/3     Action (advanced):
 kill_subprocess/0
 recall_subprocess/3     P2_SIGNAL_PROLOG()
 signal_subprocess/0     P2_WAIT_FOR_PROLOG()
 wait_for_subprocess/0   P2_KILL_PROLOG()
```

Figure 26.2: predicates used in subprocesses

26.3.12.1.2 Categories of subprocess access function

Data access functions and action functions

There are two categories of subprocess access functions:

(1) **Subprocess data access functions**

These are functions that read and write data to the area of memory shared between the two processes (labelled 'global section' in Figure 26.1)

(2) **Subprocess action functions**.

These are functions which perform some action

The data access functions are very similar to those provided for linked external code (see the accompanying External Code Manual).

The only subprocess action BIPs needed for most purposes are **create_subprocess/1** and **recall_subprocess/0**; the only subprocess interface action functions needed are P2_BEGIN_SELF(), P2_RECALL_PROLOG() and P2_KILL_SELF().

By using only these BIPs and functions the interface is kept simple and problems of deadlock and interference that may occur with more advanced features are avoided. All the functionality of external code can obtained using a subprocess without advanced features.

For clarity we look first only at the basic features: advanced features are described in §26.3.12.3.

26.3.12.1.3 The fundamental transaction

These basic features allow the following fundamental transaction to take place:

(1) Prolog sends data to the subprocess (using the BIP **send_to_subprocess/2**),

(2) Prolog signals the subprocess to start and suspends itself (using **recall_subprocess/0**),

(3) The subprocess processes the data given and writes output data to the global section,

(4) When the subprocess has finished processing it calls P2_RECALL_PROLOG() to resume execution of Prolog and to suspend the subprocess until called again from Prolog,

(5) Prolog resumes by picking up the output data with **receive_from_subprocess/1** and continuing on from there.

26.3.12.1.4 Subprocess data access BIPs

Prolog-2 provides two BIPs which allow data to be passed to and from subprocesses:

(1) **send_to_subprocess/2**
(2) **receive_from_subprocess/1**

The values that can be passed into and out of subprocess functions are atoms, strings, integers and reals.

26.3.12.1.5 Subprocess action BIPs

Prolog-2 provides basic and advanced subprocess action BIPs to control its interaction with subprocesses.

The advanced action BIPs are described in §26.3.12.3.2. At this stage you need only be aware of the two basic BIPs:

(1) **create_subprocess/1**
(2) **recall_subprocess/0**

26.3.12.1.6 Subprocess error handling

On error the subprocess BIPs execute the user-written error-handling predicate **subprocess_error/4**:

subprocess_error(Type, Errcode1, Errcode2, Goal)

Type: an atom representing the error type eg **vms, fortran, c**

Errcode1: an integer representing the high 16 bits of the full 32-bit error code for the given **Type**. (High values are 2^{16} to $2^{32} - 1$)

Errcode2: an integer representing the low 16 bits of the full 32-bit error code for the given **Type**. (Low values are 0 to $2^{16} - 1$)

Goal: the name of the subprocess BIP in error

If **subprocess_error/4** is not available then the default system subprocess error handler is used.

26.3.12.2 Compiling and linking a subprocess

26.3.12.2.1 Creating an executable subprocess

There are three stages in creating a subprocess:

(1) **Write** functions in external language (e.g. Fortran), producing source code

(2) **Compile/assemble** subprocess source to produce object code

(3) **Link** subprocess object with Prolog-2 interface objects to produce the executable subprocess

§§26.3.12.2.2-2.7 below describe these stages in full detail, with particular reference to

The Prolog-2 User Guide

Macro.

§26.3.12.2.8 explains the differences for other languages. You are strongly recommended to look at the supplied example program "subrm.mar" while reading these sections: this program contains illustrations of the use of all the features described below.

26.3.12.2.2 Writing subprocess functions

Before you can write subprocesses you need to understand the interface between a subprocess and Prolog-2.

Data is passed between a subprocess and Prolog-2 via an area of shared memory called the global section (see Figure 26.1). The subprocess accesses this data by means of the subprocess interface functions and some parameters. Prolog-2 and the subprocess synchronise with each other by means of two event flags; this allows processes to be suspended, killed and signalled.

Subprocess parameters

The subprocess parameters are variables shared between Prolog and the subprocess in the global section. Some are read-only (a subprocess should only read these) and the others can be both written and read by a subprocess.

Writing to read-only parameters will cause unpredictable and certainly undesirable results; reading writable parameters before anything has been written to them will produce meaningless results.

The parameters are all 4-byte integers, either signed (DSC$K_DTYPE_L) or unsigned (DSC$K_DTYPE_LU) — where VMS atomic data types are indicated in parentheses.

The parameters all reside in the global section, and are accessed by using the offset appropriate to each parameter in the global section (these are defined in the include file "mspdef.h01").

Parameters are read using the subprocess interface function P2_G_PARAMETER(), and written using P2_P_PARAMETER() (see §26.3.12.3 for further details of subprocess interface functions).

Subprocess parameter list

Offset 1: P2_OP   (Parameter : read only, signed)

The value at this offset is the value of Op

Offset 2: P2_NMIN (Parameter : read only, signed)

The value at this offset is the number of elements input (i.e. passed to the subprocess). This value has a maximum, defined as P2_LNIN in the "mspdef.h0" include-file

Offset 3: P2_IN

This offset indicates the start of the input elements. The subprocess should never examine the value at this offset, only pass the offset to the appropriate interface functions

Offset 4: P2_NMOUT (Parameter : read/write, signed)

The value at this offset is the number of elements output (i.e. passed back to Prolog). This value has a maximum defined as P2_LNOUT in the "mspdef.h0" include-file

Offset 5: P2_OUT

This offset indicates the start of the output elements. The subprocess should never examine the value at this offset, only pass the offset to the appropriate interface functions

Offset 6: P2_RETURN (Parameter : read/write, signed)

Its value is an integer indicating which of the recognised Return values **none** / **fail** is returned if the function is to succeed/fail respectively. If the function is in error the return value appropriate to the type of error (e.g. **fortran**, **vms**, **prolog** etc.) is returned and P2_STATUS is set to the appropriate error code. These P2_RETURN values are listed in the "mspdef.h01" include-file.

Offset 7: P2_STATUS (Parameter : read/write, unsigned)

Its value is the full 32-bit error code value which is returned when the subprocess function returns error information. This error code is split into two 16-bit integer values, which are then assigned to Errcode1 and Errcode2. Errcode2 holds the low values (0 to $2^{16} - 1$), Errcode1 the high values (2^{16} to $2^{32} - 1$).

26.3.12.2.3 Subprocess data interface functions

The subprocess data interface functions allow you to read the Input list elements and to write (and read) the Output list elements.

When reading a data item the first thing to do is to determine its type (integer, real,

The Prolog-2 User Guide

atom or string); once this is known you can call the read function appropriate to this type to obtain the value of the item.

To write a data item you simply call the write function appropriate to the type being written, together with the value to be written.

Arguments passed to interface functions

Four sorts of arguments are commonly passed to interface functions:

offset
direction
index
address

All of these are unsigned 4-byte integers.

offset: the offset of an interface parameter within the global section.

direction: an offset, either P2_IN or P2_OUT according to whether input or output arguments are being referenced.

index: indicates which of the arguments (for the given direction) is to be accessed. 0 indicates the first argument. The parameter for offset P2_NMIN/P2_NMOUT indicates the number of arguments there are; this number minus 1 is therefore the highest index value allowed.

address: the address of the subprocess's data item which holds or is to hold values passed to and from the interface.

List of subprocess data interface functions

integer P2_G_PARAMETER(offset)

Returns an integer which specifies the value of the parameter at the offset indicated

P2_P_PARAMETER(offset,integer_value)

Sets the parameter indicated by the offset as having the given signed integer_value

integer P2_TYPE(direction,index)

Returns an integer which specifies the data type (atom, string, real or integer) of the item indicated. These types are listed in the "mspdef.h01" include-file

P2_G_INTEGER(direction,index,address)

Used to transfer an integer value from the indicated interface data item, into the location pointed to by the address

P2_G_REAL(direction,index,address)

Used to transfer a real number value from the indicated interface data item, into the location pointed to by the address

P2_G_ATOM(direction,index,address)

Used to transfer an atom from the indicated interface data item, into the location pointed to by the address

P2_G_STRING(direction,index,address)

Used to transfer a string from the indicated interface data item, into the location pointed to by the address

unsigned integer P2_ATOM_LENGTH(direction,index)

Returns an integer which specifies the length of the indicated interface data item (assumed to be an atom)

unsigned integer P2_STRING_LENGTH(direction,index)

Returns an integer which specifies the length of the indicated interface data item (assumed to be a string)

unsigned integer P2_P_INTEGER(direction,index,integer_value)

Sets the indicated interface data item to the given signed integer_value. If the data item cannot be set (because of insufficient space in the global section) then P2_FALSE is returned; otherwise P2_TRUE is returned (these constants are defined in the include-file "mspdef.h01")

unsigned integer P2_P_REAL(direction,index,address)

Sets the indicated interface data item to the value of the real number stored at the given address. If the data item cannot be set (because of insufficient space in the global section) then P2_FALSE is returned; otherwise P2_TRUE is returned (these constants are defined in the include-file "mspdef.h01")

unsigned integer P2_P_ATOM(direction,index,address,length)

Sets the indicated interface data item to the value of the atom stored at the given address, with given (unsigned) length. If the data item cannot be set (because of insufficient space in the global section) then P2_FALSE is returned; otherwise P2_TRUE is returned (these constants are defined in the include-file "mspdef.h01")

unsigned integer P2_P_STRING(direction,index,address,length)

The Prolog-2 User Guide

Sets the indicated interface data item to the value of the string stored at the given address, with given (unsigned) length. If the data item cannot be set (because of insufficient space in the global section) then P2_FALSE is returned; otherwise P2_TRUE is returned (these constants are defined in the include-file "mspdef.h01")

Example of state of global section after call

After the goal

send_to_subprocess(137, [2.2, 3, 'ab', "xyzt"])

the shared data area will hold the following values:

```
P2_G_PARAMETER( P2_OP )   = 137
P2_G_PARAMETER( P2_NMIN ) = 4

P2_TYPE( P2_IN, 1 )       = P2_T_INTEGER
P2_G_INTEGER( P2_IN, 1, address_of_integer_arg1 )
Integer value at address_of_integer_arg1 is 3

P2_TYPE( P2_IN, 3 )       = P2_T_STRING
P2_STRING_LENGTH( P2_IN,3 ) = 4
P2_G_STRING( P2_IN, 3, address_of_string_arg3 )
Ascii bytes at address_of_string_arg3 are xyzt respectively
```

Data representation within the subprocess

The subprocess needs to be able to store all four types of data passed to and from the interface, namely integers, reals, atoms and strings.

These datatypes are as follows:

integer: 4-byte signed 2's-complement integer (DSC$K_DTYPE_L)

real: 8-byte D_floating point number (DSC$K_DTYPE_D)

atom: stored as a contiguous character array, each character being an unsigned byte (DSC$K_DTYPE_BU). Each array should have space for one extra byte at the end of the array — this is used by the interface routines. The length of the array (excluding the extra byte) is stored as a 4-byte unsigned integer (DSC$K_TYPE_LU)

string: see **atom** above

Validation and error checking

It is the programmer's responsibility to check that the right routines are called for each data type; this is why P2_TYPE() is supplied. However if your Prolog calls of the subprocess routines can guarantee the data type of the passed items then you will not need to check their type; but be warned that calling the wrong routine will produce unpredictable and certainly undesirable results.

Strings and atoms can potentially be very long: their maximum lengths (excluding the extra byte mentioned above) are P2_LENGTH_ATOM and P2_LENGTH_STRING, as listed in the "mspdef.h01" include-file. When getting a string or atom from the interface it is of course important that there is enough space for them to be written to, otherwise corruption will occur.

Because of this we have included functions to return the lengths of these items (P2_STRING_LENGTH() and P2_ATOM_LENGTH()), so that the space allocation can be checked before potentially corrupting routines are called.

26.3.12.2.4 Basic subprocess action interface functions

This section describes the three basic subprocess action interface functions: the advanced interface functions are described later in §26.3.12.3):

(1) P2_BEGIN_SELF()
(2) P2_RECALL_PROLOG()
(3) P2_KILL_SELF()

P2_BEGIN_SELF()

This function must always be called when the subprocess begins execution (and never called again for that subprocess). It performs an initialisation which allows the subprocess access to the shared global section and then signals Prolog (which has suspended on the **create_subprocess** BIP call) to resume. Having done this the subprocess suspends.

The initialisation includes setting the globals P2_L_VIRTUAL and P2_H_VIRTUAL (defined in "mspdat.h01"), 4-byte unsigned integers, to be the address of the start (i.e. low memory end) and end of the shared global section, respectively.

The size of the global section is a fixed number (20) of 512-byte pages.

P2_RECALL_PROLOG()

If Prolog is suspended then it is resumed running. The subprocess is then suspended (this happens even if Prolog was already running)

P2_KILL_SELF()

If Prolog-2 is suspended then it is resumed running. The subprocess is then terminated (this happens even if Prolog was already running)

The Prolog-2 User Guide

26.3.12.2.5 Subprocess calling conventions

Calling interface functions

All interface functions should be defined as subroutines with no arguments (i.e. they need not save any registers via the entry mask). Their declarations can be found in the include-file "mspfns.h01".

It is the programmer's responsibility to ensure that a subroutine never calls interface functions which interact with Prolog, when Prolog has already terminated. (If this happens then the interface function will cause unpredictable and certainly undesirable results.)

Execution of subprocess code

A subprocess must obey the VAX calling conventions on all calls to interface functions, and must not directly access the global section (named "ESI$GLOBAL_SECT") nor test or set the reserved event flags (64 and 65).

When calling any interface functions you should check the value of the global P2_FRETURN (signed 4-byte integer, defined in "mspdat.h01"); if its value is not P2_OKAY_RETURN then an error has occurred while performing the interface function, P2_FRETURN indicates the type of error (eg P2_VMS_RETURN for VMS errors) and P2_FSTATUS (unsigned 4-byte integer) holds the appropriate error code (e.g. for VMS errors this will be the VMS system service error code). See "mspdat.h01" for the values that P2_FRETURN may take.

Error reporting

VMS errors reported on subprocess interface BIPs can, if desired, be reported to Prolog as Prolog subprocess errors by changing P2_FRETURN to be P2_PRL_RETURN and by resetting P2_FSTATUS to be one of the supplementary error codes for Prolog **system** error.

If P2_RETURN shows that an error has occurred in P2_BEGIN_SELF() then the subprocess must deal with this error itself (e.g. by exiting with P2_FSTATUS as the error code), as the subprocess cannot be sure that the environment to report errors back to Prolog has been set up.

Within these conventions the subprocess can do as it will, but it should take care never to use an absolute address which might address the global section. To guard against this note that P2_BEGIN_SELF() sets the globals P2_L_VIRTUAL and P2_H_VIRTUAL to indicate the start and end of the global section.

You must take care that any new global names defined in the subprocess code are not also declared as interface globals already (all these globals are prefixed with "P2_" and are declared in "mspdat.h01").

Remember that P2_BEGIN_SELF() must be called once and once only on initial start-up of the subprocess.

Passing the result of a subprocess call to Prolog

First set the parameter for offset P2_RETURN to indicate failure, success or error. For the success case make sure that all output values are set and that the parameter for offset P2_NMOUT records the number of these values. For the error case set the parameter for offset P2_STATUS to record the error code itself.

Finally signal Prolog using the appropriate interface function (e.g. P2_RECALL_PROLOG()).

Ending the subprocess

To terminate the subprocess should call P2_KILL_SELF(). Prolog subprocess BIPs will always detect if the subprocess has terminated (even if this is not via P2_KILL_SELF()) and react accordingly. But be careful: if Prolog is suspended when the subprocess terminates, and the subprocess does not execute any interface function which will resume Prolog before it terminates, then Prolog will remain suspended indefinitely — see §26.3.12.3 on advanced action facilities for full details.

26.3.12.2.6 Compiling / assembling a subprocess

Subprocess source code will normally include declarations of the interface functions provided by Prolog (these can be found in the include-file "mspfns.h01"). Declarations of the interface parameters and of the constants used to interface to Prolog would also need to be included in the source file (these can be found in the include-file "mspdef.h01"), and of the globals used by the interface functions ("mspdat.h01").

When complete the source should be compiled/assembled to produce an object file called SPROCESS.OBJ .

26.3.12.2.7 Linking object with Prolog

To link you must have available the VAXCRTL Object Library.

First of all the files to be linked together should be specified in an options file — the file "bsubrm.opt" does this for your object file SPROCESS.OBJ . Then you should link the files to produce the executable image — the file "bsubrm.com" will link the files named in "bsubrm.opt" to produce an image called "subrm.exe". To do this you must of course have all the object files named in the options file available for linking.

26.3.12.2.8 Language differences

Languages other than Macro will use different files supplied with Prolog: a table of these is included below.

C language external code

The Prolog-2 User Guide

To conform to normal C standards, when character strings (i.e. atoms or strings) are passed into the interface functions they should be terminated with a null (\0). Similarily when they are set by these functions they will have a terminating null. The atom or string lengths should never count terminating nulls.

26.3.12.2.9 Debugging

You can use the VMS debugger to debug your subprocess program by compiling / assembling your source with the /DEBUG qualifier and by altering the link command file to include the /DEBUG switch on linking. Then if the input and output channels of the subprocess (*cf.* **create_subprocess**/3) are a terminal, the debug session will be available at that terminal in the usual way.

26.3.12.3 Advanced sub-process features

§26.3.12.1 explained the basics of Prolog-subprocess interaction; §26.3.12.2 takes you through the steps of compiling, writing and running a subprocess. This final Section introduces the more advanced subprocess facilities available in Prolog-2.

26.3.12.3.1 Advanced subprocess action facilities

Prolog-2's advanced subprocess action facilities allow a Prolog process and the subprocess to be run synchronously or asynchronously; and for the the priorities of the processes to be altered. They also allow more sophisticated creation of the subprocess and for the subprocess to terminate Prolog.

Synchronisation and flow of control

The Prolog process and its subprocess can each be in one of two states: suspended or running.

A suspended process can do no computation; it can only wait for a signal from outside which will change its state to running. A running process executes normally, can suspend itself, but cannot be suspended from outside.

Each process can activate its partner, but not suspend it; each process can suspend itself, but not activate itself from the suspended state.

At any time either Prolog, or the subprocess, or both may be running. The state in which each process suspends itself and waits for a signal from the other should be avoided, as this will result in "deadlock" where neither process is active (and each can only be activated by the other).

Predicates to control synchronisation

A number of predicates are provided which can be called from Prolog to synchronise the running of Prolog and its subprocesses. A number of procedures are provided which can be used to control synchronisation from the subprocess.

If you use predicates and interface functions which do not suspend whilst the other process is executing, then there is the risk that both processes will become suspended at the same time (a form of deadlock as each waits for the other to awaken it), or that they both be running and accessing the shared data area at the same time (when such interlock problems occur the results are unpredictable). You have been warned.

The effects of subprocess bips on synchronisation

BIP	State of subprocess		State of Prolog
	before	midway	midway
create_subprocess	not there	running	suspended
recall_subprocess	running or suspended	running	suspended
signal_subprocess	running or suspended	running	running
wait_for_subprocess	running (or deadlock will ensue)	as before	suspended
kill_subprocess	running or suspended	not there	running
halt	running or suspended (or not there)	running (or not there)	running (or not there)

When one of the above BIPs is called Prolog is, naturally, running and the subprocess may be in any state. If part of the effect of the BIP is to suspend Prolog midway through the call then it will wait for a signal from the subprocess (such as that given by the interface function P2_SIGNAL_PROLOG()). In any case, on completion of the BIP call, Prolog is, naturally, running. (The **halt** BIP never completes as it terminates Prolog.)

Table of the effects of interface functions on synchronisation

Function	State of Prolog		State of subprocess
	before	midway	midway
P2_BEGIN_SELF	suspended	running	suspended
P2_RECALL_PROLOG	usually suspended	running	suspended

371

The Prolog-2 User Guide

P2_SIGNAL_PROLOG	running or suspended	running	running
P2_WAIT_FOR_PROLOG	running (or deadlock will ensue)	as before	suspended
P2_KILL_PROLOG	running or suspended	not there	running
P2_KILL_SELF	running or suspended	running	not there

When one of the above interface functions is called the subprocess is, naturally, running and Prolog may be in any state. If part of the effect of the function is to suspend the subprocess midway through the call then it will wait for a signal from Prolog (such as that given by the BIP **signal_subprocess**). In any case, on return from the function call, the subprocess is, naturally, running. (The P2_KILL_SELF() function never returns as it terminates the subprocess.)

Process priorities

Some BIPs and interface functions are provided to allow you to examine or change the priority of both the Prolog and the subprocess processes.

These priorities can be changed by the VMS scheduler to be greater than or equal to the process's base priority. Calls to change a priority change the base priority of the process. See your DEC VMS documentation for further details.

26.3.12.3.2 Advanced subprocess action BIPs

§26.3.12.1.5 describes the two basic subprocess BIPs **create_subprocess/1** and **recall_subprocess/0**.

There are five more advanced subprocess action BIPs available in Prolog-2:

(1) **create_subprocess/3**
(2) **kill_subprocess/0**
(3) **recall_subprocess/3**
(4) **signal_subprocess/0**
(5) **wait_for_subprocess/0**

26.3.12.3.3 BIPs affecting process priorities

Prolog-2 provides four BIPs to set or show process priorities:

(1) **get_priority/1**
(2) **get_subprocess_priority/1**

(3) **set_priority_priority/1**
(4) **set_subprocess_priority/1**

26.3.12.3.4 Advanced subprocess action interface functions

(The three basic subprocess action interface functions — P2_BEGIN_SELF(), P2_RECALL_PROLOG() and P2_KILL_SELF() — are described in §26.2.12.2.4.

P2_SIGNAL_PROLOG()

If Prolog is suspended then it is resumed running. The subprocess is not suspended.

Care should be taken to ensure that Prolog and the subprocess do not interfere while they are running concurrently.

P2_WAIT_FOR_PROLOG()

The subprocess is suspended, until Prolog signals that it should resume (eg by using signal_subprocess).

Care should be taken to ensure that this function is not called whilst Prolog is suspended, or deadlock will occur.

P2_KILL_PROLOG()

Prolog is terminated immediately, regardless of whether it was running or suspended when the function was called.

Care should be taken by the user to ensure that Prolog is not performing some useful operation when it is so terminated.

26.3.12.3.5 Interface functions affecting process priorities

integer P2_GET_PRIORITY()

The value returned is the current priority of the subprocess process

integer P2_GET_PROLOG_PRIORITY()

The value returned is the current priority of the Prolog process

P2_SET_PRIORITY(integer_value)

The base priority of the Subprocess process is set to the given **integer_value**. If the **integer_value** is out of range then a Prolog (not VMS) error is set

P2_SET_PROLOG_PRIORITY(integer_value)

The base priority of the Prolog process is set to the given **integer_value**. If the **integer_value** is out of range then a Prolog (not VMS) error is set

26.3.12.3.6 Privileges and event flags

Some operations — for example creating a subprocess, deleting the process which created the current process, and changing the subprocess's priority to be greater than its creator's — require certain budget quotas or privileges. If the correct quotas or privileges are not available to you then such calls will generate a VMS error, and you are advised to contact your VAX system manager, cap in hand, to request these privileges.

For your information: Prolog suspends by waiting on the "CALL" event flag (64) and the subprocess suspends by waiting on the "RETURN" event flag (65).

27. The LINT checker

The Lint Checker scans syntactically valid Prolog files for evidence of errors such as misspellings.

Prolog programs which are quite correct may still offend the Lint Checker — for example, by including references to undefined predicates, which are to be asserted at runtime. Thus a program which produces errors in the Lint Checker need not necessarily be at fault. But the checker may detect problems which would take a long time to pinpoint using the Debugger.

27.1 What the Lint Checker reports

The Lint Checker reports the following conditions:

(1) Predicates which are undefined, not system predicates and not declared as external

(2) Predicates whose clauses are not adjacent (this often arises when a clause has been misprinted)

Suppose in the middle of a knowledge base of 50 clauses for **translate/3** you type:

```
...
translate(flea,puce,puces).
translate(louse,pou).
translate(apple,pomme,pommes).
...
```

and forget to provide a plural for **pou**. The syntax is still valid but will lead to the creation of a predicate **translate/2** with only one clause; the undefined predicate trap in your program would not help here either. But the Lint Checker would spot this error and report it

(3) Predicates which are not declared public and are never referenced. Such predicates are not necessarily otiose, because they may be referenced by a term constructed at runtime using =.. and called; however it is quite likely that the name has been misspelled or the arity is wrong

(4) Clauses for system predicates and for :- (such clauses are illegal anyway)

(5) Named variables which occur only once in a clause. These are may well be misspellings of variable names (if not, a _ would have done just as well)

(6) Wrong number of arguments to a system predicate

(7) Unbound variables in the arguments to **not**, other than _. Since **not** cannot instantiate the variable you probably did not mean to put it there.

375

The Prolog-2 User Guide

The Lint Checker does not generally check for errors which will be signalled at runtime anyway.

27.2 Accessing the Lint Checker

The Lint Checker lives in the file LINT.PRM. This file is not opened automatically at runtime; the BIP **lint/0** contains code to open it.

To use the Lint Checker type

lint.

and answer the questions:

Prolog file?
List file?
Masks?

You are asked to supply the names of a file to be checked and a report file. These should be Prolog-2 streams obeying the usual rules; for example you will get default extension .PRO for both of them. You may specify **user** to send the report to the screen.

Masking errors

If certain lint errors are not important to you then you can mask them by specifying their numbers when asked for masks; lint error numbers are given in §27.4 below.

Lint error numbers should be separated by spaces and terminated by a full stop.

If you want the Lint Checker to report all errors you should not specify any mask numbers; but you still have to type the terminating full stop and the carriage return which follows it.

27.3 Lint Checker output

The Lint Checker outputs a report which begins with the following header panel:

Lint report
===========
Prolog file: lint
Report file: printer
Error(s) masked: 5   6
Date: 21-10-86
Time: 16:23:59

It then reports the specific errors found, and finishes with the total number of errors detected.

27.4 Lint Checker error messages

The following error messages may be reported

1:   This is not a valid clause:
2:   Named variable occurs only once:
3:   The following is a clause for a system predicate:
4:   Clauses split up by a different predicate:
5:   Bad arguments to a system predicate:
6:   Predicate never referenced:
7:   Predicate never defined:
8:   Named variable in not will not be instantiated:
9:   Bad argument to call:
10: Repeat without subsequent cut:

At the end of the report the Lint Checker will tell you if it has found any errors which would prevent the file from being compiled and/or consulted. Any consultation error will also prevent compilation; but you may find your code is acceptable provided you do not wish to compile it.

27.5 A worked example

We now present an example session with the Lint Checker.

Text produced by Prolog-2 or the Lint Checker is shown in bold; text entered by the user is shown in lighter type.

?- lint.

Prolog-2 Lint checker version X.YY

Prolog file? primes

List file? (<ENTER> for A:\PRIMES.LST) user

Masks? .

Lint report
===========

Prolog file: primes
Report file: user
Error(s) masked: none
Date: 19-5-86
Time: 16:00:23

The Prolog-2 User Guide

Lint error no. 10

Repeat without subsequent cut:

do:-repeat, retract(seed(X)),Y is X+1,assert(seed(Y)),
not has_factor(X),assert(is_prime(X)),write(X),put(32),
X>1000

1 error detected

yes

Index

abort 70, 71, 156, 157, 159, 172, 173, 262, 282, 284, 288, 293, 303, 310, 312, 317, 349
abort_goal 172, 284
access mode 129
acos 116
acosh 116
actual memory 98, 101, 111
ancestor 113, 167, 290
arg 16, 176, 181, 183, 186-189, 191, 192, 194
arithmetic comparison 121
arithmetic expression 50
arity 9, 11, 16, 22, 23, 34, 49, 68, 79, 90, 94-96, 104, 116-118, 123, 126, 141, 176, 177-181, 184, 186, 189-193, 196, 200, 262, 288, 375
asin 116
assert 23, 74, 86-89, 91-93, 96, 100, 107, 148, 243, 262, 280, 282, 298, 378
asserta 89, 144, 149, 152
assertz 89
atan 116
atanh 116
atom 3, 13, 15, 16, 19, 20, 22-27, 34, 35, 47, 72, 80, 89, 104-106, 111, 114, 117, 122, 123, 129, 130, 132-134, 141, 142, 151, 175, 179-181, 184, 186, 188-194, 196, 200, 202-205, 207, 208, 213, 218, 229, 236, 243, 255, 262, 277, 293, 311, 338, 342, 350, 351, 353, 361, 364-367, 370
atomic 15, 16, 94, 362
atomprops 26, 28
backtrace 68, 69, 113, 288
bagof 17, 18
box model 160, 302
built-in predicate 155, 160, 299, 315
call 9, 12, 14, 17, 18, 28, 51, 57-60, 67, 69-72, 83, 90, 96, 98, 102-104, 110, 112, 114, 118, 123, 138, 142, 153, 154, 156, 157, 161-163, 165, 172, 174, 176, 177, 181-183, 185, 186, 188, 193, 197, 199, 200, 202, 212-217, 219-221, 223, 226, 229-233, 235-243, 254, 257, 260-264, 267-272, 276, 280, 282, 287, 289, 290, 291, 294, 299, 302, 307, 310, 312, 340, 341, 346-349, 356, 357, 358, 364, 366, 367, 369, 371, 372, 374, 377
canonical order 18, 125
clause iii, 10-16, 21, 26-28, 47, 63-66, 68, 69, 71, 83, 84, 86, 88-97, 99, 101, 102, 103, 107, 109, 111-113, 125, 141, 151, 155, 157, 158, 172, 236, 257, 288, 299, 355, 375, 377
close 30, 33, 53, 55, 95, 98, 99, 101, 105, 108, 128, 130, 132, 133, 148, 155, 184, 209, 210, 217, 250, 252, 261, 284, 314, 340-342
close_module 98, 99, 108, 184
close_stream 210, 217
comment 19, 21, 22, 28, 148, 267, 277, 279, 288, 338, 349, 350

The Prolog-2 User Guide

compare 121, 229
conlist 89, 312
consult 11, 27, 43, 45, 88, 89, 92, 93, 96, 98, 100, 131-133, 171, 210, 235, 238, 240, 241, 247, 300, 306, 317, 324, 327, 328, 338, 339, 342
context buffer 292
control-break 39, 68, 173
core 4, 5, 9, 17, 109, 158, 160, 166, 178, 226-229, 240, 245, 274, 275, 283, 288, 289, 358
create 17, 64, 67, 68, 98, 101, 103, 104, 110, 128-133, 139, 142, 143, 145, 146, 147, 148, 150, 152, 166, 170, 175, 177, 183, 200, 209, 211, 212-214, 217, 220, 223-229, 231, 232, 234, 239, 241, 242, 245, 246, 248-251, 254, 276, 307, 321, 328, 331, 332, 340, 346, 347, 348, 352, 354, 359-361, 367, 370-372
create_stream 128-131, 209, 211-214, 217, 220, 223, 225, 226, 228, 231, 232, 234, 249-251, 321
creep 5, 167
current input stream 128, 132, 133, 183, 216, 248, 259, 264
current output stream 128, 232
current_op 28
current_predicate 96
datatype 16, 130, 131
date 73, 74, 255, 322, 340, 376, 377
debug 113, 159, 160, 162-164, 166-168, 209, 246, 274, 275, 278, 279, 281, 282, 283, 286, 288-291, 297, 303, 304, 370
debug_goal 166, 167
debugging iv, 160, 164, 167, 209, 289, 370
decimals 63, 64, 72, 73, 147
decode 136-138, 153, 154, 171, 185
default_name_sys 170, 171, 277, 286, 322, 326, 328, 338, 340, 349
delete_file 340, 351
delete_stream 130, 132, 210, 217, 250, 252
display 48, 62, 124, 153, 154, 158, 160, 162, 164, 167, 210, 229-231, 239-241, 243, 245, 249, 255, 256, 278, 283, 287, 290-292, 301, 305, 309, 343
encode 138, 146, 154
erase 96, 239, 241
error iv, 24, 31, 32, 37, 48, 49, 68, 75, 84-88, 90, 103, 109, 113, 120, 131, 133, 134, 138, 140, 141, 155-160, 172, 173, 177, 178, 182, 184, 185, 198-200, 202, 205, 206, 212, 214, 215, 217, 219, 221, 222, 223, 230, 233-236, 239, 242, 245, 248, 261, 268, 274, 278, 279, 283, 284, 286-288, 291-294, 296, 297, 303, 304, 308, 311, 312, 317, 318, 324, 330, 339, 343, 344, 347, 355, 356, 361, 363, 366, 368, 369, 374-378
error handler 160, 261
error_break 158, 159, 284
error_number 159, 343, 356
exists_file 340, 351
exp 116

expand_term 27
fact 5, 12-14, 16, 17, 25, 26, 32, 33, 35, 37, 49, 51, 58, 60, 61, 74, 86, 90, 92, 96, 112, 113, 187, 253, 255, 274, 302, 309, 328
fail 14, 15, 17, 58-60, 62-64, 69-71, 73, 74, 82, 83, 85, 86, 91, 121-123, 134, 142, 145, 153, 159, 161-163, 165, 167, 173, 178, 181, 185, 188, 189, 192, 199, 200, 202, 209, 247, 282, 293, 294, 302, 303, 312, 353, 357, 363
fail_out 167
fatal error 155, 156, 159, 173, 287
file 4, 7, 30, 41, 79, 80, 82-84, 86, 87, 89, 92, 93, 98, 100, 105, 106, 108, 109, 128-131, 133, 134, 139, 140, 144, 145, 148, 150-153, 155, 156, 157, 159, 169-172, 174-177, 184, 186, 188, 190, 192, 197, 202, 203-207, 209, 210, 214, 222-231, 233-235, 237-242, 248, 249, 251, 266, 274, 276, 277, 279, 283, 292-294, 298-300, 304, 305, 307, 309-312, 315-328, 330-332, 334-342, 344-355, 362, 363, 364-370, 376, 377
files 7, 79, 88, 128, 130, 134, 139, 144, 170, 172-175, 186, 188, 190, 192, 197, 198, 206, 207, 209, 213, 222, 235, 236, 238-240, 242, 274, 278, 279, 281, 283, 284, 298, 300, 303-305, 314, 316, 319, 320, 321, 323, 327-329, 331, 332, 336-342, 345, 346, 348, 351, 352-354, 369, 375
force_error 157, 235
functor 15, 16, 22-25, 27, 90, 93-96, 104, 115-118, 120, 122, 123, 126, 129, 140, 141, 147, 157, 179, 180, 183, 186-194, 200, 213, 236, 243, 250
garbage collection 114
gc 83, 84, 337, 338
gcguide 114, 337
get 3, 5, 18, 32, 36, 38, 40-49, 52, 56, 57, 61, 63-65, 67, 68, 71-73, 83, 84, 86, 113, 118, 134, 137, 138, 140, 141, 143, 144, 163, 176, 177, 182, 183, 185, 187-189, 191, 192, 209, 210, 216, 226, 237, 239, 240, 242, 243, 245-248, 250, 253-257, 259, 260, 262-265, 267-271, 276, 284, 285, 291, 294, 295, 297-300, 308, 311, 312, 315, 317, 320, 323, 328, 340, 341, 344, 351, 354, 372, 373, 376
get0 134, 210, 216, 231, 259, 264, 299, 341, 354
getbyte 210, 216, 341, 342, 354
goal 3, 11, 12, 14-17, 27, 48, 49, 57, 60, 62-64, 69, 70, 74, 83, 84, 91, 94, 95, 98, 101, 105, 106, 112, 113, 154, 156-158, 160-164, 166, 167, 171, 172, 173, 175, 177, 182, 185, 188, 190, 192, 195, 199, 200, 212-218, 237-239, 260, 262, 274-276, 282, 284, 287, 288, 290, 291, 293, 294, 299, 309, 310, 312, 323, 332, 338, 355, 361, 366
goal_out 167
grammar rule 23, 27, 139
halt 30, 163, 171-173, 177, 276, 284, 289, 310, 314, 318, 339, 350, 356, 371
hash 83, 94-96
help iii, 4, 5, 7, 31, 39, 47, 49, 50, 53, 55, 61, 63, 64, 67, 72-74, 81, 92, 160, 163, 166, 167, 246, 248, 275, 277-279, 281-286, 289, 290, 292,

294, 295-300, 303, 305, 314-316, 354, 375
init_alloc   170, 324
initialisation file   169-171, 197, 347, 349
input   iv, 32, 51, 75, 79-81, 87, 89, 90, 100, 105, 107, 108, 110, 124, 128-134,
136-144, 148, 150, 152, 153, 158, 172, 178, 183, 185, 187, 189,
191, 193, 198-202, 213, 214, 216-218, 220, 224, 227, 229, 233,
236-240, 242, 245, 247, 248, 255, 257, 259-261, 264, 267, 268,
278, 287, 290-293, 301, 303, 310, 330, 331, 338, 341, 343, 350,
352, 353, 355, 356, 363, 364, 370
input_module   107, 355, 356
instance   10, 12, 16, 96, 119, 138, 199, 208, 211, 213, 215, 216, 218, 222,
225, 228, 231, 234, 239, 300, 315, 327, 335, 337, 341
integer   14, 16, 19-21, 25, 32, 35, 47, 83, 90, 91, 94, 115, 116, 118-122, 134,
141, 145-147, 153, 165, 167, 179-184, 186, 189-195, 198, 199,
201, 202-205, 211, 212, 214-216, 218-221, 224, 227, 229, 233,
237, 238-240, 243, 265, 267, 297, 312, 339, 356, 361, 363-366,
368, 373, 374
interface   174, 183, 188, 190, 192, 205, 211, 319, 324, 344, 358, 359
invocation number   161, 163
is/2   49-51, 115, 121, 127
is_string/2   115, 122, 123
leap   167
leash   162-166
leashing   162, 166, 168, 291, 302
length   15, 16, 34-37, 44, 115, 117, 118, 121, 122, 138, 180, 181, 190, 203,
204, 205, 213, 220, 221, 232, 237, 240-243, 266, 352, 354,
365, 366, 367
lint   iv, 67, 79, 86, 93, 275, 283, 286, 331, 336, 375-378
list   10-13, 16, 18, 22, 23, 25, 26, 28, 34-37, 44, 50-52, 55-57, 62, 65, 74, 88,
89, 92-95, 101, 115, 117, 122, 123, 126, 128, 138, 141-143,
146, 147, 150, 151, 153, 155, 157, 158, 164-166, 171, 196, 198,
200, 202, 209, 218, 227, 233, 234, 238, 241, 251, 252, 253,
255, 258, 266-268, 288, 289, 295, 297, 298, 300, 301, 306, 312,
321, 329, 339, 355, 362-364, 376, 377
listing   88, 90, 92, 93, 96, 107, 210, 275, 288, 306, 345
log   64, 87, 116, 122, 151, 153, 300
logging   64
menu   42, 163, 278, 279, 284, 285, 288, 299, 302, 305, 306
mnu file   109, 169-171, 251, 266, 274, 276, 277, 279, 283, 309, 323, 332, 334,
336, 337, 338, 348, 350
module   79, 98, 99, 101, 103-108, 148, 161, 176, 197, 237, 286, 287, 291
name   11, 12, 15, 16, 19-21, 27, 28, 32, 35, 37, 49, 53, 55, 58, 68, 72, 79, 80,
82, 87, 89-93, 95, 96, 102-110, 114, 123, 128-134, 137, 138,
140, 142, 149-151, 153, 158, 159, 163, 164, 169-172, 175-177,
179, 180, 184, 186, 187, 195, 196, 206, 210, 213, 214, 217,
218, 224, 227, 230, 233-238, 241, 243, 247, 249, 251, 254-256,
262, 265, 274, 277, 280, 281, 283, 286, 288, 290, 292, 295-297,
300, 303, 305, 313-317, 319-328, 332, 335, 338, 340, 342, 344,
345, 347-351, 354, 361, 375

nl   52, 62-64, 73, 74, 82, 112, 153, 200, 209, 210, 215, 229, 284, 286, 341
nodebug   61, 164, 166, 230, 238, 241
nonvar   16
normal error   155-157, 159
nospy   164, 166
notrace   164, 166, 289
numeric   16, 237, 241, 243, 291
op/3   24-26
open/2   130, 131, 209-211, 214, 321, 340
open_module   81, 87, 98, 106, 177, 237, 240, 277, 286, 313, 338
open_read   340, 351
open_readwrite   340, 351
operator   14, 19, 22-26, 28, 105, 109, 114-116, 119, 121, 122, 124, 139, 150,
            151, 153, 190, 196, 242, 251, 293
or/0   167
output_module   98, 106, 107, 313
phrase   10, 11
pi   116
port   5, 59, 100, 128, 161-163, 166, 174, 275, 289, 294
precedence   24-26, 28, 103, 121, 122
predicate   11, 13-17, 27, 28, 32, 34, 43-45, 49, 50, 52, 53, 55, 57, 60, 63, 65,
             66, 68, 72, 79-86, 88-91, 94-99, 101-105, 107-110, 112-114,
             125, 134, 145, 147, 150, 153, 155, 158-162, 164, 166, 172, 174,
             176-178, 180, 181, 184, 185, 187, 195-197, 199, 211, 212, 225,
             228, 231, 234, 243, 247, 252, 253, 261, 262, 266, 267, 276,
             277, 286-288, 290-292, 296-301, 303-306, 310, 312, 315, 323,
             351, 354, 357, 361, 375, 377
predicate_size   90
print   45, 51, 52, 55, 93, 142, 147, 154, 158, 167, 173, 176-178, 210, 275, 276,
        288, 291
print_ancestor   167
print_context   142, 158, 210
private   82, 86, 90, 98, 99, 102-104, 108, 140, 143, 312, 322
prompt   11, 30-32, 38, 40, 42, 43, 49, 61, 68, 70, 88, 132, 166, 169, 216, 217,
         220, 247, 261, 284, 289, 299, 300, 310-312, 314-316, 319, 338,
         346, 347
public   79, 81-83, 85, 86, 90, 99, 102-106, 108, 142, 143, 158, 166, 174, 263,
        298, 375
put/1   115, 121, 122, 134, 209, 210, 214, 343, 353
read/1   153, 154, 209, 210, 216, 259, 340, 341, 351
read_prompt   216
reading_at   341
real number   20, 73, 116, 203, 204, 365
reconsult   45, 50, 68, 88, 89, 96, 131-133, 210, 306, 318
recorded   60, 88, 96, 97
rename   13, 340, 351
rename_file   340, 351
repeat   82, 86, 153, 247, 310, 312, 313, 318, 377, 378
restart   30, 157, 172, 173, 282, 284

retract 74, 86, 88, 90-92, 96, 97, 107, 111, 144, 149, 152, 157, 378
retractall 89, 91, 97, 144, 148, 152, 287
retry 59, 167
rule 10, 12, 13, 23, 26, 27, 35, 37-39, 45-47, 58, 91, 111, 125, 139, 149, 151, 255, 318
save/5 105
save_state 170, 171
see/1 131-133, 210, 327
seeing 133, 134, 210, 317
seek 134, 209, 225, 228, 233, 234, 341, 352, 353
seek_read 341
seek_write 341
seen 15, 33, 37, 38, 51, 62, 71, 72, 86, 95, 133, 134, 210, 212, 246, 248, 255, 275, 303
serious error 155, 156, 159
setof 18, 43, 44, 46, 50, 52, 110, 125
setup_file 171
sin 22, 116, 187
sinh 116
skip 59, 71, 121, 122, 134, 163, 167, 210, 276, 319, 341, 344
skip_out 167
sort 15, 51, 57, 125, 220, 246, 250
special device 128, 130
special stream 130, 207, 209-219, 221-224, 226, 227, 229-234
spy 161-164, 166
spying 162, 164, 166, 289
sqrt 116
state 9, 28, 63, 64, 69, 72, 83, 84, 92, 98, 106, 107, 110, 113, 132, 133, 136, 137, 138, 140-143, 145-153, 158, 159, 162, 170-173, 211, 216, 225, 231, 256, 260-262, 278, 279, 282, 284, 287-289, 296, 310, 313, 314, 324, 337, 338, 342, 343, 355, 356, 366, 370-372
statistics 100, 172, 174, 283, 284, 288, 344
stdio 132, 279, 284
stream 53, 54, 89, 90, 110, 111, 128-134, 136, 153, 154, 167, 172, 183, 188, 207, 209-234, 245, 247-253, 259, 263, 264, 275, 278, 281, 289, 293, 321, 341, 343, 352-354
string 10, 16, 19, 20, 27, 34, 47, 80, 93, 115, 117, 118, 121-125, 127, 130, 134, 136, 142-144, 146, 151, 153, 154, 159, 176, 177, 179-181, 184, 186-194, 196, 202-205, 207, 208, 220, 221, 229, 232, 235-243, 258, 263, 264, 276, 279, 292, 294, 297-299, 302, 303, 304, 306, 321, 323, 329, 344, 351, 364-367, 370
string expression 117, 122
structure 93, 140, 141, 147, 200, 356
syntax error 24, 32, 49, 155, 159, 217, 278, 292, 293, 311, 312, 317, 318
system directory 170, 281, 323, 331, 333-338, 346, 347, 349, 350
tab 21, 115, 121, 122, 134, 135, 210
tail recursion optimisation 4, 112, 113, 160
tan 116
tanh 116

tell 9, 26, 35, 38, 40, 42-45, 49, 52, 53, 55, 60, 63, 81-83, 95, 131-134, 151,
       182, 210, 266, 278, 284, 298, 310, 311, 327, 352, 377
telling 31, 37, 40, 133, 134, 210, 307
term order 125
term_length 138
time 3-6, 32, 35-38, 40, 41, 44, 50, 53, 56, 57, 59, 64, 68, 69, 72, 79-82, 84,
       86, 87, 91, 95, 96, 99, 105, 110-112, 114, 128, 132, 136, 138,
       153, 158, 161-164, 169, 172, 177, 224, 227, 229, 232, 239,
       256, 260, 261, 263, 274, 275, 281, 283, 284, 290, 292, 304,
       305, 307, 308, 311-314, 319, 320, 322, 324, 328, 337, 340,
       344, 345, 370, 371, 375-377
TLI 338, 342
token_class 28, 139, 140, 143, 145, 148, 149, 151-153, 284
told 11, 34, 41, 45, 46, 52, 55, 59, 61, 74, 133, 134, 157, 210, 330
trace 58, 69, 70, 92, 161-164, 166, 278, 289, 291, 294
tracing 69, 70, 161, 162, 164, 166, 289, 290, 294
transcendental functions 116
trimatoms 111, 114, 311
trimcore 111, 114
trimlibs 99, 111, 114
trimstacks 114
tro 113
ttyflush 210
ttyget 210, 299, 341
ttyget0 210, 341
ttynl 210
ttyput 210
ttyskip 210
undefined 79, 113, 179, 190, 192, 195, 252, 253, 290, 375
unhash 96
unknown 352
user v, 7, 11, 12, 31, 33, 43, 45, 51, 63, 87-89, 100, 109-111, 128, 130, 132,
       137, 138, 144, 151, 153-157, 159, 162, 169-174, 183-185, 190,
       192, 195-199, 212, 222-224, 226, 231, 236, 247, 259-261, 266,
       267, 268, 271, 274, 275, 277, 279, 280, 288-293, 295, 297,
       301, 302-304, 306, 309, 310, 312, 316, 319, 324-326, 330-339,
       342-344, 346, 348, 349, 358, 361, 373, 376, 377
var 16, 21, 191
variable 35, 189-195, 229
variable name structure 140
varnames 92
version 3-6, 30, 39, 61, 66-68, 71, 80, 86, 87, 93, 103, 104, 142, 151, 154,
       164, 166, 169, 205, 222, 229, 243, 286, 293, 296, 314, 322,
       337, 344, 345, 377
virtual memory 4, 74, 94, 96, 101, 104, 111, 173, 206, 299
virtual_drive 279
write 4, 10, 13-16, 22, 28, 33, 34, 52, 60, 62-64, 66, 72-74, 81, 82, 86, 90-93,
       99-101, 106, 108, 112-114, 129-131, 134, 136-138, 142, 145,
       146, 147, 153-157, 166, 167, 178, 183, 184, 196-198, 200, 201,

202, 209-216, 223-225, 228, 231, 232, 234, 236, 237, 240, 241, 242, 248-250, 253, 256-262, 266, 284, 286, 310, 311, 313, 315, 318, 321, 327, 328, 330, 332, 340, 341, 347, 351, 353, 357, 358, 360-364, 378
write_depth 147
writeq 153, 154, 167, 210, 312
writing_at 341
xout 167

Free Software Offer

An advanced logic programming language
Vol. 1 Prolog-2 User Guide
Edited by Tony Dodd

The purchaser of this book is entitled to a free disk containing *Prolog-2 Tutorial* software which is sufficient to carry out the exercises in the book. The software is an exclusive version of *Prolog-2* (for PC and compatible computers) which excludes facilities for saving to and loading from an external text editor. Otherwise the interpreter is based on standard Edinburgh syntax, having DEC-10 Prolog as a compatible subset. In addition it includes a debugger, module system, predicate hashing, garbage collection, stream system, formatted I/O, full floating point operations, menu system and help system.

Simply tear off the voucher below and post to:

Intellect Books, Suite 2, 108/110 London Road,
Oxford, OX3 9AW ENGLAND

Order Form:

Please send me a copy of *Prolog-2 Tutorial* .

Name ....
Address ....
....
Signature .... Date ....